RIVER OF LIFE
CHANNEL OF DEATH
Fish and Dams on the Lower Snake

KEITH C. PETERSEN

A James R. Hepworth Book

CONFLUENCE PRESS / LEWISTON, IDAHO

ISBN 0-881090-17-5
Library of Congress Card Number 94-69720

Publication of this book is made possible by generous grants from
Lewis-Clark State College and the Idaho Commission on the Arts,
a state agency. We also acknowledge here our thanks for a substantial
gift from an anonymous patron.

Published by

Confluence Press, Inc.
Lewis-Clark State College
500 8th Avenue
Lewiston, Idaho 83501

Distributed to the trade by

National Book Network
4720-A Boston Way
Lanham, Maryland 20706

To Candy and Carol

C O N T E N T S

Chronology

c. 10,000 B.C.
  The last of the Missoula Floods, the greatest in geological history, destroy all evidence of possible earlier human life along the lower Snake River.

c. 8,000-9,000 B.C.
  People are living in the Marmes Rockshelter along the lower Snake River; the Snake River provides an essential supply of food and water to these ancient residents.

c. 1750 Nez Perce Indians acquire horses.

1802 Congress establishes the U.S. Army Corps of Engineers.

1805 Lewis and Clark journey down the lower Snake River.

1836 Henry Spalding establishes a mission near the confluence of the Clearwater and Snake rivers.

1860 Elias Pierce discovers gold on the Clearwater River in Idaho.

  The *Colonel Wright* becomes the first steamboat to navigate the lower Snake River to newly-founded Lewiston.

1861   Lewiston grows into a raucous tent city supplying goldrush miners.

1862   Lewiston becomes the capital of the new Idaho Territory.

1876   The first load of Palouse country wheat is transported down the lower Snake River by steamboat to Portland.

1896   The Corps of Engineers constructs Cascade Locks on the Columbia River as the first step in creating a year-round navigable waterway along the Columbia and Snake rivers.

1915   The Corps of Engineers constructs Celilo Canal, opening another part of the Columbia River to year-round navigation.

1930   The Corps of Engineers presents to Congress its Snake River "308 Report," outlining potential development plans for the river.

1933   Franklin Roosevelt directs the Corps of Engineers to construct Bonneville Dam on the lower Columbia River, the first Corps dam on the Columbia/Snake waterway.

1934   The Inland Empire Waterways Association is organized to lobby for an "open river" from Lewiston to the Pacific Ocean.

1945   Congress authorizes the Corps of Engineers to construct the Lower Snake River Project to bring year-round navigation to Lewiston and to generate hydropower.

1948   The Corps of Engineers establishes a new district at Walla Walla, Washington, to oversee construction of the four-dam Lower Snake River Project; the Walla Walla District will grow to supervise more construction activity than any other district in the Corps nationwide.

1952   Biologist Harlan Holmes estimates that each dam built on the Columbia and Snake rivers will kill 15 percent of juvenile salmon passing through; the Corps of Engineers refuses to publicize his report.

1955   Congress awards the Corps of Engineers first funding for Ice Harbor Dam on the Lower Snake River after ten years of effort by fishery agencies to halt construction of the project because of the agencies' concerns that the lower Snake dams will destroy Idaho salmon runs.

1961   Ice Harbor, the first of the four lower Snake River dams, comes on line.

1962   Rachel Carson writes *Silent Spring*.
            Congress authorizes the Corps of Engineers to construct a dam at Asotin, Washington.

1965   Roald Fryxell finds 10,000-11,000-year-old human bones near Marmes Rockshelter on the lower Snake River, the oldest human bones ever found in North America.

1968   Idaho senators Frank Church and Len Jordan propose a ten-year moratorium on dam building on the Snake River above Lewiston.

            The first barge transportation of juvenile salmon and steelhead around lower Snake River dams begins in an effort to preserve Idaho's anadromous fish runs.

1969   Congress passes the National Environmental Policy Act.
            Lower Monumental Dam comes on line, flooding Marmes Rockshelter.

1970   The United States celebrates the first Earth Day.

            The National Marine Fisheries Service calculates that as many as 70 percent of Idaho salmon smolts die from dam-produced nitrogen supersaturation on their way down the lower Snake River.

Conservation organizations file suit against the Corps of Engineers to halt construction of Lower Granite Dam and deauthorize Asotin Dam in an effort to preserve fish runs.

1973   Congress passes the Endangered Species Act.

1975   Lower Granite Dam completed.

Slackwater comes to Lewiston after more than one hundred years of effort to create a year-round navigable waterway from Idaho to the sea.

American Society of Civil Engineers names the Lower Snake River Project the nation's outstanding water resources achievement of the year.

Congress creates the Hells Canyon National Recreation Area and deauthorizes the Corps of Engineers' Asotin Dam.

1976   Congress passes the Lower Snake River Fish and Wildlife Compensation Plan, the largest federal mitigation effort in United States history to that time.

1980   Congress passes the Pacific Northwest Electric Power Planning and Conservation Act with a goal of giving anadromous fish equal consideration with hydropower on the Columbia/Snake river system; the act forms the Northwest Power Planning Council.

1988   Congress passes legislation prohibiting the licensing of any dam at Asotin, whether public or private.

Snake River coho salmon become extinct.

1990   One sockeye salmon manages to return to Idaho past the eight Corps of Engineers' dams on the Columbia and Snake rivers.

1991   American Fisheries Society reports that 214 salmon species in the West face extinction.

Snake River sockeye salmon listed as an endangered species.

1992   Environmentalists encourage lower Snake River drawdowns in an effort to create a more natural migration of salmon smolts; the Corps of Engineers undertakes an experimental drawdown behind Lower Granite Dam.

1993   American Rivers names the Columbia/Snake waterway the nation's most endangered river.

1994   The 9th Circuit Court of Appeals rebukes the Northwest Power Planning Council for emphasizing hydropower production along the Columbia/Snake waterway at the expense of protecting salmon.

The Northwest Power Planning Council announces an expansive salmon recovery plan for the Columbia/Snake river system.

The Columbia River is closed to commercial salmon fishing by non-Indians.

Snake River chinook salmon listed as an endangered species.

Prologue

Rivers slice through time and place. The Snake River has carved deep canyons into the landscape while it has cut through more than ten thousand years of human history. During all that time it has provided many of life's essentials for those living near it: food, water, protection, transportation, power. Studying a river like the Snake reveals much about people and place and changing times. Rivers, in other words, offer us one of our best windows to the past. As historian Donald Worster has said, "To write history without putting any water In It Is to leave out a large part of the story. Human experience has not been so dry as that."[1]

It's a warm May morning at Lower Granite Dam, isolated in the Snake River canyon in southeastern Washington about twenty-five miles from Pullman, a college town of twenty thousand—the nearest population base. Iron cables and thick yellow nylon ropes fasten a tug and barge to a steel abutment just downstream from the dam's powerhouse. Like surgical tubing connecting vessel to mainland, plastic pipes wind their way through an Erectorset-like building onto the barge and snake into cargo doors. Water draining through the tubes enters watery bays on the barge and small objects appear through the clear plastic, streaming onto the barge.

These specks are tiny fish, shimmering silver in the hose's stream—fingerling steelhead and salmon in the early stages of smoltification, the period in their lives when they turn from freshwater beings into ocean dwellers and swim in the Pacific for a few years before venturing back upstream to spawn. In a few hours the dam's fishways will disgorge slightly more than twenty tons of young fish onto the barge. At about seven to the pound, the craft will carry somewhere near three hundred thousand smolts as it sets off downstream at noon. Thirty hours later, below Bonneville Dam on the Columbia River, doors under the barge will drop open and the thousands of little fish will glide down the last hundred miles of river on their own, having taken advantage of the tug ride to bypass three hundred miles of slackwater reservoirs, thousands of predatory fish, and seven more dams on their way to sea.

It isn't hard to find humor in this situation—fish taxying downriver on a barge. A hundred years ago, millions of smolts exited to the ocean each year without artificial aid. Sixteen million adult fish annually made it into the Columbia's mouth, powering their way upstream to virtually every tributary river and creek in Washington, Oregon, and Idaho, many traveling more than nine hundred miles through some of the mightiest rivers in America, a feat roughly equivalent to swimming uphill from Dallas to Chicago. As late as the 1930s Pacific Northwesterners still told stories of spawning streams so chock-full of salmon a person could walk on their backs. But today the lower Snake and Columbia rivers are not rivers at all. They are a staircase series of slackwater pools and the young smolts—killed at dams, eaten by warmwater predators, and theatened with fatal timing dysfunctions if they fail to make it to the ocean promptly—can no longer navigate this man-made maze without help. Indeed, there is no guarantee they will survive even with this artificial taxi-barge life support system.

It would be easy to see the humor, that is, if you failed to recognize that *The Chinook*, the barge on which the fish will depart from Lower Granite Dam on this day, is a million-and-a-half dollars worth of state-of-the-art fish transportation technology, that it is only one of six sophisticated fish-carrying craft daily plying the Columbia River system during spring and summer smolt runs, and that these barges represent but a trifling percentage of the billions of dollars Americans have or soon will invest in an effort to save the Snake/Columbia anadromous fish runs.

It would also be easier to see the humor if you could ignore the people whose livlihoods await an answer as to whether the fish can be saved. There are those directly affected by each decision made about fish and dams on this river system—commercial Indian and white fishers; port employees who rely on slackwater navigation; farmers who irrigate their fields from dwindling supplies of Snake/Columbia water; aluminum workers whose jobs depend upon a steady flow of inexpensive hydroelectricity from the dams' generators. And then, of course, there are many—many—thousands more who have come to expect the cheap power that dams provide. Indeed, were it not for the Columbia and Snake dams and the economic boom they brought during and after World War II, most residents of the region would not live here today. And indeed, it is difficult to imagine that any of the nine million dwellers of the three Northwestern states will go unaffected either directly or indirectly in the upcoming struggle to determine whether the region can have both dams and salmon. All of them either rely on the river system for power or transportation, or will be asked to foot a large part of the fish-saving bill via higher power rates and taxes.

It would be much easier to see the humor if you did not know that American Rivers, the nation's largest river conservation group, named the Columbia/Snake waterway the country's most endangered river; that the once prodigious Snake river coho salmon is now extinct; that in 1990 one Snake River sockeye salmon managed to make it back to the stream where hundreds of thousands once swam. The National Marine Fisheries Service has listed the sockeye and Snake River chinook salmon as endangered. As Steve Pettit, fish passage specialist for the Idaho Department of Fish and Game has said, these endangered species listings have the potential to make the spotted owl crises—an endangered species controversy affecting a mere thirty thousand woods workers in Oregon and Washington—"look like a pillow fight." Never has there been an environmental issue in Northwest history more widely discussed and reported, and never has there been one with the potential to impact so many people.[2]

In western Wyoming, high mountain peaks shed water into creeks with names like Fox, Wolverine, Rodent, Crooked, Sickle, and Basin. Their union gives birth to the Snake River.

The Snake flows west to the Lewis, then turns south into the Jackson Hole country. Paralleling the Teton Range, it gains additional energy from the Gros Ventre and Hoback rivers before entering Idaho.

Moving west, in the days before dams and irrigation diversions, it dropped precipitously in a series of spectacular waterfalls, some of which lent their names to cities: Idaho Falls, American Falls, Twin Falls, taller-than-Niagara Shoshone Falls, Augure Falls, and Salmon Falls, all the time gathering force from the accumulated waters of the Blackfoot, Portneuf, Raft, Big and Little Wood, and Bruneau rivers.

Reaching Idaho's western border, the Snake turns abruptly north, forming the boundary between Oregon and Idaho, taking on the waters of Owyhee, Malheur, Burnt, Powder, Boise, Payette, and Weiser rivers. Flowing now with the force of one of the world's great streams, the Snake hurtles through Hells Canyon, the deepest gorge in North America. The Salmon and the Grande Ronde enter, and the river becomes the boundary between Idaho and Washington.

The Clearwater joins at Lewiston, Idaho, where the Snake turns abruptly west to arc through southeastern Washington, amassing more strength from streams like the Tucannon and Palouse before merging into the Columbia at Pasco, Washington, as the largest tributary of the Great River of the West. Before that confluence the Snake has flowed 1,036 miles (the nation's seventh-longest river), gathered water from six states, cut across a significant portion of the American West, and served as an umbilical cord, a lifeline to some of the driest and most isolated parts of the nation.

Different people have different ideas about just where it starts, but somewhere near Lewiston, where the Clearwater feeds in, most people say the "lower" Snake begins. During its last 140 miles, this portion of the river transects some of the nation's richest agricultural country, cutting a gorge two thousand feet deep, before exiting through fertile but dry desert land near its confluence with the Columbia.

Along this stretch of the lower Snake River the U. S. Army Corps of Engineers constructed four dams and attempted to build a fifth. This book is the story of how people came to settle this region and demand such river alterations—and how some eventually came to oppose them. It is a history of the long struggle to bring navigation to Lewiston and hydropower to a region; of the influence of powerful congressional representatives and booster organizations; of a clash of cultures between Indians and whites and later contention between environmentalists and developers; of the role of the federal government in Western settlement. It is also the chronicle, yet unfolding, of the conflict between native wildlife and dams. In microcosm it is, in many ways, the story of the American West.

Along with the three hundred thousand fish, a captain, a pilot, two deckhands, and one barge tender, I climbed aboard the fish barge *Chinook* and the tugboat *Idaho* for the ride from Lower Granite Dam, past Little Goose and Lower Monumental dams, to Ice Harbor Dam, near the Snake's confluence with the Columbia.

I have lived in the lower Snake River country for a quarter of a century. We residents of the inland Northwest depend upon the river to haul our crops to market, to light our homes, and to heat our schools. But we have, during the course of more than a century of white settlement, all but turned our backs on the river—so much so that the only way to really see it today is by boat. Except for a few isolated spots for a few isolated miles, you cannot drive along the lower Snake. You can zigzag across it at a few places—at a handful of bridges and over the four dams. But you can't drive near it for any extent of time, and this is inhospitable country for hikers, particularly in summer when the sun bakes the riprapped shore banks and the rattlesnakes come out. So, to most of us, the lower Snake remains an enigma in our backyard.

The Army Corps of Engineers, owners of the barge upon which I will travel and builders of the dams that have created the fish crisis, is likewise something of an enigma. Writers have long ignored this federal agency. The Bureau of Reclamation's role in watering the West has had the luxury of good historical syntheses.[3] But the Corps, with its influence centered in navigation, hydropower, and flood control, still awaits such analysis. Yet it is difficult to think of a single federal agency in the West—particularly the Pacific Northwest—that has more dramatically affected the region.

The federal government spent $33 million on Western water development in 1939. Just ten years later it expended seven times that much, and water budgets continued to rise. By the 1940s, when Congress authorized the Corps to build the lower Snake dams, one out of every four federal dollars invested in waterways development flowed into the State of Washington, and by 1960 Washington and Oregon gobbled up nearly a third of all multipurpose water project funds. Nothing before or since transformed the region so thoroughly. Historians now call the period from the 1930s to the 1970s the "dam building era" in the Northwest. During that time the Army Engineers became the nation's largest builder and operator of hydroelectric facilities, responsible for constructing the vast majority of federal dams that remade the Pacific Northwest into one of America's most important industrial regions.[4]

The tiny fish that *The Chinook* will haul on this day are an enigma, too. If you visit a fish-viewing room at any of the dams along the Columbia and Snake rivers you might see mature salmon steadily climbing fish ladders to spawning beds upstream. Designed by the Corps, these ladders have worked rather effectively since the 1930s. Strong adult fish can make it back home. The fingerlings those spawners produce, however, are rarely seen, and since they have always been out of sight, they have, until recently, been mostly out of mind. The Corps and various river development lobbyists convinced people that if they could get enough adults upstream, allowing them to lay their three thousand to five thousand eggs apiece, so many of their offspring would clog the rivers you could lose thousands at each dam and still retain the famous Northwest fish runs.

It was not actually a big lie, at least at first. Most Corps employees, for a considerable number of years, actually believed their own publicity releases and, instead of assisting small fish in their plight past dams, aimed instead at churning out ever more smolts at Corps-built fish hatcheries. They recognized there would be slaughter along the way. But they believed that if they released enough millions of juveniles every year they could get the relatively few adults to return upstream required to perpetuate the runs. Dam-fodder smolts became official government policy.

But as adult fish counts declined precipitously with the completion of each dam, it became apparent that this strategy would not work. So the Corps took to barging fish, and on this day I am riding on their prize barge attempting to learn more about these enigmas—the river, the Engineers, and the smolts—that seem destined to so dramatically influence Northwest lifestyles in the coming years.

Ed Ferrell, the barge tender, greets me as I walk on board. "Usually we don't have such high-priced help," laughs Cory Eagen, the tug's captain. But the Corps suffered a hiring freeze this spring; there will be no seasonal help to tend the fish barges. So the Engineers asked for volunteers and big Ed Ferrell—overweight in a T-shirt full of belly that hides his belt buckle, but with the massive, tatooed arms of a man who has long labored hard—signed up.

Ed Ferrell is the quintessential but often overlooked Corps employee. Although Army officers head the agency, civilians make up more than 98 percent of the Corps' work force, and for the most part they are civilians who take great pride in their work and have a tremendous loyalty to their agency. A good many are even environmentalists, and while Ed Ferrell might not describe himself as such, anyone observing the gentle way this mountain of a man handles tiny fish would know he had environmental instincts.

"Them fish are like gold in Fort Knox," Ferrell says as he gingerly scoops a dead one from the top of a holding tank as we get underway. On his previous trip he carried eighteen tons of smolts and tallied 360 "morts," as tenders call dead fish. That's an enviable survival record. But as I watch Ed dip a handful of mortalities from the tanks and toss them overboard, I know each dead fingerling hurts. Ed would like a perfect run. He would like to go the distance from Lower Granite to Bonneville without a single mort.

Ferrell has already made five round trips on the fish barge this spring. "I love it," he says. "The wind and sun. Every trip you see coyotes and deer. And I love the idea of saving fish. They're the most important thing on this boat."

Ferrell started navigational construction in 1956 on the St. Lawrence Seaway. He worked dams in Oregon, Colorado, Idaho, and Venezuela. In 1970 he began construction at Lower Granite. "I started out here shootin' dynamite," he says. "Then I poured concrete. Once we got the dam built, the Corps hired me. I've been here since. I know her from the bottom to top. They call me 'Mr. Lower Granite.' I'm just like part of the furniture." A utilityman, he speaks proudly of the concrete plug he helped lay across the river. "It's a beautiful dam," he says. And it is. "That's nicer concrete than any other dam on the river."

Ed Ferrell seems to perfectly embody the clash between the two myths in the Northwest that are primarily responsible for the current controversy over fish and dams.

First, there was the myth of the salmon, fish dating back thousands of years—exactly how far back, no one really knows. But at least eleven thousand years ago people lived along the lower Snake and Columbia and thrived largely because of the rivers' tremendous salmon bounty. Salmon were to the people of the Northwest what buffalo became to the people of the Plains, and the rituals and stories and myths about the salmon—the first salmon ceremonies and the salmon feasts—played pivotal roles in their lives.

When whites came to live along the rivers, they, too, developed their own rituals about abundant salmon, basing much of their lifestyle upon the dependable return each year of silvery hordes. The oral traditions of Columbia River commercial gillnetters ring with their own adherence to salmon ceremonies.

"It was a celebration—the fishing was a celebration," recalled one. "Every night there was a send-off. There was a party. The sun was starting to set and the men would climb down the ladders and the wives would be there and the children. The boats would take off. Then the wives would haul the lines up and then head back to the bunkhouses and light the lamps and wait to hear the sound of the hoist."

The daughter of a commercial fisherman remembered her family's version of a first-salmon feast: "My dad—the first salmon he'd catch, he'd bring it home and invite the whole neighborhood in and we would have a salmon feed. We'd slice it up in slices and it was usually a great big salmon. That's all we'd have is bread and butter and salmon and milk and coffee."[5]

The myth of the salmon grew as more residents moved to the region and began angling the rivers and streams for sport, teaching the skill of landing the big fish to each succeeding generation. The fighting spirit of the fish, their strength and endurance and ability to surmount astronomical odds as they fought their way upstream to the very gravels of their birth to spawn and then die, came to symbolize, more than any other natural resource, the spirit of the Northwest.

The only manmade artifices that could challenge the salmon allegory were the dams the fish had to battle to survive. The big federal dams that transformed the Northwest—Grand Coulee and Bonneville and all those that followed—came just when the region, like most of America, was suffering its worst years during the Great Depression and beginning to question its traditional beliefs. Then along came Franklin Roosevelt and millions of dollars of federal money and massive projects to dam and tame the nation's most powerful river. And all this created a new and powerful lore. The dams put thousands of people to work and, as folksinger Woody Guthrie wrote, their power turned the darkness to dawn. New generations of Northwesterners now proudly visited and took their children to view these wonders of the engineering world. The dams reaffirmed people's faith in their ability to transcend hard times. And the cheap power the dams produced invited more industries and more people to pour into the region, and those people, too, came to believe in the myth of the dams to eternally provide the good life. And, of course, it wasn't all mythology. Columbia River dams today generate enough power to keep sixteen Seattles lit all year long. Each of the four lower Snake dams produces all the energy needs for a city the size of Portland.

But very early on these two primal myths, salmon and dams, clashed. There is another myth, fostered by historians among others, about how people believed the resources of the West were "limitless," that we would never run out of good land to farm and big trees to cut, and that the rivers would always run full of fish. The exploiters of natural resources, of course, encouraged this parable. But people who came to extract the resources of the Northwest, including decision makers in agencies like the Corps of Engineers and the Bonneville Power Administration (which hired Woody Guthrie to write his sanguine songs about the Columbia) recognized the limits of salmon. They tried to mask their knowledge in reassurances that the region could have both cheap electricity and abundant fish, but from the time the first Columbia River federal dam at Bonneville went into operation they knew the tremendous slaughter these obstructions would bring. The federal government—and the people of the Northwest, if truth be told— at that point, in the depths of the Great Depression when Franklin Roosevelt came to offer hope and work, opted for development and dams over fish.

To say that most people in the 1930s and 1940s—including most employees of the Corps—still genuinely believed you could have both fish and dams would be true. But to say decision makers in the federal government failed to recognize that dams threatened the salmon runs would be a lie. Long before dignitaries unearthed the first shovelful of dirt to begin construction at Bonneville and Grand Coulee, fish biologists had a very good idea of exactly what would happen to the salmon, and they had loudly brought their concerns to the Corps. These biologists of the 1930s and 1940s painted a scenario of gloom that proved remarkably prescient.

And certainly by the time the Corps came to construct its dams along the lower Snake, both Engineers and fishery agencies recognized the difficulty this series of four obstructions would bring. All rhetoric about "limitless resources," and "we didn't know the problems dams would cause" to the contrary, we did make a conscious choice of dams over fish. Today we are attempting to modify that decision because the myth of the salmon proved more potent and enduring than river developers had imagined, and because a new generation of Northwesterners believes it is essential to find some balance between human development and nature.

The relative influence of the two myths changed over time. What started at Bonneville for the Corps of Engineers ended at Lower Granite. At first, as the Corps brought power to the land, the Engineers represented a symbol of hope and a brighter destiny. By 1975, when the agency completed Lower Granite on the Snake, things had changed. Bonneville, along with a couple of other famous federal dams of its vintage—Hoover and Grand Coulee—symbolized the promise big dams held for the future. Completed at a time when people grew increasingly concerned over the environmental consequences of dam construction, Lower Granite symbolized what most observers believe is the end of the big-dam era in America. The dam-building era in the Pacific Northwest was brief— spanning barely more than four decades—but it was dramatic, and people in the region will live with its consequences, both positive and negative, for many generations.

While the dams generally brought people flocking to the Northwest, they had just the opposite effect along the lower Snake. With the exception of its two population bases anchoring either end of the lower Snake—Lewiston, Idaho, (26,000) and Pasco, Washington, (24,000)—this is one of the few places in America where fewer people dwell today than before Columbus sailed from Spain. In the late nineteenth and early twentieth centuries, some whites took residence along the river, at the former seasonal homes of Native Americans. But the reservoirs flooded nearly all the habitable bottomland, and the term "sparsely populated" hardly does justice to describing the area's solitude. Like much of the West, the lower Snake River country, meagerly populated but productive, has always been a land of export. Today wheat and hydroelectricity are its most important commodities. Were it not for outside demands for these products, the lower Snake would today be undammed. The Corps' huge monoliths bisect the river not so much to serve those living near the dams as to meet the needs of others residing far away. The lower Snake country has always depended on the outside world. One cannot understand this region's local history without taking into account the influence and intricacies of national and international markets and politics.

Where, in 1805, Meriwether Lewis and William Clark found Indian villages and whitewater rapids, I saw vacant riprapped river banks and not a trace of riffles. Indeed, only a Corps publicist would still characterize this body of water as a river. Locals have come to calling it "The Great Snake Lake," and it offers few of the riverine images we romanticize —brisk-flowing, cool, clear, mountain water. Today the lower Snake is a working waterway, not a Thoreauean brook.

In the past, classic dam clashes between environmentalists and developers have focused on whether or not to flood natural areas. "Save

Hells Canyon" and "Save the Grand Canyon" have rallied public opinion in dramatic confrontations.

The present battle over the Snake differs from classic river struggles because the Snake has been dammed. In that sense it is infinitely more challenging than the fights over whether or not to dam, for this struggle will tell us whether both people and wildlife can survive in an obstructed river, as agencies like the Corps have so long promised us they can.

In this sense, too, the controversy over fish and dams along the lower Snake represents precisely the type of episode historian Patricia Nelson Limerick points to when she claims that the West is now at the vanguard of American historiography. Like a growing number of "new Western historians," Limerick has spent a career disparaging the notion that nothing really exciting has happened in the West since the romanticized frontier times; that the American West is nothing but a backwater of American history, significant only because of the efforts of a few rugged individuals who came to tame the land. [6]

To spotlight rugged individuals negates the single most important component in the development of the American West: the United States government. The government provided homesteads and gave land for schools. It offered incentives for railroads to crisscross the region. It gave money to researchers to assist farmers and brought irrigation to those farmers' lands. It offered protection from threats by humans and nature. It provided land for grazing stock, timber to feed mills, electricity to power factories, contracts to employ the masses. Yet one can read library shelves full of Western history and literature, stories of farmers and ranchers, cowboys and trappers, towns and cities, clubs and organizations, and never find mention of the federal government. That is history in a vacuum, for it ignores the most prominent thread connecting all their diverse stories.

"The history of the West," Worster wrote in 1985, "has tended to remain, against all evidence to the contrary, what it was in Thoreau's time: a saga of individual enterprise. . . . It is time that [the] emergent technological West, the West of the hydraulic society . . . be put beside the storybook West of fur trappers, cowboys, sodbusters, and intrepid adventurers." [7]

Government power, government money, government expertise, government technology, and government bureaucracy built the modern West. Some vigorous individuals traveled along and lived beside the lower Snake. But the government, through the Corps of Engineers, transfigured the river. And the historical implications of that action far outweigh all the individualistic acts of all the rugged people who ever set foot on its banks.

The Snake River struggle exemplifies Limerick's thesis, for at places like this in the American West, environmental battles frequently foreshadow similar events elsewhere in the United States and the world. We have constructed thousands of dams in the twentieth century, but we are only now learning how to live with them. Sacrifice has not played a very important part in the traditional telling of Western history. Pioneers sacrificed, but they expected theirs to be short-term suffering with ample future rewards. We now face long-term sacrifice if we are to save salmon. Now we have a chance to be heroic like our romanticized predecessors. We have both made and inherited messes. We can no longer just move on, as the classic Westerner disenchanted with her or his life could. There are no unfettered places left to go. It is time to see if we can clean things up in such a way that both nature and development can survive. Our era has the potential to be the most exciting and most ambitious in all the history of the American West, and along the lower Snake River that odyssey is well under way.

Writing Western history is something akin to being "a lawyer at a trial designed on the principle of the Mad Hatter's tea party," writes Limerick. "As soon as one begins to understand and emphathize with the plaintiff's case, it is time to move over and emphathize with the defendant. Seldom are there only two parties or only two points of view."[8]

That certainly has been my experience in investigating history along the lower Snake River. For example, it is much too easy to characterize the principal player in the story, the Army Corps of Engineers, as totally good or completely evil. The Corps is and has always been made up of many dedicated people, from Army generals to laborers like Ed Ferrell, who take great pride in their role in transforming a region. And as some of the world's best engineers and builders they did their transforming work well.

On the other hand, the Corps has never been as innocent as it has always maintained. It has never stood by passively doing "only what Congress wants," as it so often claims when it runs into controversy. Time and again on the lower Snake the Corps aggressively sought to influence Congress—usually to the joy of developers, such as its direct lobbying on behalf of dams; and sometimes to the pleasure of environmentalists, such as when the agency made an all-out effort to convince Congress to authorize the Lower Snake River Fish and Wildlife Compensation Plan, the largest in the nation at the time. To understand the story of the lower Snake requires the recognition of many points of view.

It also requires a long view. It is difficult with extended controversies such as the one along the lower Snake—where conservationists have clashed with river developers since the 1930s—to maintain interest in the topic. Cases drag on for years; characters change; people lose sight of the issues. It is easy to get excited over a short-term fish kill or a toxic spill. It is harder to understand the long evolution of competing forces that brought fundamental changes to this land. Our current environmental problems are not like Greek tragedies with short time frames and recognizable villains. Writers of history have an obligation to present the big picture.

The controversy over fish and dams, journalistic accounts to the contrary, did not suddenly arise when the Shoshone-Bannock tribe requested that the Snake River sockeye be listed as an endangered species in 1990. The story of this river, how it came to be and its significance to people, goes back through nearly two hundred years of white exploration and settlement, more than ten thousand years of native settlement, and millions of years of geologic formation. It is inaccurate to tell the story of Western history from a single point of view; it is equally wrong to pick up the story well past mid-stream. One goal of this book is to demonstrate that the conflict between the twin myths of fish and dams long predates anyone living today. It has roots in the ancient river inhabitants who relied upon the fish for food, and in later whites who envisioned the river—calmed and developed—as an avenue to profit.

We're a few hours into our barge run and Ed Ferrell is checking gauges on the tanks. The meters tell him the temperature and the dissolved-oxygen levels in the fish-holding areas. He closely monitors each, checking every couple of hours all the way down to Bonneville. The barge continually circulates river water via two huge valves and a pumping system that can handle fifteen thousand gallons a minute, making a complete water change every ten minutes so the tiny fish retain a feel for the smell and temperature of the river, essential branding if they are to return to this waterway upon maturity.

As we steer downstream we see wheat barges loading at grain ports and a few early-season campers at Corps' riverside recreation areas dotting the river banks. We bypass a dozen or more wildlife habitat areas the Corps maintains to attract deer and birds.

We reach Little Goose Dam at 3:20 and deckhand Rick Edmondson, college educated but despiser of desk work, reaches for the end of a long pole the lock tender hands down, clipping to it statistics on the cargo we're carrying. He ties us up to a float on the navigation lock wall. Now inside the lock, we are trapped by stone and concrete. At the tender's command, water pours out of the lock and we begin our slow descent to the next river level, about a hundred feet below. Once we exit the navigation lock, with the dam now looming above us, we tie up to another fish-loading area and take on forty thousand more fingerlings.

Sarah Wik, a Corps biologist, oversees the fish-loading at Goose. There is no doubt that she, like Ed Ferrell, loathes morts. When one tiny fingerling flips out of a bypass pipe onto a metal walkway, Wik descends two flights of stairs, carefully picks it up, and gently places it back into the watery stream.

Sarah Wik is part of a new generation of Corps employees. Long—and still—dominated by engineers, natural resource specialists like Wik have increased in both numbers and influence within the agency since the 1960s. She greets Ferrell heartily. She's glad he's aboard: "It costs a lot of money to have permanent Corps employees tend the barges, and it cuts young temporaries out of the system. But it has been good to introduce people like Ed to what we do. I started here ten years ago, and worked just below the powerhouse and there were people in the powerhouse who had been there longer than I who had no idea what we did out here with fish. They never stopped to see what we were doing."

Forty thousand smolts heavier, we leave Little Goose two hours after entering the lock. Halfway between Goose and Lower Monumental we pass a pleasure boat, the third craft we've seen in six hours on this isolated river. We pass Lyons Ferry Fish Hatchery, one of nine the Corps built in an effort to compensate for the fish deaths its lower Snake dams caused. "When they was building the hatchery at Lyons Ferry," says captain Cory Eagen, "I hauled all the construction equipment in."

Rick prepares a mountainous dinner of chicken, salad, bread, spuds, peaches, and beans. Ed checks the fish gauges. After dinner, all hands clear the table for five-card draw. "Ten bucks worth of chips will last you an evening if you get some good deals," Rick says as I naively ante-up.

I play for a while, find $10 isn't going to last me long, and leave with Ed to check the fish again. We read his log book from earlier trips on the fish barge. "Cold, wet, windy," "cold and rain," "ten foot waves," it says. ("At ten foot waves, you can't even drink coffee," Ed tells me. "It will jar it right out of the cup.") During one April trip they searched the water with powerful lights for a young boy swept off a pleasure boat in a big wind. No luck. They later heard he drowned.

We reach Lower Monumental Dam a little past eight in the evening; lights line the navigation lock walls. Again we drop down a hundred feet and head out downstream, the powerhouse and spillway lit like a red-and-green Christmas tree. We'll load no fish here; some day the Corps will have a juvenile fish bypass system at Lower Monumental, but not yet. Water roars through the spillway gates, all of them open this evening in an effort to flush tiny fish through the dam while avoiding the dangers of turbines. It's a relatively ineffective measure; thousands of fish are killed or eaten by predators here because there is no safe way through the dam. But fish biologists are convinced opening the spillways helps; that it is better for fingerlings to plunge down this artificial waterfall than risk virtual explosion due to drastic water-pressure changes in the turbines. So the Corps complies with their requests, despite the fact that they thus sacrifice thousands of kilowatts of hydropower as the generators lay idled for the salmon's benefit.

By 9:00 a full moon rises over the canyon and I am in the wheelhouse with Cory Eagen. "Wheelhouse" is a misnomer for this glassed-in box where the captain sits, perched thirty-two steps above the tug's deck. No wheel is in sight. Eagen leans back in a padded, swivel chair, controlling the tug with a two-inch joy stick at the end of the chair's arm, fully operated by index finger and thumb. "That moon makes it nice," he says. "With no moon you can't even see the canyon walls. It gets dark down inside this canyon." Even with the moon he frequently guides the spotlight to channel bouys to determine location.

We pass "port to port" with the cruise boat *Seabird*, but the river is quiet save for this brief activity. We reach Ice Harbor Dam about midnight and I climb up the navigation lock wall after farewells to the crew. Ed is once again out on the barge, checking gauges. "I don't sleep much on the way down," he says, "but as soon as we unload the fish and come back, I relax."

Big Ed Ferrell isn't exactly what you think of when you picture someone caring for tiny fish; nor is he the stereotypical Corps of Engineers laborer with no concern for wildlife. Ed Ferrell epitomizes the complexity of the controversy over the lower Snake, where there is seldom truly good or evil, where problems defy solutions, where money seemingly cannot buy success, where— like at the Mad Hatter's—things are not always what they seem to be, and where a waterway can be at once a river of life and a channel of death.

Part I

BEFORE THE DAMS

Chapter 1

Fire and Water

Twelve thousand years after the fact, J Harlen Bretz discovered the floods. He's lucky he wasn't there at the time.

A surging wall of water five hundred feet high moving fifty miles an hour, suspending ice, rock, and mud in raging turbulence, blasted out of Montana, crossed the Idaho panhandle into eastern Washington, and dumped into the Columbia River. The water roared out to sea, creating shock waves that pulsated like volcanic eruptions and noise more deafening than launching pads full of ascending space shuttles. It ripped all the topsoil from an area the size of Connecticut, carried huge boulders hundreds of miles downstream, and dropped a two hundred-square-mile gravel delta as far away as Portland, an area then buried under a swirling maelstrom four hundred feet deep.[1]

And this was just the last of eighty or so deluges, the greatest floods in geologic history.

The flood waters accumulated in prehistoric Lake Missoula, fed by glacial melt, snowfall, and rain. During the last ice age a lobe of the Cordilleran ice sheet scrabbled out of the north and banged into the Bitterroot Mountains, blocking the Clark Fork River. Water rose behind the dam, eventually topping the plug and slicing through, releasing torrents. These were the last days of the ice age, but it still had some force. Once Lake Missoula drained, the ice dam formed again, creating another giant lake, awaiting the time it too would breach the dam in a downstream rush. Over and over the floods pounded out upon the land, destroying everything in their paths.

Lake Missoula covered an area of three thousand square miles and held about half the water of Lake Michigan. Water stood two thousand feet deep at the dam. It all surged through the Clark Fork gap in a few days, a flow calculated at between nine and sixteen cubic miles per hour. Take the low estimate: nine cubic miles per hour is ten times the combined flow of all the rivers in the world. Calculated differently, that works out to about 380 million cubic feet of water flowing through the notch each second. The world's largest river, the Amazon, flows at about 6 million cubic feet per second; the Columbia a comparatively puny 255 thousand.

You can get a feel for the volume if you drive to Pasco, Washington, follow the Columbia downstream for a few miles, and stop near the former townsite of Wallula. Just downriver, gigantic basalt walls on either side of the river, three-quarters of a mile apart, tower eight hundred feet above the water line. This, the Wallula Gap, was narrower in pre-flood days, but it is still a useful measuring device. Stand here and imagine how much water can pass through this gap in a minute, an hour, a day. Billions of gallons. Then imagine that the Missoula floods held so much water it could not escape here, that all of the Pasco basin remained innundated for two to three weeks at a time as the floodwater reached the gap, then backed up in a deep, swirling lake awaiting its time to roar through. If you can grasp how much water this is, how much water you could pour through the Wallula Gap in three weeks, twenty-four hours a day, nonstop, you can begin to get a feel for the size of these floods.

All water converged at Wallula Gap, but it took different routes getting there, through three giant crisscrossing rivers that flowed simultaneously. The Grand Coulee tract in the west carried the greatest volume. The Crab Creek channel in the middle was fourteen miles wide. And the Palouse-Cheney tract in the east was twenty miles wide at spots and over six hundred feet deep. From this course water rushed into the lower Snake River before plunging into the Columbia.

At other places the scoured land is more spectacular: Dry Falls in the Grand Coulee featured a titanic waterfall that dwarfed Niagara. But there is plenty of humbling scenery along the Palouse tract. Travel it with someone who has a trained eye, someone like geologist Pat Seward, and the evidence of catastrophic flooding is obvious and abundant.

"These were floods of true biblical proportions," Seward said as we left the University of Idaho two days after he finished his doctorate. "You've got five thousand cubic miles of water surging out of Montana. That's five thousand cubes of water, each a mile to a side. I can't contemplate that much water. And it all came in a few days."

About seven miles north of LaCrosse, Washington, we entered the Palouse tract of what J Harlen Bretz called the Channeled Scablands. "We'll be following the flood waters from here down to the Snake," Seward explained. Our road guide suggested we could "imagine ourselves surfing the frontal waves as the waters swashed in eddies, crashed against canyon walls, and scraped against loess hills." Only a suicidal surfer could imagine that.

We topped a hill. Out of flat, cultivated farm land, steep-sided islands emerged. These are what geologists call arks. You can make your own. Get a garden hose. Lay it down on a flat piece of dirt. Turn it on to a fair trickle. Channels form as the water finds an escape, taking the easiest path. It leaves little islands of topsoil behind—miniature arks. Seven miles north of LaCrosse these islands are not miniatures. North Dakotans would call them mountains; Minnesotans would erect ski lifts.

On Highway 26 we stopped to examine a road cut, the site of a former flood eddy. Seward picked up a frying-pan-sized chunk of granite. No granite lies naturally around here; floodwaters ripped this rock out of a mountain to the north and carried it over a hundred miles. Flood-transported rocks get a lot bigger in Missoula flood country; some are the size of houses. Montana-born boulders seven feet across lie on hills above Portland, stranded when the icebergs carrying them melted in a backwash before floodwaters escaped to sea.

Continuing west on Highway 26 we traveled the Palouse River valley. Sheer basalt outcroppings form canyon rims on the north and south—hillsides once covered with topsoil, stripped bare during the floods when millions of tons of silt washed downstream. Touring this route twelve thousand years earlier we would have been under two hundred feet of water.

Making a bend into the town of Washtucna, Pat noted the opening to the Palouse River canyon, a narrow slot in a line of basalt hills. "That basalt ridge used to be intact," he said. "The Palouse River curved with the mountains, flowing below them. But the floods pirated the stream." In a couple of days, flood waters ripped a cut through the ridge, permanently altering the river's course. How much water does it take to tear a hole through a basalt mountain?

We had lunch overlooking Palouse Falls, 185 feet high, one of the most dramatic flood-created cataracts. There was no falls before the floods. Indeed, there was no river or canyon here. The canyon's basalt had buckled when one continental plate collided into another, and where the rock bent it became weak. The force of tons of water cracked the basalt at places like this, eroding part of the land, forming cascades. Palouse Falls and the stripped-bare canyon below are perhaps the most visible evidence of the force of the Missoula floods—cataract and sheer-walled, four hundred-foot-deep canyon where before there had been level land and gentle hills.

"This is where it all comes together," Seward said, stepping carefully to avoid rattlesnakes. We had stopped to over look the confluence of the Palouse and Snake rivers downstream from Palouse Falls at Lyon's Ferry State Park. Both upstream and down on the Snake, Seward pointed out flat-topped ridges dozens of feet above the water line. Where others simply saw hills, J Harlen Bretz discovered huge gravel bars. Some can be as high as twelve hundred feet and miles long, consisting of gravel, sand, and silt deposited by the floods.

We drove a few miles over the upstream bar, through what appeared to be good-sized hills. "Ripple marks," Seward corrected, "lines created by underwater currents. You know, like the little one-inch marks you see in sand along a river bank? Only these can be thirty feet high and two hundred feet from crest to crest. Imagine the power needed to create ripple marks that big." Imagine.

Water flowing upstream made these particular marks. As the floods roared out of the Palouse River they struck a high basalt knob on the opposite shore of the Snake and split in two directions, some going downstream and some up. Floods rushed up the Snake all the way to Lewiston, Idaho, about eighty miles, burying the Lewiston Valley in about six hundred feet of water. The Snake is no backyard creek. It is the seventh largest river in the United States, and by the time it reaches this point it is flowing at full power. It is no easy task to force such a river to reverse its flow. This is perhaps the only example of this phenomena on such a large, powerful stream anywhere in the world.

Arks the size of mountains; transported boulders the size of houses; ripple marks the size of football fields; gravel bars the size of hills; waterfalls and canyons formed in a day or two; rivers running upstream; thousands of miles of land scabbed clean of topsoil. This was a natural catastrophe of epic proportions. It seems so obvious now. But his colleagues nearly ridiculed J Harlen Bretz out of the profession for suggesting such a calamity in the 1920s. A modest flow of water over millions of years could create a Grand Canyon. But a deluge in a couple of days could not create a Palouse Canyon. Nature did not work that way. Or so geologists thought until Bretz came along.

The Geological Society of America awarded J Harlen Bretz its highest honor. But that was in 1979. Bretz was ninety-six. The award came from a new generation who had learned to see through Bretz's eyes. His contemporaries were less approving. To understand why, you have to go back a couple of centuries.[2]

In 1788 James Hutton wrote *Theory of the Earth*, a radical departure from the day's standard thinking. Most Western scientists of the eighteenth century believed the earth had formed in the biblical time frame of six thousand years. But according to Hutton you could not explain the earth's geology by thinking of catastrophic events packed into a few thousand years. Rather, a slow process taking millions of years created landscapes. Mountain peaks rose slowly, and eroded slowly away; it took eons to shape river canyons.

Hutton's theory left room for natural catastrophes: volcanos, earthquakes, and floods did alter terrain. Indeed, along the Snake River geologists had long agreed that the catastrophic Bonneville Flood, the world's second largest   behind Missoula—had dramatically altered the river's canyon.

G. K. Gilbert uncovered evidence of the great Bonneville Flood as early as 1878, and geologists accepted the notion of tremendous torrents of water rushing from Utah's Lake Bonneville, overflowing Red Rock Pass, and cascading down the Snake somewhere between fifteen and thirty thousand years ago. Flood waters reached a depth of three hundred feet, eroded channels, created cataracts, scabbed land, and deposited bars of huge boulders and gravel—the same characteristics Bretz noted about the Missoula floods.

Hutton's theory could accommodate a Bonneville Flood, impressive though it was. The Missoula floods were of a totally different scale. Missoula waters flowed with a volume twenty-five to thirty times greater than Bonneville. That was unimaginable to all but J Harlen Bretz.[3]

By the twentieth century, most people came to accept Hutton's ideas. But it had been difficult to wean the Western world of its biblical time frame, to convince people to think in terms of millions and billions of years rather than thousands. Geologists were not about to condone a step back to the old days of catastrophism; they were not ready to condone a radical theory from a young geologist at the University of Chicago. Imagine the outcry when Bretz proposed that a catastrophic flood similar to the one described in *Genesis* had created a vast landscape in eastern Washington.

Bretz published his first article on the Missoula floods in 1923. Others had noticed the unusual land formations of the channeled scablands. But they explained them in more traditional—and "scientific"—ways: water released as northern glaciers gradually melted formed the cataracts and canyons over millions of years.

It was a logical explanation that served the purpose of scientists without the courage or ability to think imaginatively. It was the only explanation until Bretz took the time to truly examine this unique land. Fly over the channeled scablands and much appears evident: huge ripple marks and obvious flood eddies greet even the untrained eye, and it is easy to accept the notion that a flood of unimaginable magnitude tore through this country. But Bretz did his field work, hot summer after hot summer, by walking, riding horseback, or driving an old Dodge across the scablands. From this perspective the view is different. "With eyes only a few feet above the ground the observer today must travel back and forth repeatedly and must record his observations mentally, photographically, by sketch and by map before he can form anything approaching a complete picture," Bretz wrote in 1928. It was the type of painstaking in-the-field work that made Bretz famous.

Bretz found much that gradual geological change could not explain. Only a catastrophic flood could move boulders and create gravel bars and cataracts of the size he discovered. So he published his ideas, article after article in the 1920s, and his fellow scientists condemned each in turn as "inadequate," "preposterous," and "incompetent."

Most would have caved in to the peer pressure, but not Bretz. He refined his flood thesis over nearly half a century. Eventually, through persistence and convincing arguments, Bretz held the day. By the 1950s arial photography clearly showed the flood evidence so difficult to detect from ground level.[4]

Today, no geologist really doubts that the floods occurred. They debate the number of innundations and spend time refining Bretz's theory. But they admit the floods dramatically shaped the lower Snake River country. Bretz, almost single-handedly, forced the profession to accept the concept that the earth formed by both slow evolutionary change *and* occasional catastrophic outbursts.

The Missoula floods were perhaps the most sensational event in the geologic history of the region. But to understand this geology, to know how land formed around the Snake River, you have to go back a lot farther than twelve thousand years. For that is really the end of the geological story—at least as it has so played out.[5]

The Precambrian Era covers 85 percent of the earth's 4.6 billion years. But this is a shadowy time to geologists studying the Snake. Most of the Precambrian landscape lies hidden under tons of earth detritus deposited later. The story of this country becomes a little more clear as geologists research more recent periods.

During the Paleozoic Era, 600 to 225 million years ago, much of the land around what is now the Snake River lay covered by ocean waters inhabited by unfathomable numbers of sea creatures. Their shells now form limestone deposits hundreds of feet deep. The earth's inner heat broke through its crust during the Paleozoic Era, the Seven Devils volcanos near Hells Canyon rose, and some of Idaho ascended above the salty waters. On this land forests grew and creatures left the water to find food and shelter. By 375 million years ago, insects—cockroaches and dragonflies and the like, many bugs we would recognize—roamed over these forests, unmolested by birds or other animals, which had not yet appeared. Then the forests died and became coal and peat.

In the Mesozoic Era, 225 to 65 million years ago, heat once again rose from the earth's core, and from southwest Idaho all the way into Canada old surface rock melted and became granite, the deep rock of the Idaho batholith that shapes the state's mountains. Ore deposits formed at this time, too, gold, silver, lead, and zinc deposited in cracks of the batholith, creating some of the world's richest mineral veins. Forests of cedar, sequoia, pine, and juniper replaced the palm trees now buried and turning to coal as the temperature cooled. The first birds and mammals came to the Snake River region, chasing insects and eating plants and fruits.

The modern era, the Cenozoic, came about 65 million years ago, ushered in by cold that dropped temperatures several degrees. Huge reptiles died, but some insects, birds, mammals, and small reptiles evolved and survived. The land warmed again, and for a time these creatures lived in forests much like those in the southeastern United States today, forests of persimmon, hickory, and hazel. Then the Cascade mountains folded out in gigantic wrinkles to the west, forming a rain barrier that created a drier and cooler climate on the Snake River plateau. For a while in the Cenozoic Era horses the size of dogs, camels the size of rabbits, and rhinos the size of sheep roamed the Snake River plains, gradually replaced by a tremendous variety of animals—squirrels, beavers, bears, elephants, monkeys, and more.

The Cenozoic was also the time of great lava flows in the lower Snake River region, flows that, more than any other geologic event, gave the land its shape, the greatest outpouring of lava in geological history.

Beginning about seventeen million years ago and continuing for ten million years, molten lava oozed from cracks in the earth's surface and poured over a sixty thousand square-mile area. The earth's crust cracked all the way down to the basaltic mantle that lies as a shell encircling the world, melting it and belching it out in flow after flow. It left behind what geologists today call the Columbia River basalts. Time after time the earth spewed up basalt, each time laying down layers of lava fifty to a hundred feet thick. Scientists have detected more than fifty of these eruptions in places along the Snake, and there might have been more than two hundred flows, enough lava to bury all of New England in a half-mile-deep ocean of molten rock. In some places along the lower Snake the accumulated basalt, cooled and hardened into blocks and columns, lies nearly two-and-one-half miles deep.

The lava vented from several places, but Moscow, Idaho, just north of the Snake, was a primary source. From here it flowed west, burning everything in its way, filling valleys and innundating uplands. The basalt did not flow smoothly. It created mounds, valleys, and flats, giving regions adjacent to the Snake their distinctive shape. The lava also disrupted the flow of the lower Snake, filling canyons and forcing the river to meander and assume its present course. Some geologists believe that in these days this was not Snake River water being reformed, but rather Clearwater and Salmon river flows. The Snake in those days, they say, drained through Oregon not Washington, the river gradually changing course to accept the waters and traverse the canyons molded by other streams. Because the Missoula floods ripped away so much evidence, it is difficult to read the rocks that are left, and the history of the Snake and its course remains an enigma.

After the lava finished flowing, the area of the lower Snake again cooled. The ice ages commenced about two to three million years ago. The ice gathered and then melted several times, covering all of Canada and much of the northern United States, then melting, then coming again. Each advance lasted thousands of years, with long, warm, dry periods in between. The last glacial period, the Wisconsin Ice Age, most dramatically affected the Pacific Northwest.

This advance began about seventy thousand years ago and consisted of several periods of glacial growth and retreat. The last occurred between fifteen and twelve thousand years ago, the time of the latest and largest Missoula flood.

Wisconsin-age glaciers did not creep all the way to the lower Snake, but they got within eighty miles. During this period the Snake country, now cooled again, looked much like Alaskan tundra. Archaeologists found the remains of an Arctic Fox at the Marmes Rockshelter near the confluence of the Palouse and Snake rivers. Mammoths, sometimes fourteen feet tall, inhabited the country. Bison with horn spreads of six feet also roamed the land, as did giant sloth and saber-toothed tigers. Humans were around to hunt the last of the mammoth and bison.

The giant fields of ice ground rock into a rich soil—a sort of glacial flour—and winds blew it down over the valleys and hills created by the Columbia River basalts, where it gently reformed into soft sculpted dunes. Geologists call this wind-deposited silt "loess," and it forms an icing over the lava, a sensous curving landscape of incredible fertility, topsoil over two hundred feet deep in places, some of the richest on earth.

Stand on top of a rolling hill in the Palouse country adjacent to the Snake River and you get an idea of the way all the Columbia Plateau appeared before the Missoula floods: gentle rolling hills of loess-topped basalt. The floods ripped the silt from much of the land, but they missed a great deal of property. On that land farmers eventually came to plant wheat, peas, and lentils and to seek ways to ship their products to market. They looked to the nearby Snake River for help.

And so it was that the geology of the region set the foundation for its history. The Snake connected with the Columbia and formed a network to the sea. Young salmon and steelhead used this waterway to migrate to the ocean, returning again as adults on their way to spawn, providing a staple for people who settled here. The earliest residents found shelter in caves formed from lava flows and set up homes in the warm Snake River canyon. They hunted on the grassy plains surrounding the river. Later, settlers of a different color came to the region. They extracted minerals in nearby hills and established a raucous tent city at a place called Lewiston, Idaho, and supplied the city and mines from sternwheelers plying the Snake River. Still later settlers built frame houses on low benches along the river and grew fruit on the rich soil deposited by the stream. On the plateaus above the river farmers cultivated loess-covered hills and ranchers grazed sheep and cattle in the Channeled Scablands. Towns grew up to serve the farmers and ranchers. And the Snake River became a vital lifeline for these farms and towns, a means to send crops downstream and a way to get supplies upstream; a source of power to light barns, houses, schools, and businesses.

This human history is layered over the land just as basalt is layered over Precambrian rocks and loess is layered over basalt. It reveals itself in chapter after chapter of human use and manipulation of the river. That part of the story begins with the ancients, the first people to see the river we call the Snake.

Chapter 2

The Ancients

Geologists have a unique perspective on time. Ten thousand years is a wink. Sometimes they consider it pin-point accuracy to isolate an earth-changing event within a few million years.

But in human scale, ten thousand years is an eternity. Contemplate it for a moment. Think beyond grandparents and great-grandparents. Think about more than four hundred generations of ancestors. Work your mind in a new dimension.

Archaeologists refer to the time ten thousand years ago as 10,000 B.P. ten thousand years before the present. You have to reflect far back to give ten thousand years its proper respect. Greeks constructed the Parthenon about 2,450 B.P. Moses led a group of Hebrews out of Egypt around 3,200 B.P. Egyptian Pharaohs oversaw construction of their pyramids about 4,500 B.P. Residents of the Tigris-Euphrates Valley developed a system of writing about 5,000 B.P. From that milestone you are halfway back.

Five thousand years before Mesopotamian writers, seven thousand years before Moses, and eight thousand years before Christ, people lived in a rockshelter near the confluence of the Palouse and Snake rivers. They fished the streams and hunted the plains. They gathered grains and berries. They sewed clothes. They prepared their dead for the next world. Their children swam in the water and skipped rocks and chased each other laughing along the river banks, as kids still do; their elders told stories in evenings around a fire, as oldsters still do. These were not simpletons. These people lived a complex life full of joy and grief, good times and bad.

They were some of the earliest residents of the Western Hemisphere.

On a hot summer day in 1965 Roald Fryxell trudged through a narrow bake-oven trench behind a bulldozer Roland Marmes drove. They worked just upstream from the confluence of the Palouse and Snake rivers. Dust covered their sweat-soaked clothes. Fryxell, a geologist with Washington State University's Laboratory of Anthropology, had previously uncovered artifacts in a nearby rockshelter. Now he was cutting below the land in front of the shelter to better read the area's geologic calendar. He hired Marmes, who owned the property, to bulldoze his path through time.

As Marmes scooped silt, Fryxell found bone fragments. He halted the day's work, gathered the bones, and sketched how they lay. Marmes went back to his farm; Fryxell placed the bones and drawings in his weathered pickup and drove the eighty miles to campus. Neither of their lives would ever be the same. While they didn't yet know it, Fryxell had just made one of the momentous discoveries of North American archaeology.

Richard Daugherty first became acquainted with the Pacific Northwest's prehistory as a summer intern on a Smithsonian Institution river-basin survey a couple of years after World War II. Congress had authorized the Army Corps of Engineers to build dams in the region, and archaeologists rushed to dig sites before the Engineers buried them under water. By the time I interviewed him in 1990 Daugherty was the acknowledged dean of Northwest archaeologists, a man so in tune with his passions that prior to open-heart surgery he had ordered the physician to discard his steel scalpels in favor of obsidian blades, the cutting edge of choice for prehistoric residents of the West. Daugherty owed much of his fame to discoveries made at the rockshelter Marmes and Fryxell excavated on that hot day in 1965. Daugherty had been around by then; he knew a significant discovery when he saw one. And he proved a master at garnering publicity for that particular dig.

"No one knew about the archaeology of the area before World War II," Daugherty reminisced. "There had been some work at Grand Coulee, Yakima, The Dalles. But we didn't know what to expect. We thought people had only lived here about twenty-five hundred years."[1]

One of the first sites Daugherty worked was Lind Coulee in central Washington, a place threatened by irrigation canals planned as part of Grand Coulee Dam's massive Columbia Basin Project. By the 1950s he had proven the site to be nine thousand years old, the first ancient archaeological location discovered in the State of Washington. Lind Colee excited Northwest archaeologists: there were bound to be other sites of equal or older vintage. Here in the Northwest they hoped to find evidence of some of the New World's earliest inhabitants. By 1950 Daugherty had joined the faculty at Washington State College and started the school's archaeology program. He completed an agreement with colleagues at the University of Washington: they would survey the Columbia while WSC—later WSU—oversaw work on the Snake River.[2]

Daugherty had no lack of projects on the Snake. Early Smithsonian surveys had already identified dozens of significant sites and he would uncover many more. Daugherty needed help. He would get it by developing a unique graduate program at WSU, hiring specialists from a variety of different fields to lend their expertise to archaeological investigation, people like zoologist Carl Gustafson—and geologist Roald Fryxell. "We were trying to forge a graduate program," Daugherty recalled. "But just any ordinary program wouldn't work at a place like Pullman. So we became interdisciplinary. When I hired Fryxell, only one other department in the nation had a Pleistocene geologist. But it made sense. It was ridiculous for the archaeologists to try to do geology or zoology." Washington State's multidisciplinary program, along with its rich field school along the lower Snake, soon attracted some of the brightest graduate students in the country. And on the lower Snake River they uncovered a treasure trove.

John McGregor, grandson of the founder of one of Washington's largest agribusinesses, first took Richard Daugherty to rockshelters near the family's huge ranch in the early 1950s. "He showed me what came to be known as the Marmes Rockshelter, but I dismissed it because I thought it was too low and would have been under water nine thousand years ago," Daugherty recalled. So Daugherty and his crews dug other sites along the Snake. They found excellent material, some of it more than six thousand years old. They also discovered many more places deserving excavation. Richard Daugherty would not return to Marmes until 1962.

Daugherty and his crew set up that summer of 1962 at the mouth of the

Palouse River to excavate the Palus Indian village site. "We had a few years to dig, more than eighty known sites, and little money," Daugherty remembered of those days. "You know you are going to miss some sites. You just hope you select the right ones. I decided to work the Palus village site. As we were setting up camp at the village, I remembered Marmes, just upstream, and took some people to do some test excavation. We started getting some interesting stuff." Indeed, they found so much interesting stuff that Daugherty moved his crew from the village to the rockshelter, working it in the summers of 1963 and 1964. "I got ahold of Fryxell and told him he had better take a look at this."

Daugherty, Fryxell, and crews dug in the rockshelter intermittently for three summers, finding dozens of artifacts and the remains of several humans. It was all valuable and interesting, but this was a hectic time for Washington State University archaeologists. The Army Corps of Engineers had completed Ice Harbor Dam in 1962. They would soon finish Lower Monumental and move on to build two additional dams upstream. Daugherty knew dozens of lower Snake prehistoric sites deserving excavation before backwaters flooded them. He had small crews, little money, and less time. But Fryxell, intrigued by the potential to uncover a long geological record in the soft silt in front of the rockshelter, would fit Marmes into his busy schedule, giving it what time he had.

Roald Fryxell was a Renaissance man. In an era when most academics specialized in narrow topics, Fryxell took a broader view. One of the younger generation of geologists who grew up admiring J Harlen Bretz, Fryxell, like Bretz, was an inveterate field geologist who spent much of his time in the Channeled Scablands fleshing out Bretz's theories. "Knowledge is a continuum, like the sphere of the earth but with the uninterrupted vastness of a universe," he wrote. "Our formal academic categories are as arbitrary and artificial as the lines of latitutde and longitude we scribe on a globe. . . . Each worker stands within the expanding field of his own perception. . . . To fetter his education or his intellectual growth with the boundaries of traditional disciplines is, to say the least, short-sighted."[3]

Fryxell's imagination, the quest for knowledge that led him to dig the trench in front of Marmes Rockshelter, also earned him national respect. The Washington senate named him one of the state's "Distinguished Citizens," and the National Aeronautics and Space Administration selected him as one of the first scientists to examine soil from the moon. He applied techniques he developed at Marmes to handling those lunar core samples.

But that all lay in the future on that hot day in 1965 when Fryxell discovered bone fragments in the dust behind a bulldozer. Back at campus he unloaded his find, placing it in the laboratory safe. It would be November before he would return to the site. Then he and Daugherty retraced his steps, dug a little deeper, and found more bone fragments. The dozer could not have tipped these into the ditch from higher ground; these came to lie there naturally. Given their depth—many feet below the ash line created by Mt. Mazama's eruption that formed Oregon's famed Crater Lake 6,700 years earlier—these had to be ancient.

Back Daugherty and Fryxell went to the laboratory where Carl Gustafson studied their bones to determine if they were human. It took about a year-and- a-half before Gustafson could give the fragments much attention, but he then announced they came from people.

Fryxell returned to the trench as often as possible, but he had other duties: sites to excavate, classes to teach, papers to write. Finally in the spring of 1968, with Lower Monumental Dam nearing completion, its reservoir waters about to flood the site, WSU turned its full attention to the Marmes Rockshelter. Crews dug during a wet spring and hot summer. They came across burial sites and artifacts, and found bones of numerous individuals. They radio-carbon dated some and were stunned with the results: the human remains dated from 9,000 to 11,000 B.P.

But while they now knew the site's importance, Daugherty and Fryxell had just about run out of time and money. This is when Richard Daugherty began to exert the public relations skills that are as much a part of his reputation as his archaeological knowledge.

Powerful politicians had come to know Daugherty over the years because of his effective lobbying for salvage archaeology. President Lyndon Johnson appointed him one of fifteen members of the Advisory Council on Historic Preservation, and Washington senators Henry Jackson and Warren Magnuson appreciated his tireless work. "So one day I called Magnuson's secretary, told him about our ancient Marmes bones, and told him we needed $80,000. He said, 'Come back to Washington.' So, we packed up one of the 'Marmes Man' skeletal remains, strapped them into an extra seat on the plane, and flew off." When they landed, Magnuson arranged for a press conference in his office. Reporters from the major press associations, magazines, and newspapers snapped photos and fired questions as Fryxell and Daugherty unveiled the oldest documented human remains ever found in North America to that time. That press conference touched a regional and national imagination. Perhaps no North

American archaeological dig has attracted more public attention than would the upcoming work at the Marmes Rockshelter. "Marmes Man" became front-page news in papers from coast to coast.

Not only were the Marmes bones old, they were also uniquely located: overlying those ancient remains were layer upon layer of evidence of human use of the rockshelter, extending into the twentieth century. Here was ten thousand years of human history, condensed into one small area, waiting to be uncovered, a discovery of extraordinary significance. As Hannah Marie Wormington, president of the Society of American Archaeologists said, "The odds against finding such a complete package of evidence within one site again are so great it is almost impossible." The site, she said, "is like a calendar of the centuries."[4]

Warren Magnuson would pull strings with his old Senate colleague Lyndon Johnson. Johnson would, for the first time in American history, issue a presidential order that an archaeological site be protected. The National Park Service would declare Marmes a national landmark. Fryxell, Daugherty, and their crews would unearth spectacular remains of nearly thirty individuals. A small community of groupies would form around the dig, sometimes more than a thousand spectators watching the archaeologists at work. Vendors would sell Marmes Man mugs and Marmes Man bumper stickers. And the Army Corps of Engineers would construct a levee to protect the site from the rising waters of Lower Monumental Dam, and the levee would fail, and the site would flood, and archaeologists and engineers and politicians would blame each other, and one of the West's most significant archaeological sites would wind up under forty feet of water. But that was all in the future.[5]

Roald Fryxell and Richard Daugherty generated national publicity at Marmes because they uncovered evidence in a debate dating back to the fifteenth century when Christopher Columbus thought he had discovered a New World, only to find others already living there. People began a long speculation about how and when Columbus's Indians had arrived.

At first Europeans believed unknown pilots, perhaps ancient Carthaginians, had sailed the Atlantic and settled America.

Next came the idea that the ancient Continent of Atlantis had once connected Spain to the Americas. When it sank, so some people theorized, it stranded early colonizers in the New World.

Then came a persistent belief about American Indians being part of the exiled Ten Lost Tribes of Hebrews who had spread over the world, somehow making it to the Western Hemisphere.

In 1589 a Jesuit missionary named Jose de Acosta wrote a remarkable book. Nearly 150 years before Vitus Bering sailed the Alaskan strait named for him, while Siberia was nothing but a blank spot on world maps, de Acosta speculated that Indians had not arrived by sea and had not crossed the Atlantic. Rather "savage hunters driven from their homelands by starvation or some other hardship" journeyed overland through Asia to America.

In 1856 Samuel Haven wrote *The Archaeology of the United States*, the most influential tract published on American archaeology to that time. The first Americans came from Asia, he firmly stated, having crossed the Bering Strait. Many still questioned the hypothesis, but by mid-nineteenth century people increasingly believed Indians arrived first to the western coast of the Americas, not the eastern.[6]

At first they thought these ancient settlers arrived by boat. Gradually, however, de Acosta's concept of people walking from the old world to the new gained adherents. If people walked, they needed something to walk on, and that something was Beringia, a piece of property connecting Siberia and Alaska that was at times a thousand miles wide. It is popularly known as the Bering Land Bridge, though it really did not resemble a bridge at all. This was broad country with rolling hills, indistinct from the Siberian and Alaskan lands it connected. People traveling here would have believed they were traversing more of the same type of country they had already explored, not crossing a bridge to a new world.

Beringia lay exposed because glaciers trapped tremendous amounts of moisture. Less than 3 percent of the earth's water is salt free, and most of that is locked in glaciers. Today's ice sheets hold so much water that, should they melt, oceans would rise three hundred feet, covering places like Los Angeles and New York. Yet today's glaciers contain only a fraction of the water they held during the ice ages. During the last ice age glaciers cleaved so much water that ocean levels shrank lower than two hundred feet below today's water line. And Beringia appeared.

For much of the period from ten thousand to twenty-five thousand years ago ice caps held enough water that people could have walked from Asia to Alaska. At earlier times, during earlier ice ages, the land bridge also appeared. During one of these periods tribes of hunters first followed herds of mammoth and other large game into Alaska. As glaciers melted,

Beringia drowned, isolating the wanderers, who then scattered across two continents.

Some archaeologists believe America's settling began early. Louis Leakey, famed hominid hunter of Africa, once claimed a site in California showed evidence of human occupation over two hundred thousand years old. That would mean humans considerably unlike us had crossed the Arctic land bridge, a hypothesis most find unlikely since such primitive people probably could not adapt to harsh northern climates. Although some archaeologists think they have found evidence of human occupation of North and South America more than forty thousand years old, that record is sketchy.

Modern *homo sapiens* evolved thirty-five thousand years ago or so, and about ten thousand years after that Beringia lay exposed as a land bridge. Most investigators agree that sometime during Beringia's last appearance someone stepped onto Alaska and discovered a new world. Speculation runs high as to just when that momentous event occurred. But there were people in the new world thirteen thousand years ago, and possibly considerably before then.[7]

Beringia was broadest precisely when North American ice was thickest. Gigantic glaciers, the Laurentide in the east and the Cordilleran in the west, covered Canada with hundreds of feet of ice, blocking the southern migration of Beringian wanderers. However, interior portions of Alaska, a zone archaeologists refer to as the Alaskan Refuge, remained ice free, and here the Asian nomads lived and hunted.

Population grew, testing the refuge's ability to provide sustenance. While population increased, the great ice sheets receded. As ice melted, sea levels rose, inundating Beringia. With the possibility of their retreat to Asia eliminated, these early Americans, searching for food, found an ice-free corridor between the Laurentide and Cordilleran glaciers: a narrow, rugged passage through Canada. After an arduous journey through an inhospitable land, some bands eventually arrived at the southern Canadian border, looked out upon the plains abutting the Rocky Mountains, and proceeded on; in a remarkably short period of time—some say as little as a thousand years—they settled places as distant as the Great Lakes and California, Mexico and Peru, Florida and Argentina. Theirs was one of the great accomplishments in human history.[8]

Such is the generally accepted theory, although some archaeologists have different ideas about how and when people migrated south. Still, if these first Americans entered the United States through Canada's ice-free corridor, they had to have arrived near either the east or west slopes of the Rocky Mountains. Archaeologists debate this point, too. Perhaps groups came to both sides almost simultaneously. Regardless, it is possible that the first person to see the United States crossed the Canadian border west of the Rockies, somewhere between eastern Washington and western Montana, just north of the Snake River. From that point other bands followed, chasing herds and livelihoods, moving east, west, and south, populating the continents. And it is possible that some of these earliest Americans lived along the lower Snake River, a warm place with ample shelter and food. The Missoula floods tore away any proof of settlement prior to the last flood about twelve thousand years ago. But after that, people definitely inhabited the lower Snake, leaving behind evidence of the way they lived.[9]

It was one of those issues that divided kindred souls: do you save migrating salmon or preserve a prehistoric site? People usually do not have to make such choices. The Army Corps of Engineers hoped not to, but it got caught in the middle and became a scapegoat in a doomed salvage operation.

Once Washington State University archaeologists concentrated on Marmes in the spring of 1968 they quickly uncovered riches. They found a tiny, perfectly preserved, ancient sewing needle. They located weapons, hundreds of artifacts, and the bones of animals, and they could tell what these people ate and how they lived. And, of course, they uncovered human remains.

Each week brought provocative new evidence of early life in the Americas. The archaeologists worked frantically but they were running out of time. Lower Monumental Dam would soon flood their site.

They established a tent city and hired a bigger crew. They erected a mess hall and stretched electricity lines. They often worked from 6 a.m. to midnight, digging, sifting, cataloging. By August archaeologists had removed five thousand cubic yards of dirt, much of it with brushes and dental picks. They had also screened nearly two hundred tons of earth through small mesh. Yet they daily discovered more rich cultural material. They needed more time. That is when Richard Daugherty asked his friend Warren Magnuson for help.

In mid-summer of 1968 Daugherty and Fryxell had requested the Walla Walla District of the Corps of Engineers to build a dike around the

Marmes site. But the Corps discarded the idea: it did not have the money or authority for such construction, it claimed. Indeed, the District's official stance on matters of archaeology and Indian reburial in those days could best be described as an effort to get by with as little expense as possible. If Indian tribes or archaeologists requested money to investigate sites or demanded reburial, the District attempted to pass the project on to the National Park Service. "If the worst were to happen and demands were made on Lower Monumental, Little Goose, or Lower Granite for reloca-tion of prehistoric burials," bluntly wrote District Engineer Colonel Robert Giesen in a letter to his superiors in 1968, "we would attempt compromise in form of construction of minor, token memorials." Noted Harry Drake, Chief of the Engineering Division at the District in June 1968, a levee at Marmes would be "quite an expensive alternative. It looks like the proper alternative is fast digging" by archaeologists.[10]

Daugherty then approached Magnuson and the senator asked Congress for $1.5 million to build a levee—this at a time when the entire federal budget for archaeological work nationwide was about a million dollars annually. The House of Representatives killed his proposal. Undeterred, Magnuson took his case directly to President Lyndon Johnson. No American president had ever ordered funding to preserve an archaeological site. Weeks passed. Late October arrived with no presidential decision. The Corps pressed Magnuson to withdraw his request but the senator refused. The Engineers then urged the President not to authorize levee construc-tion. But on the last day of October Johnson ordered the Corps to build a protective dike around the Marmes archaeological site.[11]

The Corps had hoped things would not come to this. The Engineers were in a difficult situation. To fish biologists, the date Lower Monumental Dam went into operation would be critical. After long negotiations with fishery agencies, the Corps agreed to begin filling the reservoir by December 1968 to allow time to test fish-passage equipment prior to the annual spring runs. But Lyndon Johnson's order threw this schedule out of kilter, and fishery agencies protested.

The fishery agencies were adamant about a December reservoir filling and they had the Corps on the defensive. In April 1968 the Corps had completed John Day Dam on the Columbia. It proved an immediate dis-aster for spring salmon runs. The Engineers had not installed turbines in the powerhouse, so all water plunged over John Day's spillways, resulting in deadly nitrogen supersaturation poisoning downstream. And the adult fish-passage facilities malfunctioned. All in all, biologists estimated the dam killed more than twenty thousand adult salmon that spring. The fiasco forced the Corps to listen much more receptively to fishery agency demands at Lower Monumental. The Corps was in the proverbial hard spot, chastised by archaeologists who sought delays in the dam's schedule, and fish biologists who wanted the agency to proceed apace. This seemed a sure lose-lose situation. And it was.[12]

There is a "potential fish passage crisis at Lower Monumental Dam," the Oregon State Game Commission wired Senator Mark Hatfield. "While we are in sympathy with archaeological investigations . . . we have no alternative but to oppose this particular project as serious fish passage problems would very likely result," wrote the Idaho Fish and Game Department to Senator Frank Church.[13]

Harry Drake, Walla Walla's engineering chief, didn't especially like the idea of building a levee, either. But he never doubted the Corps could successfully build one. "The Chief of Engineers met me in a hotel room in Lewiston," he recalled, "and said, 'LBJ wants a dike, so have at it boys and don't worry about the cost.' We'd built these cofferdams all up the river and had good success, so I thought 'no sweat.'" But the Corps had no time to investigate intangibles, like deep fissures in the volcanic basalt that could spurt water behind the protective levee. It had its orders: construct a dike and complete it by the end of February 1969, allowing a few weeks to test fish equipment before the spring runs.[14]

On a cold, rainy November 2, more than two hundred people gathered under umbrellas at the Marmes site to watch Magnuson turn the first spade of dirt for the levee. Representatives from the Smithsonian Institution and national archaeological societies attended. Roald Fryxell's father traveled from Illinois. It was a good day with smiles and congratulations. But some Engineers had reservations about the proposed breakwater.

"We are concerned that this [levee] design may not fully protect the archaeological digging site," wrote the North Pacific Division's chief of engineering in an inter-departmental memo before work began. Rushed to meet their February deadline, the Corps had no time to test levee alternatives. They never doubted the dike would hold. But water backed up by the dam could fill the levee from behind. The Corps recognized the problem and proposed to solve it by pumping the seepage back into the river. But the Engineers underestimated the amount of water that would gush in at Marmes. Their pumps never had a chance.[15]

Roald Fryxell was concerned, too. He knew something about geology and feared water would ooze through an old fracture. To prevent it, he encouraged the Corps to construct a small horseshoe-shaped dike just large enough to protect the rockshelter and the land below it, leaving the fracture to harmlessly vent water into the Lower Monumental reservoir. "We didn't have any idea what the Corps meant when they said 'We'll build a levee,'" Daugherty noted. "We thought it would be small, but they moved in huge equipment. Fryxell was skeptical, but you figure the Corps has built a lot of levees, they must know what they are doing." The Corps opted for a larger levee because the Engineers believed they needed a firm basalt abutment upon which to anchor their dike, and Fryxell's small horseshoe did not offer that security.[16]

Levee construction continued through the winter, and the Engineers finished it on time. In February the Corps began filling Lower Monumental's pool. As the impoundment reached the Marmes site, water roared into the levee from the fissure behind the dike, just as Fryxell had predicted. Forty-five thousand gallons each minute. The Corps started their huge pumps, shooting streams of water over the dike. But it didn't take an engineer to realize the pumps could never keep pace with this gusher.

The Corps opened Lower Monumental's flood gates, allowing workers to locate the problem. They discovered a leak much greater than the Engineers had anticipated and figured how to fix it. But to secure the site would take time, and the Corps had no time if it was to save migrating salmon. Marmes was doomed.

The Corps worked with Daugherty, Fryxell, and their team to protect the site. Crews covered the ground with giant sheets of plastic and poured truck loads of fill on top to prevent water from sloshing through and destroying the fragile stratigraphic record. Finally, the Corps ordered the site evacuated. They pulled their pumps. Archaeologists watched as forty feet of water quickly covered one of North America's most valuable prehistoric sites.

For a while the Corps contemplated "dewatering" Marmes, claiming all they needed was authorization and money—about $3 million. Roald Fryxell gamely prophesized that he would one day climb back into the trench that had made him famous. But the authorization never came. Optimism turned to gloom and bitterness.

Fryxell blamed the Corps for not taking his advice and constructing a smaller dike. Following his lead, editorialists throughout the Northwest chastised the Engineers. "An abysmal failure to protect America's greatest archaeological treasure," claimed the *Seattle Post-Intelligencer*; "A tragedy recognized throughout the Pacific Northwest and in other parts of the world," wrote the Spokane *Spokesman-Review*.

The Corps, embarrassed, attempted to explain. While admitting they had underestimated the rate of seepage, they had based flow estimates upon the best available evidence. It would have been unsafe to construct the smaller dike Fryxell wanted. Curiously, though, the Engineers' little-publicized "After Action Report" listed as one dewatering option the construction of a short levee from the canyon wall to about midpoint of the original levee, a proposal remarkably reminiscent of Fryxell's.

In the popular mind the Corps—America's dam builders—bungled a simple job. But in reality Marmes drowned due to an unfortunate string of events. If only archaeologists had begun excavating earlier. If only Congress had authorized money to construct the dike in the summer of 1968, allowing ample time to plan and build a suitable breakwater. If only Congress had provided funding to dewater the site once it flooded. If only fish runs had not been seriously damaged at John Day and fishery people had not pressured the Corps at Lower Monumental. If only circumstances had changed, archaeologists might know much more about the ancients who came to settle the lower Snake River after the last Missoula flood. [17]

But they know much, thanks to archaeological work undertaken at an impressive series of prehistoric locations all along the river. The National Park Service and the Corps spent thousands of dollars on archaeological investigations, a salvage operation yielding some of the most significant information ever uncovered about early life in the West. Marmes was the most publicized and probably the most significant of the lower Snake archaeological digs. But there were dozens of others—Strawberry Island, Alpowa, Seed Cave, Davis Bar, Windust Caves, Thorn Thicket, Wawawai, Squirt Cave, Granite Point, Three Springs Bar—and from materials uncovered at these, archaeologists have pieced together the story of early people along the lower Snake River.

They divide life here into five phases. The earliest, dating from about 10,000 to 8,000 B.P., is the Windust. The Cascade phase runs from about 8,000 to 4,500 B.P. and the Tucannon from 4,500 to 2,500 years before the present. The Harder phase takes life up to about the year A.D. 1750 and the Numipu postdates 1750. [18]

The lower Snake canyon today is inhospitable—scrabby rattlesnake country. But this land looked different eight to ten thousand years ago, during the archaeological Windust phase. In those days it was cool country. Fryxell's team found the jawbone of an Arctic fox inside the Marmes rockshelter. Residents didn't travel to the Arctic to catch it. Flood plain vegetation more resembled a tundra than today's desert. Nearby north slopes and river banks probably held wooded patches, for archaeologists also found the remains of red fox and pine marten, animals of the forest.

Life had rhythms for ancient river dwellers; survival dictated that. During early spring people fished and gathered roots on flat land near the river and the plains above. Later they picked berries on wooded hillsides. Then came summer hunting on the uplands. Fall found people back at the river catching salmon. Mobile during much of the year, the river people concentrated in winter along the warm stream banks in and around rockshelters. Not all activity stopped. They probably harvested river mussels during cold months when water levels dropped and certainly hunted game that wandered to the river banks. But winter generally provided a time of rest for the upcoming gathering seasons.

We sometimes stereotype these early people as big-game hunters. Those along the lower Snake did stalk big animals. They fabricated razor-sharp blades and hunted deer, antelope, and elk, driving animals past hunters lying in ambush who threw spears with atlatls, devices that, in essence, extended a spear-thrower's arm, enabling him to hurl projectiles twice as far and with greater force than when throwing unassisted. The earliest residents domesticated dogs that probably helped hunters track game. These settlers might have also trapped big game in man-made, camouflaged pits. They ate fresh meat or prepared it for winter storage, fashioned hides into clothes, and cracked animal bones to expose nutritious marrow.

Archaeological evidence indicates that these earliest Snake River inhabitants relied more on big game than fish. But fish bones don't preserve well, and there is no reason not to believe that salmon also formed a significant part of their diet. For the salmon were abundantly in the river by then.

The salmon, like the ancient residents of North America, have a shrouded history. Most biologists now believe that the Pacific salmon—genus *Oncorhynchus*—developed from the genus *Salmo*, to which the European brown trout and Atlantic salmon belong. At one time, early in the Pleistocene Era, *Salmo* inhabited all the northern hemisphere. At some point a stock of the genus became isolated and gradually developed characteristics distinguishing it from other *Salmo* populations. This stock became *Oncorhynchus*, and itself eventually split into several species—coho, chinook, sockeye, chum, pink, and perhaps a few others—scientists still debate the number of Pacific salmon species. *Salmo* never left the area, steelhead trout—*Oncorhynchus myskiss*—being the most famous Northwest representative of the genus. And the Pacific salmon continued to share some important characteristics with its Atlantic counterparts, including an incredible jumping ability that originally gave *Salmo solar*—"salmon the leaper"—its name.

Pacific salmon—anadromous fish that are born in freshwater, spend most of their lives at sea, and return to freshwater to spawn and die—came to inhabit virtually every river and creek from California to Alaska. The Snake system, with its associated tributaries, became one of western America's most important salmon-producing streams. Archaeological evidence uncovered so far indicates that the earliest river dwellers had not yet developed the technology to harvest the fish *en masse* as later residents did. But these early inhabitants no doubt took substantial numbers with spears and apparently trapped some in weirs. Eventually, salmon would provide a nutritional food bank for people of the lower Snake, nature making deposits every year and humans withdrawing to meet their needs. The river people came to depend upon salmon, and poor runs could bring disaster. But the runs were normally good, providing a reliable food source. Salmon were even more important than buffalo became to the people of the Plains—more easily caught, and more abundant. No wonder the people of the lower Snake developed elaborate rituals and feasts dedicated to the fish, rituals continued into the twentieth century by native peoples of the region, ceremonies thanking the fish for returning and sacrificing themselves for the people.

Blessed with a prolific food supply, these ancient river inhabitants developed a sophisticated lifestyle. They carved finely crafted bone needles as small as modern embroidery needles. They stitched skin clothing. They sewed waterproof bags allowing them to transport drinking and cooking water from the river. They split crushing, chopping, and scraping tools from basalt slabs and fabricated delicate blades from crystalline rocks, blades sharper than modern surgical scalpels. They developed a trade network with neighboring peoples and treasured the tiny seashells they bartered for, seashells from an ocean four hundred miles away.

Small groups of people, perhaps two or three families, lived in the Marmes Rockshelter, at Windust Caves, and at other ancient sites along the lower Snake. Occupying these primarily during winter, they had time to speculate on life and death as they ate well from the year's gathered supplies. Indeed, they had considerable leisure time, their entire surroundings serving as vegetable garden and feed lot. Theirs was not an unremitting struggle to survive, and during leisure hours they developed rituals and refined religion. The residents of Marmes, for example, cremated their dead, perhaps as a way of preparing them for their next life; Daugherty and Fryxell unearthed at Marmes the oldest evidence of cremation ever found in North America.

Over thousands of years, life gradually changed for the river's inhabitants. They moved out of caves and rockshelters into semi-subterranean pithouses. They replaced atlatls with bows and arrows. They grew more adept at catching salmon, weaving nets to capture the fish and using lines and sinkers. Life took a dramatic change somewhere in the early eighteenth century when horses migrated to the region.

Of the lower Snake River's five phases of Indian life, the last, the Numipu, is the shortest, a little over 150 years, a period in which the river's native people rapidly reached their ultimate technological development and just as quickly declined, decimated by white diseases, chased from most of their homes by white settlers. That era began with horses.

Traffic went both ways on the Bering Land Bridge. People came to the Americas, but the Americas boasted at least one significant export: the horse. Thousands of years ago horses roamed the American prairies. But they died out. That is, all except the ones making their way over the land bridge to Asia. Once in the Old World, domesticated horses became the most important means of transportation in Asia and Europe. Conquering Spaniards reintroduced horses to the Western Hemisphere. Some escaped onto the plains of North America and multiplied. Southwest Indians traded these to nomadic tribes in the north. The horse culture spread quickly, and by the early 1700s the lower Snake's Nez Perce probably owned some.[19]

Nez Perce tradition says the tribe's first horse was a white mare heavy with foal purchased from the Shoshone, the Nez Perce's southern neighbors and rivals. The mare lived in a village along the lower Snake at the mouth of Asotin Creek, and that horse and her colt spawned the thousands of Nez Perce horses the tribe eventually owned.

Probably within a generation of obtaining their first horse or horses the Nez Perce learned how to use them, and with that knowledge came a dramatic lifestyle change. First the horses served as pack animals, replacing dogs with their greater carrying power. Then Nez Perce learned to ride. Once they acquired this skill the Nez Perce and their Palouse Indian neighbors became masters of horsemanship.

Thousands of horses thrived on the rich grasslands of the lower Snake country, protected from harsh winters and isolated from natural predators. The Nez Perce and Palouse counted their wealth in horses, and they were wealthy indeed. Perhaps alone among the Indian peoples of North America, the Nez Perce and Palouse practiced selective breeding. They castrated poorer stallions and traded inferior stock to neighboring tribes.[20]

Small bands of Nez Perce wanderers, who had previously ventured across the Bitterroot Mountains on foot to hunt buffalo, now took to riding horses, enabling them to travel farther and carry home more dried meat and hides for clothing and shelter. Instead of sending a few foot travelers, whole villages now crossed the Lolo and other trails. They also could now more easily travel to multi-tribal fishing grounds, such as The Dalles along the Columbia. Horses took Snake River people to the plains above the river to gather roots and grains, and to hunt deer and antelope. The horse brought other changes. Snake River residents could now construct larger pithouses because they could drag larger poles to the river. Increased mobility introduced Snake inhabitants to other lifestyles. They borrowed the concept of the tipi from Plains Indians, developed a more elaborate system of constructing graves, and acquired new tools.[21]

Obtaining horses changed lower Snake lifestyles, but patterns established over thousands of years continued. During spring, summer, and fall the river people hunted and gathered from temporary villages on the plateaus. Since they could now travel farther, their diets became more diverse. They ate rabbits, deer, elk, bear, antelope, buffalo. Men hunted larger animals while women and children trapped smaller ones. While men hunted, women gathered roots, berries, nuts, and seeds, particularly kouse and camas roots dug with sharpened sticks.

Despite the ability to travel more widely, salmon remained a staple food. Each spring—and to a lesser degree each summer and fall—the river filled with salmon. The Indians of the lower Snake waited expectantly for the first sign of their arrival, then caught hordes. They built rock and driftwood platforms from shorelines and netted the struggling fish. They built weirs of willow brush and poles. They caught some with hooks and lines. What fish they did not eat immediately they split open, cleaned, and dried on wooden racks in the sun or smoked and stored for winter use.[22]

Through more than ten thousand years of human settlement the lower Snake had gone from tundra cool, to a lush period when the river banks supported a rich diversity of plant and animal life, to a dry desert-like climate. Through it all, people relied on salmon. Archaeologists are not quite sure how direct the lineage is between the Nez Perce, Palouse, and other river inhabitants of historic times and the ancients who occupied sites like Marmes. There is no doubt that the Nez Perce speak a tongue stemming from one of the oldest-known language stocks in North America. It could be that the earliest residents to settle this region, those evacuees of the Alaska Refuge so many thousands of years ago, are distant relatives of the river people encountered by whites. Later arrivals also appeared along the lower Snake. After ages of unions and divisions, these may have developed into the river people of the eighteenth, nineteenth, and twentieth centuries.

What is clear, however, is that throughout this long period of settlement, people of the lower Snake depended on salmon. Salmon, more than anything else, tied the horse people of historic times to the ancients of the Marmes Rockshelter. By the late-twentieth century the Nez Perce Indians no longer relied on dwindling salmon runs for primary sustenance. But the salmon still held religious and spiritual significance, a reminder of an ancient way of life along the river. When dams came to threaten the salmon's existence, the Nez Perce and other Idaho Indians became vocal and significant players in efforts to preserve the runs.

Ten thousand years after a wandering band found home in a rockshelter near the confluence of the Palouse and Snake rivers, Roland and Joanne Marmes farmed the land surrounding it, raising cattle and irrigating crops.

Then the Corps of Engineers condemned part of their property and the Marmes family moved their home to higher ground.

Then the state highway department condemned more of their property to make way for an access road to a new state park, and the Marmes family moved their house again.

Then the Corps of Engineers condemned their house because it now sat along a proposed recreational trail that would tour hikers through the region's rich geologic and archaeologic history. Finally the Marmes family moved completely off the land they had farmed for years.

"We didn't make any money" from the well-publicized Marmes

excavation, Joanne Marmes reflected. "We just went down in history and you can't send two kids to college on that."

During the course of all the moves, Roland and Joann Marmes divorced and Joanne's brother, who ranched just upstream on land the Corps also condemned, committed suicide. "He just never was happy after he got off the ranch," she said.

Roald Fryxell wasn't particularly happy, either, the way things turned out. "We received considerable criticism both within the academic community and without, that the $1.5 million appropriated to save the [Marmes] site with a levee could be put to better use," he said. "Archaeologists felt it could be better spent on basic research. Maybe it could, but we had no such option. The money was appropriated for a levee." Fryxell made a national reputation at Marmes, but, frustrated because he could not complete his work there, he grew irritated at what he considered unwarranted sniping by academics jealous of his notoriety.

Richard Daugherty and Roald Fryxell had a falling out at Marmes. "Roald was very bright," Daugherty observed later, "but he would fly into a project and never write it up. He moved from Marmes to the lunar project, and then was removed from that. His life was coming apart—like everything important had been done."[23]

But Fryxell stayed at Washington State University, hoping to once again find the spark that had so stimulated him at Marmes, that had launched a career that seemed destined for brilliance. He turned to Lind Coulee, the place where his mentor Daugherty had first discovered evidence of ancient life as a young archaeologist. He hoped to use some of the sophisticated techniques he and Daugherty had developed at Marmes to uncover even more information at Lind Coulee. He pushed himself, traveling the lonely eastern Washington highways at ungodly hours, trying to fit archaeological excavation into a demanding teaching load. Lind Coulee finally killed him. On May 18, 1974, while driving home to Pullman in a borrowed Volkswagon with no seat belts, Fryxell fell asleep. His car jumped a ditch and rolled twice. Roald Fryxell, age forty, died instantly.

He was thirty-one years old on that hot summer day in 1965 when he walked behind Roland Marmes's bulldozer and discovered America's oldest human remains. Both men's lives changed dramatically from that point. And the world came to know more about America's first settlers. But the site Marmes and Fryxell worked now lies under forty feet of water, the Corps-built levee retaining quiet water resembling a reflecting pool. The road Fryxell traveled so many times to dig this site is closed to the public;

you can only get there by water now. Occasionally boats pull up to the levee and their occupants, oblivious to all the excitement this property witnessed in the 1960s, try a little crappie fishing.

Marmes perhaps holds more secrets. In the 1970s contractors for the National Park Service dove into the pool and found the site pretty much as Fryxell and Daugherty had left it. It still might hold fragments of a puzzle that future archaeologists will uncover, parts that will help to explain more about the earliest residents of the lower Snake—the ancients. [24]

Chapter 3

The Seekers

In that stretch of the Snake River that separates Idaho from Oregon and carves Hells Canyon, the deepest gorge in the United States, the section Grace Jordan once described as "flinging itself between its pillars with special frenzy," you can still get some appreciation of the way the lower Snake churned in the days when the seekers arrived, in that time before dams and stagnant pools replaced whitewater.[1]

Some seekers came to the lower Snake to make maps, claim land or souls, trap furs, explore; others came for gold; some arrived to farm. They brought transformations that dwarfed the alterations of the Missoula floods. They opened the country, saw its potential, and almost immediately demanded changes on the river, changes that would smooth the obstacles impeding navigation, preventing this part of the river from ever again "flinging itself . . . with special frenzy."

October 10, 1805: Nez Perce Indians on horseback watch Meriwether Lewis and William Clark enter the Snake River. Thirty-three people and one dog in five canoes ride low in crystal clear water, loaded with supplies soaked from an upstream dunking.

It was about 5:00 p.m. on a Thursday. Clark, Lewis, Sacajawea, Ordway, York, and the others of that expedition, explorers with names burned into a nation's memory, paddled out of the Clearwater into the lower Snake, the first non-Indians to see its "greenish blue" water with shoreline of "open Plain on either Side." And from that moment the river's history changed.[2]

Lewis and Clark's Corps of Discovery awoke early the next morning, sculled six miles through swift water, and stopped for breakfast. They descended the Snake, what Clark called "Lewis's River," going ashore at a Palouse Indian[3] village to barter for fish, roots, and dogs. (The Corps had limited hunting success and dogs satisfied the men's hunger for meat.) Following breakfast they proceeded on, navigating nine violent rapids during the day.

They made another thirty miles on October 12, until they reached what later navigators called Texas Rapids. "The Indians had told us [it] was very bad," Clark wrote. "We found [it] long and dangerous about 2 miles in length, and maney turns necessary to Stear Clare of the rocks, which appeared to be in every direction."

October 13 dawned dark and rainy, but the party negotiated the rapids without mishap. There were few Indians here, but at a different time of year the boaters would have witnessed the bustling village of Palus, largest community on the lower Snake, just yards downstream from the rockshelter later called Marmes, where ancient river residents had once made their home.

Early the next morning they glided under "a remarkable rock verry large and resembling the hill [hull] of a Ship." Monumental Rock would later give its name to a dam. Palouse Indians escorted them through several treacherous rapids this day, but even expert guidance could not prevent one canoe from striking a rock, upsetting all people and supplies. The explorers beached on an island after making only fifteen miles.

The party passed eleven islands and several rapids on October 15, some "verry bad and dificult." They camped at the head of Fishhook Rapids because Indian guides warned them of difficulties ahead.

With an Indian canoe at its head the expedition negotiated the rapids the next morning, one boat hitting a rock, forcing a painstaking unloading. At Five Mile Rapids, rather than risk boating through, crew members portaged a hard three-fourths of a mile with heavy craft and supplies. Then the Corps floated down the last few miles of the Snake to its juncture with the Columbia. During their time on the lower Snake they had passed more than thirty rapids worthy of noting; upset two canoes; experienced heat, cold, wind, and rain; and made the first written observations of the river.

The following year Lewis and Clark traveled the country again, but not on the same route. In 1806 they trekked overland along the old Nez Perce Trail south of the river, reaching the Snake near Alpowa. They camped the night of May 4 just outside of present-day Clarkston, Washington, then continued their journey east the next day. They hurried along the Snake this time, anxious to return home. But Lewis took time to make some prophetic remarks about the land surrounding the river. "This country would form an extensive settlement," he wrote, "the climate appears quite as mild as that of similar latitude on the Atlantic coast if not more so and it cannot be otherwise than healthy; it possesses a fine dry pure air. . . . I have no doubt but this tract of country if cultivated would produce in great abundance every article essentially necessary to the comfort and subsistence of civillized man." It proved to be an accurate prediction.

Following Lewis and Clark a kind of who's who of western explorers came to the lower Snake—David Thompson, Donald McKenzie, Peter Skene Ogden, Jedediah Smith, among others. Yet despite all this early exploration, people had a hard time figuring just what to make of the place, whether it was good country or bad. Early reports ranged from those of Meriwether Lewis, who saw glowing potential, to those like Alfred Seton of John Jacob Astor's Pacific Fur Company, who found little to praise. "The country is plane, not a tree to be seen," he wrote, "a barren sandy desert producing a little wormwood [sagebrush], & in some places a few miserable tufts of grass."[4]

In 1828 English botanist David Douglas, namesake of the Pacific Northwest's most famous evergreen, traveled the land and seconded Seton's opinion:

> We rose always at daybreak, and camped at 3 or 4 p.m., during which interval, the thermometer commonly standing in the shade at 108 degrees of Farenheit. . . . In the cool of the evening we generally made fifteen or twenty miles more. Except that good water may be obtained, there is nothing to render the country superior, in summer, to the burning deserts of Arabia. Salmon are caught in the river . . . but they are neither so plentiful nor so good as in the Columbia.[5]

Though they were not yet sure of the country's potential, people continued to examine it. In 1841 Charles Wilkes's United States Navy expedition scouting the Pacific Rim sent a few men inland to explore the Walla Walla and lower Snake region. By this time the country had garnered considerable publicity in eastern newspapers, stories written largely by missionaries and their families. Their reports were generally favorable, but William Breckenridge could not figure what all the ballyhoo was about and cast his lot, in the long, confusing littany of whether this was a rich land or poor, with those opting for the latter. "It appears to me," he wrote, "that we certainly must have viewed it in a very different light from the Majority of Writers that have come out so boldly in its favor." Not two acres out of a hundred north of Walla Walla would pay the farmer for his trouble, he predicted.[6]

If observers could not make up their minds about the land's quality, missionaries had no doubts about the region's potential for conversions. In 1832 the *Christian Advocate and Journal* of New York carried the story of four Indians who had traveled from the inland Northwest to St. Louis seeking the "whiteman's Book of Heaven." The American Board of Commissioners for Foreign Missions responded in 1835 by sending Marcus Whitman and Samuel Parker west. Whitman returned after meeting with Nez Perces at the fur traders' rendezvous at Green River, but Parker continued to the lower Snake country.

Parker, a keen observer, left the most detailed description of the land since Lewis and Clark. He found the confluence of the Clearwater and Snake to "combine many advantages for a Missionary station." While Parker admitted that the nearby prairie country had a "want of summer-rains" making it impossible for "some kinds of grain [to] flourish," he noted that cattle and horses grew fat on the rich bunchgrass, and—like Lewis and Clark—he predicted a prosperous settlement.[7]

Parker left for the East before missionaries Marcus Whitman and Henry Spalding arrived at Fort Vancouver on the Columbia River in 1836, but Hudson's Bay Company Chief Factor John McLoughlin informed them of Parker's suggested missionary sites at Walla Walla and along the Clearwater River, where they respectively settled and worked diligently —but with increasingly limited success—until Cayuse Indians killed Whitman and others at his Walla Walla mission in a classic clash of cultures.

The Whitman massacre of 1847 launched a decade of Indian-white confrontations. After news of the Whitman deaths reached the Willamette Valley, a group of Oregon Volunteers entered the Walla Walla country seeking revenge. The Volunteers never did track down the guilty Indians, but in 1848 the Cayuse themselves turned over five of their members, who were tried at Oregon City and hanged. The Indian "war" of 1847-48, militarily indecisive and probably unnecessary, had important consequences on the lower Snake. Whites unjustifiably accused Palouse Indians of siding with the Cayuse murderers of Marcus Whitman. Though inaccurate, that image held until the second outbreak of hostilities in the 1850s when the Palouse paid for their unfortunate reputation.[8]

By the early 1850s contact between Indians and whites in the Inland Empire increased as emigrant trains, peddlers, prospectors, and railroad surveyors entered tribal lands. Settlers worried such incursions might lead to conflict, so in 1855 Washington's first territorial governor, Isaac Stevens, convened a two-week council in Walla Walla. According to an agreement Stevens thought he had wrenched from the gathered tribes, the Indians agreed to confinement within several large reservations. Whites could now freely settle in and travel through the non-reserved lands.

Isaac Stevens was pleased as he rode out of the Walla Walla Valley on June 16, 1855. For five days his party journeyed northward to the Snake. They followed that river a few miles, noting cornfields and orchards cultivated by Nez Perces and Palouses influenced to take up farming by Henry Spalding. Observing this land, Stevens cast his opinion with those who predicted a future wealth of settlements. He found this "a delightful rolling country, well grassed and arable," and was convinced the hills would make "a remarkably fine grazing and wheat country."[9]

As Stevens continued east, he assumed he had solved problems between Indians and whites in the inland Northwest. But Congress did not approve his treaty, and within a few weeks gold discoveries in Colville drew whites across reservation land. Indians killed seven intruders, some of whom they accused of stealing horses and raping women. They then repelled a hastily organized military expedition, and what began as a police action turned into war. Cayuse, Yakima, Spokane, Palouse, Coeur d'Alene, and other tribes united in an effort to prevent erosion of their ancestral lands.

In 1857 the army constructed a military post known as Fort Walla Walla as a way of keeping peace. Tempers calmed for a while, but in the spring of 1858 hostilities flared when, almost simultaneously, a small group of Palouse Indians stole some army cattle and Colville miners petitioned the army for additional protection after rumors spread that Indians had massacred a group enroute to the diggings.

Colonel Edward Steptoe took four companies into the Palouse country to discipline the cattle thieves, crossing the Snake at Alpowa. Predictably, the cattle rustlers evaded the cumbersome army troops. Steptoe continued toward Colville. Spokane and Coeur d'Alene Indians, alarmed at this military invasion, intercepted the soldiers and attacked near Rosalia. Following a hard battle, Steptoe retreated in the middle of the night, making it to the Snake River where Chief Timothy's friendly Nez Perce ferried the exhausted troops to safety on the south shore. It was the most significant military crossing ever along the lower Snake, preventing Steptoe's name from going down in American history with the less fortunate George Custer. Once on the other side of the river, Steptoe withdrew to Walla Walla.

News of "Steptoe's Disaster" swept the Pacific Northwest. Army commanders ordered Colonel George Wright to retaliate, and Wright did his job ruthlessly.

Wright brought a show of force never before seen in the interior. Moving from Fort Walla Walla in the summer of 1858, he commanded twelve companies. He built the only fort ever established on the lower Snake. Fort Taylor, named for an officer killed during Steptoe's wild flight, barricaded with basalt rock and alder logs, lay on flat land at the Tucannon River's mouth. Wright garrisoned it with one company, then pressed on into the plains. In a series of battles over the next month he inflicted heavy casualities, killed hundreds of horses, and destroyed stores of food. Facing destruction, the Indians ended hostilities and the United States Senate finally ratified Stevens's treaties of 1855. Although the government forced no immediate removal of interior tribes to designated reservations, Indian control over ancient lands ended, clearing the way for white domination of the lower Snake.[10]

Lieutenant John Mullan nearly lost his life along the Snake while stationed at Fort Taylor in 1858, grappling hand to hand with an Indian. But in the next year he returned to the same place and crossed the Snake River while constructing his famed 624-mile military road from Fort Walla Walla to Fort Benton, connecting the Columbia/Snake waterway with the Missouri/Mississippi system.

Of all the river's early travelers and explorers, Mullan most poetically saw the region's potential:

> Night after night I have lain out in the unbeaten forests, or on the pathless prairie with no bed but a few pine leaves . . . with no pillow but my saddle, and in my imagination heard the whistle of an engine, the whirr of the machinery, the paddle of steamboat wheels, as they plowed the waters. . . . In my enthusiasm I saw the country thickly

populated, thousands pouring over the borders to make homes in this far distant land.[11]

During the 1850s, war suppliers laboriously hauled materials up the Columbia on barges or small scows to Walla Walla. In 1858, R. R. Thompson and L. W. Coe decided upon a better way. They constructed a steamboat above Celilo Falls to run along the upper Columbia and lower Snake rivers. They completed their boat in 1859, named it the *Colonel Wright* after the hero of the Indian campaigns, and hired Len White to guide it. In 1859 he piloted the first steamboat on the Columbia above The Dalles, taking supplies to Fort Walla Walla, and in the next year made it to the mouth of the Palouse, where the army established a forward supply base.[12]

Thompson and Coe made a lot of money and White proved the Columbia/Snake waterway navigable—at least by an able and courageous pilot. The same year Len White got as far as the Palouse River, Elias D. Pierce discovered gold above Lewiston. White would lead an array of pilots and boats serving the lucrative mining trade, plying the lower Snake River in that stream's most glorious era of steam navigation. By then, so many white miners, settlers, and entrepreneurs were crossing through the lower Snake region that the era of exploration effectively ended.

The explorers—Lewis, Clark, Thompson, McKenzie, Douglas, Parker, Stevens, Steptoe, Wright, Mullan, and others recorded their impressions of the river, its valley, its people, and the plains surrounding it. They, some of the most noted explorers in the American West, preceded and invited the most dramatic change ever to a region forged by fire and water and inhabited for thousands of years. And the most prophetic of them, people like Lewis and Clark, Parker and Mullan, accurately predicted the settlement ahead.

After Colonel George Wright quieted the Indians, invasion of the inland country commenced unabated. Prospectors led the way. Some searched on the legal side of the Indian/white territorial lines Isaac Stevens drew in 1855. Others, like Elias D. Pierce, ignored that treaty document.

As miners pressed into crags and valleys of the inland Northwest, finding few promising claims, they looked enviously to the Bitterroot Mountains, a place that appeared hopeful: here were steep slopes ravined by creeks and rivers, places where prospectors might mine profitably with nothing more sophisticated than a pan or sluice box. The best routes into these enticing mountains all required crossing Nez Perce lands, and Pierce saw no reason not to travel them.

Elias Pierce was one of those rugged, tireless, fearless, aggressive nineteenth-century fortune seekers people later produced movies about. Except in his case the world simply forgot.

Pierce fought in the Mexican War, prospected in California, and traded with Indians, traveling lonely trails few other whites dared tred. In 1852 he bought horses from the Nez Perce Indians, staying in their country just long enough to convince himself he could find gold there if he spent time searching. But there is no sense chasing after gold if you think you can make money more easily. So Pierce sidetracked again to California to work on an irrigation project, then ventured to British Columbia when the Western rumor mill churned stories of easy pickings there. Not finding his bonanza in either place, he returned to Walla Walla and began again to trade with Indians. Six years after his first trip, E. D. Pierce re-entered the Nez Perce lands he believed held gold.[13]

In 1858 Pierce stopped along the Clearwater River where he hoped to test his theory. But with Indians battling intrusive whites throughout the inland Northwest it seemed an inopportune time to begin prospecting, even in friendly Nez Perce country. Pierce waited out the hostilities.

Early in 1860 he returned to the Clearwater with a companion and found a few cents worth of color. It wasn't much, but finding real treasure, Pierce believed, required only more time, more people, and more supplies. "[I] knew I had the . . . destiny of that country, and that I could flood the entire region with good reliable men at my option," he later wrote. First he would have to overcome opposition from a few people with more scrupples about obeying government treaties.[14]

Indian agent A. J. Cain, stationed in Walla Walla, tried detering Pierce, even though the prospector assured him his discoveries lay outside the Nez Perce reservation line. Despite Cain's admonitions, Pierce went back to the Clearwater, found more gold, and brought the news to Walla Walla. Pressure on Cain grew. Businessmen, eager for trade, weren't about to sit idly while an Indian agent barred potential customers from the gold fields. [15]

Pierce would return to the Clearwater yet again in 1860, this time with ten men. They found ore in nearly every stream. Their success electrified the West. Newspapers in Portland, Puget Sound, and California reported the discoveries, and by late 1860 hundreds of miners had entered the country, many of them settling in a new town called Pierce.

In April 1861, recognizing they could no longer restrain miners from Nez Perce lands, A J Cain and Edward Geary—superintendant of Indian affairs for Oregon and Washington—convinced Lawyer, a Nez Perce head man, to relinquish mining grounds north of the Clearwater in exchange for $50,000. There is no indication any of the money ever reached the Nez Perce, but it really did not matter. The ink had hardly dried on that paper before white miners began violating the new agreement, too.

Each day more prospectors streamed into the country. In open violation of the law, many ventured south of the Clearwater into the Salmon River country. Soon infringements became flagrant, none more so than the establishment of Lewiston, a town that boomed into a thriving trading center at the confluence of the Snake and Clearwater rivers, smack in the heart of sacred Nez Perce land.

By 1862 white population in Washington Territory east of the Cascade mountains surpassed that on the west side. A year later, President Abraham Lincoln, responding to political pressure from settlers who felt isolated from the seat of government near Puget Sound, established Idaho Territory. The new territory embraced all of present-day Idaho and Montana and most of Wyoming, and Lewiston became its capital.

Soon government officials began pressing the Nez Perce for access to even more land, hoping to legitimize the trespasses at Lewiston and in the mining regions. A new treaty conference held in May 1863 drove a final wedge between two factions of the Nez Perce. In June some Nez Perce head men, including Lawyer, signed a treaty the government's negotiator boasted "relinquished . . . nearly six millions of acres . . . at a cost not exceeding eight cents per acre." Other head men, such as Joseph, Big Thunder, and White Bird, refused to sign. In the name of the Nez Perce, Lawyer gave up 90 percent of former reservation lands. Although the treaty "legalized" the new white settlement at Lewiston, it also foreshadowed difficulties between whites and non-treaty Indians that led to the Nez Perce War of 1877 and the famous, elusive trek of Chief Joseph.[16]

Although it changed a region and helped start a war, Elias D. Pierce's discovery did not help him much. He missed out on the good claims by spending his time negotiating for rights to construct a wagon road into the mines, a road that proved profitless. Later he retired to Indiana to live miserably off his veteran's pension. In 1892 Indiana's representative to Congress petitioned on his behalf for the government to compensate the former adventurer for "services rendered to his country in the early days of the West." The request never made it out of committee. Pierce died penniless five years later. He didn't even leave enough money for a funeral or headstone. His obituary read simply that he had "spent 20 years in California in its early days." It made no mention of an Idaho town named for him in the heart of the gold country he discovered or of the dramatic impact of that golden discovery upon the lower Snake River country.[17]

Even after fifty-five years of exploration by Lewis, Clark, Thompson, and all the rest, Idaho's Clearwater gold fields lay in isolated, primitive country. But discover enough color and prospectors will go most anywhere, as they did to the Clearwater. Steamboats provided their transportation. Steamers carried more than sixty thousand miners, traders, gamblers, bartenders, dance hall girls, entrepreneurs, and curiosity seekers into the Idaho mines between 1861 and 1863. Some of the boats stopped at Wallula on the Columbia River, leaving passengers to continue their journey overland. But many ventured on, up the cascading waters of the lower Snake, all the way to Lewiston. The *Colonel Wright*, piloted by Leonard White, the first boat and the first captain to steam into the lower Snake in 1860, also pioneered the route to Lewiston in 1861.[18]

White unloaded his supplies and passengers and turned around. It had taken three-and-one-half days to churn and pull his boat upstream from The Dalles. He returned in eighteen hours. The Columbia and Snake were fast-flowing rivers, and only courageous captains attempted them. But the trade proved lucrative. Steamboatmen could get rich taking supplies and people upstream and carrying gold down. Once White proved the lower Snake navigable, others followed, and soon the *Spray*, the *Cascadilla*, the *Tenino*, the *Okanogan*, and the *Nez Perce Chief* joined the *Colonel Wright* in supplying Lewiston.

Seen from one perspective, riding sternwheelers along the Columbia and Snake was the lap of luxury. Henry Miller made the boat trip to the mines in 1861, observing "gentlemen . . . who view the scenery, smoke Havana cigars, and quaff Champagne cock-tails." Passengers could eat food better prepared than at most hotels, frequently including fresh-caught salmon ceremoniously presented in elaborate dining salons.[19]

But the lower Snake remained a wild river; the thirty or so rapids Lewis and Clark encountered still endured. This was no opulent excursion for steamer crews. At times even a fearless captain like Len White failed to get through. Generally, from November through April the Snake ran too low for steamboats to navigate. During the height of the gold rush Lewiston merchants became so desperate they offered bonuses to the first boat making it upriver in the spring.

The best navigation, from late spring through early summer, came when high water covered rocks and flattened rapids. Even then, steering a course through the Snake required skill. Come too early and you might have to moor in a place a few miles above the Snake's confluence with the Columbia, a safe refuge rivermen called Ice Harbor, where you could rest unscathed as ice chunks flowed downstream. Get too close to a canyon rim and you might run onto a gravel bar.

Even if you encountered no serious problems you still had to negotiate places like Pine Tree, Palouse, and Texas rapids, places that remained rough no matter the time of year. Henry Miller described the ordeal at Palouse Rapids:

> The ascent . . . baffles all generally received notions in regard to steamboat navigation. In three quarters of a mile there is an ascent of at least six feet. The water is lashed into billows capped with foam, and the feat of ascending them looks fool-hardy. But we take a running jump right into the centre of the rapids; and inch by inch the boat goes bravely up. The waves strike her sides as if she were thumping on the rocks. Sometimes the "upper-tow" will carry her ahead half a length at a time, and then she will stand trembling for minutes in a place, or sheer from side to side as if complaining at the labor forced upon her. In an hour and a quarter we made three-quarters of a mile.[20]

And that represented an easy trip. Come upon such cascades during shallow water and Miller's ascent would appear to have been made in a speed boat. In low water crewmen ventured ashore with a huge piece of timber, wedged the timber between rocks above the head of the rapids, and fastened a line around its middle. Then they ran the line to an iron capstan on the boat's fore deck. As the rope coiled around the capstan, the engines churned mightily and the boat literally drug itself upstream. You didn't make three-quarters-of-a-mile per hour doing that. As more boats plied the lower Snake, rivermen sank iron rings into boulders and used these to secure their lines, a more reliable and durable navigational aid.

Although it was no easy task negotiating the lower Snake, skilled boatsmen completed the runs without mishap in the 1860s. Lewiston grew complacent: townspeople no longer worried about whether or not boats would make it, only when they would arrive. And the business community grew impatient, especially after prospectors discovered color in the Boise Basin. Why not send boats farther upstream, all the way to Boise, and supply those gold fields from the territorial capital?

Lewiston dispatched a scouting expedition to determine the navigability of the river to Boise. The town's newspaper, the *Golden Age*, enthusiastically reported the result:

> They found nothing in the river to impede navigation whatever. . . .
> The Snake is navigable for steamers, and will be much safer to travel
> than the river is from Lewiston to the mouth. . . .
>
> A new route will now be opened for steam, the results of which
> cannot now be foretold. We shall penetrate Nevada and Utah
> Territories by steam, as it is well known that it is only 90 miles from
> Fort Boise to Salmon Falls [and] . . . Salmon Falls is within 250 miles
> of Salt Lake City. [21]

The only thing between Lewiston and Fort Boise, that is, was 135 miles of river, dozens of rapids—and Hells Canyon. One suspects Lewiston's glowing report did not dupe experienced riverman Thomas Stump. He had no doubt read less-rapturous stories about Hells Canyon. But he felt up to its challenge.

Stump had replaced the ubiquitous Len White as captain of the *Colonel Wright*, and though Stump lacked White's flamboyance, he was a skilled and adventuresome boatman commanding the most versatile steamer on the river. In 1865 he set out from Lewiston, churning and winching his boat up the canyon for four-and-one-half days until, about eighty miles above town, the current casually tossed his sternwheeler onto a jagged reef that ripped away eight feet of bow. Stump beached his vessel, repaired the bulkhead, and turned back to Lewiston, covering the distance in three-and-a-half hours. The trip proved too much for the sturdy boat and after its attempt up the canyon its owners salvaged only the engine.[22]

The middle Snake River would never be navigable. Lewiston failed to benefit from the Boise gold run, and the Clearwater/Salmon gold fields played out. Miners moved to Boise, Virginia City, the lower Kootenay, Helena, and other western bonanzas. As population shifted south Lewiston stagnated. Boise became the territorial capital. Soon only one boat a week traveled to town. The lower Snake quietly awaited its next rush, its next influx of steamers. That boom came from tilling the soil, not digging for minerals.

Miners needed food and farmers followed them inland. Most settled around Walla Walla and tilled the flat valley floors, believing the steeply sloped hillsides nearer the Snake unproductive.

Stockmen moved into the lower Snake region, and their cattle and sheep grew fat on the luxuriant bunchgrass of the hills. Soon eastern Washington cattlemen trailed stock to British Columbia, Montana, Oregon, Puget Sound, and Idaho, eventually driving them all the way to Cheyenne, Wyoming, to sell to buyers from Omaha and Chicago.

But the region proved inhospitable to beef ranchers. A series of cattle-killing winters decimated herds. Of an estimated ten thousand cattle in the Walla Walla area in 1861, perhaps only a thousand survived that year's harsh storms. The winter of 1880-81 left stacks of sun-bleached bones visible to settlers for decades. Although a few herds remained, the cattle boom ended with that devastating winter.[23]

The most dramatic revolution in lower Snake River history came when someone discovered that farmers could profitably till the steep hills above the river. The hills proved to be fruitful indeed. Covered with the fertile loess deposited by glacial winds, the Palouse and surrounding regions had some of the richest topsoil in the world and soon yielded some of the nation's most abundant grain crops. Wheat quickly became king.[24]

People would never make money on such abundance, however, unless they could ship it to market. Before the 1880s no railroads crossed the country, leaving only one alternative: transport wheat to the Snake River and ship it to Portland by steamboat. No simple task, that.

The first problem came in getting wheat to the river banks. In places, the lower Snake cuts a canyon more than two thousand feet below productive farm land, and the richest agricultural country lies in the elevations highest above the river. The simplest solution was to plunge down the canyon rim by horse and wagon over primitive roads. Sometimes cargo drivers tied logs behind to slow their descent. The roads themselves contained many switchbacks and in places enterprising farmers constructed turntables that

allowed wagons and teams to negotiate sharp corners in lazy-Susan
fashion. But this was no way to get huge crops to market, and inventive
settlers searched for other methods.[25]

Major Sewell Truax constructed a 3,200-foot-long grain chute down the
banks of the Snake in 1879, but his effort hardly became an instant success. Workers had to unsack wheat at the top, pour it into the four-inch
pipe, then resack it at the bottom—time-consuming work. Besides, friction
often ruined the grain. After a couple of years Truax installed baffles. They
slowed the fall and lessened friction damage, but then his chute clogged.

Primitive though it was, Truax's device proved more efficient than
hauling wheat downhill by wagon, and within a few years other chutes
lined both sides of the river. The bucket tramway, an even more ingenious
solution, soon replaced them. Farmers loaded wagons full of sacked wheat
and journeyed to the head of the nearest tram. There they unloaded the
wheat sack by sack, placing each sack on an arm-like metal projection attached to heavy cables, an early version of the chair lift. Poles and towers
running up canyon walls supported the cables.

Bucket trams ran by gravity: the loaded wheat going down forced unloaded "buckets" up in a perpetual motion. The trams had two major
advantages over grain chutes. They created no friction, and workers had
no need to unsack and then re-sack wheat prior to shipping.

Area farmers constantly sought faster methods of shipping grain to
riverbanks. Their search led to the most efficient method devised to get
wheat down mountain slopes prior to trucks and highways: the rail tram.
Wooden tracks covered with strap iron coursed down the hillside. A cable
with a car attached to each end looped over a pulley at the top. Workers
loaded the upper car with wheat and, when started downhill, it pulled the
empty buggie up. Half-way down, the tracks split so the cars could pass
each other.

Some of the Snake River grain conveyances operated into the 1940s. Originally developed to haul grain to steamboat landings, they survived by sending crops to railroad sidings long after steamers ceased plying the river. But
their peak operation came in the glory days of Snake River steam navigation, when the "wheat fleet" supplied the world with Inland Empire grain.

Imagine Liverpool, England, in the 1880s. A four-masted sailing ship
docks. Workers hurry into the hold and begin unloading cargo. They stack

endless sacks of wheat on the wharf. An exchange-board clerk tallies the shipment, making his way down a list of wheat-producing regions that send grain to this, the world's largest wheat exchange: India, Russia, Australia, Germany, Chili, Atlantic Coast of United States, Pacific Coast of United States. Finally the clerk comes to the heading "Walla Walla" and makes his mark. He probably doesn't stop to think about the journey those Walla Walla sacks have made. If he does, he must contemplate an improbable venture.[26]

"Walla Walla" was a catch-all term for a large wheat-producing region. Some of Liverpool's wheat did come from Walla Walla, sent from there to the Columbia River to begin its downriver journey. But most wheat came from the lower Snake River region where it was grown on steep hillsides and harvested with huge teams of horses and mules. Farm laborers sacked the wheat in the field and carried it by wagon to the rim of the Snake River canyon. Then they sent it down that sheer chasm by tramway.

At the river's edge workers took wheat off the tram, loaded it onto hand trucks, marked each bag's quality, variety, weight, and owner, then stored each bag in a warehouse built on piers over the river. When a steamboat pulled up, warehouse workers reloaded the sacks onto hand trucks and hauled them up wooden planks to restack them in the boat's cargo hold. Once loaded, the boat headed downstream.[27]

The steamboat negotiated the rapids of the lower Snake and the Columbia until reaching the unnavigable falls at Celilo. There workers removed the wheat, loaded it onto railroad cars, portaged it around the rapids, then re-loaded it onto another boat for the short journey to the Cascades where it was again unloaded, portaged, and re-loaded before landing at a dockside warehouse perched on spindly piling along the riverfront in Portland.

At Portland, laborers stockpiled the wheat in a warehouse, then later removed it, sack by sack, and loaded it once again onto a sailing vessel that tugboats maneuvered to the Columbia River's mouth. From there sails went up and the wheat started on a four-to-five-month journey around Cape Horn to England, where it was unloaded and tallied as "Walla Walla wheat" by an employee who probably had no idea where Walla Walla was and had no reason to care about the astonishing journey these sacks had made.

The wheat fleet of tall-masted sailing boats gave Portland's harbor a unique ambiance. The initial shipment of Northwest wheat went from Portland to Liverpool in 1869. By the 1880s more than a hundred tall-masted vessels serviced the city. It was a spectacular sight, a crowd-pleaser to both residents and tourists.

Upstream at small towns along the lower Snake River, sturdy little sternwheelers serviced the ports. Although the boats were less spectacular, the residents of these towns looked upon their "wheat fleet" just as admiringly as any Portlander. Without these steamers, Portland would have had far fewer ships at its docks, for the Inland Empire increasingly provided the bulk of wheat shipped from the Rose City to England.

The first load of wheat went down the lower Snake in 1876, making its way from Almota to Portland. It proved to be a lucrative trip, and the Snake River's wheat fleet soon numbered sixteen steamers—more than had ever catered to miners—bringing machinery, supplies, and mail upstream, hauling wheat down. In days before railroads, the lower Snake served as an essential lifeline to residents along and above the river. A network of towns, farms, and transportation systems emerged. Tall wheat ships brought prosperity to Portland. But the Snake River's squat sternwheelers provided more than that to the Snake region. For those who chose to live in the country of the lower Snake they made survival possible.[28]

Although most people resided on the prairies above the river, farming homesteads and trading at towns that sprouted up every few miles, some people also lived directly along the river and a good number of communities grew up there, too. Some, like Asotin, Clarkston, and Lewiston still endure. But for the most part, those Snake River towns are gone. Call the roll of those places and conjur images of a former way of life: Ainsworth, Almota, Ayer, Farrington, Grange City, Illia, Joso, Levey, Magallon, Matthews, Moore, Page, Penewawa, Riparia, The Riviera, Scott, Sheffler, Silcott, Simmons, Snake River Junction, Walker, Wawawai.

Colorful as many of these communities were, they really amounted to little more than way stations: landings where steamboats pulled ashore to service passengers, to load wheat, to unload supplies. Or, later, places where trains stopped to accomplish the same. Once transportation improved, once the prairie lands got their own train service and the steamers quit landing and the trains rolled hurriedly through, the residents of the little river towns quietly passed their lives. None of these communities ever boomed for an extended period, although boosters liked to brag that their burg would surely become an important riverside metropolis one day. With the exception of the three biggest towns, about a hundred residents were the maximum for the river villages. Although most continued to exist into the 1960s, only the three largest Snake River communities survived the arrival of slackwater.

Except for Lewiston, Clarkston, and Asotin—the three having a combined population in the 1990s of about forty thousand—the lower Snake was always sparsely populated. A good many dreams died along that stretch of the river. Dozens of entrepreneurs at places like Almota and Riparia and The Riviera went broke waiting for booms that never came.

For some people, the river was never more than a way to make money, and when their dreams of profit were dashed, the dreamers tended to move on. But to hundreds of generations of native peoples, and to a significant number of later white residents, the river was always more than a place to reap profits. To them it was a home. They grew attached to the place. They learned to adapt and accept what the land would give, and, if they didn't prosper, they at least lived peaceful lives. One of those was Ben E. Kelley. "A boy living along the river doesn't keep a diary but remembers certain events," Kelley wrote late in his life. "When he gets up in the morning he gives a brief glance upriver to guess about what time it is and then a close scrutiny of the river nearby to see if anything was floating by or if the river had fallen or was rising."

A boy living along the river learned to respect it. "The year I was six I went to school to Mrs. Blyton's across the river," Kelley reminisced. "When I first started going over in the fall when the river was low, my father would sit in the stem with a paddle to steer . . . while I rowed the boat. Soon I became a good enough oarsman that they let me go alone—with much hand waving and watching until I tied up on the other side a quarter of a mile away. Once or twice a high wind would come up making huge whitecaps. I would go down and make sure the boat was securely tied and make signs I would stay with the Blytons that night. . . . Some evenings as I rowed back the salmon were jumping all around me." [29]

Long before the environmental era of the late twentieth century, an emotional schism developed between those who learned to accept and appreciate what the river naturally offered—people like Ben Kelley—and others who believed the Snake could provide much more. If people could master this river, said some, bury its rapids, provide year-round navigation, they would open a lifeline. Create an open river to the sea and the inland Northwest—particularly Lewiston and Clarkston—would prosper. The lush interior farmlands would become the world's wheat basket. And those who controlled that trade, who could economically ship this abundance to market, would get rich. An open river would serve that demand. It appeared that simple. But the dream took a hundred years to realize.

Chapter 4

An Open River

Had they contemplated the protracted construction of Cascade Locks, promoters might have gained some inkling of just how long it would take to open the rivers all the way from Lewiston to the Pacific Ocean.

The boiling rapids at the Cascades of the Columbia, downstream from The Dalles, Oregon, halted navigation. Entrepreneurs countered whitewater with imagination: they ran mule trains along the river banks and for 75 cents per hundred pounds portaged "emigrants effects" around the falls. Eventually the Oregon Steam Navigation Company took over, replacing mules with a small locomotive, Oregon's first.

The detour accomplished its task but consumed too much time for the dreamers who envisioned a day when boats would steam directly through the Cascades. In 1876 Congress authorized the Army Corps of Engineers to construct a canal to achieve that goal. Two decades later they were still working at it. People came to joke that only ancient pioneers could remember when the job had begun. Nevertheless, when completed in 1896, the locks proved effective. Boats carrying thousands of tons of material slipped easily past the rapids. As an added benefit, railroads lowered rates to compete with the paddlewheelers; freight rates from The Dalles to Portland plummeted.

Merchants and farmers lobbyied for more navigational aids to allow steamers to pass all the way to Lewiston. It seemed a no-lose situation: either steamboats would carry their cargo more cheaply than railroads, or railroads would lower rates to beat the competition. The next obvious obstruction to an open river was Celilo Falls, upstream from The Dalles.[1]

An Open River Association formed in Portland. Working with wheat growers in the interior, it pressured Congress for a canal along the eight miles of river foaming through Celilo's boulders. Congress responded by authorizing the Corps of Engineers to construct another passageway. The Corps built an impressive concrete, stone, and metal ditch with a series of locks, sixty-five feet wide and eight miles long, completed in 1915.[2]

Northwesterners celebrated the accomplishment in a manner appropriate for a destiny-changing event. A dozen river towns, all hoping to become prosperous ports, observed the occasion with "Open River" commemorations. There were speeches and parades, baseball games and fireworks, carnivals and banquets. A boatload of excursioning dignitaries, commencing at Lewiston, celebrated all the way to Astoria, where the Columbia empties into the Pacific.

The oratory oozed with optimistic predictions for the inland Northwest. "Civilization may well make here its most splendid achievements," prophesied Marshall Dana, one of the canal's staunchest supporters. Joseph N. Teal, another open river stalwart, seconded that opinion: "The Inland Empire will be an empire in fact as well as in name—an empire of industry, of commerce, of manufacture and agriculture; and the valleys of the Columbia and the Snake will have become one vast garden, full of happy homes and contented and industrious people."[3]

No community rejoiced more boisterously than Lewiston, the isolated Idaho town that had long pegged its visions of growth and prosperity upon a navigable waterway. The town's newspaper called May 15, 1915 "Lewiston's Greatest Day," a day when twenty-five thousand people came—by boat, train, auto, team, afoot—to commemorate the "Open River to the Sea." One hundred guns saluted the sunrise and a hundred more ushered in the night after a day of festivities. Thousands of school children throughout Idaho studied the event and its importance to their state's future through a series of lectures on the open river instituted by the state superintendent's office.

Yet it did not take long for the splendid dream of those 1915 celebrants to shatter. Hardly had the Celilo Canal opened when Columbia and Snake river steamboating collapsed. In hindsight, it seems obvious why.

Sternwheelers had become outmoded, unable to compete with the speed, efficiency, and greater carrying capacity of trains. Once tracks crossed into the wheat regions the boats had no hope of seriously threatening railroad dominance. Railways simply lowered rates until steamers lost

their freight trade. By 1919 the new locks at Celilo, opened with such fanfare just four years earlier, lay virtually idle—simply "boondoggling," critics came to jest. From 1921 to 1930 the canal had no commerce at all.[4]

With the glory days of the great wheat fleets ended and railroads shipping grain to market, it appeared to some pessimists that the Columbia/Snake
river system would never become a significant navigational way. But there
were those who continued to dream: open rivers had brought prosperity
elsewhere; they could do the same here. In fact, the long battle for a navigable
water course from Lewiston to the Pacific had really just begun.

Pacific Northwesterners did not invent the concept of open rivers, of
course. Egyptians built canals four thousand years before the birth of
Christ. The Erie Canal of the 1820s touched off an interest in inland
navigation in the United States. The federal government became involved
in 1824 with the first in a series of congressional acts aimed at improving
navigation. Soon the Eastern United States became linked with a system of
navigable waterways.[5]

By the 1870s steamboat operators had increasing difficulty competing
with the low rates of the railroads that connected the east and west coasts.
As railroads came to dominate shipping, however, they raised their prices
and residents of inland areas clamored for relief. Increased competition
appeared the best method of forcing lower rates, and in those years only
an inland waterway system could compete with railroads. Improvements
in marine technology—including propellors adaptable to shallow-draft
vessels and the development of towboats and barges capable of carrying
huge loads—provided the means to contest the railroads.

President Theodore Roosevelt believed in the cause of inland navigation,
but he also advocated maximum multipurpose development of the nation's
rivers. In 1908 he wrote:

> Our river systems are better adapted to the needs of the people than
> those of any other country. . . . Yet the rivers of no other civilized
> country are so poorly developed, so little used, or play so small a part
> in the industrial life of the nation as those of the United States.
>
> It is poor business to develop a river for navigation in such a way as
> to prevent its use for power, when by a little foresight it could be
> made to serve both purposes. We can not afford needlessly to

sacrifice power to irrigation, or irrigation to domestic water supply, when by taking thought we may have all three. Every stream should be used to the utmost.[6]

Roosevelt aimed his words primarily at the U. S. Army Corps of Engineers. In those days, the Corps believed rivers had one primary purpose: navigation. All other river uses were subordinate. Roosevelt strongly disagreed, and among members of his Inland Waterways Commission, only the Corps' representative dissented from the president's multipurpose views. The Corps' advocacy of the primacy of navigation went a long way back.

Congress formally established the Corps of Engineers in 1802 and in 1824 directed the agency to clear snags from the Ohio and Mississippi river. The General Survey Act gave the agency comprehensive surveying authority. The Army Engineers now assumed responsibility for a wide array of civil works, including the clearing of rivers; the construction of lighthouses, public buildings, monuments, and bridges; the exploration and mapping of the West; and the surveying and planning of canals, roads, and railways. Even so, the Corps concentrated its power in programs to improve harbors and ease navigation on the nation's rivers. By the mid-nineteenth century the Corps of Engineers dominated federal water programs. When it became involved in flood control, however, it temporarily lost favor.[7]

In 1861 Army Engineers Andrew Humphreys and Henry Abbot staked their reputations—and that of their agency—on a monumental study of Mississippi River flooding. Their report became gospel to generations of Army Engineers. Discounting the potential for jetties to remove sediment, and dams and reservoirs to ease flooding, Humphreys and Abbot proposed instead to construct levees—ever higher and longer; whatever proved necessary to hold back the silt-strewn, raging river.

Then came a persistent critic: bridge builder and river pilot James Eads, who, in the 1870s, constructed small jetties in the delta. Eads's breakwaters washed away sediment and created a deeper channel less prone to flooding and open for the first time to ocean-going traffic.[8]

This embarrassment—and the Corps' continued insistence that structures such as jetties and dams were merely ineffective fads, that levees provided the surest long-term flood control solution—ended the Army Engineers' monopoly of government water projects. Congress discovered that the Corps had not cornered technical expertise. In ensuing years it granted increasing authority to Corps' competitors for federal water money: the Mississippi River Commission, the Geological Survey, and most importantly, the Reclamation Service. Frustrated in its effort to solve flood problems, the Corps backed away from "multipurpose" river developments, cleaving more single-mindedly to navigation as its primary responsibility. If the Army Engineers could not monopolize all aspects of waterway development, they would hold tight to navigation and insist that it dominate other river uses. They would fight multipurpose projects that combined navigation with hydroelectricity, irrigation, and flood control—projects that could just as well be constructed by other federal agencies. Multipurpose developments threatened navigation's dominance and therefore the Corps' dominance. Consequently, the Corps opposed Theodore Roosevelt's multipurpose plans in 1908.

But significant legislation in the 1920s and 1930s, combined with a new post-Humphreys and Abbot generation of Corps leaders convinced of the bonanza multipurpose development would bring to their agency, transformed the Army Engineers once again into the nation's dominant water resource institution.

The 1925 Rivers and Harbors Act directed the Corps and the Federal Power Commission to estimate the expense of surveying the nation's navigable rivers. The 1927 Rivers and Harbors Act actually authorized these river surveys, based on estimates the federal agencies had previously submitted and published in House Document 308, which came out in 1926. Known as "308 Reports" after that House document number, these studies became basic planning tools for navigation, flood control, irrigation, and hydroelectric power generation. By the mid-1930s the Corps had prepared more than two hundred. Now eagerly touting dams and multipurpose endeavors, the Corps recommended gigantic construction projects throughout the nation.

The Corps began reaping benefits from its 308 recommendations when Franklin Roosevelt became president. The federal government authorized Bonneville Dam on the lower Columbia River in 1933, one of the Corps' first important multipurpose efforts. The Flood Control Act of 1936, which authorized more than 250 projects, further enhanced the Corps renewed leadership role in multipurpose water resources construction. No longer advocating "levees only," the Corps now launched a dizzying era of dam-building, many constructed in the Pacific Northwest, and most providing multiple benefits. If navigation alone could not justify construction, the Corps could perhaps demonstrate the cost-effectiveness of a project by including flood control, hydropower, irrigation, recreation, and other benefits. Tally them in. Rather than fighting multipurpose dams, the Corps now recognized that such projects would bring the agency work, money, and power, and the Corps became the most important dam builders in the United States.[9]

The Corps of Engineers, active in the Pacific Northwest long before Bonneville Dam, undertook its first regional civil works project in 1866, clearing snags on the Willamette River near Portland. In the 1870s the Engineers cleared and dredged the lower Columbia, and in the 1880s it began constructing jetties at the river's mouth. Completion of the Cascade and Celilo canals in 1896 and 1915 solidified the Corps' reputation as the dominant regional waterways agency.[10]

Cascade and Celilo created a primitive version of an open river that permitted transportation all the way from Portland to Lewiston by intrepid pilots in sturdy boats traveling at high water. The lower Snake, though, remained treacherous. The Corps could build a dozen canals on the Columbia, but until it did something about Snake River rapids, for most of the year Lewiston's "port" would remain an illusion.

To gain better access to that Idaho town, the Corps began clearing snags and rocks from the lower Snake in the 1880s. They blasted rock, constructed dikes, and brought in a government steamer, the *Wallowa*, to dredge and remove debris. Yet local farmers and merchants wanted more, and in 1907 they pressured the Washington legislature to take the unusual step of giving $125,000 to the federal government for the Corps to use in creating a truly open river along the Snake and Columbia. Most of the money went into channel clearing on the Snake.[11]

Despite these efforts, shipping along the lower Snake steadily declined. The Open River Transportation Company operated between Lewiston and Celilo Falls from 1905 to 1912 before going bankrupt. No river commerce existed on the Snake from then until the Corps finished Celilo canal in 1915, when the Columbia River Transportation Company operated between Portland and Lewiston during high-water months. In 1920 one boat made five round trips between those cities, but then, except for short-hauls between railroad stations along the river, all shipping on the Snake ceased.[12]

Even when boats could ply the lower Snake they usually came at the wrong time. Spring and high water were best for navigation, but harvest came in the fall. Railroads increasingly provided the only option for grain growers, and farmers grew disenchanted with that choice as rates skyrocketed.

By the early 1930s products went by barge for 50 cents a ton from Duluth, Minnesota, to Buffalo, New York, a distance of about a thousand miles. Boats towed freight from Kansas City to Chicago—approximately 550 miles—for $1.94 per ton. At the same time, farmers in the interior Northwest paid railroads $4.80 a ton to ship wheat to Portland or Seattle, a distance less than four hundred miles. These farmers thought it unfair that the federal government assisted shippers elsewhere yet did so little for them. The lower Snake River provided an artery to the sea. The government, they argued, needed to recognize that stream's potential and open the river to year-round navigation.[13]

"An open river does not mean merely the completion of the Celilo Canal, blowing out a few rocks at the rapids and scraping the gravel off of a few shoals," complained Captain W. P. Gray, longtime pilot of the Columbia and Snake rivers. "It means dams with locks on the Snake . . . to submerge the rapids, reefs and bars." He spoke in 1915 while Celilo gleamed glossy new. Even then river advocates like Gray knew that canal alone was inadequate. Over the years they would organize into a confusing array of advocacy groups demanding further improvements.[14]

There was the Columbia & Snake River Waterways Association, the Western Inland Waterways Corporation, the Umatilla Rapids Association, the Inland Empire Maritime Conference, the Tri-State League, the Columbia Valley Association, and various others of short life and little influence. The organizations sometimes bickered among themselves: those based in Portland or along the Columbia naturally wanted the Columbia developed first; those centered in Lewiston sought improvement of the Snake.

Still, most groups had several things in common. They pursued a series of locks and dams along the Columbia and Snake rivers to create slackwater from Lewiston to Portland. They advocated multipurpose projects that could produce hydroelectricity and aid irrigation, although they viewed these benefits as tangential to navigation. They organized public opinion to pressure Congress. And they expected that, once Congress authorized river improvements, the Army Corps of Engineers would undertake the task because, as Lewiston's Arthur Ward, a leading open river advocate exaggerated, the Corps was "thoroughly disinterested and completely competent."[15]

The river advocates, however, proved too splintered to be effective. They needed unity and a strong leader. They found those attributes in the Inland Empire Waterways Association and Herbert G. West.

Advocates of river improvements got along fairly well as long as little money was involved. The federal government spent such tiny sums on the Columbia/Snake system that all river associations could at least agree on one goal: they wanted the government to invest much more.

When Franklin Roosevelt became president, however, regional animosities swelled. Much sooner than anyone expected, Roosevelt directed the Army Corps of Engineers to construct Bonneville Lock and Dam. Open river supporters should have rejoiced, and some did, particularly in Portland, because the dam would create work for idle Portland residents, become a tourist attraction, aid shipping to the city, and generate electricity for local markets.

But upstream Columbia River residents, concerned because the Bonneville project called for locks too narrow to allow sea-going vessels to navigate beyond that structure, saw few benefits for themselves. Umatilla business people demanded larger locks and immediate authorization for an additional Columbia River dam near their city.

Meanwhile, Lewiston's open river advocates split with their former allies on the mid-Columbia. They saw no reason why Umatilla should get a dam before the lower Snake. "Development on the Columbia River should follow similar development on the lower Snake River—not precede it," argued the Lewiston-based Western Inland Waterways Corporation. And mid-Columbia groups, they claimed, jeopardized all future river development by advocating larger Bonneville locks. Expensive sea locks, which would bring no immediate benefits to Lewiston, would cost $7 million above the hefty $32 million the federal government had already set aside for Bonneville, possibly diverting money from Snake River improvements. Besides, some powerful Eastern congressmen already believed the sparsely populated Pacific Northwest received too much federal largesse and might revolt if asked for more. "If more millions should now be secured for sealocks at Bonneville it is readily conceivable where the open-river project may end—stranded on the limb of the tree," warned the *Lewiston Morning Tribune*.[16]

Amidst this atmosphere of squabbling, the chambers of commerce of several Snake river towns called an open river meeting at Lewiston in February 1934, pledging that delegates would take no official vote on any course of action: this would be an informational gathering only. More than three hundred people arrived.

The night before that Lewiston conclave a group of men met quietly in Walla Walla, Washington, and determined to disregard the ''no official vote'' sanction. The next day B. M. Huntington, president of the Walla Walla Chamber of Commerce, rose before the conference urging delegates to approve a seven-point set of principles. Point one recommended seagoing locks at Bonneville. Point two advocated immediate construction of a dam at Umatilla. Only by point three did Huntington address the idea of locks and dams on the lower Snake. It was a proposal with priorities guaranteed to anger, and it did. The conferees refused to vote. Undeterred, the rebels met again the next day in Walla Walla and organized a new organization destined to succeed where so many others had failed. They called it the Inland Empire Waterways Association (IEWA).[17]

The IEWA offered pragmatism where others had promoted regionalism. Its primary purpose was to get slackwater to Lewiston. But IEWA members realized they would need to compromise along the way. If they had to placate some Northwesterners by supporting sea locks at Bonneville, they would do that. If they had to lobby for a dam at Umatilla, they would do that. They would do what needed to be done, they would appease those needing appeasement.

The IEWA promised a united front, but other river associations remained leary, unwilling to abandon their causes to join to an upstart group. Herbert G. West, the first managing secretary of the IEWA and for decades its organizational wizard, gave them no alternative. West proved tireless and ruthless in his efforts to build IEWA's membership, even at the expense of other organizations. When some groups declined to pay membership dues West chastised them: ''Other organizations wish to take some of the credit but nevertheless the glaring truth is that this Association alone has started the ball rolling for . . . development.'' It was not long before West's aggressiveness, combined with IEWA's effectiveness, drove all other waterway groups into extinction.[18]

West proved an excellent choice to manage the association. He promptly got himself appointed to President Roosevelt's National Resources Committee and to the Water Resources Committee of the Pacific Northwest Regional Planning Commission. Within these groups he labored for a unified, systematic development of the Columbia and Snake waterway and soon attracted powerful allies.[19]

At the same time, West toiled for grassroots support. "It was door to door work, in those days," he recalled of the association's first years. "A $5 donation was big money. It was nothing to work all day in the office, then drive fifty or a hundred miles to address a night meeting of farmers."[20]

Both West, the indefatigable promoter, and the Inland Empire Waterways Association profited. The IEWA became one of the most potent water development organizations in the nation. And West, who had moved to Walla Walla from Portland in 1930 as the district representative of a small mercantile firm, became one of the region's most influential citizens, serving as the town's mayor and becoming a first-name chum with some of the nation's most powerful legislators. In 1959 the Army awarded him a Certificate of Appreciation for Outstanding Civilian Service. Ten years later the Department of Defense made him the second recipient in the nation of its Civilian Service Medal. "Through his efforts," the 1959 citation read, "he helped to gain for the Corps of Engineers and the Army great prestige and public support." The Army did not exaggerate. As much as any other person, Herbert G. West brought slackwater to Lewiston, creating work for hundreds of Army Corps of Engineers employees.

Almost immediately after its organization the IEWA won a significant victory, and soon other river associations either joined with it or simply ceased business as membership dues increasingly rolled to the new group. In the summer of 1934 West and other IEWA members prepared background materials for the Corps in support of sea locks at Bonneville. When Secretary of the Interior Harold Ickes, a key Roosevelt advisor, traveled to the dam site, West met him and pressed the case. In August the Corps announced a change in plans. It now found sea locks at Bonneville fully justified. The IEWA took perhaps more credit than it deserved in winning approval of the larger locks, but in the eyes of many open river advocates it had proven its effectiveness.[21]

In this early triumph IEWA initiated three strategies destined to become its hallmark. First, while development of the lower Snake River remained its highest priority, the IEWA took a broad view and championed water improvements throughout the Northwest. Second, it worked closely with the Army Corps of Engineers. And finally, West recognized that the only way to do business with Washington, D. C., was to become familiar with power brokers there, and he came to know his way around that town very well.

West understood that the Corps of Engineers would not consider Snake River projects until it had completed Bonneville and made improvements to the mid-Columbia navigation channel. Rather than complaining about lack of attention to the Snake, he threw his organization behind the Columbia projects, adroitly biding time and winning friends at the Corps.

His patience paid off. Bonneville's completion provided two new sources of ammunition for IEWA in its open river campaign. First, shippers used the locks. In 1937, the year before the Bonneville locks opened, fifteen thousand tons of freight went through the nearby Cascade Canal. Two years later, three hundred thousand tons went past Bonneville. The new locks proved river transportation a viable alternative to railroads, provided rivers truly were navigable.[22]

At the same time Bonneville's hydropower created an even greater need for slackwater. "The industrial utilization of the power developed at the Bonneville and Grand Coulee dams raises for immediate consideration the related problems of transportation and markets," noted the Pacific Northwest Regional Planning Commission. "The immediate improvement of . . . channels . . . to Asotin . . . will partially solve the problems of transportation and markets for industries using the power generated."[23]

West and the Inland Empire Waterways Association developed a close relationship with the Corps. West made the acquaintance of all District Engineers serving in Portland, and, after the Walla Walla District formed in 1948, those who came to his town. He played golf with them, entertained them in his home, planned gala banquets when they arrived and when they left. No District Engineer escaped Walla Walla without a resolution of appreciation from IEWA.[24]

Herbert West cultivated a symbiotic relationship with the Corps. Only the Corps could bring the improvements he coveted, but he let the Corps know it could rely on him for help, too. Officially, the Corps does not promote its own recommendations. It provides information enabling Congress to make decisions. Unofficially, however, the Army Engineers are very adept at marshalling political support for projects they favor. One of their most effective methods is to work through lobbying groups like the IEWA. When Division Engineer Colonel Thomas Robins urged the Association in the 1930s to work for Columbia River improvements as a prelude to Snake River work, IEWA carried the Corps' charge into

Congress. In 1970, with the Walla Walla District embroiled in an environmental controversy over Lower Granite Dam, District Engineer Colonel Robert Giesen suggested a counter-campaign of pro-dam publicity by IEWA. These were just two of numerous occasions when IEWA came to the aid of the Corps, becoming the agency's "unofficial" lobbying arm.[25]

While Herbert West recognized that he needed the Corps, he knew his most important allies would be representatives in Congress and influential bureaucrats in the federal government. During every legislative session from 1934 until he retired in 1967, Herb West appeared before Congress, testifying to the need for slackwater development in the Pacific Northwest. It was not like he breezed into town, sat before a congressional committee, gave testimony, and left. In these well-planned, exhausting trips, Herb West usually traveled with a large entourage, sometimes twenty or more influential IEWA members. Their itinerary was always full.

During its week in Washington IEWA delegates began each morning with a briefing breakfast. Then they scheduled meetings throughout the day with the most influential people in town. They would, of course, touch base with the Corps—usually first thing. But they would also meet with the Department of the Interior, the Bonneville Power Administration, the Bureau of the Budget, the Interstate Commerce Commission, the National Water Commission, the Department of Transportation, the Atomic Energy Commission, and presidential staffers. These were not office calls on lowly federal employees. Normally IEWA had direct access to the highest official's office. In between meetings they testified at hearings and hosted parties for Northwest congressional representatives. When they got home, delegates wrote their thoughts about the meetings, and Herbert West planned how to improve the next year's invasion of Washington. Noted Dwight Eisenhower's assistant director of the Bureau of the Budget in 1956, "Of the many delegations who come to Washington to discuss water resource development with us, [IEWA] always ranks at the top in clarity and forcefulness of presentation."[26]

During important legislative proceedings affecting river development, West was a whirling dervish. Not only did he write, call, and cajole Congress, he also lined up chambers of commerce, port officials, petroleum companies, local and state politicians—whomever he thought had influence—to write, call, or cajole. And he always maintained flexibility. The means to the end really did not matter. If he believed, as he did in the 1930s, that he could most strongly advocate Snake River development by stating that the region, served by navigation, would be better able to provide homes and jobs for dust-bowlers evacuating the Midwest, then he would make that case. If he believed, as he came to in the 1940s, that Snake River dams would never win authorization on navigational merits alone, then he would tout the importance of hydroelectricity. If he believed, as he did in the 1950s, that fishery agencies might thwart dam construction, then he would argue for including fish-passage facilities at the river-blocking monoliths.

Herbert West and the Inland Empire Waterways Association eventually got their way. The Corps of Engineers constructed the dams creating a year-round navigable channel to Lewiston. But it was a long struggle. Not until 1945—eleven years after IEWA formed and eighty-five years after Len White first piloted a steamboat into the Snake River—did Congress authorize the Lower Snake River Project. It would be another thirty years—ninety-nine years after the Corps began construction on the Cascade Canal—before the Army Engineers finished the last dam in that system, bringing slackwater to Lewiston. Open river advocates won their war in tiny increments. The Snake River dams are a testament as much to perseverance as they are to engineering ability.

Chapter 5

"Construct Such Dams as Are Necessary"

Build the dams, Herbert West said, and development will follow. He said it to Congress, port districts, chambers of commerce, schools, farmers.

Build, and the Snake River will become a lifeline to one of the world's richest agricultural regions. Break the stranglehold of railroads, and freight charges will plummet. New industries will rise. Population will escalate. Build, in other words, and the inland Northwest will become that "empire of industry, of commerce, of manufacture and agriculture" that open river advocate Joseph N. Teal had predicted in 1915 upon the completion of Celilo Canal.

But the government would not authorize dams unless their economic benefits outweighed construction costs. Railways already adequately handled the region's freight, so there was no need for expensive locks. And the dams' power would go unused in the sparsely populated Pacific Northwest.

Herbert West found himself in a Catch 22: the region had inadequate development to justify the projects, yet if the dams went unconstructed the region would never develop.

Some environmental groups in the 1960s and 1970s criticized the Army Corps of Engineers for steadfastly siding with developers in advocating water projects that brought profits for business and work for Engineers.

Those development groups that sought authorization for lower Snake dams might have wished for such a relationship. For years the Army Engineers claimed they could find no economic justification for major river construction and dashed the hopes of business people and Northwest congressmen who sought construction of dams and locks on the lower Snake.

As early as the 1890s Pacific Division Engineer Colonel George Mendell bluntly and pessimistically told Congress he found extensive navigational work on the lower Snake infeasible: river traffic had virtually disappeared and steep canyon walls isolated the river from prime agricultural lands.[1]

Yet these obstacles did not deter adherents who continued to press the case for an open river. The Lewiston Commercial Club lobbied Idaho's congressional representatives for a survey determining the river's navigational feasibility. In 1915 they got federal funding for their survey, but not the desired results. The Army Engineers again found no justification for expensive work along a little-used river.[2]

In 1924 river boosters persuaded the Corps to survey again, and so commenced one of the most undignified assaults ever made on the river. Three Army officers, including Division Engineer Colonel W. J. Barden, boarded the government steamer *Umatilla* at Lewiston. The *Umatilla*, built for shallow water on rivers like the Snake, drew only three and a half feet. But even that trifling draft proved no match for the Snake at low flow. The boat clumsily proceeded downstream stern-first, raked itself over rapids and occasionally grounded on rocks. A few miles downstream the party disembarked at Riparia and waited two days for a storm to pass. When it didn't, the Engineers abandoned the cause and caught a train to Seattle.

Obviously having seen enough of the river, Barden wrote, "I do not think a channel of [5 feet] could be obtained and maintained" at a reasonable expense. He addressed only the simple task of blasting rocks and removing shoals. He did not even contemplate the much more complex and expensive job of building dams. In 1924 that seemed merely a pie-in-the-sky dream of a few unrealistic Lewiston residents.[3]

In 1932 Lieutenant Colonel Thomas Robins, Pacific Division Engineer, conducted another review of the lower Snake in response to congressional resolutions. The colonel pointed to the Celilo Canal, sitting virtually unused, and cautioned against hurried development on the Snake that might only result in similar unwise federal expenditures. He urged caution, recommending only minimal channel clearing in the foreseeable future. First develop the Columbia, he suggested, determine whether river traffic justified additional expenses, and only then proceed up the Snake.[4]

Open river adherents protested. Columbia and Snake river improvement should not be "split up and constructed piece-meal," stormed Arthur Ward of Lewiston's Western Inland Waterways Corporation. "It should be authorized and constructed as a whole." Development advocates sympathized little with Robins's plea for caution merely because the waterway had little existing traffic. "It has always been my theory," wrote the traffic manager for Lewiston's largest industry, Potlatch Forests, "that once barge transportation was established it would build for itself new tonnage which is not now moving." Build the dams and increased river traffic and regional development will follow.[5]

To determine the region's attitudes about an open river the United States Senate conducted hearings in Portland and Lewiston in 1932, shortly after Robins had made his recommendations. Governors, legislators, and representatives of open river associations pleaded for speedy and simultaneous construction of dams on the mid-Columbia and lower Snake. Galleries of farmers, river pilots, shippers, and business people cheered. In two days of testimony only the Corps' Robins opposed immediate Snake River construction. Again he urged caution: take the projects one at a time. Although outnumbered, Robins's voice proved the most influential to lawmakers who valued the Corps' technical expertise in such matters. Congress would not authorize dams on either the Columbia or the Snake in 1932.[6]

In 1933 the Army Engineers submitted their long-awaited Snake River "308 Report" and it proved another disappointment for developers. In addition to Pacific Division Engineer Robins, the District Engineer and Chief of Engineers also found dams and locks unjustified. The region did not need hydropower, and virtually no shippers used the river. Benefits did not come close to equaling costs.[7]

A few months later Lewiston hosted the open river rally that spawned the Inland Empire Waterways Association, and Herbert G. West began his long campaign to bring slackwater up the Snake. The IEWA initially had no more luck convincing the Corps of the dams' justification than had earlier organizations. But when the association pressured legislators, Congress at least ordered the Corps to continue studying the Snake.

A 1936 Corps of Engineers report recommended a dam on the Columbia at Umatilla as well as a series of ten locks and dams between Pasco and Lewiston on the Snake. That was the good news. The bad news for IEWA came when the Corps still did not advise Snake River construction until it had completely finished four massive dam projects planned for the lower and middle Columbia.[8]

The following year Robins penned a more favorable report to Congress. He also considered the possibility of ten dams along the lower Snake, but concluded that four would provide adequate navigation. For the first time he spoke of "indirect benefits," thus coming to the side of IEWA in the long controversy over whether to first build and then wait for development, or wait for development before building. Low-cost water transportation and cheap power would bring agricultural and industrial maturity, Robins claimed. He sounded like Joseph Teal and Herbert West.[9]

In the Corps of Engineers' complicated heirachy, Robins's report next went to the Board of Engineers for Rivers and Harbors, which agreed dam construction would stimulate regional growth and seconded his recommendation for authorization. As the last step in the review process, Major General J. L. Schley, Chief of Engineers, studied the document. Schley concurred that dams would bring development but he did not believe such potential regional benefits justified federal expenditures. Although Robins was finally willing to gamble that the dams would pay for themselves by creating a demand for navigation and hydropower, Schley was not. He vetoed the plan.[10]

This 1938 review was the most positive to date by the Corps. Still it was hardly enough for Herbert West. He worked closely with Northwest congressional delegates and convinced them to introduce twenty-four measures in the 1930s, all requesting navigational improvements on the Columbia and Snake. Without Corps' endorsement, however, West would fail. Congress relied heavily on the Army Engineers' recommendations. As long as the Corps did not completely support river development, Congress was unlikely to authorize Snake River dams.

The 1930s ended with the Corps more favorably disposed toward Snake River slackwater than at the decade's start, but still skeptical. The Engineers had convinced themselves that river development would bring economic growth, but Congress proved unwilling to authorize dams based solely on future potential. In the 1940s, however, as the nation came to make economic decisions that had seemed purely speculative in the 1930s, the situation changed dramatically. Finally Congress agreed to a series of dams along the lower Snake River. But even then authorization did not come easily, for the Snake River dams had detractors nearly as influential as their supporters. And the detractors would delay congressional authorization for quite a while.

Some opposition came from people jealous of any federal money flowing to the Inland Empire. The proposed Snake River project rekindled old animosities between northern and southern Idaho and eastern and western Washington. Puget Sound business people fought authorization because they viewed an open river as an open door luring inland trade to Portland rather than Seattle and Tacoma.[11]

But western Washington's protest proved mild compared to southern Idaho's. Idaho's major population surrounded irrigated land in the south. People lived close to the Snake River and depended upon it to water their crops. As Congress considered developing the lower Snake, southern Idahoans worried that the Army Engineers might appropriate their farm water for downstream navigation and power production. "For 30 years there has been discussed the possibility of converting the lower Snake river into a navigable stream to Lewiston," wrote a Boise civil engineer in 1941. "Southern Idaho business men have slept through this discussion . . . on the part of northern interests, that some day this navigation progam would rob south Idaho of a vast agricultural empire."[12]

The Corps tried to allay fears. "This office . . . does not want to get into any political arguments," Portland District Engineer Colonel C. R. Moore wrote, "but it seems ridiculous to consider the improvement of the river below Lewiston for navigation as in any way adversely affecting irrigation interests." Lower Snake dams could create navigable reservoirs by utilizing flows entering the Snake after it left the irrigation districts, waters fed by the Salmon, Clearwater, Grande Ronde, and other rivers.[13]

The Corps could, in the 1940s, diffuse the irrigation argument, but the underlying causes of concern were more deeply rooted. Southern Idaho business interests fought the Snake River plan primarily because they feared it would bring an economic boom to Lewiston at the expense of Boise. Animosities between the two communities went back to the 1860s when Boiseans "stole" the territorial capital from Lewiston, and residents of the two cities had never really stopped sniping at one another.[14]

A power struggle in the Pacific Northwest between the nation's two biggest dam builders, the Army Corps of Engineers and the Bureau of Reclamation (formed by Congress in 1902) created an even more serious obstacle to lower Snake development. With an increase in multipurpose water projects around the nation, the line separating major responsibilities between the two agencies blurred. No longer did the Bureau construct projects only for irrigation and the Corps for navigation. Both now built dams providing multiple benefits, and turf wars increased as each fought for a share of the federal largesse making its way to the Pacific Northwest. The Army Engineers and the Department of the Inerior's Bureau clashed repeatedly. Franklin Roosevelt's Secretary of the Interior Harold Ickes became so frustrated with the Corps that when Arthur Maass wrote one of the most critical books ever penned about the Army Engineers, Ickes glee-fully consented to write the foreword. "One way to describe the Corps of Army Engineers," Ickes alleged in Maass's *Muddy Waters*, "would be to say that it is the most pervasive lobby in Washington. The aristocrats who constitute it are our highest ruling class. . . . Within the fields that they have elected to occupy, they are the law—and therefore above the law." [15]

The Bureau of Reclamation vigorously resisted a bill debated in 1941 to authorize the Corps to build dams along the lower Snake. The Interior Department viewed authorization as a threat and encouraged the House Committee on Rivers and Harbors to reject the proposal, or at the very least insert an amendment that in essence gave the department veto power over all Corps activities along the river. Such opposition might not have been the decisive factor, but when the Secretary of the Interior speaks forcefully against a water project it has an effect, and Congress refused to authorize the Snake River project in 1941. [16]

In 1944 Interior attempted to attach a similar amendment to legislation then being discussed. The IEWA countered, "We do not object to the Corps of Engineers consulting with the Secretary of the Interior . . . but certainly we do not want them to be subservient." Subservience proved to be a moot point; Congress once again refused authorization. [17]

The next year Congress did authorize the dams, but Interior's objections continued. In 1947 it denounced the modest irrigation benefits the Corps claimed for Ice Harbor Dam on the lower Snake, stating that the Bureau of Reclamation's Columbia Basin project—part of Grand Coulee Dam—could easily provide all the irrigation the Pasco region needed. It was a futile complaint brought by an agency that had lost the major battle. [18]

While IEWA soothed sectional differences and the Corps insured its primacy over the Bureau along the lower Snake, open river advocates faced another opponent: railroads. Western Washington might lose a little trade, southern Idaho worried about Lewiston's economic growth, and the Bureau of Reclamation fretted about loss of influence. But railroads had more serious reasons to fear navigation. Bringing barges up the Columbia and Snake rivers to Lewiston might bankrupt the railroads along those rivers. Railways had invested a great deal of money building lines to tap the Inland Empire's lucrative wheat trade. They were not about to sit idly while groups like IEWA advocated inexpensive barge competition. Fighting unremittingly against lower Snake dams, the railroads had plenty of influential congressional representatives on their side. They proved a worthy rival for Herbert West.

If one person finds a market, others usually appear to help share the profits. Steamboat companies reaped the early rewards of the lower Snake region's gold and crops. But railways soon followed, criss-crossing the land with track. By the time Celilo Canal opened, railroads were entrenched and sternwheelers never regained their foothold.

Various railroads along the lower Snake contended for routes and business, but they always united in one effort: go to any extreme to eliminate the threat of water-borne competition. Dealing with steamboats proved no particular problem. When the Cascade and Celilo canals opened, railways simply lowered rates and the slower, smaller steamers went unused. The same happened when railroads built along the lower Snake: they bankrupted the steamboat companies.[19]

In the twentieth century, navigation technology began to change. Now tugs and barges could haul tremendous loads inexpensively. The railroads could not and did not ignore this threat. It was unfair for the federal government to subsidize river transportation, they complained, conveniently forgetting the huge land-grants the nation gave railways in the nineteenth century.[20]

The IEWA attempted to thwart this railroad opposition. When the Corps questioned the wisdom of lower Snake development and pointed out the abysmal history of navigational improvements along the Columbia and how railroads had put shippers out of business there, Herbert West countered that things had changed. Barges could now effectively compete with railroads. Besides, even if railroads continued to secure a large share of the traffic, locks would pay rich benefits to inland farmers because competition would force railroads to permanently lower rates.[21]

Throughout the 1930s, however, the Corps steadfastly disagreed with IEWA. The Engineers said they could not justify navigational improvements simply to lower freight rates.[22]

The arguments raged for years between southern and northern Idaho, eastern and western Washington, the Bureau of Reclamation and the Corps of Engineers, railroads and adherents of navigation. Those opposing Snake River development successfully stymied the efforts of groups like IEWA to obtain congressional authorization for locks and dams. Try as they might, Herbert West and his congressional allies failed.

Despite West's vigorous efforts, the lower Snake might never have been dammed had World War II not intervened. The war changed the American West more than any other event, save perhaps the gold rushes of the nineteenth century. The debate over dam construction suddenly and radically shifted. Now open river advocates no longer based their case primarily on navigation. They had the leverage of another issue: the sudden need for hydropower. Hydropower would dramatically increase project benefits over construction costs. Congress would finally authorize the lower Snake project.

Thomas Robins's plans for an orderly and cautious development of the Columbia River ended the day Franklin Roosevelt took office as President of the United States. Searching for ways to employ masses of laborers, Roosevelt ignored Robins's plea for caution in favor of huge federal dams hundreds of miles apart on the Columbia. The Bureau of Reclamation would build Grand Coulee, and the Corps, Bonneville.

Completed several years later, these monoliths proved what Herbert West had long suspected: once built, dams would attract development. That development came, however, not because of improved navigation but because of inexpensive hydroelectricity. Bonneville and Grand Coulee initiated an astonishing period of dam construction in the Pacific Northwest, and the dams transformed the region into a major industrial center.

Prior to Bonneville and Grand Coulee, the Corps remained skeptical about the region's need for hydropower. In a typical assessment for that decade, the Engineers reported to Congress in 1934 that "The prospects for marketing of power . . . are not encouraging." Many others similarly believed the Northwest would soon face an energy glut. Critics referred to Bonneville as a "dam of doubt" and called Grand Coulee a "white elephant in the wilderness." Generators would rust, spillways crumble, transmission lines go unused. In this thinly populated region there simply was no place to market the huge amounts of electricity these dams would produce, let alone the many thousands of additional kilowatts to come if dams went up along the lower Snake. When Bonneville came on line in the late 1930s, however, the economics of Northwest dam building changed dramatically. Development did follow the dams.[23]

More specifically, the aluminum industry followed the dams. Spurred by the need for inexpensive aluminum for airplanes during World War II, the Aluminum Company of America constructed the region's first plant at Vancouver, Washington. Soon, five other factories in Washington and Oregon produced the metal. The Bonneville Power Administration (BPA), established to market the vast new stores of hydropower in the Northwest, encouraged this aluminum incursion. Bonneville referred to the businesses as "direct service industries" and rather than channel them through intermediaries like power companies, Bonneville sold thousands of megawatts of electricity at ridiculously low prices directly to the aluminum plants. Small wonder the Northwest aluminum industry boomed despite being thousands of miles from its sources of raw materials and its prime marketing regions. Bonneville needed the aluminum industry to soak up its excess hydropower, and the companies responded by providing nearly 70 percent of BPA's revenues in the 1940s.

By the 1950s the Pacific Northwest manufactured nearly half of all aluminum produced in the United States. By the 1990s alumina ore was by far the Columbia/Snake waterway's biggest import. The aluminum industry then employed nearly eight thousand people, payed total wages of about $500 million annually, and burned more than three thousand megawatts of electricity each year. The industry by then was still a major player in the Northwest economy, but the Northwest had changed considerably since the 1940s: it had many more people and many more businesses. The Boeing airplane company, for example, dwarfed all the aluminum companies combined in number of workers (with nearly a hundred thousand) and in total payroll ($5.5 billion), but Boeing used only a fraction of the electricity (one hundred megawatts). As the ability to produce ever-more hydropower without dire environmental consequences diminished, many Northwest residents came to question the region's continued courting of the aluminum industry.[24]

In the 1940s, though, the Pacific Northwest loved aluminum companies and the economic expansion they brought. And the BPA loved the companies' energy-gulping pot lines, each pot requiring hundreds of kilowatts of electricity to maintain heat at 1,742 degrees, hot enough to transform powdered ore into molten metal. As early as 1947 the BPA predicted that the "Pacific Northwest will continue to experience an acute power supply problem for years to come" (the first in a long BPA litany of exaggerating the region's true energy needs), and urged continued construction of federal hydroelectric dams. The aluminum industry contracted for every kilowatt of energy unused by households or other businesses. There was no power surplus, the BPA said. The region was rapidly growing, and Northwest residents became convinced they needed more hydropower to attract more industry.[25]

So now it suddenly appeared the region needed all the power federal dams could generate. For the first time Congress proved willing to seriously consider a series of dams along the lower Snake. In 1944 both Senate and House committees approved a lower Snake project proposal, but Congress again delayed authorization because of confusion about the number of dams the Corps intended to build. Some Engineers believed four sufficient to produce the slackwater and hydroelectricity desired. Others opted for six, and some, ten. Although ten dams represented a duplication of construction, they would eliminate the costly relocation of railways because reservoirs would remain low enough to permit use of existing tracks. Four to six dams would necessitate expensive track relocation, but less construction duplication. No one seemed to know just how many dams to build, and Congress refused to authorize this uncertainty.[26]

The Corps could not resolve the issue without further study, but hesitated to undertake expensive studies unless Congress authorized construction, another Catch 22. Finally, Congress bridged the impasse by ignoring it, authorized the Corps to "construct such dams as are necessary" to provide slackwater along the entire lower river, and left it to the Army Engineers to decide the number best suited to meeting that goal. Congress passed Public Law 14 on March 2, 1945, ending the long struggle for authorization.

In the following two years the Corps conducted a number of studies and consulted with various government agencies to determine the number of dams necessary. Building four dams would require construction of the highest lock lifts (more than one hundred feet) ever designed in the world. The Corps questioned whether migratory fish could negotiate such a series of tall obstructions. On the other hand, a four-dam system was the most cost effective and would produce more hydroelectricity.

State fishery agencies, while questioning whether fish could survive any additional dams along the Columbia/Snake waterway, reluctantly agreed four dams were better than six or ten. Although several years of operation at Bonneville demonstrated strong fish could pass both upstream and down over one dam, fishery people feared the cumulative effect of numerous obstructions. The Idaho Department of Fish and Game summed up the opinion of Northwest fishery agencies: "After giving thought to the many problems involved, we feel that possibly less harm may be done by the four-dam plan [although] this letter is in no way intended as an endorsement . . . for construction of [any] dams in the Snake River." The reaction helped convince the Corps to build four dams. On April 23, 1947 the Chief of Engineers instructed the North Pacific Division to proceed with plans to construct four dams between Pasco and Lewiston.[27]

Eighty-five years after Captain Len White piloted the *Colonel Wright* up the Snake and first envisioned a year-round navigable river, Congress authorized the lower Snake River project. The Inland Empire Waterways Association, grain growers, barge companies, and chambers of commerce celebrated. Railroad workers viewed the project apprehensively. And those concerned with preserving fish runs harbored serious reservations. Still, it appeared in 1945 that developers had won. Little did Herb West and his allies know it would be another three decades before the Corps would finally complete the inland passageway to Lewiston; that the contest for authorization would pale in comparison to battles over approving money for actual construction; that there lay ahead many unforeseen compromises to protect the natural environment. Most of those who fought for the dams in the 1920s, 1930s, and 1940s would be dead before the first barge finally plowed through slackwater to Lewiston in the 1970s.

Part II

FISH vs. DAMS

Chapter 6

Battle for Ice Harbor

Optimistic and generous near the end of World War II, Congress authorized the Corps of Engineers to construct four dams along the lower Snake River. It also instructed them to build the long-debated multipurpose dam at Umatilla, Oregon, on the Columbia, later named for Oregon Senator Charles McNary, and to erect Lucky Peak Dam near Boise. The new work overtaxed the capacity of the Portland District office and in 1947 the Corps' North Pacific Division Engineer approved formation of an extra district. He appointed Colonel William Whipple to select a site for the Army Engineers' newest headquarters.[1]

Whipple traveled to Pendleton. He investigated Pasco. He sounded out the residents of Boise and Spokane. Finally, he selected Walla Walla. The ubiquitous Herbert West had some influence on that decison.

West provided Whipple and his small staff with temporary office space in Walla Walla. He encouraged entrepreneurs to form the Blue Mountain Housing Company and construct permanent homes for Corps employees. His efforts paid off and Colonel Whipple became the first District Engineer.

Whipple quickly assembled his key staff and the District began hiring engineers and support workers. "Walla Walla District started fast right off the bat," recalled Harry Drake, who arrived from Corps offices in Oklahoma and later became chief of the engineering division. Eventually, Walla Walla became the largest construction district in the entire Corps bureaucracy, principally because of the massive work it undertook along the lower Snake.[2]

The Walla Walla District would erect and oversee the dams, build new recreational facilities, provide access to new ports, and create jobs bringing economic growth to the lower Snake region. It would construct the world's largest steelhead fish hatchery, transport juvenile fish downriver by barge in a unique conservation effort, and oversee a multi-million dollar plan to compensate for fish and wildlife losses, the largest federal compensation plan in American history to that point. The District would win awards and face burning criticism. It would be an exhilarating and bumpy road for the District. In the decades following World War II the Lower Snake River Project would become a textbook-style study of the nation's changing attitudes toward development and preservation.

On a cloudy afternoon, May 9, 1962, Vice President Lyndon Baines Johnson, voice raspy from bronchitis, stepped to a podium constructed specifically for his massive frame—forty-seven inches on the speaker's side, sloping gently upward. Build it differently and risk incurring the considerable wrath of this temperamental politician. So the Corps of Engineers, in charge of festivities that day, built it just as the vice president requested. Standing in front of that podium, Lyndon Johnson pressed a button ceremoniously activating Ice Harbor Dam's generators and told the gathered crowd that this was only one in a string of dams soon to dot the Snake. In fact, the river would some day boast a series of impoundments all the way from Pasco, Washington, to Weiser, Idaho, producing millions of kilowatts of electricity. "A prudent people will not allow the endowments of nature to waste away," he declared. "On the Columbia there are only three reaches of river left without power development," and within a few years, Lyndon Johnson promised, the federal government would see to those, damming that water as well.

In 1962 neither Lyndon Johnson nor any of the senators, governors, congressmen, and lesser luminaries present from three states could foresee a time when advocating the damming of a free-flowing river would generate more boos than cheers. Still, even in 1962 Lyndon Johnson should have had some inkling of the changing times ahead: conservationists had already come close to thwarting dam builders at Ice Harbor, and they waged that battle long before the environmental era of the 1960s and 1970s. On the other hand, there is no evidence that conservationists showed any concern when developers first proposed a dam at Ice Harbor, more than half-a-century before Lyndon Johnson's appearance.[3]

Engineers and developers had always looked longingly at the irrigation and hydropower capacity of the Columbia River system. The Great River of the West held more untapped energy than any other stream in the nation. It split some of the country's richest agricultural land, soil that needed only water to become fertile. The river's greatest tributary, the Snake, held nearly equal potential. Pick most any spot along these two streams and you could build a dam that would produce the energy and provide the water that could make a place prosper. A person need not be a genius to discover attractive dam sites. Still, even in the early days before the rivers became fairly clogged with dams, some places held more appeal than others. A combination of water velocity, nearby irrigable land, and firm canyon walls made a site especially appealing. One such place lay just upstream from the Snake's confluence with the Columbia, near Pasco, Washington, at Five Mile Rapids.

Old timers used to tell the story of an unsuspecting passenger on a Northern Pacific train stepping into the Pasco depot during a brief stopover. To visit Pasco in those days was to know a dusty, dry, wind-blown hamlet with few people and, by all appearances, fewer possibilities. But in America's dry West appearances seldom stopped town boomers, land speculators, and entrepreneurs. Eager and ever-hopeful real estate dealers descended upon the Pasco station every day at train time to pitch their sales speeches to unwary passengers. One agent, the old timers said, approached a particular traveler and extolled Pasco's potential. "All this place needs for success and prosperity," he bragged, "is good people and water." Replied the passenger: "That is all that Hell needs."[4]

Still, the realty man had a point: Pasco did need only people and water, and of the two, water was much more important. On the surface it would seem relatively simple to irrigate Pasco lands: the town sat at the junction of two of the West's greatest rivers, the Columbia and the Snake. But the good farm lands lay above the streams and pumping irrigation water uphill proved a confounding challenge. So most early Pascoans staked their hopes on a grandiose scheme to transfer water from the Palouse River, more than seventy miles away, through a complex system of irrigation canals, flumes, and reservoirs. In 1893 more than two hundred men and dozens of horses began excavating, but the depression that year abruptly terminated their work.[5]

Eastern financiers revitalized the project in 1897, but after three years of hard work, heavy expenses, and no profit, the corporation permanently abandoned the scheme.

Buoyed by Congress's passage of the Newlands Act in 1902 and its formation of the Reclamation Service (forerunner of the Bureau of Reclamation) another group of local residents reorganized in 1904. If private enterprise could not divert Palouse River water to Pasco, surely the federal government could. And the federal government did come to the region, setting off wild speculation that Pasco's desert would finally blossom like a rose. For nearly two years, as many as forty engineers studied the problem of building a dam on the Palouse River and transporting water to a hundred thousand acres.

By 1906 the Secretary of the Interior seemed poised to approve the Palouse Project, but then F. H. Newell, chief of the Reclamation Service, reconsidered. He found the enterprise too expensive. Instead, the service would irrigate 450,000 acres in the Yakima Valley, a project destined to become one of the agency's most successful, for this water would begin transforming central Washington into the nation's leading supplier of apples. Of course, that proved little consolation to people at Pasco who complained that "senile . . . officials" using "high-handed treachery" had blindsided their endeavor.

Undaunted, Pasco residents sought other sources of irrigation, turning their attention now to the nearby Snake River. First, the Burbank Project, a privately capitalized venture, placed a pump on the south bank of the Snake and irrigated nearly five thousand acres. But too few landowners enrolled to pay the company's bills. Furthermore, by the early twentieth century water levels at Five Mile Rapids had declined drastically during the summer growing season because large irrigation projects in Idaho diverted much of the Snake's flow. The Burbank Project stumbled along for a few more years but eventually dried up—literally and financially.[6]

Visionaries made two other attempts to dam Five Mile Rapids. Both sought to take advantage of the strong current in order to provide the necessary power to pump irrigation water uphill. Both would have built at precisely the location where the Corps of Engineers eventually constructed Ice Harbor Dam.

In 1907 the Benton Water Company proposed a low dam across the Snake, an idea the Pasco Commercial Club promptly endorsed. Such a structure would "greatly improve" the Snake as a "national water highway" the club predicted, and simultaneously provide water for irrigation and power.

Both the United States House of Representatives and Senate passed a bill permitting dam construction in 1908, but President Theodore Roosevelt, that persistent champion of multipurpose water development, pocket-vetoed it. The Five Mile dam failed to meet his standards; with better planning a dam there could serve the needs of even more people.

Interest in the project faded for several years until respected engineer E. G. Hopson of Portland revived it in 1916 by producing a report for the Pasco Chamber of Commerce, successor to the Commercial Club. "There appears to be quite a favorable possibility of development on a large scale," Hopson argued. He claimed water backed by the dam could irrigate nearly seventy-five thousand acres. As for secondary benefits, the dam could not only improve navigation by eliminating one of the lower Snake's most treacherous rapids but it could also produce power. Hopson's proposal won the endorsement of both Pasco-area irrigationists and open river advocates, who viewed it as an important step in the long struggle to create a navigable channel to Lewiston.

The Five Mile project languished during World War I but boosters promoted it again shortly after the armistice. Both the State of Washington and the U. S. Reclamation Service investigated, but neither found much promise, the Reclamation Service noting pessimistically, "Further improvements on Snake River [at Five Mile Rapids] are unjustified." That 1926 document virtually ended all Reclamation Service/Bureau of Reclamation activity on the lower Snake.

When people began seriously reconsidering federal improvements to the lower river in the 1930s they almost always looked to the nation's other dam builders, the Army Corps of Engineers. And each Corps' proposal for a series of dams—whether four or six or ten—to bring slackwater to Lewiston included construction at the important Five Mile site. Eventually the Corps did build its dam there. And eventually the Burbank/Pasco area benefited from irrigation. As it turned out, however, the two projects were unrelated. Ice Harbor's irrigation was negligible compared with its hydroelectric and navigation benefits. The Pasco desert bloomed in the 1950s and 1960s primarily from waters diverted from the Grand Coulee/Columbia Basin project, not from those of the nearby Snake. Even so, irrigation boosters had been the first to envision a dam at the big rapids near the river's mouth, a dam the federal government eventually built. Nevertheless, by the time the Corps became involved at Five Mile Rapids it faced critics earlier dam planners had not: conservationists concerned about the obstacle's impact on fish.[7]

The Columbia/Snake system is home to various anadromous fish—those that migrate from freshwater to the ocean only to return when mature to spawn in native streams. There are steelhead, shad, smelt, and several species of salmon. Steelhead and salmon are the prizes. Although similar, they have one important difference: Pacific salmon always die after spawning while steelhead may live to repeat their arduous cycle.

And that lifecycle truly is arduous. An adult female salmon may lay three thousand to five thousand eggs. Like so much in a salmon's life, minute timing then becomes critical. A male's sperm remains viable for a very short time; an egg lying in water for even three minutes becomes virtually inpenetrable by sperm. Once her eggs are fertilized, the exhausted female covers them with pebbles. Then she and the male drift downstream; their once strong, sleek bodies now become flaccid, unable to fight stream currents. Spawning is their last act. Afterwards the fish slide into holes or wash onto banks, die, and become part of nature's food chain, providing sustenance to bears, birds, wolves, coyotes, and other carnivores, or rotting away to fill the stream with nutrients.

Salmon eggs lie in gravel about fifty days before hatching into alevins, embryonic fish feeding on attached yolk sacs. Once it has consumed the yolk sac, the alevin becomes a fry. It eats drifting organic matter and hunts small insects. When the fry push free of the gravel and enter the stream, they begin their lives as both prey and predator. It is a time of great attrition. Salmon boast a remarkable hatch rate. Often as many as 99 percent of a female's eggs become alevin, but these immense numbers are critical: as few as a hundred young fish might survive to the fingerling stage from a hatch of three thousand eggs.

Up to eighteen months can pass before the fish attempt their journey to the sea, which usually begins in spring when rivers run fast and high. During this downstream saga they undergo a physiological transformation called smoltification that enables them to adapt to saltwater. In fact, they become entirely different creatures during their migration. No longer are the fish at home in the sweet, cool freshwater of a mountain creek. Instead they pursue the bitter rush of acrid saltwater through their gills—something akin to puppies suddenly taking to trees. Biologists don't understand how salmon know that there is a sea at the end of their odyssey, but some urge carries them onward and increased glandular activity predisposes them to seek an ocean they have never seen. When the call of the sea arrives, it comes upon hordes at once. Millions of tiny fingerlings turn nearly instantaneously from the security of their shallow streams to the uncertainty of a riverborn migration that will carry them past a gauntlet of hungry predators ranging from squawfish to seagulls. The young salmon do not swim to the sea, however; they drift to it along moving waters. Change a rapidly flowing river into a series of slow-moving slackwater pools and the disruption to this ancient migratory ritual can prove fatal.

The smolts might travel nearly a thousand miles before reaching saltwater. There they roam in estuaries close to the seashore, but eventually move to open waters and may swim as many as four thousand miles a year, all the time avoiding sharks, seals, rays, and dolphins. After one to five years in the ocean, salmon return to the river that first transported them to sea. For days or weeks they pause to re-adjust their systems from saltwater to fresh, then fight their way upstream to spawn within a few feet of their own birthplaces.

The system is not infallible. A few confused fish breed in unfamiliar waters. Biologists believe this, too, is part of a grand scheme: just enough salmon detour to different streams to ensure the vitality of the species and create new strains in the gene pool.

Most anadromous fish, though, return to their birth waters, drawn by their senses and an almost magical ancestral and personal memory that remains one of the great mysteries of nature. Salmon have a sense of smell completely foreign to land creatures. Millions of minute receptors decode watery messages. Indeed, the fish's brain is nearly given over to interpreting smells. Salmon and steelhead can also detect minute temperature and chemical changes in water. Beyond this, the fish have developed something far beyond what we call a memory, a process of imprinting that probably began before birth, for it seems genetically tied in unfathomable ways to thousands of generations of ancestors, a cumulative recollection probably unmatched by any other creature. No matter how many thousands of miles a fish might swim at sea, it can always unwind that memory and use that inestimable sense of smell to find its way home. We call a salmon's brain "tiny" in the condescending way we usually describe wildlife, but we will never fully understand, and we can never match, their astonishing ability to find home.

Salmon fast on their spawning runs. They must live off fat stored from their time at sea. If delayed too long by dams or other obstructions, their foodstores can give out before the fish reach their spawning grounds.

Salmon are extraordinary jumpers. Watching the fish surmount rapids and falls as high as ten feet—the rough equivalent of a twenty-foot bar for an Olympic high jumper—Caesar's legions gave the Atlantic salmon its generic name *Salmo*, the leaper. Salmon will exhaust themselves and die attempting to jump a barrier to their home rather than enter an unblocked stream. Place a dam in the water with no provision for fish passage and you wipe out the migratory pattern. The complete obstruction of the lower Columbia at Bonneville, for example, would have terminated all fish runs in the Columbia River and its tributaries above that point, including the Snake.[8]

A myth has developed about the callous attitude of early Army Engineers in the Pacific Northwest toward the preservation of anadromous fish runs. Specifically, the myth claims the Corps did not seek fish-passage facilities at Bonneville Dam, the lower Columbia's first great multipurpose project; that only after unrelenting public pressure did they compromise. The myth is wrong.[9]

Aware of migratory fish problems well before the federal government authorized Bonneville, the Corps had already installed fish-passage facilities at projects on the Willamette River and at Ballard Locks in Seattle. As the agency began surveying the Columbia system for potential dam sites in the 1920s, Division Engineer Colonel Gustave Lukesh wrote, "In connection with tentative design of dams for Columbia River and certain tributaries it appears that provision should be made for the passage upstream of fish, especially salmon, migrating to breeding places." Nearly a year before the federal government authorized Bonneville in 1933, Portland District Engineer Major Oscar Kuentz emphasized that "studies must be made to determine the best method of passing the salmon over the [proposed] high structure."[10]

The myth asserts that the Corps designed Bonneville sans fish ladders, adding them only after public outcry. In fact the Corps' initial design, submitted to Congress in 1933, included fish-passage facilities. Facing pressure from the federal government to get unemployed people working immediately at Bonneville, the Corps had no time to develop detailed fish-passage plans. Yet the original budget included $640,000 for fishways. True, fish passage—once the Engineers completed final planning—eventually cost over $7 million. The Corps greatly improved the original plans, many additions coming as a result of public concern, particularly from

Columbia River commercial fishing interests. Regardless, it is inaccurate to say the Corps showed indifference toward fish. Forced to act quickly during the project's initial planning stages, the Corps subsequently cooperated with state and federal fishery agencies and commercial fishing interests, funding significant research studies. Once this research determined the need for more comprehensive fish-passage systems, the Engineers agreed to expand their original concepts.[11]

The effort seemed to pay off, for at first Bonneville appeared to be a success. The Department of the Interior noted that salmon climbed the fish ladders with "far less effort than their forebearers that fought upstream through the swirling rapids that are now buried beneath fifty feet of water," while the Oregon Fish Commission considered the operation "entirely successful."[12]

Even in the midst of this success some remained skeptical. All Bonneville actually proved, they claimed, was that most strong upstream and downstream migrants could overcome one large dam. While praising Bonneville's success, the Interior Department's Bureau of Fisheries also warned that the cumulative effects of more dams might doom anadromous fish. As early as 1938 biologists realized that some fish died attempting to pass the dam. Later studies showed mortality rates for downstream migrants to be as high as 15 percent. Lose that many fish at each dam and the string of federal projects proposed from Bonneville to Lewiston could exterminate Idaho's anadromous fish. Fishery people could live with Bonneville, but they would fight to prevent dams on the lower Snake, the gateway to some of the most significant salmon and steelhead spawning grounds in America.[13]

Concerns about the lower Snake project's impacts on fish first surfaced at an open river hearing in Lewiston in 1937. With one exception, speakers that day unanimously endorsed a Corps of Engineers' plan to dam the Snake. Although V. E. Bennington, a member of the Washington State Game Commission, chose not to directly oppose the dams, he pointed out that the Corps had proposed an insubstantial amount of money for fish passage when compared to the millions that had proved necessary at Bonneville.

Bennington found no allies during the hearing. In private conversations following the meeting, however, he made some significant converts, telling representatives of the Inland Empire Waterways Association they could expect a "considerable fight" from both commercial and game fishing interests unless they worked with the Washington departments of Game and Fish to secure fish passage facilities. The IEWA promptly passed a resolution requesting the Corps to seek additional money for fish conservation at Snake River dams.[14]

The alliance between fishery agencies and the IEWA would be short-lived as the agencies stridently fought lower Snake dams. In 1945 an Oregon chamber of commerce urged the IEWA to "adopt measures to effectively combat" the "highly organized" opposition to Snake River dams by fish and wildlife agencies. "These agencies are going out of bound," the chamber claimed, "and we contend that in some activities they are exceeding their authority."[15]

Even the Corps' Assistant Chief of Engineers Thomas Robins, a man generally sympathetic to fishery concerns during his tour of duty in the Pacific Northwest, grew exasperated with the increasing animosity of fishery advocates. Testifying before Congress in 1941 he noted that Bonneville fishways had been eminently successful and claimed he had every reason to believe fish could safely pass in both directions over Snake River dams fitted with similar facilities. The dams' turbines were "absolutely incapable of hurting the fish. If you could put a mule through there, and keep him from drowning he would go through without being hurt. Before we put the wheels in, we carried on experiments with fish, and proved conclusively that the pressure of the turbines will not injure fish." It was a broad statement.[16]

Actually, the turbines at Bonneville and other Columbia River dams did kill fish, although researchers eventually found that the barriers also created numerous other, more serious difficulties for the migrants unrelated to turbine mortality. Dams, in other words, killed fish in a variety of ways. Still, Robins's comment provided fuel for advocacy groups like the IEWA and became almost a soundbite, a sort of shorthand, knee-jerk defense mechanism: "since turbines don't kill, dams are safe." In later years the IEWA frequently repeated the assertion that turbines were harmless to fish. Dam advocates so frequently used the image of passing a mule (sometimes a horse or cow) through the turbines that it became part of the region's folklore. Ignoring the many non-turbine mortalities dams caused, the IEWA and its allies conveniently concluded that dams posed no serious cumulative effects. More important, in the 1940s many members of Congress came to equate this supposed turbine safety with dam safety.

Although fishery agencies and some commercial fishing organizations attempted to scuttle congressional authorization of the lower Snake projects, they entered that fray too late and with too little power to combat organizations like the IEWA that had advocated a series of dams for years. Besides, in the 1940s, most people viewed river development as a national asset rather than an environmental liability. When Congress authorized the projects in 1945, conservationists changed their tactics. Unsuccessful at blocking authorization, they now attempted to convince Congress to with-hold construction funds in order to prevent the Corps from building the structures. Fishery advocates drew their line at Ice Harbor, not only because the Corps proposed to build it first, but also because they believed if they could stop Ice Harbor, Congress would never agree to construct the other three projects upstream. On the other hand, if Ice Harbor went up, it would be virtually impossible to halt construction of the remaining dams. And, facing growing evidence of the destructive cumulative effects of dams, fishery officials in the 1940s had good reason to believe four dams on the lower Snake would permanently obliterate the anadromous fishery of the Columbia's major tributary. They prepared to battle the Corps and its development allies like the IEWA. The decades-long animosity and frequent mistrust between fishery agencies and the Corps in the Pacific Northwest, a division that has affected natural resource policy in every part of the region, can be traced to this no-holds-barred fight over Ice Harbor. Fishery biologists had dissented, cajoled, and protested before. They now determined to do more. This time they would fight to defeat the Engineers rather than simply try to find ways to make the best of another dam situation.

By the late 1940s fishery biologists had begun re-evaluating their initial glowing commendation of fish-passage facilities at Bonneville. In 1947 the Interior Department proposed a ten-year moratorium on further dam con-struction on the lower Snake and Columbia, allowing biologists time to study fish needs. The department, congnizant of hydropower re-quirements in the region, claimed the Bonneville Power Administration could obtain necessary electricity from dams constructed elsewhere, in places less vital to fish than the lower Snake. Even so, the Interior Department waffled, concluding that if the lower Snake's power eventually proved essential the "salmon run must if necessary be sacrificed." Rather than attempting to permanently halt dam construction, the department proposed its moratorium as a way of gaining time to investigate the best ways to mitigate fish losses: "The Government's efforts should be directed toward ameliorating the impact of this development upon the injured interests and not toward a vain attempt to hold still the hands of the clock."[17]

The IEWA and other development interests opposed the ten-year freeze. So did the Corps of Engineers, which viewed the work stoppage as antithetical to its plans for orderly river development. The Engineers believed Bonneville proved it possible to pass fish in numbers large enough to insure the preservation of runs and did not agree that the cumulative impact of additional dams would bring disaster. "Although the conditions at Bonneville Dam and at the Snake River Dams may be dissimilar in some features," wrote Portland's District Engineer in 1947, "in view of the experience of the functioning fish facilities at Bonneville Dam, this office still is of the opinion that the Snake River Dams will not eliminate the runs of migratory fish on that stream."[18]

In 1947 the Columbia Basin Interagency Committee (CBIAC), formed the previous year by various federal and state agencies as the first planning agency to oversee use of waters on the Columbia River system, interviewed experts on fish, power, irrigation, and flood control and discovered a "plethora of opinion" but a "paucity of fact" surrounding fish migration and the problems dams posed. Even so, in September the CBIAC recommended against the moratorium. Another effort had failed, but the fishery agencies were not ready to give up. Instead they stepped up the intensity. And as the fishery people heightened their campaign so too did Herbert West and the IEWA. This was destined to become a long, bitter fight.

The case against the dams centered on two aspects of fish survival: the highly publicized efforts to pass mature fish over the blockages and the much-less ballyhooed but technically more difficult problem of getting young smolts through them. Indeed, another myth has developed concerning fish and dams along the Columbia/Snake waterway, this one perpetuated by the Corps of Engineers, the Bonneville Power Administration, and hydropower advocates. This myth states that in the 1930s and 1940s, when the Engineers began constructing Northwest dams, fishery biologists worried only about passing adult fish and expressed no concern about getting juveniles to sea. "When hydroelectric dams were originally constructed in the Northwest it was believed that providing adequate upstream passage over the dam was sufficient to sustain salmon and steelhead runs," reads a publication of the Northwest Power Planning Council, a statement frequently repeated by employees of the Corps and hydropower advocates in public meetings and during conversations. It is a convenient myth, for it absolves the Corps and BPA of much of the blame for the extreme losses of juvenile fish the dams would eventually cause, losses that would lead to exterminating or endangering several species. "We just didn't know," becomes a familiar refrain. But the Corps did know. So did the Bonneville Power Administration.[19]

It is true that biologists now know much more about the problems dams cause downstream-migrating juveniles than they did in the 1930s, 1940s, and 1950s. And it is also true that the popular press focused principally on upstream-swimming adults. These were, after all, the fish tourists visited dams and spawning streams to see, and anglers attempted to hook. Juveniles, on the other hand, were virtually invisible. But it is more a deception of recent political convenience than a statement of facts known at the time to say the Corps was unaware of the difficulties its river work caused smolts. As fish advocate Ed Chaney—who came to the Northwest in the 1960s as a Columbia River fish biologist for the Oregon Fish Commission—noted, "We have known slackwater would be a problem with juveniles for decades. It is revisionist history to say these guys didn't know what they were doing." And the record bears out Chaney's charge.[20]

As early as 1934 the Bureau of Reclamation recognized the difficulty of attempting to get juvenile fish past a major dam. Largely because of this vexing juvenile problem, the Bureau chose to provide no fish passage at Grand Coulee, and that dam forever blocked the upper Columbia to anadromous fish. In 1947 biologist Harlan Holmes began studying juvenile mortalities at dams and discovered some turbines could be "literal sausage grinders." In 1952, when Holmes estimated that Bonneville Dam killed 15 percent of juveniles passing through, the Corps refused to publicize his report. In 1948 the U. S. Fish and Wildlife Service stated of the proposed lower Snake dams specifically, "Adequate facilities can be provided for the upstream passage of fish. . . . The potential loss of downstream-migrating fingerlings presents a more serious problem. . . . The lower Snake River dams collectively present the greatest threat to the maintenance of the Columbia River salmon population of any project heretofore constructed or authorized." Although later Engineers sometimes conveniently forgot their agency had arrived at this conclusion so early, by 1954 even the Corps came to recognize this position. Walla Walla District Engineer Colonel Fremont Tandy admitted to a convention of Idaho sporting groups that year, "The basic element of the anadromous fish problem as related to water resource development is the downstream passage of fingerlings propagated in areas above the locations of high dam projects. We are confident . . . that we can pass adult migrants upstream over dams of any height, but we have yet to learn how to pass them downstream successfully." After tests that year showed tremendous juvenile mortality, Ray Oligher, a Corps biologist who started working at McNary Dam in 1954, recalled, "We knew then there would be deaths. We got real concerned."[21]

When the Department of Interior's 1947 moratorium failed, it fell to state fishery agencies, commercial fishing businesses, and, to a lesser extent, sports fishing groups to pursue the case against dams on the lower Snake. And they did not hesitate to describe the proposed dams for what they in fact turned out to be: fish killers.

From the beginning these opponents centered their arguments on the cumulative damages dams inflicted upon the fish. In 1951 the Oregon Fish Commission estimated that of one million juveniles approaching Lower Granite Dam, the furthest upstream of the four planned along the Snake, only 316,000 would live to see the downstream side of Ice Harbor, the last dam on that river. They would then confront four more dams on the Columbia before entering the ocean to face years of predation at sea. That estimate of 25 percent killed at each dam eventually proved to be high, but the commission had made a strong, graphic case. In addition, upstream migrants could expect problems, too. Some fish would be unable to negotiate all eight dams, or if they did, they would find that reservoirs had flooded their spawning beds. The difficult struggle over the dams might exhaust the fatty reserves the fish had stored during their time in the ocean. Summarizing the case against the dams the director of Washington's Department of Fisheries wrote Congress: "The future of the Columbia River salmon industry, the second greatest renewable resource of the Pacific Northwest, hangs in the balance over the decision of Congress regarding the appropriation of funds for Ice Harbor Dam."[22]

Fishery people knew they faced an onerous task because plans for a newly industrialized post-war Pacific Northwest required significant new blocks of energy, much of which had to come from hydropower. Dam opponents needed to step gingerly, but they believed they could convince Congress the nation could have its power without jeopardizing Columbia and Snake river fish runs.

Congress had agreed to authorize the lower Snake project only because of power. Indeed, by 1948 the Army Corps of Engineers projected that 82.5 percent of the benefits from the four-dam project would come from power, 15 percent from navigation, and a piddling 2.5 percent from irrigation, flood control, and recreation. These were multipurpose dams, but one purpose clearly dominated.[23]

When the issue became one of building dams with primary benefits of power rather than navigation, the fishery interests had an opening. The Corps *had* to build on the lower Snake if the dams' principal objective was getting barges to Lewiston. When the mission shifted from navigation to electricity, however, fishery agencies alleged that the Northwest possessed many other potential locations for hydroelectric dams, sites less harmful to anadromous fish.

"There are 387 dam sites that are undeveloped in the Columbia River basin," wrote the director of the Washington Department of Fisheries in 1951. "These sites are capable of producing between thirty and fifty million kilowatts of hydro-electric power. Among these sites only a minority . . . are objectionable from a fisheries standpoint." To fishery agencies the logic seemed clear: build less-detrimental dams before blocking fish on the Snake River. Alternative dams could produce more electricity. And, by calculating a potential $9 million annual loss because of depleted or exterminated fish runs, they could generate it far less expensively. Indeed, the lower Snake dams would, in the opinion of the Washington Fisheries Department, "create some of the most expensive electricity in the United States."[24]

As alternatives to lower Snake dams, opponents proposed to first attain maximum generating capacity at Grand Coulee and Bonneville, then build projects on the upper Columbia and its tributaries where Grand Coulee had already obliterated fish runs. As dam foes accurately noted, these two measures would produce much more hydroelectricity than all four lower Snake dams combined. Finally, if Snake River development proved necessary, fishery advocates urged the government to first dam Hells Canyon and other locations upstream, preserving the lower Snake and its entrances to the important Clearwater and Salmon river spawning grounds. The debate over damming Hells Canyon would eventually pit conservationists against developers in one of the nation's longest, most significant environmental battles, a fight environmentalists would win. Interestingly, in the early skirmishes, not all conservationists opposed dams in one of the nation's most scenic gorges—at least not if building in Hells Canyon would preserve a free-flowing lower Snake.[25]

State fishery agencies took their case directly to the people and to Congress. "All too often in the past fishery management agencies have suddenly been presented with an approved major dam project and told that they were, in the shortest time possible, to design and devise fish passage facilties," wrote John Biggs, the frustrated director of the Washington Department of Game. "In the past, the fisheries scientists of this Department have maintained an absolutely non-partisan position with regard to the political aspects of the development of the Columbia River," stated John Hurley of Washington's Department of Fisheries. At Ice Harbor they determined to take a different approach. This time they would be heard early and often.[26]

The Washington departments of Fisheries and Game, the Oregon Fisheries Commission, and the Oregon Game Commission all played active roles. They testified before Congress, providing scientific information. But they had done that before. This time they abandoned any attempt at "objectivity," speaking out specifically against the dams. And they did "not leave a rock unturned in getting the proper information to the right people at the proper time." For example, the Washington Department of Fisheries lobbied congressional representatives; supplied Seattle newspapers with information noting their side of the case; sent telegrams opposing the dams during times when congressional committees considered appropriations bills; and, in an unusual letter headed as "the most important that the Department of Fisheries has ever addressed to you," requested sports fishers to urge congressional representatives to defeat the "fish-killing dam" at Ice Harbor.[27]

The aggressive campaign put Herb West and the Inland Empire Waterways Association on the defensive. The IEWA had occasionally needed to counteract arguments of those few hostile to lower Snake dams, especially railroads. Opposition, however, had never before been as loud, organized, or broad-based. This required renewed dedication. But West would join this contest, no holds barred. And he would win.

Herbert West and the IEWA probably believed they, too, fought to preserve fish. After all, the association effectively supported increased appropriations for lower Snake fish-passage devices. But the IEWA remained convinced you could have fish and a dammed river, too; or, more pessimistically, if one or the other had to be sacrificed, better it be fish than development.

At first, West and the IEWA tried to convince Congress that dams did not hurt fish. In fact, West went so far as to say they helped. Ignoring the argument about dams' cumulative impacts, he emphasized what some had said about Bonneville in the 1930s: by smoothing rapids these monoliths actually eased upstream salmon migrations. As for downstream migrants, West assured politicians that "with modern turbines, the fingerlings are not chopped to bits, nor do the salmon break apart from water pressure." It was the old "mule can pass through" argument. Despite West's assertions, the House of Representatives continuously denied funding for construction at Ice Harbor, partially because many representatives remained concerned about fish passage. Frustrated in his efforts to persuade Congress the dams were harmless, West in 1955 tried a different tactic: he unilaterally declared scientific victory. He testified to Congress that recent tests had shown fish could pass over dams "without irreparable damage to the Columbia River fishery resource." Fishery agencies immediately attacked his statement as "erroneous and misleading," claiming it "had no technical basis in fact."[28]

Having had little luck persuading Congress of the dams' safety, West sought other causes for the Northwest's decreased fish runs. His bogeymen became those who fished the rivers. Greedy Indian, commercial, and sports fishers, not dams, were primarily responsible for declining returns. It was an argument that would be repeated often by dam builders and power producers in the decades to follow. And it had some merit.

Beginning with the advent of the Columbia River's commercial canning industry in the 1860s, commercial fishers had taken a severe toll, as had, to a lesser extent, Indians and sports fishers. However, due to a variety of new laws and seasons, runs had largely stabilized by the 1930s. When federal dams came, fish faced yet another obstacle, and runs of wild salmon and steelhead again plummeted. Unless the debate's focus could be shifted from dams to other fish-kill causes, the lower Snake might never gets its development. So the Corps of Engineers joined West in making the case against commercial fish operations. Officials at the Corps' Walla Walla District, for example, grew impatient at continual construction delays in 1955. The North Pacific Division had formed their office primarily to construct McNary and the four lower Snake dams. They had completed McNary. If Congress continued to refuse funding for Ice Harbor there might well be no reason for the District to exist. So the District attempted some persuasion of its own, despite the agency's rhetoric that it never lobbies, instead doing only as Congress wishes. After a year of observing fish passage at McNary, like West, the Corps announced a scientific victory. Results there, the Corps asserted, "discount considerably the claims of the fish industries that dams on the river are a hindrance to the anadromous hordes;" enough fish had eluded the real culprits, "the commercial fishermen's nets and sportsmen's lures," to insure survival.[29]

Reaction came swiftly. The Oregon State Fisheries Director demanded that the Corps correct misunderstandings created by the news release and take steps "to avoid the release of such material in the future." The *Astorian Budget* labeled the statement "dangerous . . . government . . .

propaganda." The Columbia River Salmon & Tuna Packers Association claimed it was "based on such flimsy and inconclusive premises that we cannot avoid the thought that the document was prepared and issued for the purpose of retaliation against the industry because of its opposition to certain projects the district would like to undertake." And Oregon Senator Richard Neuberger, an ardent supporter of Ice Harbor Dam, chastised the Corps for its "flagrant partisanship."[30]

The response had an effect. The Army Corps of Enginners suddenly appeared more like partisan infighters than purveyors of technical expertise above such political squabbling. The agency's hard-fought reputation as servants rather that persuaders of Congress was threatened. Brigadier General Louis Foote, North Pacific Division Engineer, wrote to Neuberger that he regretted the incident and reprimanded the Walla Walla District.[31]

The Corps would not again be so outspoken during this debate. But as Congress continued to refuse funding for Ice Harbor, the Walla Walla District funneled information to Herbert West, who became even more vocal. "It is high time that the people who are dependent on the fishing industry for their livelihood should stop their blind, unreasoning attacks on progress and development," he wrote the executive secretary of the Columbia River Fishermen's Protective Union. He accused Alvin Anderson, director of the Washington Department of Fisheries, of "a complete lack of understanding of the overall water resource development program . . . a biased opinion, and a closed mind which is unworthy of one occupying a public position." The Washington Department of Game was "not particularly interested in the fisheries program . . . in the Snake River area; but, rather, [are] permitting themselves to be used as fronts for other groups and organizations opposed to the extension of inland navigation and further hydroelectric power development in the Northwest."[32]

The results of all the lobbying and accusations proved inconclusive. It is unclear whether any of this sniping would have eventually convinced Congress one way or another. The decisive factor in getting money released for the Snake River dams—just as it had been key to getting them authorized—was hydropower. Once again Herbert West, the champion of inland navigation, found himself relying upon the crutch of power. Once again he would argue adroitly, for it really did not matter to him why the dams were built, just so long as they were.

The Pacific Northwest economy, which had blossomed robustly during World War II, stagnated in the immediate post-war years. The region still relied too heavily on its two historic legs of economic dependence: agriculture and forestry. Dam proponents argued that building the lower Snake dams would stimulate the economy. Construction would employ people and create much-needed hydroelectricity, encouraging more diverse industry.[33]

Those were old arguments, going back to New Deal days, and it is doubtful they alone would have convinced Congress to unleash construction funds. In the 1950s, however, dam advocates could also plead the cause of national defense, and they specifically noted the immense power requirements of the Atomic Energy Commission's Hanford Operations, located near the proposed Ice Harbor Dam.

A presidential report in 1951 outlined a need for four to four-and-one-half million more kilowatts of power to meet critical national defense programs in atomic energy, chemical production, and the manufacture of aluminum and other metals. The IEWA noted in a slick publication titled *Power for Defense* that completing just three dams in the Northwest—Ice Harbor, The Dalles, and Hells Canyon—could provide nearly half of these national demands.[34]

The Atomic Energy Commission aided the cause. In 1950 Hanford's manager wrote Washington Senator Warren Magnuson of his concern that the Bonneville Power Administration—facing increasing power requests and no immediate new supplies—could not meet Hanford's growing needs. He suggested Ice Harbor could serve as the AEC's exclusive power source. That idea failed. Hanford would not have a private dam. But the AEC kept up the pressure. In 1952 the agency wrote Magnuson that negotiations with BPA indicated a critical upcoming power shortage, just when Hanford needed vast amounts of additional energy to meet requirements for its enlarged facilities. "It does appear to us," the agency noted, "that the proximity of the Ice Harbor Dam to our Hanford Works would be a feasible and sound means of strengthening the Bonneville system so that they would have added system capacity to enable them to supply Hanford with its increased requirement."[35]

The fishery interests counter-attacked. "Any Pacific Northwest power shortage that exists now is not the product of the salmon problem," wrote Robert Schoettler, director of the Washington Department of Fisheries, "but a result of the power agencies failing to develop non-controversial sites while ignoring the pleas of the fisheries people and the general public."[36]

Still, it proved difficult to argue against the Atomic Energy Commission and national defense, particularly with the nation at war in Korea. Wrote Oregon Senator Wayne Morse to a constituent critical of his support of Ice Harbor and other proposed lower Snake dams:

> I haven't any doubt about the fact that the dams will unquestionably create some loss to the fishing industry, but I don't think to any such degree as is feared.
>
> However, . . . I have always been frank with the fishing industry by telling its representatives that when one in my position has to make a choice between what he thinks is essential to the adequate defense of his country and the economic interests of some particular segment, I think it is clear that my vote should be on the side of strengthening our defense.
>
> In the years ahead, we are going to need every kilowatt of electric power we can generate in this country, if we are going to maintain our superiority over Russia in the field of atomic defense. Whatever sacrifices the American people find are necessary they must be willing to make, and I think that applies to the sportsmen of the country as well as to every other group.[37]

The power issue had enabled fishery agencies to expand their arguments in the 1940s. Once it became clear the Snake River dams' primary purpose was power, not navigation, fishery advocates could legitimately point to other sites in the region that could generate more electricity with less environmental damage. But the power issue, and Cold War fears of insufficient energy to fuel the nation's atomic program, ultimately defeated them. In reality, though, it seems the fishery people were doomed from the beginning. One reads the newsletters and correspondence of the IEWA and is struck by the firmness of its resolve, by its absolute conviction that its cause was just. Herb West never doubted his eventual victory.

Such confidence is missing in the writings of fishery people, even the state fish agencies that lobbied hardest. From the beginning they fought Ice Harbor from a mentality of failure. They wanted to defeat this dam, but the best they really hoped for was delay. Their pessimism began in the 1940s when the Department of Interior, in advocating the ten-year moratorium, admitted that "the present salmon run must if necessary be sacrificed." The Washington Department of Fisheries reflected a similar attitude in later years. "We recommend building of upriver dams first, thereby saving our second greatest renewable resource until its sacrifice is actually required by the over-all economy of the region," the agency telegraphed Congress. Another time it wrote that it was a "mandate [of] the Department of Fisheries . . . to preserve the fisheries resources of the Columbia River as long as is economically possible." The agencies only hoped to delay the inevitable until the dams proved absolutely necessary. To wage successful battle with true believers like Herbert West, one must also be a true believer.[38]

As it turned out, the fishery agencies achieved almost all they had originally sought. By the time political wrangling over Ice Harbor concluded, the debate had taken nearly ten years, the length of the lower Snake moratorium proposed in 1947.

During this period of delay, the Corps of Engineers helped to allay conservationists' fears by hiring Milo Bell, one of the nation's leading experts on fish passage and something of a folk hero to fishery biologists, to design its fish facilities. Bell, along with Harlan Holmes, designed fish ladders at Bonneville in the 1930s at a time when, according to Oligher, "we knew virtually nothing about ladders. To a lot of people's surprise, the Bonneville ladders worked well." Holmes and Bell then designed ladders at McNary, and the Corps hired Bell to diagram Ice Harbor's adult fish-passage system, much to the fishery agencies' gratification. The Engineers also made models of fish-passage devices at Ice Harbor, invited critiques from fishery agencies, then redesigned facilities to meet biologists' concerns. Once McNary went on line in 1954 the Corps cooperated with state agencies to test that dam's fish-passage capabilities, applying lessons learned there to the lower Snake projects. One of the lessons came from observing that, despite earlier Corps' statements about mules safely traveling through turbines, Bonneville's and McNary's turbines did kill substantial numbers of juvenile fish. The turbines sucked in air as well as water and the air created a vacuum under turbine blades. Migrating juvenile fish hugged the underside of these blades and literally exploded in that vacuum. So research at McNary led to a new turbine design, first used on the lower Snake dams. The design created a steady, even flow of water through the turbine, provided more clearance between blades, and still efficiently produced electricity. Turbines themselves would not pose major problems to fish along the lower Snake.[39]

Although fishery agencies got their "moratorium," it did not come solely because of their political clout. They had had their day. For a few years in the late 1940s and early 1950s they helped persuade Congress to delay lower Snake dams. But there was another reason Congress withheld construction funds. Fiscal conservatives, particularly in the House of Representatives, sought to cut federal spending. As the years passed, the debate over Ice Harbor revolved more around budget concerns than fish issues. By 1952 the IEWA, the Corps, and others had probably convinced a majority in Congress that fish could be safely passed along the lower Snake. Still, another four years rolled by before Ice Harbor construction began. The difficulty for dam proponents from 1952 to 1956 was not so much the fishery people. The thorn was a new man in the White House, and a new policy concerning federal dam construction.

In 1950 the Corps requested $12 million for Ice Harbor, an appeal President Harry Truman supported. But Congress eliminated the item for two reasons: concern over fish and runaway government spending.[40]

Truman favored Ice Harbor, convinced of its ability to produce cost-effective power for defense, especially for the AEC's growing needs at Hanford. His budget requests of the early 1950s included multi-million dollar items to start construction. Although Truman's requests usually made it past the Senate Appropriations Committee, the joint Senate-House Conference Committee repeatedly defeated them, usually because of fiscal concerns.

In his last budget request to Congress in January 1953, Truman included nearly $5 million for Ice Harbor construction funds, and it finally appeared Congress might agree to spend the money. But Dwight Eisenhower took office a few weeks later and proclaimed a policy of "no new starts" for federal multipurpose dams, a procedure intended to curb federal spending and encourage local and state governments, as well as private enterprise, to share more costs of river development. He eliminated the Truman Ice Harbor request in his revised budget, and in this honeymoon period between Congress and the White House, Congress granted the president's wish.

With Eisenhower in office the task for dam supporters became harder. Now they had to battle both a hostile House Appropriations Committee wary of federal dam expenditures and the White House.

To people who appreciate the lower Snake dams, Herbert West is a hero, an unflagging advocate of construction. But it is unlikely the dams would today stand had it not been for the equally ardent support of

Washington Senator Warren G. Magnuson. Year after year in the 1950s he carried the Ice Harbor banner into congressional battle. Year after year Congress defeated him. After one painful loss a frustrated Magnuson wrote, "It is as if the Congress had taken action which would stop development of oil and gas wells in the Southwest, or coal fields in Pennsylvania or West Virginia. Hydroelectric power represents a source of energy fully as vital as oil, gas or coal."[41]

But Magnuson kept inching closer to victory, kept making converts. Finally, his shrewd political maneuvering paid off in 1955. Rather than wage a floor fight that year and risk censure from Eisenhower and his "no new starts" congressional allies, Magnuson quietly persuaded the Senate-House Conference Committee to amend the president's budget to include a modest $1 million appropriation to begin Ice Harbor construction. Fishery agencies, in the words of salmon advocate Anthony Netboy, were "caught napping by this parliamentary maneuver." When they did not protest, Congress passed the measure. Eisenhower, unwilling to veto an entire omnibus bill over such a triffling amount, signed it. Magnuson, West, and all the other dam supporters finally had a foot in the door. As the IEWA proclaimed, "We have broken the log jam with respect to the development of the Snake River, and . . . we should be able to push our program . . . ahead rapidly towards final conclusion."[42]

Ice Harbor represented the first federal hydroelectric start during Eisenhower's administration. "They're not going to like it but they'll have to take it anyway," a gleeful Magnuson exulted. "Years ago I told a group in Lewiston that one day there would be a Coast Guard station in their community," Magnuson later reminisced. "I think they thought I was a little bit touched." But Magnuson laughed last. He had a vision of slackwater lapping all the way to Lewiston's shores and he lived to see it. A direct descendant of the open river advocates of the 1870s, Magnuson brought to the task enough political muscle to accomplish the dream. It was a "memorable acheivement," editorialized the Pasco newspaper in 1957 after the Corps finally began Ice Harbor construction. "The supporting cast is very long—and richly deserving of credit—but it is Washington's Warren G. who is entitled to take the solo encore."[43]

The Corps quickly began spending its million dollars by constructing an access road to the site. In 1956 it built a cofferdam to divert the river away from the construction area. More money came from Congress and "dirt really began to fly," in the words of a Walla Walla District news release, in February 1957 when earth movers began excavations for the dam itself. Ceremonies attended by Senator Magnuson and other political luminaries on June 2, 1957 commemorated the placing of Ice Harbor's first concrete. The officials dropped a piece of parchment, carefully wrapped, into that cornerstone block. The message read:

> Here below the surging waters of the Snake River and below the thousands of tons of one of man's largest creations, we place this memorial to you, the far-future generation.
>
> Here, in the early years in the atomic era, the people of the United States exhibit faith in the future by placing the first concrete of a great dam to provide the benefits of peaceful living for the people of our nation.
>
> By the nearness of one of the world's largest atomic energy installations and awareness of the forces of destruction on tap around the world, we humbly pledge our efforts in the peaceful traditions of our great nation, the United States of America.

In November 1961 the Corps began filling the dam's pool (named Lake Sacajewa after the only woman in the Lewis and Clark party). Ice Harbor generated its first power in December.

Workers laid out thirty-five million pounds of reinforced steel and covered it with tons of concrete. They excavated more than a million cubic yards of rock and dirt, in some places digging more than a hundred feet below the original river bottom to reach firm bedrock. They relocated miles of railroad track, built fish ladders on both shorelines, and installed a vertical-lift navigation lock gate weighing seven hundred tons, the world's highest single-lift lock.

When they were finished the dam across the Columbia's largest tributary was more than half-a-mile long, rose 130 feet above the river bed, and backed a reservoir thirty miles long. The dam could generate 270,000 kilowatts of electricity, with empty bays for additional generators the Corps would add in the 1970s.

As Lyndon Baines Johnson took the podium in May 1962 to dedicate the latest dam on the Columbia River system, that concrete plug had already submerged Five Mile, Fish Hook, Pine Tree, Haunted House, and other rapids, places of turbulence that had slowed the progress and endangered the lives of navigators from Lewis and Clark to Len White. The dam itself sat just below a kidney-shaped bay where intrepid captains formerly tied up to allow chunks of ice to flow past. "Ice Harbor" they had called it, and the name stuck.

"We have had to fight for every inch of the way so far for our Northwest development," wrote Charles Baker, president of the Inland Empire Waterways Association during the height of the battle for Ice Harbor. "And apparently, we are going to have to fight down to the last dam."[44]

Prophetic words, those. As he stood addressing the genial crowd on that May day in 1962, Lyndon Johnson anticipated a time when placid water would replace rapids all along the lower Snake and giant turbines would generate thousands of kilowatts of electricity. His was an accurate vision, for the fishery people had been right: build Ice Harbor and it would prove impossible to halt construction of Lower Monumental, Little Goose, and Lower Granite. Still, Lyndon Johnson could not have predicted it would be another thirteen years before slackwater finally arrived at Lewiston. Federal budget difficulties would delay work and fishery advocates would make one last stand before bowing to the Corps. In addition, the Army Engineers would face a litany of changing regulations and suffer delays as the nation grappled with increased concerns about the natural environment. Charles Baker had been right. It would be a long fight before other dignitaries mounted a podium to dedicate the last dam on the lower Snake.

Chapter 7

A Seaport for Idaho

In comparison to Ice Harbor, opposition to Lower Monumental, thirty miles upstream, was mild. Fishery people had taken their stand at Ice Harbor and lost. Now they worked with the Corps to make the most of a situation they feared would never be good. They would make only one more significant protest along the lower Snake—at Lower Granite—but that would not come until the 1970s.

When the National Wildlife Federation testified against allocating Lower Monumental construction funds, the Inland Empire Waterways Association chided it for its "age-old emotional approach to the fish problem, offering no solution and no effort to reach a solution." The conservationists now seemed out of step; no one in Congress paid much heed to the Federation's pleas.[1]

By adhering to his "no new starts" philosophy, Dwight Eisenhower again proved a more formidable adversary than conservationists. Once again, Warren Magnuson outflanked the former general in a House-Senate conference committee, obtaining construction funds in the summer of 1960. In a letter to Herbert West, Magnuson described the effort:

> Looking back on that Conference Committee, Herb, I believe the Lower Monumental start is one of the biggest achievements ever!
>
> Actually, [the] 1955 . . . Conference when we got Ice Harbor [money] was . . . by comparison only [a] tea party.
>
> Same old story, isn't it Herb. Only delay, until we push them into taking action![2]

Magnuson had freed a modest $1 million for start-up, but that was all he needed. With the door opened, construction appropriations flowed steadily. The effort to preserve the Marmes archaeological site created the only significant controversy at Lower Monumental.

The Corps named its new dam after a large rock creased with vertical basalt columns, a landmark Lewis and Clark had called "Ship Rock" but later travelers renamed Monumental Rock. In February 1969 the Engineers began filling the dam's reservoir. Considerable debate did surround the naming of Lower Monumental's pool. Congress took no action for many years but in 1978 decided upon "Lake Herbert G. West." Herb West died in 1974. With the possible exception of Warren Magnuson, no other person was more responsible for this and the other three reservoirs stretching from Ice Harbor to Lewiston. It was a fitting memorial.[3]

In June 1965 the Walla Walla District signed the largest civil works contract in Corps of Engineers' history to that time. The contract granted $72 million to a California construction conglomerate to build Little Goose Dam about thirty miles upstream from Lower Monumental. The Corps completed this project with the least controversy of any of the four lower Snake dams. Nonetheless, for a brief time it appeared Little Goose might not be finished any time soon. To understand why requires some knowledge of hydropower and how it is marketed in the Pacific Northwest.[4]

Electricity cannot be stored. It must be used at the exact instant it is produced. This characteristic has served to tie together vast regions of the country with mazes of power lines supplying electricity to places of need. Obviously, the sparsely populated lower Snake required less power than its four federal dams would produce. Emanating from the dams are huge power lines that race electricity elsewhere. Thermal electricity is more expensively and less flexibly produced than hydro. Regardless of the supply source—coal, oil, gas, or nuclear energy—heat and steam provide the basis of thermal plant production: heat yields steam which emits electricity. Thermal plants can generate vast quantities of electricity, but they cannot always produce it efficiently at the time of greatest demand. Thermal plants provide what electrical suppliers call "base load" requirements. There are times, however, when society needs additional, short-term energy, usually early in the morning as people awaken, turn on appliances, and heat coffee, and again at night as they fix dinner and sit down before their television sets. Since electricity cannot be stored, and since thermal plants are something akin to elephants—powerful and efficient once they get going but cumbersome getting started—hydropower often supplies these "peak load" demands. Water behind a dam represents potential energy that can be tapped as easily as turning on a faucet. No heat is involved, and response time is nearly instantaneous. During most of the day while thermal plants supply base requirements, dam turbines might sit idle, then spin into action during times of maximum need.

Because of its peak load potential hydropower is much in demand, and the Columbia/Snake basin produces more hydroelectricity than any other American river system. Naturally, there are people in other parts of the country who have looked enviously at this source of abundant power and dreamed of tapping it. In the 1960s they finally did, courtesy of the Bonneville Power Administration (BPA).

When Franklin Roosevelt sent the Bureau of Reclamation and the Corps of Engineers to build Grand Coulee and Bonneville, he touched off a great debate over who would market the power from these and other Northwest dams. Some said the Bureau should sell it; some said the Corps. Roosevelt's New Dealers opted instead for a new, independent agency, the Bonneville Power Administration. Since the late 1930s, BPA has marketed all electricity produced by federal dams and power plants in the Pacific Northwest. Selling millions of kilowatts of energy to public and private companies, BPA came to control the largest bloc of power in the West.

When Congress authorizes the Corps of Engineers to build a dam, it does so only if benefits exceed costs. Along the lower Snake the bulk of the return on investment had to come from the sale of hydroelectricity. If the Corps was to receive construction money from a Congress enamored of benefit/cost ratios, then the BPA had to find some way to profitably sell the energy Corps-built dams would produce.

The BPA proved itself an aggressive vendor by constantly seeking new sources of energy and places to market it. In the early 1960s its efforts led the agency into the field of international diplomacy.

The Columbia's headwaters lie in Canada, and the BPA (as well as the Corps and the Bureau of Reclamation) understood that regulating stream-flow there would create immense benefits for power, navigation, and flood control in the United States. Before the days of dams, natural Columbia River streamflow at the Canadian border could annually range from a low of 14,000 cubic feet per second to a high of 550,000 per second, depending upon the season. The government could build dams at every available

site in the United States and still lack control of Columbia River water:
too much of its flow depends upon activity in that stretch of the stream
winding through Canada. For example, even with dams on the United States
portion of the Columbia and lower Snake, augmented by others on tributaries, the Corps contended it could never fully protect the lower Columbia region against major flooding without more reservoir storage in Canada.
And by the 1960s Columbia River dams in the United States produced
only about one-third of their potential hydroelectricity because the Corps
and Bureau had no dominion over streamflow north of the border. The
Corps of Engineers had also studied a tremendous energy source on the
Kootenai River near Libby, Montana. But a dam there would back a reservoir into Canada, an action requiring Canadian permission. Obviously, all
this called for some negotiating between countries.

Consequently, in 1964 the United States and Canada signed a water rights
treaty they had negotiated for nearly twenty years. It committed Canada
to constructing three huge dams that could back 15.5 million acre-feet of
water and help regulate streamflow into the United States. In exchange,
the United States would pay Canada more than $300 million for the resulting
downstream power, navigation, and flood control benefits. Half of the additional electricity generated downstream as a result of the treaty would
revert to Canada by the year 2003. In addition, the Corps could build Libby Dam.

Because the agreement promised Canada $300 million, the BPA had to
find a way to earn the money. The agency intensified ongoing negotiations
within the United States to market some of its vast stores of energy to the
more densely populated Southwest. With the final Canadian Treaty docu-
ments being processed, Congress approved the biggest transmission project
ever undertaken in the United States, "the intertie," an intricate network
of high-voltage electric lines that stretch across eleven Western states from
Canada to Mexico. At the time of negotiations in the 1960s, planners primarily envisioned the intertie as a means of marketing surplus energy from north
to south. But electricity can flow both ways along power lines, and as the
Northwest has grown, it has also received benefits in the form of surplus
power from the south. Most power needs in the Southwest come in the
summer as people turn on air conditioners. In the Northwest, just the opposite occurs as residents require more energy for winter heat. The intertie
assists both regions in meeting increasing seasonal demands.[5]

In the midst of all this high-powered negotiating, Herbert West and Warren
Magnuson turned to Congress for start-up money for Little Goose

and Lower Granite dams. While the Canadian Treaty and the intertie eventually aided their cause, for a time it looked like all that treaty-and agreement-signing would only bring more delays.

After Canada and the United States had completed most of their negotiations, but before Congress had approved the intertie, BPA administrator Charles Luce appeared before Congress to request a delay in Little Goose and Lower Granite construction. The BPA now feared an energy surplus in the Northwest.[6]

This testimony from a former ally in lower Snake development angered Herbert West. Even if the dams added to an energy excess, farmers needed them for navigation, he claimed. "We will have to enlist every bit of strength that possibly can be brought to bear" to keep the projects on schedule he warned IEWA members.[7]

Luckily for West and other Snake River promoters, the BPA soon returned to the fold. In August 1964, just four months after Luce's pessimistic testimony, Congress approved the intertie. Now the energy demands of the Southwest could absorb the electricity that Lower Granite and Little Goose would provide. Indeed, the BPA predicted just one year later that its power needs would more than double in the decade ahead. It once again welcomed dams on the lower Snake.[8]

The Corps signed its gigantic Little Goose construction contract, and in 1970 workers completed the dam: a 2,600-foot-long structure whose backwaters inundated the island that gave the concrete monolith its name. [9]

Little Goose survived the waxing and waning of the Canadian and intertie negotiations with only a mild delay in scheduling. That delay, however, pushed construction of Lower Granite Dam forward into a new environmental era, one that guaranteed a lawsuit and a struggle nearly as protracted as that at Ice Harbor.

Things began well enough for the Corps at Lower Granite. Congress appropriated initial construction funds in 1965, and for two years preliminary work went as expected: contractors built a cofferdam, laid an access road, dredged a navigation channel. By 1967, however, President Lyndon Johnson found himself in a political and economic bind. Protests of U. S. involvement in Vietnam multiplied while the economy stagnated. Congress, led by powerful Northwest representatives like senators Warren

Magnuson, Frank Church, and Mark Hatfield, continued to appropriate funds for Lower Granite, but in an effort to combat inflation, Johnson's budget executives refused to spend the money. The Corps did what work it could at the dam site, but as the *Lewiston Morning Tribune* editorialized about Johnson's promise to give the nation both guns and butter, "The economy couldn't stand the heat, and Lower Granite was one of the largest and first lumps of butter to melt."[10]

President Richard Nixon, taking office in 1969, proved equally reluctant to increase civil works spending, and his first budget allocated no money for Lower Granite. Dam proponents hauled out their lobbying arsenal and detailed the many reasons why the government should finish the project.[11]

They claimed the region needed Lower Granite's electricity to avert a power shortage in the 1970s and noted that the Corps had already spent more than $40 million on the dam—wasted money unless the Engineers completed their task. Each year of delay brought inflationary increases to the final price tag. Further, the three dams downstream would do Lewiston no good unless the Corps also built Lower Granite, since slack-water remained forty miles from the city.[12]

Northwest legislators continued efforts to pry appropriations loose, but for the first time their key advocate balked. Warren Magnuson, out of favor in a Republican White House, believed it unlikely Nixon would release enough money to construct all authorized waterways work in the Northwest. He wanted Lower Granite, but another project took priority: a third powerhouse at Grand Coulee.

It remained for Oregon's Republican Senator Mark Hatfield to lead the charge for continued orderly development of the Northwest's rivers. In a long impassioned letter to Nixon he urged a "re-examination of priorities in federal spending to upgrade the position of funds for water resource developments" in order to avert "an unbelievable [negative] impact upon the economy of the Northwest."[13]

That letter and continued lobbying by the IEWA and others brought results. In December 1969 the executive branch released funds for Lower Granite. The Walla Walla District opened bids for the main construction contract in March 1970 and work began two months later.[14]

Dam proponents had many reasons to seek immediate construction funds at Lower Granite, but underlying all was a growing fear. In 1969 dam advocates sensed public opinion moving away from overwhelming support for the lower Snake project to concern. Dam adherents had good reason to worry, and they were shrewd enough to know they needed to get moving at Lower Granite or the dam might never be built. Lower Granite construction was beginning at a time of rising environmental concern both locally and nationally.

In the spring of 1969 Don Thomas, an editorialist on Lewiston's KRLC radio, began questioning the wisdom of completing Lower Granite. Could Idaho salmon and steelhead make it past one more barrier? Was it not more economical to halt development at Little Goose and truck supplies to ports there? Would Lewiston's long-awaited slackwater reservoir become little more than a polluted pool as industrial, farm, and mining chemicals settled in the dead water along its shorelines? As Idaho's Republican Senator Len Jordan noted, "It is the first time I have ever heard of any criticism of building a dam down river from Lewiston by those who live in Lewiston. It shows some kind of a shift."[15]

It did show some kind of shift, but like many "revolutions," this one actually was more evolutionary than abrupt. One of Lower Granite's benefits would provide flood control for Lewiston and perhaps prevent innundations like those that occurred in the 1890s and 1940s. The Flood Control Act of 1936—which launched the Corps on a dam-building frenzy—had actually initiated a growing nationwide controversy between conservationists and Army Engineers. According to the language of that act, the federal government could authorize flood control projects so long as the "benefits to whomsoever they may accrue are in excess of the estimated costs." Congress added the clause in a good-faith effort to curb "pork barrel" spending. But the act gave expansive latitude in calculating the figures. Noted Idahoan Keith Higginson, who served in the 1970s as head of the nation's other great dam-building agency, the Bureau of Reclamation, "When a congressman would ask me about a project's benefit/cost ratio, I would say, 'Congressman, I can find you any benefit/cost ratio you want.'" The act, indeed, provided for flexibility, and the Corps and Bureau could adeptly find the "benefits" required to justify most any project's costs.[16]

Building dams—usually big ones—increasingly became the flood control alternative of choice precisely because of benefit/cost requirements. Despite earlier reservations, the Corps became multipurpose champions after 1936. In order to justify ever more flood control projects, the Corps eagerly tacked onto its dam proposals additional multiple benefits for hydropower, recreation, irrigation, or water supply. What might start as a simple local request for flood relief could easily become a huge dam providing "multiple benefits" for an entire region. Constructing multipurpose projects from coast to coast, the Corps grew dramatically into an agency funded at hundreds of millions of dollars annually. But as the Corps enlarged, its critics also grew bolder.[17]

Conflict arose because the "whomsoever" benefitting from federal multipurpose projects generally were either people living on or hoping to develop the flood plain or those who wanted profit from other changes brought by a federal dam—such as navigators, port districts, and industries that used huge amounts of electricity. Only rarely did those interested in aesthetics, fish, or wildlife benefit. After years of lobbying by conservationists, Congress eventually addressed some of this imbalance by developing formulas to monetarily compute the value of hunting and fishing days and fish and wildlife resources lost or gained as a result of water projects. Many environmental losses, however, proved irreducible to monetary terms. Aesthetics never entered into computations. Nor did the value of simply preserving natural areas for future generations.

Conservationists had some success in the post-World War II period. Perhaps most importantly, they persuaded Congress to pass the Fish and Wildlife Coordination Act of 1946 and its 1958 revision. The 1958 law required that "equal consideration" be given wildlife and development. A major milestone in the American conservation movement, it provided that fish and wildlife not only be considered but actually enhanced at federal water projects. It was a conservation law with teeth.

Conservationists also gained some highly publicized successes by defeating individual federal dams, the most celebrated being the 1950s effort that halted construction of the Bureau of Reclamation's proposed inundation of Echo Park on the Colorado River. Just as the Fish and Wildlife Coordination Act of 1958 marked the beginning of important legislation improving conservationists' ability to shape water development, the Echo Park fight heralded a new era of environmental activism. Echo Park brought national attention to the need for wilderness preservation. A few years later a woman ushered in the modern environmental age.

Occasionally, someone writes a book that transforms a nation's attitude, as Rachel Carson did in 1962 with *Silent Spring*. By exposing the harmful effects of indiscriminate pesticide use she, more than any other person, launched the environmental era. During the next eight years that era blossomed. In 1969 Congress passed the National Environmental Policy

Act (NEPA). On April 22, 1970 the nation celebrated Earth Day, an out-pouring of environmental concern that attracted millions. Popular, influential books about the environment whetted the public's appetite. [18]

Although some had criticized the Corps of Engineers in earlier times—the fight for Ice Harbor Dam certainly proves that—well into the 1960s the agency's image remained largely favorable: the Army Engineers built projects and the nation profited. But by the late 1960s the Corps came under vicious attack. A more fitting villain could hardly be imagined. Not only did the Corps alter nature in an epoch of rising preservation consciousness, it was also headed by Army officers at a time—during the Vietnam War—when the military suffered its worst public relations image. Luridly titled books excoriated the agency: *Dams and Other Disasters*, *America the Raped*, *The River Killers*. [19]

Critics brutally attacked benefit and cost ratios. They claimed federal guidelines provided so much flexibility the Corps could justify any project. Benefits went primarily to local developers, while the entire nation paid the bills. Others said the Corps included speculative benefits by hypothesizing, for example, that development might increase commerce on currently unused waterways. Still other critics argued that economic analysis could never compensate for some of the most significant losses on dammed rivers: destroying natural resources, flooding valleys and forests, submerging historic sites, disrupting ecological systems, threatening fish, or eradicating wildlife species. [20]

Environmentalists believed they finally found the key to controlling the Corps with NEPA. The National Environmental Policy Act mandated that federal agencies consider the environmental consequences of their actions. All agencies would produce environmental impact statements for projects significantly affecting the environment's quality. The statements would describe adverse effects and discuss alternatives and would circulate for comment among other federal, state, and local agencies and the public at large. Best of all, it would open decision-making to wide scrutiny.

The Corps did change with NEPA. No longer could the Army En-gineers listen only to developers when seeking local support. The Corps entered into a continuing dialogue with environmental groups and fish and wildlife agencies. It formed an Environmental Advisory Board. It enlarged its environmental resource staffs at all districts, staffs that came to include employees as acutely aware of the need for environmental protection as any Sierra Club member. Some writers came to praise the Corps as the outstanding federal bureau in dealing with environmental concerns. What had formerly been one of the most despised federal agencies became one of the most lauded.[21]

Still, many people doubted the depth of change at the agency. The main problem, in the opinion of many environmentalists, was the Corps' tremendous backlog of projects authorized by Congress before the significant conservation and environmental legislation of the 1950s and 1960s. Projects like Lower Granite Dam. "Today we can clobber them on new projects which are poorly conceived," noted Brent Blackwelder of the Environmental Policy Center in the 1970s. "The problem is with all the old boondoggles authorized by Congress back in the Forties and Fifties, which are still not built. The Corps clings to them like a bulldog. These projects never die, they just fall into a coma for a while, then get revived." Indeed, getting Congress to deauthorize a Corps project proved nearly impossible. While Congress permitted precious few new starts of major dams after NEPA, the Corps had a wealth of previously authorized projects to pursue.[22]

Further, NEPA set no priorities for environmental enhancement: each federal office established its own. In the Corps' case, a major priority—not uncharacteristic of an agency priding itself on technical knowledge—was to produce complex, long, and detailed environmental impact statements. The Engineers soon realized that courts never ruled an EIS inadequate because it said too much, and the size of the Corps' statements ballooned. Developing the "ultimate" EIS frequently became the agency's focus rather than NEPA's broader goal of enhancing environmental quality. Although the Corps sought comments from environmentalists, public participation in the planning process remained reactive. The Corps produced the impact statements and could reject any suggestions as long as it indicated reasons for doing so. Noted one scholar studying the impact of NEPA upon the Corps: "The Corps was not immoral; rather it was amoral, merely responding project by project to whatever pressures developed in a given instance. . . . It gave Congress all the environmental protection that it requested, and then left the rest up to the individual political desires of the communities involved in individual projects. The actual weight the Corps gave to environmental values in any given project thus tended to be unpredictable and . . . not . . . subject to any kind of consistent control."[23]

So amidst the rejoicing about how the Corps had changed, some critics questioned whether it really had. To them, the Army Engineers merely latched onto the environment the same way they had earlier converted to multipurpose development: by espousing environmental protection the

Corps could increase both its budget and staff. To many, the Corps remained the same old agency: it talked environmental protection, but what it really wanted was to engineer nature's control. The Corps could never let nature be. Leaving nature alone would not benefit the agency. But controlling nature—in "environmentally sound" ways—could bring the Engineers vast new work.

Despite all the environmental legislation, the Corps remained largely a construction agency. "Build they must" some environmentalists accused and, using the mocking logo of a beaver to represent the agency, others claimed the Engineers' slogan should be "Keep Busy." There was truth to the accusations. By the 1970s the Corps had grown into a massive federal agency with more than thirty thousand employees. Some of those workers could operate projects already constructed. But to keep that many people employed required that this bureaucracy find ways to build new things. The Corps' answer was not to stop building, but to build for the good of the environment. Many environmentalists interpreted NEPA and other protective legislation as a mandate to preserve nature. But the Corps never saw it that way. To the Corps the mandate had just changed: they would still build, but differently. Noted one Chief of Engineers in the 1970s: "We're going to build waterways, but they're going to be the best waterways in the world. It's the same challenge, but we'll be doing it in a way that becomes a plus in our natural treasury of resources." To the Corps the issue was never whether nature could or should be controlled, the issue revolved around finding the best way—the way most appropriate to the times—to control it.[24]

Lower Granite Dam would be built in this atmosphere of changing national consciousness and the Corps' reaction to it. Idaho Senator Len Jordan had been one of the first to recognize a shift in local opinion concerning the project, but soon others also noticed the rising tide of environmental awareness. Harry Drake, then chief of the Walla Walla District's engineering division, later reminisced about those days of rising environmental consciousness. He laughed about it in the 1990s, but in the 1970s the changing attitudes caught the District unaware:

> On the very first Earth Day in 1970, Lewis-Clark Normal School invited the Colonel to Lewiston to discuss Lower Granite Dam. But the Colonel said, "Hell, no," so he told me to go! They put me in a

chair in the middle of the gym and a couple hundred students sat around me. They all had loaded questions. They'd clap at their questions and boo at my answers. They even grilled me about the pollution we were causing in Gary, Indiana, because that city produced steel for the dam![25]

Dam proponents knew if they could begin Lower Granite construction immediately, environmentalists would have a hard time stopping it. And, as it turned out, environmentalists were destined to lose. Headed by the Association of Northwest Steelheaders, however, their opposition would be vocal.

The Steelheaders made a preliminary effort to halt Lower Granite in 1969 when Senators Church and Jordan suggested a ten-year moratorium on dam building above Lewiston. The group sought to extend that work-stoppage downstream to include Lower Granite. At first they appealed meekly. But, emboldened by heightened national interest in the environment and recognizing the need to act fast after the Nixon administration released construction funds, the Steelheaders became more aggressive. Still, they might not have made such a trenchant stand had it not been for gas bubbles.[26]

Force more air into water than it can transfer back to the atmosphere and water supersaturates. Too much oxygen, argon, carbon dioxide, neon, or helium does little damage. But air is 78 percent nitrogen, and water supersaturated with nitrogen kills.[27]

Rivers become naturally supersaturated when waterfalls carry trapped air deep into plunge pools. Nature generally balances itself, and supersaturated water rarely becomes a problem in free-flowing streams where riffles and cascades allow dissolved gases to escape. This process is called equilibration, and the Snake and Columbia Rivers were always in equilibrium— until people started building dams.

Plunging water over a dam's spillways, particularly during spring freshets when rivers run fiercely, places an overabundance of air in the river below. One or two dams generally create few serious problems if ample free-flowing water downstream allows gases to dissipate. But a river transformed into a series of slackwater pools eliminates the air's escape route, producing supersaturation. Too much supersaturation creates gas bubble disease. Killing too many fish with gas bubble disease invites the public's wrath, as the Corps of Engineers discovered.

Divers have long understood that nitrogen supersaturation kills. A deep-water diver is subjected to pressure that forces nitrogen into his or her bloodstream, where it dissolves. Unless the diver slowly returns to the water's surface and allows time for his lungs to eliminate excess nitrogen, bubbles will form in his bloodstream and cripple him with the bends.

Gas bubble disease creates a similar problem in fish. As they move from one area to another, fish maintain a balance in their bloodstreams consistent with the river's nitrogen and oxygen concentrations. If the fish has lived in supersaturated water, its blood supply contains the same supersaturated concentration levels as the stream. These concentrations of nitrogen and oxygen generally cause no problem until the fish moves to water of a different pressure (when it surfaces, for example). At that point, the fish's bloodstream naturally releases the excess gas via bubbles.

The spectacle of Columbia/Snake river fish exposed to nitrogen supersaturation attracted widespread notoriety. "The results are horrible and deadly," noted a writer in _Outdoor Life_ in 1972. "In a heavily afflicted fish, bubbles of free nitrogen appear under the skin and in the fins, tail, and roof of the mouth. Eyes protrude or hemorrhage, and in extreme cases they are actually blown out of the head. Fish blinded in this dreadful manner have been known to live long enough to beat themselves to death against the concrete barrier of a dam that they could no longer see."[28]

It was a true statement, but its sensationalism missed the main point. Most fish suffering from gas bubble disease never show symptoms. Air pockets simply block blood vessels and kill fish before bubbles form on exterior surfaces. In addition, the disease kills in other ways. Fish surviving one dose of supersaturation from a dam are more prone to die from a second dose—such as at the next downstream dam. Even if fish survive nitrogen supersaturation, the disease damages tissues, and fish become more susceptible to infection and predation. Gas bubble disease strikes adults as readily as juveniles.

During equilibrium a stream is 100 percent saturated with air. Supersaturation is anything above that. Fish have the ability to survive a little increase. But in 1969 and 1970 Northwest scientists recorded intolerable levels of supersaturation: nearly 130 percent along the lower Snake and Columbia down to Portland; almost 150 percent below Mc-Nary Dam. Fish agencies had originally recommended that the Corps pass water over its spillways to aid juvenile fish moving downstream, allowing the fingerlings to clear the dam without passing through deadly turbines. But now they realized this strategy only increased supersaturation deaths.

With John Day, Lower Monumental, and Little Goose dams all coming on line within two years of each other, the river quickly became a channel of death. In anticipation of the time when increased demands would dictate the need for more generators, the Corps constructed each dam with empty turbine bays. Fearing that allowing the full force of the river to rush through empty bays might structurally damage the dams, the Engineers sent a lot of water over spillways in foaming cascades, supersaturating the river. The highest levels of supersaturation also occurred at precisely the wrong time. Just as most migrating fish attempted to make their way up or downstream, the dams discharged millions of gallons of spring runoff. By 1970, after Little Goose opened, the National Marine Fisheries Service calculated that supersaturated gases killed 70 percent of Snake River smolts.

State fish agencies had warned of various fish-passage problems at Ice Harbor as early as the 1930s, but the agencies had never attracted grass-roots support. Fears of wholesale deaths from nitrogen supersaturation brought out people *en masse*. Many claimed the Corps should have foreseen the difficulty. "The nitrogen problem is not new," charged Annette Tussing in *Field and Stream*. "Its supersaturation at dams has been recognized for fifty years. . . . But the Corps wasn't listening." [29]

Actually, embryonic (but little publicized) studies of gas bubble disease dated back to the 1850s. The first scientific paper on the potential danger of nitrogen supersaturation at Columbia River dams, however, did not appear until 1966, and researchers still underestimated the severity of the problem until water flowed through John Day Dam in 1968. [30]

John Day stood incomplete that year. The Corps filled John Day's reservoir, but it had neither completed turbine installation nor adequately tested fish-passage facilities. All water flowing downstream went over the spillways and supersaturated the stream below. An estimated twenty thousand adult chinook salmon died, and hundreds of them washed ashore or floated downstream for all to see. Scientists now intensely began studying gas bubble disease. Indeed, most of what researchers know about supersaturation they learned after the events at John Day in 1968. The Corps sponsored many studies and experimented with methods to alleviate the problem. Although the press continued to chastise the Engineers, most fishery people noted that the agency worked diligently to find a solution. [31]

With Lower Monumental and Little Goose nearing completion, the Corps and fishery agencies investigated both short-and long-term remedies. They knew the dams would only increase nitrogen supersaturation and they came upon a partial solution: never again put a dam into operation without at least one turbine in place. The turbines would enable some water to ease through the dam rather than crash over its spillways. Not only did the Corps agree to this, Walla Walla District Engineer Colonel Richard Connell encouraged the North Pacific Division to "strongly push to have all additional [turbine] units funded on an expedited basis." Congress, however, proved unwilling to release the millions of dollars this would cost. Besides, installing a turbine or two at Lower Monumental and Little Goose would not entirely solve the problem. So the Corps and scientists sought other remedies.[32]

A solution the Corps originally thought would be temporary proved successful enough to become part of its permanent operations. The National Marine Fisheries Service transported juvenile fish by truck and airplane past the Snake and Columbia dams and their supersaturated waters and released the fish below Bonneville. First undertaken experimentally in the late 1960s, the Corps took over the program that became known as Operation Fish Run. Still, the taxi system neither aided upstream migrating adults, nor helped those millions of smolts that escaped barge and truck collection facilities. It was only a partial remedy to supersaturation. Research continued.[33]

The Corps knew it could eventually diminish the problem by regulating spring flows at upstream dams like Dworshak on the Clearwater. But in the late 1960s and early 1970s, with its upstream projects incomplete, the Corps lacked adequate control over the river. It needed a timely short-term solution to prevent both the deaths of millions of fish *and* a public relations disaster.

The Corps and researchers thought they had struck upon the ideal solution with perforated bulkheads. If the Corps allowed the river to rush unchecked through empty turbine bays, it could damage dams. Slotted bulkheads slowed the flow and protected the structure while theoretically allowing fish to pass through the dam unharmed. The massive, multi-million dollar steel gates allowed excess water and fingerling fish to go through unused turbine bays instead of over spillways and thus dissipated the water's energy and lowered nitrogen levels. The bulkheads, which the Corps dubbed "holey gates," worked well in model tests. But sometimes David-scale models do not reflect reality at Goliath-size dams. Rushed into place at the insistence of politicians, the public, and fishery agencies, the holey gates brought the Corps colossal grief.

While the IEWA and fish agencies encouraged a crash program for the gates, Northwest representatives maneuvered funding through Congress. The Corps installed them at Little Goose, Lower Monumental, and Ice Harbor. They performed admirably in reducing nitrogen supersaturation. "Everything looked fine . . . for awhile," noted the Corps. But as an Environmental Protection Agency official later summed up, "We fell on our faces."[34]

Although the holey gates lowered nitrogen levels, they proved lethal in other ways. Some fish died when they smashed into the slotted bulkheads. If they managed to find their way through the holes, they often emerged dazed and injured, easy prey. The National Marine Fisheries Service speculated that as many as 50 percent of fish passing through the bulkheads died, and the Corps removed the gates, once again upsetting impatient observers. Longtime dam supporter, Senator Bob Packwood of Oregon, who had labored hard to secure money for the bulkheads, rebuked the Corps:

> I am distressed. . . . I have consistently expressed my concern to the Corps about the nitrogen problem and frequently questioned if the bulkheads were indeed the real solution, pointing out the great cost involved. . . . The slotted bulkheads obviously were not as practical as anticipated, and we are now faced with continued high waters, high spills, and physical fish damage if the bulkheads are utilized, and supersaturation of nitrogen if they are shut down. Either way we and the fish suffer. . . . We have wasted both time and money.[35]

The Walla Walla District researched other ways to eliminate supersaturation. Finally, the Corps and fishery agencies hit upon a better solution and gave it another catchy name, "flip lips." Flip lips are ledges installed near the base of a dam's spillways, just below the tailwater surface. Except for very infrequent floods, water rushing over the spillway is directed along the flip lip surface and disperses horizontally, settling over large areas of the river, dissipating nitrogen. With evidence from models that the flip lips worked, the Corps began installing them—and they did help solve the supersaturation problem. Now, however, it was 1972. A lot of supersaturated water had already passed over the dams.[36]

"I have to go all the way back to the slaughter of the buffalo to match the kind of total wipe-out that is threatened in the Columbia," said Tom Knight, information officer for the Washington Department of Game. "And it took longer to finish off the buffalo."[37]

In 1969 an estimated 20 percent of chinook juveniles migrating downstream died from gas bubbles. In 1970 the estimated kill reached 70 percent, and biologists stated that more than 30 percent of steelhead smolts showed symptoms of the disease. The deaths increased. In 1971, nitrogen supersaturation claimed as much as 90 percent of the smolt run. At those levels scientists estimated about two-and-a-half million salmon, one million steelhead, and forty thousand gamefish—perch, bass, sturgeon—died in one year.[38]

Some questioned the accuracy of the figures. Claimed Will Sivley, the former chief of the Walla Walla District's engineering division two decades after the supersaturation crisis of the early 1970s, the fish-kill statistics "were gross estimates of a very questionable character." Fishery biologists would have strongly disagreed with that assessment. But by the early 1970s everyone, including the Corps, understood that nitrogen supersaturation killed. "Two more years like 1970 and the salmon and steelhead fishery may become a thing of the past," warned Idaho's Governor Cecil Andrus.[39]

Of all those vexed by the nitrogen deaths, none proved more of a thorn to the Corps than the president of the Northwest Steelheaders Council, Arthur Solomon of Spokane. "Our fish are dying by the thousands every day," he protested. "The Columbia River system is suffocating." Arthur Solomon and the Steelheaders worried about declining fish runs for some time. But the increased deaths by gas bubbles convinced them to take aggressive action to preserve anadromous fish runs on the Columbia and Snake. Their solution: sue the Corps of Engineers in an effort to halt construction of Lower Granite Dam.[40]

In March 1970 the Association of Northwest Steelheaders and seven other conservation organizations filed suit against the Corps, seeking not only to halt Lower Granite construction but also to deauthorize Asotin Dam, planned for the Snake River above Lewiston. According to the Steelheaders' complaint, building these dams violated citizen rights to due process guaranteed by the Constitution, as well as rights protected by the National Environmental Policy Act of 1969.[41]

The Corps fought back. It noted that, with authority from Congress, it had spent millions of dollars on fish research and fish-passage facilities along the Snake, had held numerous public hearings, had testified frequently before Congress. Consequently, the Corps contended it had violated no due process laws. Further, since Congress authorized the dams long before NEPA's passage, that law did not apply. The Corps filed a motion to dismiss.

After the distressing reports of the 1970 nitrogen supersaturation kills, the Steelheaders filed an amended suit broadening the original's scope. Now the conservation association alleged that Lower Granite violated the Water Pollution Control Act and the 1958 Fish and Wildlife Coordination Act. It sought to designate the Snake River from Asotin to Almota—below Lower Granite—as a national preserve, precluding any further dam construction.

These were the opening salvos in a complicated struggle. In the summer of 1970 the State of Washington entered the lawsuit on the side of environmental groups. Rather than seeking a halt to Lower Granite construction, the state wanted to force the Corps to consult with state fish and game agencies to determine adequate compensation measures, as required by the 1958 Fish and Wildlife Coordination Act. The Corps contended it had already conferred with fish agencies, and that, in any event, the state's case lacked merit because the 1958 act had no authority at Lower Granite, which was authorized in 1945, thirteen years before the act took effect.[42]

But Washington Department of Game officials believed the unusual step of entering the lawsuit justified. "It is our position that the Corps has consistently ignored the [1958] Coordination Act," noted State Game Director Carl Crouse, "and in so doing has not given proper recognition to the mitigation of fish and wildlife losses."[43]

The strong language and blatant legal move were guaranteed to generate responses from those who had worked years toward completing the inland waterway to Lewiston. Port districts in Idaho threatened to file a counter suit. Chambers of Commerce condemned the State of Washington. The Inland Empire Waterways Association filed a brief in federal court opposing the lawsuit, claiming a Lower Granite work stoppage would bring severe economic loss.[44]

The Corps of Engineers also undertook a public relations campaign that included supplying information to dam supporters willing to write letters to newspaper editors; establishing a speakers' bureau of "local opinion molders"; and encouraging pro-development groups such as the IEWA to send out pro-dam news releases. The District's Real Estate Divison suggested that Walla Walla's Public Affairs Office take the offensive by producing a movie of the Lower Granite shoreline as it existed in 1970 to "show the present violence to the environment from cattle feed yards, slaughter houses, auto junk yards, decrepit houses and buildings, trash and garbage dumps . . . and other pollution and filth problems . . . explaining how we will eliminate these problems by construction of Lower Granite."[45]

These low-key efforts might not have generated much controversy, but when the Corps published a brochure responding directly to the Steelheaders' accusations, even the U. S. Fish and Wildlife Service, which had previously remained on the sidelines in the lawsuit and debate, grew impatient. In a letter released to the press, the Service challenged as preposterous the Corps' assertions that it could pass fish over the dam "with very little delay or loss"; that the dam would not "adversely affect water quality but will eliminate many sources of pollution"; that fishermen would still be able to catch steelhead in slackwater reservoirs; and that "the amount of fish in the river is expected actually to increase." Admitted Willard Sivley, looking back at this period when the Corps came under increasing scrutiny by environmentalists: "We got tired of so many people taking pot shots at us and we wanted to take some back. So we published the brochure. It wasn't too smart."[46]

Although the District's efforts to influence public opinion largely failed, its actions insured Lower Granite's completion. The Corps filed a number of legal motions to dismiss the Steelheaders' suit, bringing delays that allowed construction to continue. More significantly, it refused to slow construction while the complicated legal proceedings wound their way through the courts. When announcing it would forge ahead, the Corps notified Congress: "To delay [projects such as Lower Granite] pending final court decisions, where we expect to eventually prevail on the merits of the case, would be contrary to the best public interest and would encourage more vexatious law suits seeking to stop or delay other projects." Despite court proceedings, the Corps awarded the construction contract in 1970.[47]

As workers built the dam, lawyers debated its merits. In December 1971 federal judge William Goodwin dismissed the lawsuit against the Corps. "It is within the province of the Congress . . . to proceed, to alter or to stop" construction, he wrote. But "it is beyond the power of this court to determine what course the Congress should follow." Lower Granite by then stood nearly half complete. The state and Steelheaders appealed, claiming courts did have jurisdiction over federal agencies violating NEPA or the Fish and Wildlife Coordination Act.[48]

In 1973 the U. S. Court of Appeals reversed the lower court decision and urged plaintiffs to reinstate their suits. With the dam now nearing completion, the Steelheaders and State of Washington quickly filed again. Finally, in 1977, U. S. District Judge Manuel Real ruled largely in favor of the Corps, primarily because the issue had become "moot for the reason that the four dams on the lower Snake river have been constructed and are in operation." The Corps' decision to continue construction despite the lawsuits proved an effective strategy. The judgment, however, did not entirely favor the Corps. Finding that the Engineers had inadequately studied and reported on fish and wildlife resources, the judge ordered the Corps to file supplemental reports regarding plans to enhance fish runs. Judge Real, in other words, required more than mitigation for losses; he also ordered that fish runs be enhanced. For a few years the Corps complied with the judgment by funding studies to determine enhancement concepts. Then in the early 1980s President Ronald Reagan's Office of Management and Budget eliminated the program's money, terminating the Corps' enhancement studies. The Corps made no vocal protest of this cut in funds and quietly ceased abiding by the court's order. As salmon runs declined precipitously in the 1980s, most observers forgot about Real's injunction requiring enhancement. By then, mere survival seemed a task daunting enough.[49]

Still, after all the years of litigation, the Steelheaders could point to some success. They had not stopped Lower Granite, but some in the association never believed that possible: the dam was too far along by the time they began the suit. Upstream from Lower Granite, Congress had authorized the Corps to construct another dam at Asotin. To many parties in the suit, halting this structure was the main objective, and there is no doubt that the Steelheaders' case helped turn public sentiment against Asotin Dam.

Despite the rising environmental consciousness of the 1960s and 1970s, there was never much chance environmentalists would stop Lower Granite. Unlike the struggle at Ice Harbor, this outcome was never seriously in doubt. Slackwater reached Lewiston on February 15, 1975, and Lower Granite generated its first electricity in April. On June 20, 1975 the sternwheeler *Portland* steamed into Lewiston marking the end of three festive days of dedicating the "Northwest Passage," making Lewiston, at long last, a seaport. It was the biggest river celebration since the completion of Celilo Canal in 1915.

The Corps of Engineers dispatched a host of officials while governors

and congressional representatives from Oregon, Washington, and Idaho attended. Port districts, chambers of commerce, and the Pacific Northwest
Waterways Association (recently renamed from the old IEWA) all came.
Perhaps the proudest attendee was Washington's Senator Warren
Magnuson, who had battled and maneuvered for decades for this day.
"The nay-sayers said it couldn't be done, shouldn't be done, and wouldn't
be done," he boasted at Lewiston. "But over 35 years ago we planned for
the future and during all the years since that time we have all worked
together. And now today we can stand here in Lewiston—over 400 miles
from Bonneville where it all began in 1933—and we can tell the nay-sayers
that we have succeeded where they said we would fail."

Idaho's Senator Frank Church added his accolades: "It is an achievement
so exceptional that envious communities will forgive us as we all go aboard
this month's pleasure cruise on the waters of self-congratulation. . . . A
community that started from the deck of a wooden riverboat now wel-
comes home its descendants, the steel tugboats."

Idaho Governor Cecil Andrus claimed the navigable waterway "will en-
rich our daily lives through international trade."

Despite the concerns of many environmentalists in the late 1960s and
early 1970s, only three protestors showed up, carrying signs saying, "The
Corps goes free, the Snake is dead" and "Damn the Corps, not the rivers."
No one paid much attention, but Idaho's governor added a somber note to
the festivities. "Before I accept this structure," he said at Lower Granite, "I
want to point out that the cost of this system has been horrendous, both in
dollars and in cost to our natural resources." Andrus challenged Congress
and the Corps to solve the problems of fish migration. "We should not
wring our hands," he admonished. But resolving the problems of fish
migration was destined to become a struggle as thorny as the fight to bring
dams in the first place.[50]

The National Society of Professional Engineers named the Lower Snake
River Project one of the ten outstanding engineering achievements of
1975. The American Society of Civil Engineers (ASCE) proclaimed it the
nation's outstanding water resources achievement that year, while the Pacific
Northwest Council of the ASCE called it 1975's outstanding civil
engineering achievement in the Pacific Northwest.

And so, after more than a hundred years of effort, in 1975 Lewiston
became a seaport. By the 1990s Herbert West's dream of development
following the dams had, at least partially, come true. Grain elevators,
warehouses, and small industries today dot the river bank at eight ports

warehouses, and small industries today dot the river bank at eight ports along the lower Snake. The Columbia/Snake river system, dammed and stilled, rivals the St. Lawrence Seaway and Mississippi River as the greatest man-created navigational network in the nation.

Still, things have not turned out exactly as Herbert West and the dam proponents envisioned. For a hundred years visionaries predicted an economic boom of seismic proportions once Lewiston became a seaport—more jobs, more workers, larger payrolls, new businesses, more services, a higher standard of living. The Corps of Engineers did its best to encourage that euphoric thinking. In the mid-1970s, as it pressed to complete Lower Granite amidst rising concern about that dam, its glossy publications spoke of "significant industrial growth," "far-reaching ramifications [on] . . . the economy," "a large quantity of newcomers" to the Lewiston Valley. But the bonanza never came. There has been some economic growth; some new development at the valley ports of Wilma, Clarkston, and Lewiston. And the local chambers of commerce will tell you the cities are better off than before slackwater. But there has been no economic or population growth on a scale developers had promised. Admitted Port of Lewiston manager Dale Alldredge in the late 1980s, "The arrival of slackwater by itself didn't turn us into that economic mecca that was foreseen when the whole system was designed."[51]

Tugboats can now travel up and down the river, but during the course of completing this massive project public attitudes changed. Biologists had always worried about the dams' impact on fish. In the 1940s and 1950s they were in a minority. As the Corps and developers considered constructing one more dam above Lewiston, however, they ran head on into an increasing groundswell of opposition. The four dams the Corps built are really only part of the lower Snake River story. The whole story includes the history of the proposed dam at Asotin that the Corps did not build, that rare project in the anals of Corps of Engineers' history, the dam Congress took back.

Chapter 8

Asotin

The dividing line is often imprecise when people refer to the "upper," "middle," and "lower" Snake. But, as the Corps of Engineers discovered, making that distinction can mean much when a dam is at stake.

When the Corps presented Congress its Snake River 308 report in 1934, Portland District Engineer Major Oscar Kuentz divided the document into two sections to facilitate discussion. In those days the Corps used only the terms "lower" and "upper" when referring to the Snake River, and, for convenience, Kuentz declared that the town of Asotin, Washington, separated the two. His decision had merit: there were important differences in the river above and below Asotin. Above, the Snake narrowed, flowed over rapids, and churned through Hells Canyon; few people lived in the surrounding country. Below, the river grew wider and its banks supported more people. Kuentz believed the government should develop only that part of the river below Asotin because "it is only in that section that improvements to benefit navigation are of sufficient importance to justify expenditures of public funds." Above Asotin, power showed greater potential than navigation. As it had when reporting on other Columbia and Snake river dams in the 1930s, however, the Corps denied that the region needed dams built primarily for hydropower.[1]

Actually, the Snake narrows and becomes more rapid a short way above Asotin, and had Kuentz created his division point farther upstream—say where the Grande Ronde enters the Snake, an equally logical spot—there would probably today be a dam at Asotin.

But Kuentz chose Asotin, and Congress, on the Corps' recommendation, authorized the Lower Snake River Project to include dams bringing slackwater to that town but not beyond. It granted no authority for a Corps dam at Asotin until 1962. By then national consciousness was changing and many people viewed dams as liabilities rather than assets. Facing political pressure from environmentalists, Congress would eventually deauthorize Asotin, a rarity in Corps history. Asotin is a testament to what might have happened to all the lower Snake dam proposals had authorization come a few years later than it did for Ice Harbor, Lower Monumental, Little Goose, and Lower Granite. In that event, the lower Snake might today still be free-flowing.

In the mid-1950s the Walla Walla District proposed as its next Snake River project a series of three dams above Lower Granite: one at Clarkston, one at Asotin, and one eight miles above the Grande Ronde at China Gardens. The Engineers eventually dropped the Clarkston proposal, but by 1958 both the District and North Pacific Division recommended constructing Asotin as the next logical step in the development of the lower-to-middle Snake River.[2]

Whether in the 1930s or the 1950s, Asotin Dam always had dubious navigational benefits. Few people lived above the dam to benefit from slackwater transportation. As a result, even more than on the Lower Snake River Project where hydropower produced greater than 80 percent of total benefits, Asotin would be a dam built preeminently for its electricity. And in 1960 Lieutenant General Emerson Itschner, the Army's chief of engineers, found power alone insufficient justification. Ignoring District and Division recommendations, he omitted Asotin from the Corps' list of projects seeking congressional authorization. "The dam looks promising as a power producer," he admitted, "but the navigation benefits do not appear to be sufficiently assured to warrant authorization." Some day navigation potential might improve. Until then, Itschner refused to recommend an Asotin Dam.[3]

The Inland Empire Waterways Association rallied a lobbying effort. Herbert West viewed Itschner's action as a temporary setback, not total defeat. "The Chief of Engineers, in effect, has said, 'not now, but come back . . . and let's take another look,'" he wrote IEWA members. "We will win this fight as we have others. This is only a slight delay."[4]

The IEWA encouraged politicians to speak out for Asotin, and Idaho

Governor Robert Smylie became one of the chief of engineers' principal critics, firing off letters to Washington encouraging a dam. Meanwhile, IEWA hired an engineering company to re-figure the Corps' economic data. The Seattle firm found $405,000 more in annual navigation benefits than had the Corps. That figure brought Asotin's benefit-to-cost ratio up to 1.72 to 1, a more favorable margin than eight other Columbia Basin projects Itschner had approved.[5]

The new figures placed the chief in an awkward public relations position having recommended a number of dams with less economic justification. So the chief's office reconsidered and in 1962 recommended Asotin for congressional authorization. Once again, IEWA and its allies lobbied hard. No one seriously opposed the project and Congress authorized it in 1962.

Despite the engineering firm's rosy forecast the Corps' Washington office remained skeptical about the dam's navigation benefits. As a result, debate raged over whether or not to include navigation locks, delaying a possible early construction start and allowing opposition forces to gain strength.

Although the chief of engineers eventually agreed to recommend Asotin, his office differed with the Walla Walla District and North Pacific Division about whether or not to install locks. The regional offices recommended they be included, the chief disagreed. About the only use for locks would be to provide access to rich limestone deposits at a Snake River site known as Lime Hill or Lime Point. In rejecting the proposed locks the chief wrote, "At this time, the uses of limestone from this source . . . and the savings in transportation costs, are not sufficient, in my opinion, to warrant the inclusion of a lock for barge navigation."[6]

The IEWA, port districts, and other dam advocates, strongly supported by Idaho's Senator Frank Church and Representative Compton White, Jr., protested the decision. In 1963 the Senate requested the chief to review his ruling. The chief ordered the Walla Walla District to reinvestigate.

Those advocating locks faced a dilemma: the chief of engineers would probably recommend against them if they served only a single-purpose, yet there were few other reasons to include locks at Asotin other than to transport limestone downstream. Recognizing the difficulty of changing the chief's opinion unless it found other reasons to justify locks, the Walla Walla District asked local groups to help uncover other possible uses—an example of a Corps district not merely doing as Congress asked, but of attempting to encourage development groups to work on its behalf in order to incorporate additional features in an authorized project.[7]

Lock advocates tried hard, but with limited success. In a report to the Corps, the Port of Clarkston found that some wheat would find a market if slackwater went further up the Snake, and predicted shippers would also haul timber products. Eleven pages of its thirteen-page report, however, centered on limestone. Congressman White suggested that locks would encourage industrial development. Senators Warren Magnuson and Frank Church wrote that "dramatic changes in the region's economy since the original design of the dam for power only will justify inclusion of a navigation lock in the interest of both human and natural resources." But these were vague allusions to what *might* happen. In the final analysis, try as they might, lock advocates unearthed no valid reason to justify navigation other than to gain access to lime. To make matters worse, economic justification for single-purpose "lime" locks weakened as the years wore on.[8]

In 1960 two major Pacific Northwest cement companies expressed an interest in Asotin's limestone. But when Congress initially authorized the dam without locks, both companies found better and cheaper deposits elsewhere, and by the mid-1960s no one wanted Lime Point's material. Despite unanimous support for locks at a Lewiston public hearing in 1965, the Walla Walla District changed its 1962 opinion and recommended constructing the dam without navigation facilities. By the time the debate subsided it was 1967, and, although the Corps did not yet know it, the question of whether or not to build locks had become almost moot. Forces that would eventually defeat the proposal to build any dam, with or without locks, stood ready to take the offensive.[9]

Dam opponents opened their fight against Asotin by questioning a miniscule benefit in the Corps' reckoning of Asotin Dam economics: the merits of proposed slackwater recreation.

As its 1977 deputy director of civil works observed, the Corps had not always recognized the importance of recreation at its projects. "Around our first reservoirs we treated recreation as a nuisance to be avoided," testified Brigadier General Drake Wilson. "Then we reluctantly tolerated it, then allowed minimum development provided someone else would pay for it." As the public's leisure time increased, however, Congress provided a significant incentive for the Engineers to augment their recreational program.[10]

In 1932 Congress extended the Corps' authority to consider recreational boating when planning navigational improvements, and the Flood Control Act of 1944 recognized recreation as a legitimate function of federal water projects. Still, these measures merely permitted the Corps to develop recreation facilities; they did not mandate them. Even more important, the Corps had to exclude the monetary benefits produced by recreation when determining a project's economic feasibility. The Engineers still had little motive to build recreational sites.

But after World War II the Corps entered a changed recreational world. People had increased leisure time and more money to spend. Swift advancements in boating technology encouraged boaters to seek lakes and reservoirs. By the early 1960s a federal study found that nearly half of all recreationists preferred water sports. Recreation at man-made lakes grew faster than any other outdoor activity. And many fishing groups, who had more-than-occasionally opposed Corps dams, now claimed that, if they needed to be built, they should at least be completed with recreation in mind. "It's time that the economic importance of outdoor recreation was recognized," wrote an author in *Field and Stream* in the 1950s. "Some dams are necessary . . . but there is no reason why, in designing them, recreational uses should not be considered."[11]

In 1964 Congress passed the Federal Water Project Recreation Act (WPRA). It enabled the Corps and other agencies to calculate recreational benefits when determining project economics. Now recreational development could partially justify the construction of marginal multipurpose projects by tipping the benefit-to-cost ratio in favor of construction. Not surprisingly, the Corps suddenly advocated the merits of reservoir recreation wherever it sought to build a dam. It became one of the world's largest recreational agencies.[12]

While many conservationists viewed WPRA as a victory forcing the nation's largest dam builder to finally consider recreation at its reservoirs, some environmentalists came to abhor the act once the Corps increasingly relied on recreation to help justify dam construction. The problem, said environmentalists, arose because the Corps viewed all recreation alike: a visit to a powerhouse or a day waterskiing ranked equally with backpacking or canoeing. And the Corps was right, as long as the battle remained on financial grounds. Indeed, waterskiers probably contributed more to the economy than canoers. Environmentalists found themselves arguing aesthetics while the Corps presented economics.

Every Corps project faces the fundamental issue of whether developed recreational facilities are superior to natural ones. On one hand, development provides greater access. There is no question that, in most cases, more recreationists use reservoirs than the free-flowing rivers they replace. But as the number of free-flowing rivers decreased, public demand to preserve remaining ones grew. By the 1960s virtually every major natural area had advocates desiring that it remain unaltered, and the debate over river development heated. In no place was that contest hotter than along the undammed portion of the Snake River.

The Corps of Engineers estimated that Asotin would derive 99 percent of its benefits from electricity and less than 1 percent from recreation, but those proposed recreational benefits sent up a red flag spurring dissention. Those who supported the dam, partially because of its supposed recreational advantages, argued from a different set of values than those opposed to the structure.

"The recreational potential of the Asotin reservoir is striking," noted a consulting group the Lower Snake River Ports Association hired. "It will be possible to travel by pleasure craft on slack water to the lower end of the Grand Canyon of the Snake River . . . and to the mouth of the . . . famous 'River of No Return.' Here, in some of the most primitive and spectacular scenery in the country it is possible . . . to hunt deer at dawn, Chinese pheasants and quail in the morning, and to fish for steelhead . . . in the afternoon. . . with a good chance of success in all three." [13]

The Sierra Club, which led the fight against Asotin in the 1960s, dissented. The Corps' reservoir would ruin a great scenic treasure. "We believe that *quality* of recreation also is an important consideration," countered the Club's Brock Evans. "In the particular case [of] that part of the Snake River to be impounded by the Asotin Dam, it may be that the type of experience of traveling up or down a great living river is a higher type of . . . experience than that offered by one of many similar reservoirs which already exist on both the Snake and Columbia Rivers." [14]

But the Corps preferred to count numbers and maintained that more people—particularly family boaters—would use the reservoir than the free-flowing stream it replaced. Additionally, since Asotin would flood only twenty-six miles of the Snake, "there would still be many miles of open river available to the adventurous boater," noted Major Harold Matthias, Walla Walla's acting district engineer in 1969. His predecessor, district engineer Colonel Robert Giesen, had shared that sentiment. "In the development of any water resource project, it is realized that some of the natural beauty of a free-flowing intermountain river is lost, particularly for those who revere this type of stream," Giesen wrote Senator Warren Magnuson in 1967. "Creation of a long narrow lake in the Snake River canyon makes possible other types of recreation . . . at the same time creating a beauty of a different variety which we feel offsets the losses. Our experience has been that the Columbia and Snake River dams with stable pools have created very scenic and beautiful bodies of water. These reservoirs are utilized heavily by many more people than would have been able to enjoy the streams in their natural state."[15]

The Corps estimated ten thousand visitors annually used that part of the river they would flood, but thirty thousand would come once the dam created slackwater. When a 1973 Washington Department of Game study showed sixty-five thousand people-days of usage annually along the free-flowing river, or more than twice the number the Corps estimated for reservoir use, the Corps had lost a significant argument in its arsenal: the Asotin Dam would bring no recreational economic benefits. By then, however, the issue was nearly irrelevant. Forces opposed to the dam had gained too much strength. Led by the Sierra Club, public opinion had dramatically shifted. Brock Evans described the Club's involvement in spearheading this changing attitude:

> For about three years' running (1967-69), I would get word from our people in Washington, D. C. that the Corps of Engineers was making another request for more "study" funds for this boondoggle of a project. I would immediately get out an alert, burn up the wires to our people in Lewiston and Clarkston, and to some of the sportsmen around the state, and we would pour in a flood of mail to Senator Church and the Washington State delegation, urging that funds be deleted.
>
> These pressure tactics worked. . . . Gradually over the years we were able to build a backfire of local sentiment against the project.[16]

By 1969 numerous individuals, institutions, and organizations had joined the Sierra Club in opposing Asotin. The *Lewiston Morning Tribune* recapped the changing times:

> The joy with which this area greeted congressional authorization of

the proposed Asotin Dam—just seven years ago today—is recalled by most of us now as extremely simplistic. . . .

In the years since 1962 we have become less sure than we were then of the invulnerability of our environment and less inclined to alter it for alteration's sake. . . . It used to be that our grandchildren would thank us for building that dam; now they will thank us if we don't, more than likely, and we know it.[17]

In a series of stinging editorials against the Corps' request for Asotin study funds in 1969, the *Tribune* argued against appropriating any money for the dam. "We don't think a dime should be spent on this project until somebody other than the prospective builder has found good reason for building it," the newspaper opined, a remarkable turnabout for a publication that had supported Snake River development for nearly a hundred years. Other papers, most significantly the influential Portland *Oregonian*, also came out against congressional appropriations.[18]

The Pacific Marine Fisheries Commission urged Congress to refuse Asotin funding. Other agencies and organizations joined in, worried about the loss of another stretch of natural river, fearing potential harm to anadromous fish, and questioning whether the Northwest needed additional power.[19]

The Corps attempted to stem the groundswell by repeating time-worn projections of upcoming energy needs. "The Bonneville Power Administration [predicts] . . . a major resource deficit of 780,000 kw in the 1974-75 power year with increasing deficits in the following years . . . to the point that by 1978 this region is faced with a 3,000,000 kw deficit," the North Pacific Division informed the Chief of Engineers. "Asotin should come on the line at the earliest possible time."[20]

The Inland Empire Waterways Association, as usual, supported the Corps' request for funds to study the project in 1969. But this time the IEWA would lose. This time dam opponents flooded Congress with mail. As a result, and at Idaho Senator Frank Church's request, the Corps dropped its petition for planning funds.[21]

Frank Church became a darling of environmentalists in the 1970s, a senator with a huge wilderness area named in his honor. But he had not always opposed damming the Snake. As a junior senator he even endorsed a controversial dam in Hells Canyon, an area long revered by naturalists. "A high dam at Hells Canyon," he said in 1957, "would prove a great stimulant to the entire Northwest. It would bring to Idaho, in generous measure, benefits of the kind that have enriched our neighboring states from such mighty government dams as Grand Coulee, Bonneville, Shasta and Hoover. . . . This we owe, not only to ourselves, but to our children and our grandchildren." Throughout the 1950s and 1960s he vigorously supported the four dams of the lower Snake project, even when environmentalists opposed Lower Granite. And he pushed hard for Asotin authorization in 1962.[22]

By the late 1960s, however, Frank Church began to question further dams along the Snake, particularly those threatening the pristine beauty of Hells Canyon. He spearheaded a drive that would permanently prohibit dam building in the nation's deepest gorge and lead to congressional deauthorization of the Asotin project.

Few stretches of American rivers have endured as much controversy as the middle Snake. For decades people argued about whether this reach of water should be dammed, and if so, by whom.[23]

In the 1940s and 1950s the debate centered on who would build dams, not whether they should be constructed. It became the nation's most publicized battle between private and public power concerns. Both the Corps of Engineers and the Bureau of Reclamation surveyed potential dam sites in Hells Canyon, sites that could produce enormous amounts of public electricity. Fishery agencies generally remained quiet about these dams. They concentrated instead on defeating Ice Harbor, a project they viewed as much more destructive to fish runs than obstructions upstream.

The real culprit for public power advocates was not conservationists but President Dwight Eisenhower and his "no new starts" policy for federal hydroelectric projects. Echoing administrative sentiments, in 1955 the Federal Power Commission sided with private interests and granted the Idaho Power Company a permit to construct three middle Snake dams: Brownlee, Oxbow, and lower Hells Canyon. Frustrated in their loss, public power advocates solicited and won United States Senate approval to construct a dam so high it would flood the three Idaho Power sites. But the House of Representatives rejected that proposal, and Idaho Power's first dam went on line in 1958.

Even with the dams built, the lower (and most dramatic) part of Hells Canyon remained undammed. But not because of conservationists, who were just beginning to speak out against destroying this pristine part of the river. Rather, squabbles over who should build again stymied construction. Four private firms proposed to construct a high dam at one site, while the Washington Public Power Supply System sought to build a still higher dam a short distance away. The Corps of Engineers, also hoping for action in the canyon, proposed a series of dams from Lower Granite all the way to the Idaho Power Company's downstream project. And the Corps frequently clashed with the Bureau of Reclamation, which also had designs there. Indeed, Hells Canyon was a dam-builder's dream, a treasure-trove of hydropower potential. Virtually every private and public dam-building agency active in the Pacific Northwest aspired to construct something there. The long, complicated, and heated debate raged through the late 1950s and 1960s. Eventually, the focus shifted from who should build to whether to dam this scenic gorge at all.

In 1964 the Federal Power Commission granted permission to the four private firms to construct their high dam. Public utilities and conservation groups appealed, and eventually the United States Supreme Court heard the case. Overruling the commission in 1967, the court ordered it to consider the possible advantages of public development. By this time, however, environmental groups adamantly opposed any development along the middle Snake, and even the Department of the Interior, whose Bureau of Reclamation had long desired to build there, reconsidered obstructing this stretch of wild water.

Located precisely where the Corps had led many people to believe the "lower" Snake ended and the "middle" Snake began, protagonists largely left Asotin out of the early controversy surrounding Hells Canyon. But in the late 1960s dam opponents often included it with other "middle" Snake dams they considered of dubious merit. Less and less did they view Asotin as an inevitable extension of the four-dam "lower" Snake River project.

In the late 1960s two unusual political bedfellows combined to help preserve the middle Snake and Hells Canyon. Idaho's Democratic Senator Frank Church now opposed dams of any type in Hells Canyon, largely on aesthetic grounds. Idaho's Republican Senator Len Jordan formerly lived along the middle Snake and had attachments to the place. Even so, environmentalists suspected his intentions when he sought a dam-building moratorium. In 1954, as Idaho's governor, he had favored federal construction in Hells Canyon, so long as these power-producing monoliths did not interfere with southern Idaho's future irrigation demands. In the late 1960s environmental activist Annette Tussing, after interviewing Jordan, claimed he had not really changed his mind in the intervening years. He still opposed federal dams not because of their threat to the canyon's scenic wonders but because he continued to fear a federal power dam might require water useful to irrigate southern Idaho. If the feds could build a dam and also guarantee adequate water for upstream irrigation, fine. But that seemed unlikely in the 1960s and 1970s. "There are many sources of power," he stated in 1971, "but the one essential element in making the desert bloom is water." Though they reached the same conclusion by approaching the issue from different perspectives, both Jordan and Church came to advocate a temporary halt to all dam construction along the middle portion of the river. Their combined efforts stalled dam building and in the process doomed the Asotin project.[24]

In 1968 Church and Jordan proposed a "ten-year moratorium on any further dam building between the Hell's Canyon [Idaho Power Company] project and the Asotin site, in order to keep Idaho's water options open pending further study on use." The United States Senate held lengthy hearings over the issue, pitting developers against environmentalists in a classic confrontation that lasted years. In session after session, Congress refused to approve the moratorium. But in session after session Jordan and Church re-introduced the legislation, successfully postponing everyone's dam-building plans.[25]

In 1973 Republican James McClure replaced Jordan. Working with Church, Idaho governor Cecil Andrus, and other Northwest politicians, McClure advocated an even more comprehensive proposal to halt dam construction. Now the Idaho senators collaborated to fight for a Hells Canyon National Recreation Area (NRA) prohibiting dam building by anyone along the middle Snake. Environmentalists supported the NRA; public and private power interests opposed it. By 1974 it appeared Church and McClure had enough support to pass the legislation, and the Senate approved it. Idaho's Representative Steve Symms, however, led stiff opposition to the bill in the House, and it died in committee. Finally, in 1975, the same year the Corps finished Lower Granite Dam, Congress created the Hells Canyon National Recreation Area, and President Gerald Ford signed the act into law. As Frank Church, the man who had supported so many dams elsewhere, noted during NRA dedication ceremonies: "I think that as we look ahead in this age when we display such arrogant pride in man's work, it is a welcome thing, once in a while, to celebrate the preservation of God's work."[26]

Throughout the long debates over the moratorium and NRA, developers and preservationists argued whether to include Asotin Dam in the restrictive legislation. The Church and Jordan moratorium sought to temporarily halt dam construction *between* the Idaho Power Company's last dam and Asotin. Many people, including the Corps of Engineers, believed such language allowed construction *at* Asotin. Indeed, the two sponsoring senators differed over whether their moratorium affected this dam site. Frank Church clearly expected the resolution to prohibit construction at Asotin. Although the dam site itself technically lay outside moratorium boundaries, Church argued that "the proposed Asotin Dam would back water for 26 miles into part of the stretch of the river which the moratorium bill would protect." Clearly, he did not want the Corps to build Asotin, at least for ten years. Jordan, on the other hand, now convinced that the Corps could build this dam without destroying irrigation potential in southern Idaho, wanted Asotin excluded from the moratorium. He intended for the Corps to carry out necessary plans and eventually begin construction, even if Congress passed the moratorium resolution.[27]

Once Congress began debating the specifics of a Hells Canyon NRA, however, Asotin clearly lay outside its protective boundaries. That worried many environmentalists who wanted all the undammed part of the river, not just the section through Hells Canyon, preserved. In 1971 the House Public Works Committee inadvertantly authorized the Corps to expend $500,000 at Asotin. That brought the project, until then largely ignored in NRA deliberations, clearly into the spotlight. A perplexed Oregon Senator Bob Packwood wrote to the Corps, following the House action, "I am sure I do not have to bring to your attention the degree of public concern about this project." He wondered how the Corps could justify seeking such funding in the midst of so much controversy.[28]

Actually, the Corps was blameless. Earlier in the year Congress had asked the agency how much it could spend at Asotin in the near future should Congress authorize the money. The Corps responded with the $500,000 figure. The House committee then included that amount as a tiny part of a huge omnibus public works measure, and the proposal slipped by Northwest congressional representatives. The Corps reassured Northwest politicians it had no intention of beginning work at Asotin without the obvious approval of Congress.[29]

Within a few months of this episode the Corps informed the Senate that since "plans for the ultimate development of the Snake River are still highly controversial and subject to great change," it had moved Asotin from its list of "active" projects to "deferred" status. That did not satisfy environmentalists who wanted it not just "deferred" but "dcauthorizcd" to prevent future efforts to rally support for a Corps-built dam. By then, Asotin had few friends in Congress. In 1973 even Idaho Representative Steve Symms, a vigorous opponent of the Hells Canyon National Recreation Area, introduced legislation to deauthorize Asotin. "No matter which way you turn, there is very little justification for building Asotin Dam," he stated. But while it willingly moved the dam to deferred status, the Corps' Walla Walla District refused to recommend deauthorization. As a result, and because influential groups still supported the project, Church and McClure sought to permanently prohibit a federal dam at Asotin. They received strong support from Daniel Evans of Washington, Robert Straub of Oregon, and Cecil Andrus of Idaho, the Northwest's three governors. "The deauthorization of the Asotin Dam proposal is very strongly supported by all of us," they wrote Congress. "The destructive impact such a dam would pose to economically vital Snake-Salmon River fish runs is flatly unacceptable to us." Although the Hells Canyon National Recreation Area did not extend to the site, the bill's final version contained a clause specifically forbidding the Corps from building there. Congress had at last deauthorized Asotin, thirteen years after approving it. Other than a little core drilling to find a suitable damsite, the Engineers had done no work. Yet Asotin had been one of the most controversial projects in Walla Walla District history.[30]

For a number of years some development groups, particularly the Inland Empire Waterways Association—now renamed the Pacific Northwest Waterways Association (PNWA)—hoped to persuade Congress to reauthorize Asotin. Trying to marshall support for the project, John Tuttle of the PNWA claimed in 1979 that Asotin was "inadvertently deauthorized" as part of the legislation creating the Hells Canyon National Recreation Area. But Tuttle was wrong. There was nothing inadvertent or ambiguous in Congress's action.[31]

But Asotin seemed a dam that refused to die. Although the NRA prohibited the Corps from building there, it did not ban private interests. Asotin enjoyed less protection against dam building than did property within the NRA boundaries; the federal government could still permit a private dam there. Throughout the 1970s and 1980s the issue of whether-or-not to construct a dam at Asotin continued to surface.

In 1977 Washington Governor Dixie Lee Ray endorsed a hydropower dam at Asotin. Two years later, seventeen Pacific Northwest electric cooperatives sought a Federal Energy Regulatory Commission (FERC) permit to investigate the feasibility of an Asotin dam. At the instigation of environmentalists who hoped to kill all Asotin dams once and for all, the Bureau of Outdoor Recreation (BOR) in 1977 began a study to determine the feasibility of adding thirty five miles of the Snake River to the nation's Wild and Scenic Rivers System, a segment specifically including the Asotin dam site, thereby prohibiting dam-building by any public or private interest. [32]

The BOR requested the Walla Walla District to participate in the study and the Corps rather reluctantly agreed. It recognized that most of those favoring wild and scenic status did so to prohibit construction at Asotin. Paul Fredericks, the District's representative to the study group, recommended that Corps' involvement "be limited to providing input on benefits foregone and impacts on our currently authorized activities." The District clearly did not care to be seen as attempting to prevent wild river designation because "we will be in the minority and be accused of trying to keep the Asotin project alive." On the other hand, many District employees still favored a dam at Asotin, primarily to help eliminate what had become an embarrassment for the agency: the continuous need to dredge the waters in front of Lewiston and Clarkston because of siltation in the Lower Granite reservoir. The Corps had not anticipated such dredging because the agency believed its Asotin Dam would trap the sediment upstream, in the less populated—and less visible—reservoir be-hind that edifice. Now that the Corps could not build at Asotin, some Engineers still hoped someone would construct a dam there to eliminate the costly dredging downstream. [33]

So, while officially remaining neutral during the BOR's study process, the District did note that failure to construct the dam would result in an estimated power loss of $23 million annually and prevent access to deposits of limestone. Nonetheless, the BOR recommended that the reach be included in the Wild Rivers System. The Department of the Interior, however, advised against inclusion and Congress refused to pass such legislation. Those desiring a dam at Asotin still had an opening. [34]

The controversy at Asotin came to a head once again in 1988 when a private firm, Asotin Hydro Company, a subsidiary of Consolidated Hydro of Greenwich, Connecticut, requested a preliminary FERC permit to study a two-hundred-foot-high dam backing a reservoir twenty-six miles long. Reaction came swiftly.

The dam "would generate electricity the region doesn't need and make money for stockholders who have never seen the river," editorialized the Moscow *Idahonian*. A variety of groups—including environmental organi-

zations, jetboaters, outfitters, city councils, and county commissions—
formally opposed the permit.[35]

The Asotin County Public Utilities Commission was one of the few
regional organizations to waver over dam construction, a considerable con-
trast from the 1950s and 1960s when developers spoke out boldly for
Asotin. But even the PUD tempered its advocacy. The PUD filed a
counter proposal primarily to block other entities from building in its
backyard. Under federal regulations, public agencies received first permit
priority even if filing after a private corporation, and the first public agency
seeking a permit held priority over all other public organizations. The
PUD took its stance primarily to assure itself that if anyone built at Asotin,
it would be the PUD, not a private out-of-state company.[36]

And, to the concern of many, the Corps, after all these years, still
refused to give up entirely on the idea of a dam at Aostin. When
representatives of the Connecticut firm visited the Walla Walla District,
the Corps continued to express interest in the project. "In addition to
power benefits that would be derived," the District wrote, "a dam at
Asotin would be very effective in reducing the large sediment load that is
being deposited in Lower Granite Reservoir."[37]

The two permit requests, coming after a long lull at Asotin, and the
Corps' continuing interest, once again awoke those opposed to further
dams on the Snake, particularly Idaho Senator McClure. He introduced
legislation prohibiting FERC from licensing any dams along the Snake
from Asotin to the NRA boundary. In November 1988 President Ronald
Reagan signed the bill into law, closing the last loophole at Asotin. The
federal government could neither build there nor could it license a private
or public dam. Environmentalists had won a significant, long, and
hard-fought battle to prevent dams upstream from Lower Granite.[38]

Chapter 9

Fish vs. Dams

Not many people lived along the Columbia River in 1861, but a few fishermen caught salmon, selling them fresh locally or shipping them smoked, salted, or canned to distant markets. By 1866 commercial canneries processed more than 270,000 pounds, and by 1880 canned salmon ranked second (behind only lumber) in Pacific Northwest exports.[1]

In those days, millions of fish made their way up the Columbia and into the Snake River and its tributaries, and commercial fishers along the Snake also prospered. William O'Brien of Weiser, Idaho, about 230 miles upriver from Lewiston, began fishing commercially in the late 1870s. Like others up and down the Snake and Columbia, he seined, using a net 350 feet long and 12 feet deep. With two other men, a horse, and a boat, he hauled the seine over the same stretch of river, time after time, day after day during the salmon season. O'Brien sold his fish to farmers, fish merchants, hotels, and restaurants. By 1894 nine other commercial fishing outfits had joined him in the vicinity of Weiser. Together they harvested more than 2,600 salmon and 4,000 steelhead that season.[2]

O'Brien was but a small part of commercial fishing operations along hundreds of miles of rivers on the Columbia/Snake system. Seine nets and fish wheels—a much more effective way of removing fish from the water—dotted the rivers, extracting more salmon than nature could supply on a reharvestable basis. By 1884 canneries along the Columbia produced more than forty-two million pounds of fish. Dependable marine engines allowed fishermen to move to the ocean in 1905 to begin sea trolling, and in 1911 commercial businesses along the Columbia processed nearly fifty million pounds. But by then some people understood that these tremendous yields could not last. The technological efficiency had already intersected harvestable potential. As early as 1894 the United States Commissioner of Fish and Fisheries declared it "beyond question that the number of salmon now reaching the head waters of streams in the Columbia River basin is insignificant in comparison with the number which some years ago annually visited and spawned in these waters."[3]

In 1877 Washington Territory imposed a salmon season on the Columbia in an effort to preserve the fishery. Oregon followed with similar regulations the next year. Both Oregon and Washington passed laws regulating the type of gear fishers could use. Eventually, both outlawed fish wheels, traps, and seines. Concern over salmon and steelhead also spawned a patchwork of conservation groups. But these organizations (and often-conflicting state laws) could not meet the needs of a shrinking resource.

While admitting that this hodge-podge of fishing regulations could never preserve the salmon runs, the U. S. Commissioner of Fisheries in 1885 believed artificial propagation offered a solution. Oregon developed its first fish hatcheries in the 1870s, and by the 1930s several of them operated in the Northwest. They seemed to many a technological salvation. But a new commissioner of fisheries—in 1937—challenged the praises previously lavished on artifical rearing. "How ill-founded was his faith in the all-effectiveness of [fish hatcheries] in maintaining or restoring the fisheries," wrote the commissioner about his 1885 predecessor. [4]

By the 1930s state laws, along with commercial fisher's own restraint, had eased the over-fishing threat to anadromous fish. Environmental degradation of fish habitat had become a much more serious problem. Still, throughout the latter part of the twentieth century, commercial fishers remained the purported bogeymen. In particular, representatives of the Corps of Engineers, the Bonneville Power Administration, and other dam and hydropower advocates who long refused to acknowledge their own complicity blamed commercial fishers for ever-dwindling fish runs. These continuing accusations came despite strong evidence that by 1938 (the year Bonneville Dam went on line) fishers took from the river only what nature could replenish. That is, by 1938 it was clear the fish could survive if they only had to deal with commercial fishing. Still, laws and regulations continued to squeeze commercial fishers and distract attention from other, more serious fish-killing practices. In 1938 commercial fishers could work the Columbia River 272 days of the year. By the 1990s they could fish the Columbia for a couple of weeks in February, occasionally for a few days in August and September, and two or three days a week in October. In 1994 the river was completely closed to commercial fishing. And yet the fish runs deteriorated. "After fifty years of cranking down on harvest, you'd think we'd have some results," complained commercial fisherman Kent Martin in 1992. "We need to look a hell of a lot less at harvest and much more at habitat."[5]

Indeed, Northwest fish habitat was by then a mess, and commercial fishers were blameless. Agriculture destroyed fish-rearing grounds by polluting streams with animal wastes, pesticides, and herbicides. Soil erosion—from inappropriate farming methods—buried spawning beds. Altering stream channels and siphoning off water for irrigation dried up spawning gravels. Over-cutting trees close to waterways increased sedimentation and erosion while raising stream temperatures. Gold dredging destroyed spawning beds and flushed sediments downstream to bury other spawning areas. Temporary dams installed to divert water for placer mining characteristically went up without fish ladders and sometimes completely destroyed tributary runs of anadromous fish. Domestic and industrial pollution killed fish.[6]

Still, the fish—strong and adaptable—could have survived both the degradation in habitat and the pressures from commercial fishing. What many could not survive were dams—the big dams and little dams that mushroomed across the Northwest. By the end of World War II more than three hundred dams filled the Columbia River Basin—only two, Bonneville and Grand Coulee—having been constructed by the federal government on the Columbia main stem. Most of these were tiny splash dams and irrigation diversions. Along the Snake River, however, some larger structures proved more worrisome. Swan Falls Dam, constructed and expanded over a period of years in the early 1900s, rose without a usable fish ladder and destroyed a considerable portion of the upper Snake River fish runs. In the 1950s Idaho Power Company's three-dam complex in the middle Snake blocked access to an extensive habitat for chinook and sockeye salmon and steelhead. Idaho Power attempted to install fish-passage systems at the dams but bungled the efforts, thus destroying some of the Snake River's premier fish grounds. By the early 1950s, even before the Corps began constructing Ice Harbor Dam, half of the original spawning habitat for anadromous fish in the Columbia River system had been destroyed or blocked.[7]

Clearly, the Columbia River fishery was a resource in trouble before the federal government began its major dam-building program along the Columbia and Snake rivers. But fishery experts knew the situation would only get worse once the Corps began constructing massive multipurpose projects.

Those big federal dams, even when equipped with fish-passage facilities (and some, like Grand Coulee, were not), can deplete fish runs in many ways, not all of them apparent in the 1930s when work started on Bonneville. Reservoirs can flood the shallow gravel beds fish use to spawn. Smolts migrating downstream can be killed in turbines or, if they survive, can arrive below a dam stunned: easy prey for seagulls, squawfish, and other predators. Fish flushed over spillways to reduce turbine mortality might succumb to increased nitrogen supersaturation. Stressed too much while passing over spillways, fragile young salmon also become susceptible to bacterial kidney disease, a serious killer. Upstream migrating adults sometimes cannot detect fish ladder entrances, and even if they do, they usually spend more time in the river than in pre-dam days, all the while subject to more stress, more disease, more pollution.

Even those fish that survive face the threat of timing dysfunctions. Approximately 50 percent of the Columbia River's chinook salmon and steelhead populations originate in the Snake River system. With the completion of Corps of Engineers dams along the Snake and Columbia, a trip that formerly took an Idaho smolt about twenty-two days from its Salmon River birthplace to reach the ocean had increased to fifty-four days. Delays in getting to the sea frequently cause smolts to die or lose their migratory urge and revert to a non-anadromous life cycle. If an adult salmon, which rarely eats once it enters the river, does not make it to spawning grounds on time it, too, can die, having depleted its store of fatty energy.[8]

Dam-caused fish mortalities became depressingly clear over the years. Annual adult counts of chinook salmon over Ice Harbor Dam declined from 94,301 during the first year of operation in 1962 to 23,175 in 1991. Sockeye dropped from 1,118 in 1963 to 1 in 1992. Snake River coho became extinct in the 1980s. It is impossible to accurately estimate the number of salmon in the Columbia system prior to the incursion of white settlers, but scientists believe at least sixteen million adult fish annually entered the river. That number had dwindled to fewer than two-and-a-half million by the 1990s, all but about three hundred thousand of those being artifically reared in hatcheries. And while fish agencies continued to squeeze commercial fishers, limiting seasons and catches, no knowledgeable observers by then really questioned the principal culprit: federal dams killed far too many juveniles. Wrote Wesley Ebel of the National Marine Fisheries Service, "The drop in adult return percentages reflects losses of juveniles due to fish passage problems in the Snake River—not to adult losses at dams, nor to ocean mortality, nor to increased fishing pressure in the ocean, nor even to the river gillnet fishery."[9]

To continue basing primary blame on habitat degradation from logging, farming, and urbanization, or on commercial fishers, as the Corps of Engineers, Bonneville Power Administration, ports, and sports fishing organizations often do, only obfuscates the issue. Habitat improvements could still help the fish. But by the 1990s fishery biologists had ably demonstrated that federal dams accounted for more than 95 percent of salmon losses on the Snake/Columbia system. Of course, biologists had known that for years. But for decades the considerable political clout and public relations ingenuity of the Corps and BPA effectively delayed action aimed at addressing the real problem—dams. This delay, for which the Corps, BPA, and their political allies are largely accountable, destroyed several species of Snake/Columbia river anadromous fish and jeopardized others.

As early as the 1930s the federal government recognized that its dams killed fish and wildlife, and it began legislating a plethora of regulations to ameolorate the problem. Federal laws, however, did nothing to solve the essential problems created by dams. At best the laws only delayed the day when entire species faced extinction.

Through the 1936 Fish and Wildlife Coordination Act and its 1946 and 1958 amendments the Corps became involved in mitigating losses its dams inflicted. But the acts helped little in preserving Columbia River fish runs. As the Corps' Edward Mains wrote, "The Fish and Wildlife Coordination Act is a relatively complex law, and is subject to various shades of interpretations by reasonable men." The Corps' decentralized structure allowed it considerable autonomy in interpreting such laws from district to district. Not surprisingly, adhering to the act's provisions "ranged from good to fair, to too-little too-late, to none," noted the Pacific Northwest Regional Commission. After all, the act and its amendments required only that fish and wildlife be given "full consideration." In practical terms the Corps could accomplish this—and frequently did—by simply appending state and federal fish agency studies to their reports to Congress. If Corps decision makers at either the district, division, or national level opted to exclude suggested fish-protection measures, they almost invariably retained enough flexibility to legally do so. Of course, these same vague guidelines sometimes permitted Corps decision makers concerned about environmental protection to justify greater fish protection than the original authorization intended.[10]

Though ushered in with great hopes, the National Environmental Policy Act (NEPA) of 1969, like the earlier Fish and Wildlife Coordination Acts, proved vague enough to allow the Corps to adhere to the letter of the law while ignoring its intent. In 1980 Congress passed yet another act designed specifically for the Columbia River system, one that seemed guaranteed to aid anadromous fish. Indeed, many considered the Pacific Northwest Electric Power Planning and Conservation Act the most ambitious effort in the world to restore fishery resources.

In 1979 the National Marine Fisheries Service had considered protecting some varieties of Columbia River salmon under the Endangered Species Act. Concerned that such designation would remove the salmon issue from regional control and wreak economic havoc, Northwest congressional leaders persuaded Congress to instead pass the Northwest Power Act, giving the Bonneville Power Administration authority to protect, mitigate, and enhance fish resources affected by hydroelectric projects. At the same time the act required the BPA to ensure that the Pacific Northwest retained "an adequate, efficient, economical, and reliable power supply." Indeed, aluminum companies' continued requirements of cheap electricity were as important in getting Congress to pass the act as were concerns about salmon. Just how the BPA was to allocate water for these two sometimes-conflicting goals would be greatly debated in the 1980s.

The measure created the Northwest Power Planning Council. The council, a multi-state agency with two governor-appointed representatives each from Montana, Idaho, Washington, and Oregon, is charged with establishing equity among the Columbia system's myriad users and for doubling the number of salmon in the river, from 2.5 to 5 million. Its very composition seemed to doom the council to failure. Representatives from Montana, for example, frequently shared little with downstream interests in Washington and Oregon. "They have something to gain if they're successful [at increasing fish runs], but we don't have a salmon run to return," commented one of Montana's members in the early 1990s. Consequently, Montana skeptically viewed proposals to drain water from its system in order to assist juvenile salmon. Further, the council never developed a way to meet its twin obligations of increasing fish runs while retaining the region's supply of inexpensive hydroelectricity. In the words of outspoken council chairman Ted Hallock in 1991, during its first decade the council was "totally dictated to by the power industry." For ten years it focused on trying to increase fish stocks in ways that would have little or no negative impact on hydroelectric generation, primarily through expansive fish hatchery production. The council paid little attention to "the things that were killing the fish." By 1992 the council had proven ineffective at augmenting salmon runs. Even more worrisome, many biologists claimed its insistence on producing more and more hatchery stock brought drastic reduction in wild fish, which had to compete with the new hordes for food and habitat. Noted R. Keith Higginson, Director of Idaho's Department of Water Resources, former Commissioner of the Bureau of Reclamation, and hardly a rabid environmentalist, "The Power Council has been around for over a decade, spent about $2 billion, and the fish runs are still going to Hell." In 1994 the 9th Circuit Court of Appeals also strongly rebuked the council's efforts on behalf of fish: "Rather than asserting its role as a regional leader, the Council has assumed the role of a consensus builder, sometimes sacrificing the act's fish and wildlife goals for what is, in essence, the lowest common denominator acceptable to the power interests."[11]

The problem with all of these well-intentioned laws was that the Corps could act legally and the fish would still suffer. The provisions either did not directly affect the agency or were written broadly enough that the Engineers could technically fulfill their legal obligations without really improving the fishery resource. Further, fishery advocates and environmentalists found the agency unwilling to allow any tampering with ultimate control over "its" dams. For years, and to some extent today, the Corps' view was, "These are our dams and we'll operate them as we see fit." And the agency proved just as adamant about relinquishing control over the fish that happened to swim past their structures. When Oregon Senator Charles McNary in the 1930s advocated splitting management at Bonneville Dam between the Corps and a proposed Columbia River Administrator, the Corps opposed the recommendation precisely because of fish: "Neither this Department nor any other agency will be in a position to assure the preservation of the highly important salmon fishery on the Columbia River unless it has full and complete control of the operation of the dam," wrote the Chief of Engineers. In 1970, when some critics wanted state fishery agencies given ultimate authority over fish runs, the Corps again defended its primary role in fish passage at its Columbia and Snake river dams. "We have the desire, manpower, and professional capability to effectively operate our fishway systems . . . without having the fishery agencies tell us what to do," wrote Pacific Division Engineer Brigadier General Roy Kelley.[12]

A further difficulty arose because the Corps acted at once as several bodies operating largely independently of each other. Dealing with the agency was like trying to squeeze a ball of mercury. There was seldom a single set of rules for "The Corps." While the Office of the Chief of Engineers in Washington determined general policy, it left execution to its division and district personnel. In the Northwest, for example, three districts—Walla Walla, Seattle, and Portland—operated under the North Pacific Division, which operated under the Office of the Chief of Engineers. Environmentalists frequently complained they never knew how such a decentralized agency made decisions. Not only did similar environmental arguments and tactics fail to work from district to district, but often the rules changed dramatically within districts because the Corps brought in new District Engineers every three years, and a new District Engineer could bring with him a whole new set of allegiances. During the period of planning and constructing the lower Snake River projects, for example, the Walla Walla District had eleven District Engineers, some of them quite sympathetic to fishery concerns and some who could hardly be troubled by such matters. It made a great deal of difference under whose watch fish preservation proposals made their way to the District's headquarters.

Despite its decentralized nature, the Washington, D. C., office never gave districts complete autonomy, and residents of the Pacific Northwest—including some Corps employees—grew frustrated because local Corps officials frequently sought to do more for fish than the Corps' upper echelons would allow. Longtime Walla Walla District biologist Ray Oligher recollected some of that frustration when recalling his trip to Washington, D. C., in the mid-1970s to advocate on behalf of the Lower Snake River Fish and Wildlife Compensation Plan, the most expensive mitigation proposal in American history to that time: "We spent two days in Washington and it was a tough sell. There was only one biologist in D.C. at the time. They were 3,000 miles away from the issue and they were money handlers who could care less about salmon."[13]

In 1988 a frustrated Norma Paulus of the Northwest Power Planning

Council alleged that the Washington, D. C., office had "declared war on fish." Indeed, Army Engineers in the East frequently were less sensitive to fish problems than those in the Northwest. Director of Civil Works Major General H. J. Hatch wrote the North Pacific Division in 1987 that he was "not convinced that the fish survivability goals you are attempting to achieve are justified, appropriate or something the Corps must accomplish." Lieutenant Colonel Kit Valentine of the Washington Office of Environmental Overview toured fish facilities along the lower Snake that same year and chastised Walla Walla District officials, noting that the Corps' Washington officials had questions about "when enough is enough." He reminded District personnel that the Corps' primary concerns were flood control and navigation and that the "environmental- natural resources program with the U. S. Army Corps of Engineers" had "a limited visibility and a low priority." He also expressed concern about the many arrangements between the North Pacific Division and various fish and wildlife agencies to preserve fish runs.[14]

Anadromous fish returning to the Snake River in the late twentieth century faced a dammed channel of death, a potentially unsolvable problem exacerbated by conflicting authorities and ineffective federal laws. In the period from the 1970s into the 1990s the Corps of Engineers and other state and federal agencies pumped hundreds of millions of dollars into fish preservation efforts while maintaining the dams at peak operating efficiency for electrical production, navigation, recreation, and irrigation. Nowhere in the world had society spent anywhere near as much money to preserve fish runs as on the Columbia River system. Despite all that money, the fish continued to die. The experiences along the Snake and Columbia rivers proved only one thing: the legislators who passed the Northwest Electric Power Planning and Conservation Act hoping to avert a potential economic crisis brought by an endangered species listing were living a pipe dream. It would prove impossible to have low hydroelectric rates, free navigation, and viable fish runs in the Columbia/Snake waterway.

One could take the case of the Lower Snake River Fish and Wildlife Compensation Plan as a perfect example of a noble federal program underachieving its expectations. There is no doubt the compensation plan, at one time the largest federal mitigation program in American history, has helped to buy time in the struggle to preserve fish and wildlife. But it has not become the panacea many had hoped. The Corps of Engineers has spent more than $220 million, plus an estimated $10 million annually in operating expenses, to compensate for fish and wildlife losses its dams caused along the lower Snake. Ninety percent of that money financed fish mitigation measures. But it will take more than a multi-million dollar compensation program to preserve the fish and wildlife threatened by those lower Snake dams.[15]

The condensed history of the Lower Snake River Fish and Wildlife Compensation Plan is this. In 1959 the Walla Walla District requested the U. S. Fish and Wildlife Service to submit reports outlining the effects of the four lower Snake dams and suggesting ways in which the Corps could compensate for lost resources. Fish and Wildlife completed reports on the first three dams, but by 1966 the Corps believed the anticipated costs for project-by-project mitigation were too high. So the Corps asked the agency to furnish a single report on the four dams as a unit.

In 1971 the agency completed its assessment. The Walla Walla District provided comments, and Fish and Wildlife submitted a final compensation plan in 1972. During the next few years the Corps held a series of public meetings concerning the plan, revised it again, and in 1976 Idaho Senator Frank Church introduced legislation enabling the District to compensate for losses. Just minutes before Congress adjourned on October 1, it passed the Water Resources Development Act, which included the Lower Snake River Compensation Plan. On October 22, just one day short of a pocket veto, President Gerald Ford signed the act into law.

The bill authorized $58.4 million—a figure later dramatically increased—for mitigation on the Snake. It called for the acquisition of 24,150 acres of wildlife habitat and fishing and hunting access, as well as the construction of nine fish hatchery complexes.[16]

The real history proved much more complicated than this summary. In the 1970s the Walla Walla District came to support the concept of lower Snake compensation, aggresively making the case for mitigation before sometimes-reluctant Corps officials in Washington, D. C. The District, however, had not always thought highly of paying millions of dollars to atone for fish losses, and in the late 1960s some fishery agencies chastised the District for proceeding too slowly.

"We were changing things," the District's Willard Sivley recalled of those days of massive construction along the lower Snake. "Whenever you change things, you upset people. We tried to balance the demands of many groups. We learned a great deal in the process. That we preserved fish runs at all is something of an environmental miracle."[17]

Sivley landed his first job at the Walla Walla District in 1950. He worked through the ranks and eventually served as chief of the engineering division from 1973 until he retired in 1980. Recognizing the importance of fish and wildlife and the Corps' increasing responsibilities toward them, the agency in 1963 sent Sivley to the University of Michigan for a master's degree in natural resources. As chief of the planning branch he became one of the primary molders of the Corps' lower Snake compensation plan. Joining him were Bert McLean and Ray Oligher, two of the Corps' pioneering biologists, who had also come to the District in the 1950s. It was unusual for Corps districts to feature any staff biologists in those days, let alone two, and certainly it was rare for a district to send an engineer to school for a degree in natural resources. "I think Walla Walla District was pretty progressive in terms of the environment," Sivley recollected.

In the late 1960s the Corps of Engineers entered a period of transition. It moved from an agency primarily concerned with construction to one that assumed greater responsibility for preserving natural resources. The Corps hired its first biologist in 1938, but by the mid-1960s it had fewer than seventy-five natural resource personnel nationwide. Then the situation began to rapidly change. By 1972 the Army Engineers had four hundred people working nationwide in its environmental operations. That number grew to nearly five hundred a few years later—a dramatic increase, but still a tiny minority at the huge federal bureaucracy.[18]

In 1970, however, the Corps remained development oriented and frequently clashed with fish and wildlife agencies over their respective responsibilities. The North Pacific Division, frustrated at the delay in completing the lower Snake compensation report, blamed the Fish and Wildlife Service for the long-overdue plan.[19]

Fishery people had a different perspective, accusing the Corps of deliberately causing the delays because it refused to provide needed information. Indeed, as the Washington Attorney General's office informed the Corps, it was precisely because of this perceived inaction that the Washington Department of Game entered into the Northwest Steelheaders' Lower Granite lawsuit against the Corps.[20]

Despite the various charges and counter-charges, the Fish and Wildlife Service did complete its draft compensation plan and submitted it to the Corps. The Corps had concerns about the report, especially its recommendation for constructing several multi-million dollar fish hatcheries. "While propagation has a role in the total mitigation plan, we disagree that it need be the major element," wrote Division Engineer Brigadier General K. T. Sawyer. But the Corps would not win this argument; it would build fish hatcheries. Ironically, by the 1990s as fish biologists increasingly questioned the wisdom of so many hatchery fish competing with dwindling wild strains, the Corps could legitimately note that fishery agencies themselves were primarily responsible for the millions of fish placed in the river system annually because they had demanded huge hatcheries as a part of the Lower Snake River Compensation Plan. The Corps proved less willing to point out that its alternative had not been to attempt to improve wild runs, but merely let "nature" take its course. Doing so would have surely resulted in even more alarming fish deaths.[21]

By the 1970s, when fishery deterioration on the Snake became apparent to everyone, the Corps willingly cooperated with fishery agencies in persuading Congress to pass the compensation plan. Indeed, the magnamity of the Corps' proposal surprised many people, both within and outside the agency. As Sivley characterized it, "When we first started talking about a $58 million mitigation program in the early 1970s, we staggered a lot of people."[22]

Sivley was unsurprised when Corps officials from Washington occasionally visited the District and "accused us of caving into local people and spending too much on fish." But even in the Northwest, some people disapproved of the compensation plan.[23]

The most expensive item in the plan, construction and operation of fish hatcheries, troubled several agencies. Virtually all costs incurred by the hatcheries had to be returned to the federal government from the sale of electricity generated at the four dams. That meant passing on the costs of hatchery construction to electricity users in the form of higher rates. Ken Billington, executive director of the Washington Public Utility Districts Association, claiming his organization was "stunned" by the project expenses, questioned whether the Corps had not sought much more compensation than legally necessary. The Bonneville Power Administration shared this sentiment. Noted BPA administrator Donald Hodel, "We are greatly disturbed at the magnitude of the compensation measures proposed . . . and the extent to which payment for such compensation is intended to be allocated to power revenues." With the destruction of fish by now clearly apparent, however, neither the Corps nor Congress proved willing to incur further wrath from Northwest residents and environmental groups. Congress would direct the Corps to build hatcheries despite objections from power marketers.[24]

The Walla Walla District ended up remodeling or building nine hatchery complexes. These were to produce more than twenty-seven million salmon and steelhead annually, the number believed necessary to insure an annual return of 132,000 adult fish.[25]

While fish received most of the publicity surrounding the lower Snake compensation issue, the plan proposed to mitigate for wildlife losses, too. The controversies involving fish hatchery construction paled compared to those surfacing when the Corps attempted to compensate for wildlife deaths caused by its four-dam project. And while it is convenient to blame a federal agency like the Corps for fish and wildlife destruction, sometimes the complications go far beyond bureaucratic foot-dragging to essential societal rifts over whether and how to atone for such losses.

River edges—riparian zones as scientists call them—are wildlife oases. Flood soils deposited along river banks over thousands of years create lush floral habitats attractive to a diverse lot of birds and animals. Consequently, riparian zones are among the richest ecosystems on earth. Even in country as dry as the land through which the lower Snake River flows, the riparian community teems with life. This region looked barren and desolate to early explorers, but it always held wildlife. In 1972 an estimated 22,000 pheasants, 57,000 quail, 20,000 partridge, 52,000 chukars, 120,000 mourning doves, 8,400 cottontails, and 1,800 deer lived within a half mile of the river's edge between Pasco and Lewiston. Islands and shorelines provided additional resting, nesting, and feeding habitat for thousands of migrating waterfowl.

Dams inundated virtually all of this land. These birds and animals could not simply move on when the reservoirs rose. The Snake's hardscrabble uplands offered little to entice or support such animal settlement. By 1987 Washington Department of Game officials estimated that the lower Snake supported only 2,000 game birds; that furbearing animals had plummeted from 13,000 to 500; that the 95,000 wintering songbirds formerly along the river then numbered only 3,000. The Corps would try to save some of these animals, but said mitigating for some species, particularly non-game animals, would not be "economically justified." These included lizards, snakes, mice, gophers and several other types of rodents, as well as birds of prey such as osprey and hawks—precisely the types of species humans often consider "lower rung" and consequently frequently omit from mitigation proposals.

Of course, just as dams did not solely kill fish, the loss of Snake River riparian lands to reservoirs did not exclusively bring such wildlife losses. Other human actions—such as an increased use of toxic farm chemicals and sacrificing wildlife habitat and wetlands to development—also took their toll. But the reservoirs remained the primary culprits, and mitigating for these wildlife casualties proved to be one of the most complicated aspects of the Lower Snake River Fish and Wildlife Compensation Plan.[26]

The compensation plan called for acquiring 24,150 acres. It would be difficult to obtain that much property without getting it through condemnation, and those living near the lower Snake were not about to sit idle while the government took away their farms and ranches.

By the early 1970s the Corps had grown used to controversy regarding fish, but it had not anticipated the contention that would surround land acquisition for wildlife. Looking at the situation retrospectively, perhaps the District should not have been surprised. As one specialist noted in 1979 at a national conference on compensation, "The mention of mitigation in agricultural circles conjures up a wide range of attitudes—most of which are hostile."[27]

By the 1970s the United States annually lost more than six million acres of farm land to development and soil erosion. Farmers in some areas adamantly demanded that "not one more inch" be relinquished. At the same time, environmentalists clamored for fish and wildlife compensation, a conflict bound to lead to confrontation as Congress increasingly required federal agencies to mitigate despite farmers' concerns.[28]

The Lower Snake Compensation Plan proposed acquiring 8,400 acres for upland game-bird production and hunting, 15,000 acres contiguous to lower Snake River project lands for chukar habitat and hunting, and about 750 acres of fishing access. The District would purchase the chukar land; the State of Washington, with money provided by the Corps, would acquire the property for upland game and the bulk of the fishing access; the State of Idaho would buy about fifty acres of fishing access, again with Corps funds.[29]

The Corps held a series of public meetings to solicit input prior to congressional authorization of the compensation plan, and it became immediately evident that many people opposed these far-reaching measures. At a 1973 public hearing in Colfax, Washington, participants unanimously opposed any increase in government ownership of local lands. Not only were farmers concerned about losing property, they also worried about potential problems stemming from increased hunting. At one point the Walla Walla District considered separating the fish portion of the compensation plan from the wildlife portion. Some in the District believed the fish proposals would pass Congress more easily by themselves. State fish and game agencies, however, insisted on keeping the package together. They feared that separating the two components might doom the less-popular wildlife compensation altogether.[30]

Despite the clamor, Congress passed the compensation plan. Opponents became more outspoken. They had several concerns. Many protested the loss of local property control and a resulting drop in tax revenues. "The Federal and state governments already own approximately one-third of this county," declared Columbia County Commissioner Vernon Marll. "Further acquisition . . . by Federal and state agencies would serve only one purpose—to lower the economic base and set a trend toward the eventual destruction of the economy of Columbia County."[31]

Most, though, specifically denounced the Corps' right to condemn land. On a trip to the Walla Walla District in 1976, Chief of Engineers Lieutenant General John Morris explained that the Corps always attempted to purchase lands via the willing buyer-willing seller approach. But "if no one wants to sell, then I'm left with a problem that I can't resolve." The Walla Walla District recommended that the agency purchase lower Snake compensation lands only on a willing seller basis, but Morris worried about the precedent this might set. "If we go that way," he asserted, "it will be the only place in the United States where land is acquired by this manner. Such a plan could be extremely difficult to administer on a national basis." In 1976 the chief's office overruled the District's recommendation: much to the concern of local Engineers, the Corps would condemn land if necessary to obtain mitigation property.[32]

This decision brought strong protests from local residents, many of whom misunderstood the complicated Corps decision-making process and believed Walla Walla District officials had misled them. "All through the . . . hearings the people were told the . . . compensation would be done on lands acquired *only by willing sellers*," charged one. "If this is to be changed, we feel the whole program should be sent back to the District office and further hearings be held so the people involved have an opportunity to express their views."[33]

Columbia County's commissioners suggested the Corps confine its mitigation projects to existing state and federal lands. Only a minority, though, thought the Corps could achieve adequate compensation on existing government property—much of it rip-rapped riverbank lands or unproductive canyon sides. But Northwest politicians recognized a groundswell when they saw one and encouraged the chief of engineers to reconsider the Corps' condemnation proposal. Idaho's Senator James McClure joined Washington's Henry Jackson and Warren Magnuson in opposing "the Corps of Engineers' authority to acquire land or easements for that plan through condemnation proceedings." The governors of Washington, Oregon, and Idaho likewise fought the idea. The chief of engineers finally backed down, despite the precedent this might set. The Corps would first attempt to purchase all necessary land via the willing seller concept. It would also wait until 1983 to determine whether it needed to pare down the number of acres purchased, revert to condemnation, or find suitable alternatives, such as paying farmers to plant wildlife forage.[34]

In 1983 the Walla Walla District prepared a special report to Congress about its purchases of off-project lands, a pessimistic digest: "Owners do not want to sell strips of land through their holdings. They do not want to enter into perpetual easements that will be a burden to their heirs, to future owners, or that will affect the saleability of their land. Owners do not want unlimited public access on their land, they want to be able to control public use and hunter/livestock interactions." After five years of trying, the Washington Department of Game and the Corps had made precious little progress in acquiring acreage for wildlife mitigation.[35]

Despite the setbacks, Walla Walla recommended again in 1983 that "it would be inappropriate to abandon [the willing seller] concept." The Corps and the state would try again. The Corps also agreed to acquire land only with the concurrence of county planning commissions.[36]

Most important, the Walla Walla District, in an effort to break the impasse in land purchases, made an even more significant recommendation. The Corps suspected that its biggest difficulty came from landowners unwilling to chop up farms to sell small parcels meeting the specific compensation plan requirements or to sell perpetual easements for hunting on private lands. So the District recommended that it and the Department of Game purchase entire farms and ranches, even though some land so bought might not meet ideal compensation standards. The request went to the chief of engineers' office, which approved it in 1985. In 1986 Congress authorized this modification. For the first time the Corps seemed optimistic it could purchase the requisite property.[37]

Yet criticism of the Corps continued, particularly from its partner in the compensation plan, the Washington Department of Game. Bruce Smith, the department's eastern Washington regional director, suspected that Washington, D. C., Corps officials did not share Walla Walla's aim of fully implementing the compensation plan's acquisition goals. When the District informed the department that only $200,000 of a requested $1.7 million would be available for land acquisition in 1987, Smith exploded. "They've left us high and dry once again," he charged, "and we can't seem to get through the layers of Corps administration to identify an accountable party."[38]

Actually, the culprit was President Ronald Reagan's executive department, which the next year eliminated all money for land purchases. In fiscal year 1990 Congress gave the District $861,000 for property acquisition. The five-year clock for completing land acquisition recommended in the 1983 special report to Congress then began ticking. All land purchases had to be completed by fiscal year 1994 and some District employees still questioned the goals' achievability. "Already [Walla Walla District] believes that an extension of the FY 1994 'sunset provision' will be needed to fulfill the objectives of the Compensation Plan," wrote Richard Carlton, the District's real estate division chief.[39]

The Corps' problems and frustrations were many. When the District and State of Washington identified usable land with owners willing to sell, county planning commissions had to approve the purchase. Just meeting those requirements would have been difficult. But there were other problems as well. Owners frequently expected more than the land's appraised value, while other purchasers competed for the limited parcels available.

Overriding all these difficulties was a lack of dependable funding. "Many times in past years," Carlton wrote, "we have cultivated prospects and initiated our contacts with individual owners only to inform them in a few months that we cannot make an offer due to lack of funding. This destroys our credibility as a reliable and earnest buyer in the market place. It is imperative to the overall success of the Compensation Plan that adequate and more predictable levels of funding be sustained." As the 1990s began the Corps had only purchased approximately four thousand of its twenty-four thousand acre goal.[40]

Preserving wildlife threatened by the Snake River dams drew less attention than fish issues, but there were similarities between the two experiences. Most significantly—and not surprisingly—it became clear in both instances that while people generally favored the concept of environmental protection in the abstract, many resented such protection "in their backyards," with personal costs involved. The same farm organizations that had fought for the lower Snake dams and benefited from the reduced freight rates they brought, now opposed the idea of surrendering property to aid wildlife or paying higher property taxes due to increased federal land ownership. Like utility users elsewhere in the Northwest, they wanted the dams' benefits and generally agreed it would be nice to save animals. When it came time to pay the bills, however, they balked. Northwest farmers, like Northwest utility users, refused to face reality. They wanted the nation's cheapest electricity, a federally subsidized navigation system that guaranteed inexpensive grain shipment, and abundant fish and wildlife. Something would have to give. As the region entered the 1990s, the only things to have given to that point were fish and wildlife.

The Lower Snake River Fish and Wildlife Compensation Plan would play a significant role in efforts to save the Northwest's anadromous fish. Grand as it was, however, fishery biologists always knew it alone would not be enough. Indeed, the compensation plan would actually be a minor part of federal outlays to save Columbia/Snake river salmon and steelhead; it would only mitigate for losses brought by construction of lower Snake dams. The compensation plan goals fell far short of restoring fish runs to their pre-dam levels, and although biologists recognized the improbability of again seeing sixteen million adult fish annually swimming the Columbia/Snake system, they wanted considerably more than were there when dam construction began on the lower Snake. Environmentalists and fish biologists increasingly demanded that the Corps and BPA do much more than merely "compensate" for losses dams caused. They concentrated their efforts on forcing the Corps to develop ways to get smolts safely past the dams.

At the time the Corps constructed Ice Harbor Dam, most public attention focused on adult fish survival. Salmon produced so many eggs that the Corps chose to ignore scientific warnings about massive smolt deaths. It believed that if its fish ladders could guarantee a significant adult return rate then the adults would produce enough offspring to insure the preservation of fish runs, even if tens of thousands of juveniles died at each dam. Consequently, Ice Harbor had fish passage only for adults; smolts had to fend for themselves.

Even though adult fish also die at dams, enough do survive to insure runs—if the dams killed fewer juveniles. As studies began to reveal the number of smolts that actually died at each dam, as well as the devastating cumulative effects of dams, the Corps came to realize it needed to improve juvenile survival rates or face the ongoing wrath of fish biologists, environmentalists, and—more importantly—Congress.

Actually, fishery agency concern over juveniles quickened with the completion of McNary Dam on the Columbia in 1954. The agencies began marking smolts, then placing them in the river above the dam and netting them below the dam in order to determine mortality going through the structure. The tests were a bit primitive at first. "A couple of studies showed that more got killed than had been planted above the dam," recalled Corps' biologist Ray Oligher. "But the tests did show there were deaths. That was when we got concerned."[41]

When studies found that McNary's turbines killed some of the smolts, the Corps developed safer turbines for the lower Snake dams. The studies also demonstrated a dramatic escalation in predation with dam construction. The rivers always hosted predators—birds and fish that feasted on smolts—but warm, slow-moving reservoirs encouraged even more, including several varieties introduced to the Columbia system as game fish. Salmon smolts attract predators by pooling up behind dams before moving through. "I've stood and looked down over a dam and all you could see were walls of squawfish," noted Oligher. "For juveniles it was like swimming into the jaws of hell." So the Corps experimented on the lower Snake with ways to more safely pass smolts. At first, some of the solutions seemed a little rudimentary. But the Walla Walla District was on the cutting edge of juvenile bypass research: nowhere in the world had anyone tried anything so grand.

The Engineers had designed a sluiceway to divert ice and trash around Ice Harbor Dam. In the 1960s the agency drilled holes from the sluiceway into turbine intakes to provide access through the dam for juvenile fish. Because the dam had no fish-guidance devices, however, the smolts had to voluntarily find their way to the sluiceway openings. Further, those fish that did make it into the sluiceway hurtled past the dam so fast that some were stunned. They became easy victims for predators downstream. Even so, the sluiceway proved safer for fish than going through turbines—or over the spillway and dying of nitrogen supersaturation.[42]

The Corps did not build a sluiceway at Lower Monumental Dam, but the Engineers embedded a juvenile collection pipeline along its entire length. Again constructed without a guidance system, the pipe proved even less effective than the converted sluiceway at Ice Harbor.[43]

Juvenile fish that did not go over a dam's spillway or through one of the rudimentary passage systems were suddenly swept down 120 feet below the surface into the turbine intake. In 1969 scientists came upon the idea of lowering huge screens into the water behind dams to deflect the young fish before they entered the turbines. They are called "traveling fish screens" because they use an endless belt of heavy nylon mesh mounted like a vertical treadmill to prevent clogging by debris. The deflectors force the fish into slots in the dam where they are guided by lighted openings to a long tunnel or channel that transports them around the deadly turbines and spillway.[44]

The screens were still experimental when Little Goose went on line in 1970, so the Corps opted for a bypass system identical to Lower Monumental and encountered similar problems attracting young fish. In 1973 the Corps installed traveling screens at Little Goose, and the number of juveniles safely bypassing the dam increased dramatically.[45]

The state of the art had changed significantly by the time the Corps built Lower Granite. This dam's juvenile bypass system was the most elaborate of any of those designed during original construction along the lower Snake. It was the first dam on the Snake or Columbia with submersible screens installed at the time of construction. As a result, its bypass system attracted an estimated 50 percent of salmon and 75 percent of steelhead juveniles. Lower Granite and Little Goose also featured fish-loading areas. These became heavily used, beginning in 1977, with the District's most publicized fish-passage endeavor, Operation Fish Run.[46]

In 1968 the National Marine Fisheries Service (NMFS), under contract with the Corps, began transporting juvenile fish by truck around dams on the Snake and Columbia, releasing them below Bonneville. This un-orthodox "migration" lessened fish kills at the dams and delivered the tiny fish to estuaries in a timely manner. Preliminary reports indicated survival rates twenty times higher than for fish left to find their own way downstream. At first the Corps and NMFS viewed the project as an experiment, a temporary means of saving fish until the Corps could construct hatcheries to produce ever more sacrificial smolts. But each year the operation expanded, with NMFS transporting 154,000 fingerlings in 1971 and 435,000 in 1976.[47]

The year 1977 came in dry, one of the worst droughts in Northwest history. Light snowfall forced those who controlled the multipurpose dams of the lower Snake and Columbia to make difficult decisions. Power companies wanted all available water stored to meet later energy demands. Young fish, however, needed a steady water flow to help move them downstream. The Corps, fishery agencies, and power marketers reached a compromise: greatly expand Operation Fish Run. The District added a new dimension to the fish transportation system that year when it transported nearly five-and-one-half million smolts downriver by barge. In 1981 the transportation project became a permanent part of Walla Walla District operations. By the end of the 1980s the Corps freighted more than twenty million fish annually in sophisticated million-dollar barges.

State fish agencies, Indian tribes, and the Corps praised Operation Fish Run, especially in its early years, and especially in low-flow seasons. Indeed, the Corps probably spent more time and money publicizing this program than any other environmental endeavor it undertook in the Northwest, touting it as one of the agency's most innovative conservation efforts nationwide. And few doubted that transportation helped. Had it not been for barging, the drought of 1977 would have been disastrous for steelhead and salmon smolts. Operation Fish Run, renamed the Juvenile Fish Transportation Program in 1981, proved its effectiveness in numerous other low-flow years in the 1980s. In 1976, Wesley Ebel of the National Marine Fisheries Service enthused, "We can work wonders with this transportation system, particularly with the steelhead trout. . . . It seems possible that we can establish adult runs of both steelhead trout and salmon in far greater numbers than existed before."[48]

That proved an optimistic prediction. Gradually, fishery officials criticized the Corps' over-reliance on transportation, and the program became one of the Walla Walla District's most controversial projects, pitting environmentalists and biologists against the Engineers and their navigation/hydropower allies in a long debate over the most effective way to preserve dwindling fish runs. Young steelhead did remarkably well in the barges, and the juvenile transportation program led to greatly increased survival and return rates. Indeed, the transportation system probably kept steelhead off the endangered species list in the early 1990s. By then, thanks primarily to the juvenile transportation program, steelhead populations in the Snake were relatively healthy, at least for hatchery stock. Steelhead smolts are about twice the size of most chinook salmon juveniles, however, and considerably sturdier. Research indicated that salmon did not stand the stress of transportation nearly as well. The Corps frequently modified the system to lessen stress on juveniles, but the survival rate for young chinook never approached that of steelhead.

"We barge more and more, and fewer salmon are coming back," charged Andy Brunelle, environmental specialist in Idaho Governor Cecil Andrus's office. "It's not working." Seconded biologist and fish advocate Ed Chaney, "This is a huge scientific hoax, perpetuated by the Corps because they have become so fanatical about it. They have cooked the data. This is religion being passed off as science. But it shows how powerful groups like the Corps and BPA are. They can still have people believing these fairy tales about the benefits of barging." As Cecil Andrus's office bluntly stated in a slick brochure castigating the Corps and BPA for reliance on transporting smolts, "Barging salmon is not legally, socially, or biologically acceptable for endangered Snake River salmon." In 1993 an alliance of environmentalists, along with the states of Oregon and Idaho, brought a lawsuit against the Corps and NMFS claiming that barging actually contributed to the salmon's decline, but lost the case.[49]

Still, by the 1990s the juvenile transportation system had powerful supporters. When Governor Andrus encouraged the Northwest Power Planning Council to initiate a permanent annual drawdown of lower Snake reservoirs in an effort to flush—rather than ferry—juvenile salmon to the sea, the Corps, power companies, and navigators spoke forcefully against the measure. Consequently, despite mounting evidence that taxing simply could not insure chinook survival, no matter how many million the Corps might transport, the council opted instead to try once more to increase the efficiency of barging.[50]

By the late 1980s federal and state fishery agencies and Indian tribes had won some concessions from the Corps and its fish transportation program managers. The Engineers reluctantly agreed to "spread the risk" in high or normal streamflow years by placing some juvenile fish back into the river below dams rather than attempting to transport them all. It became increasingly apparent, however, that the rudimentary juvenile bypass systems (converted sluiceways and the like) at many Snake and Columbia

River dams simply could not insure juvenile fish survival, even in good water years. The fishery agencies advocated better, more sophisticated bypasses, but sometimes they ran afoul of Engineers who did not always share their belief in the need for better fish facilities.

With its stated goal of restoring fish runs to levels existing prior to construction of lower Snake dams, the Northwest Power Planning Council emphasized two key components of a recovery program: fish hatcheries and juvenile bypass systems. Increasing hatchery production alone would not sufficiently improve fish runs if juveniles could not make it past the dams. The council could finally see the folly of the "salmon fodder" method of producing more and more smolts in the hopes enough would survive the downriver slaughter to ensure the runs' stability. Further, the council believed bypasses necessary to protect dwindling runs of wild salmon and steelhead.

The Walla Walla District agreed with the need to modernize bypasses at two lower Snake dams, Lower Granite and Little Goose, and in 1983 began meeting with fishery agencies and tribes to determine a suitable system. All participants agreed to construct a fish flume at Little Goose. Although more expensive than traditional pipeways, flumes had been used effectively at a few smaller dams in the Northwest.

In 1985 the Corps began testing several types of flumes, but debates over the relative merits brought delays. First planned for operation in 1987, the Corps did not complete the Little Goose system until 1990. When finished, the Corps of Engineers' first fish flume was the latest in bypass technology. Huge structural-steel towers supported an outdoor corrugated steel flume nearly half a mile long, covered with a vinyl sun screen. Now, rather than a dark, rapid trip through pressurized pipe, young fish flowed at the speed of a natural stream in sunny light. The bypass cost $9 million and the Corps proudly unveiled it during international festivities surrounding the twentieth anniversary of Earth Day. [51]

The Northwest Power Planning Council also wanted the Corps to upgrade the system at Lower Granite and construct new bypasses at Lower Monumental and Ice Harbor. Although the Corps agreed with the improvements for Granite and, eventually, Monumental, the Engineers insisted that an expensive bypass system at Ice Harbor was economically unjustified. Their resistance touched off a heated confrontation over the best way to preserve Northwest fish runs. [52]

According to the Corps, the Lyons Ferry Fish Hatchery, constructed as part of the Lower Snake Compensation Plan and located upstream from

Lower Monumental, made a new bypass and collection facility at that dam economically feasible because the system could capture millions of smolts entering the river at that point. No smolt-producing streams enter the Snake between Lower Monumental and Ice Harbor, however, and there are no hatcheries on the river. The Corps maintained it could not justify a bypass system at Ice Harbor because it could capture and load onto barges enough juveniles at the three upstream dams to insure that adequate numbers of smolts made it to sea. The Corps' obstinance about the Ice Harbor bypass system angered fish agencies and some key Northwest politicians.

The issue came to a head in 1988. Northwest congressmen, particularly Idaho Senator James McClure and Oregon Senator Mark Hatfield, worked a 1987 proposal through Congress that enabled the Corps to spend $8 million on lower Snake bypass systems, including design work at Ice Harbor. Accompanying the funding came a report that provided specific instructions on how to disburse the money. But the Office of Management and Budget (OMB) and the Corps balked. Claiming such congressional reports had no binding, they refused to spend the funds as instructed. Technically, the Corps and OMB were correct about the report, but their decision nevertheless provoked Northwest congressmen who believed Congress's intentions were clear. Despite congressional protests, the Corps refused to reconsider. Major General H. J. Hatch, the Corps' director of civil works, chose to expend only $4 million, and then not on the bypass construction as outlined by Congress. The Engineers instead would use $3 million to purchase two new juvenile fish transportation barges and $1 million for additional studies to determine the bypass systems' cost effectiveness.

The Corps' stance emerged as the opening volley in a complicated debate. The primary issue centered not on whether fish should be saved, but how best to save them. The Corps specifically questioned the wisdom of a multi-million dollar bypass system at Ice Harbor. According to Corps' figures, the system would return only thirty cents in benefits for each dollar expended. Fishery agencies challenged the Corps' mathematics.

An even larger issue emerged in the Corps' affection for the Juvenile Fish Transportation Program. "We believe transportation is more efficient and productive than bypass," claimed Walla Walla District Engineer Colonel James Royce. Given enough barges, the Corps believed it could save more fish for less money by barging than it could by installing bypass systems at Ice Harbor and the Columbia River dams. "Even with improved passage around dams, you'd still have reservoir mortality," declared Walla Walla

District biologist John McKern. The Corps proposed to solve that problem by giving all the fish it could catch a ride to the ocean.[53]

Fishery agencies, tribes, and conservation groups sought to wean the Corps from its dependence on barging. There was, of course, the issue of whether chinook salmon could really survive transportation. The debate, however, proved even more complex. No dams below McNary on the Columbia—the one immediately below that river's confluence with the Snake—had barge-loading facilities or bypass systems. That meant that smolts had to get through the last three dams on the Columbia as best they could. According to Steve Pettit of Idaho Fish and Game, unless the Corps built more bypasses, fish entering the river below McNary would be left "high and dry." Further, the Corps does not catch every fish at its collecting dams, and those missed would be at risk if downstream dams had no bypass systems. "The Corps takes great pride in the juvenile transportation system," observed Pettit. "But it is not the only answer. We also need bypass systems."[54]

Despite the many allegations on both sides and legitimate differences of opinion over how best to preserve fish, the Corps' refusal to spend money in the way Congress requested drew reprimands. "It gets disturbing when Congress takes action on something like this and you say that you're not going to honor it," Idaho's Senator McClure remonstrated the Corps. "We consider your response to be completely unacceptable in its policy intent" he and Senator Hatfield wrote to the OMB. "I'm outraged," stated Idaho Representative Richard Stallings. "It's very clear what Congress intended." It was heavy artillery, and it had an affect.[55]

While most critics blasted the Corps, like so many issues concerning fish preservation in the Northwest, this one was highly complex and much bigger than a disagreement between the Engineers and Congress. It was actually a battle between the Democratic Congress and Republican President Ronald Reagan's White House. "What we have here is probably not the Corps of Engineers as the villains," claimed Oregon congressman Les AuCoin, "but the Office of Management and Budget, which is trying to squeeze funds . . . [is] putting pressure on the Corps to not release these funds."[56]

The Reagan administration believed the federal government had over-invested in various programs to save Northwest fish. Consequently, it wanted to scale back expenditures in the hope that state governments would fill the void. But in this particular battle Congress ultimately prevailed. When legislators went back into session they specified exactly how the Corps should spend its money. And the Walla Walla District began expending it along the lower Snake precisely as Congress dictated: it appropriated design funds for a new Ice Harbor bypass system. It did so reluctantly and unenthusiastically, however, still believing Ice Harbor's bypass system was economically unjustified. In a 1990 information paper the Walla Walla District noted, redundantly and somewhat petulently, that with new collection and bypass systems at the three dams above Ice Harbor, "construction of fish facilities at Ice Harbor is questionable."[57]

The figures get a little staggering: $50 million spent on fish-passage systems at the four Snake River dams at the time of construction and millions more in retrofitting them with juvenile bypasses; $220 million for the Lower Snake Compensation Plan and $10 million annually in operating expenses; millions more in the Juvenile Fish Transportation Program, scientific research, satellite tracking and monitoring systems, and staffing at laboratories and fish-counting facilities. It hardly seems unusual that, when the Bonneville Power Administration announced plans in 1992 to spend an additional three billion dollars over ten years to assist anadromous fish on the Columbia/Snake system, hardly anyone noticed. By then Northwesterners had become accustomed to expending astronomical sums in efforts to preserve their primary wildlife symbol.

What did surprise a lot of people was just how little success resulted from those huge expenditures. In the minds of most Northwesterners, things were not supposed to turn out this way. Sure, they enjoyed and sought cheap electricity and subsidized navigation. But most people—probably even most employees of agencies like the Corps and BPA—truly believed, at least at one time, that they could enjoy these benefits and have fish, too. As the region entered the last decade of the twentieth century, many began to question that possibility.

When the Corps commenced building its dams in the Northwest, the public looked upon them as aiding not only society but also the environment. Social critics like Lewis Mumford wrote about electricity's ability to eliminate urban pollution. Vast quantities of cheap hydropower in places like the Northwest had the potential to forge a utopian society. Thus, when the BPA hired folksinger Woody Guthrie to write propaganda about hydropower development on the Columbia, local residents believed his lyrics told the simple, honest truth. "Roll on Columbia, roll on," he wrote. "Your power is turning the darkness to dawn." While a few fish advocates agonized over the harmful effects of dams, most Northwesterners believed the dams symbolized both the beginning of a regional economic boom and an antidote for the pollution that plagued more-populated regions. Although no one used the exact terminology in those days, the dams were an environmental boon.

Northwesterners came to live well off the dams' cheap hydropower, irrigation, and navigation. They grew increasingly dependent upon them. And while fish biologists, commercial fishing organizations, and a few others continued expressing concern about fish, not too many people paid attention. After all, anyone could visit a federal dam and watch huge salmon steadily make their way up the ladders past the fish-viewing windows. Surely there could be no problems as long as big fish kept returning year after year. The federal agencies that operated the dams and sold the electricity proved reluctant to admit to declining numbers of returning salmon. And the fish did have remarkable abilities to cross the huge barriers thrown in their path. It might well have been that with just a few less dams, the Northwest could have had its hydropower, its navigation, its irrigation, and its fish, too.

But the few fishery biologists of the 1930s who warned of the cumulative effects of dams eventually proved right. Throw up too many obstacles and even these hardy, strong fish will become extinct. And when it came time for tiny fingerlings to negotiate eight dams between Lewiston and the sea, with the hundreds of miles of warm, slow-moving, predator infested water in between—when it came to that time with the completion of Lower Granite in 1975—it quickly became apparent that something had gone wrong with the dream: Northwesterners could not have the benefits of eight massive dams and fish too—at least not without more sacrifice than they had so far been willing to accept.

At that point, in the late 1970s, a belated panic set in and Northwesterners sought multi-million dollar options to help insure fish runs while maintaining a free navigable waterway and cheap electricity. For more than a decade-and-a-half residents of the Northwest tried to convince themselves that, with the proper infusion of technology, innovation, and money, they could still have their fish and their power and their shipping. And they proved willing to throw hundreds of millions of federal dollars into that effort.

By 1990, however, the hoax had been exposed. Even this mighty river system was helpless to provide all the water that Northwesterners demanded for fish, irrigation, power, navigation, urban water supply, and recreation. Its magnificent fish could not surmount every obstacle placed in their way. By 1990 it was clear that the dams had truly endangered the salmon just as surely as hunters had once endangered the buffalo. By 1990 the only issue remaining to resolve was whether Northwesterners would finally prove willing to sacrifice to save the salmon, and how drastically their lifestyles might change should they be so willing. As the region entered the last decade of the twentieth century, the threatened runs of Columbia and Snake River salmon became the Northwest's most critical environmental issue.

Chapter 10

Endangered Species

Fish tie a huge region together. What happens on the continental divide affects fishing in Alaska and northern California. The region is all intricately connected and interconnected. And then you get all the political connections: state vs. federal; state vs. state; federal vs. federal; upstream vs. downstream; tribe vs. tribe. And then you get all the players—fishermen, irrigators, navigators, hydropower users, biologists. It is boxes within boxes, and the boxes are infinite. We are in a mess. It seems almost beyond human ability to deal with it.

Ed Chaney

In the high mountainous center of Idaho, nine hundred miles from the Pacific Ocean, Redfish Lake in the Sawtooth National Recreation Area spawns some of the world's most distinctive fish, *Oncorhynchus nerka*, the sockeye salmon. Although related to other salmon species of the Pacific Rim, the sockeye runs by a different clock. Most salmon hatch from eggs in cold mountain streams, spend a little time adapting to the freshwater where they will eventually return to spawn, and then make a beeline to the ocean. Snake River sockeye also hatch in shallow gravel beds, but they remain in the safe confines of Redfish Lake for up to two years before riding spring freshets to the sea, where they live for two or more years. Before they return to the lake at the base of the Sawtooth mountains their nine hundred mile return journey through the Columbia, Snake, and Salmon rivers takes them further while climbing higher (6,500 feet) than any other North American salmon.[1]

The sockeye enter the Pacific weighing a few ounces and take on a blue-tinged silvery color (some people call them bluebacks). They develop into the slimmest and most streamlined of all salmon species. Before returning to Idaho they gain three to eight pounds. They give their home lake its name by turning bright red just before they spawn. Sockeye are closely related to the smaller kokanee salmon, the primary distinction being that the kokanee spend their entire lifecycle in freshwater, maturing in lakes before returning to their birthing beds to spawn and die.

Despite the perilous and arduous journey from Idaho to the ocean and back, Redfish Lake once supported thousands of sockeye. In the 1890s commercial fishermen on the Columbia caught more than a million sockeye annually, making sockeye the second most important fish of the stream, behind only chinook salmon. Not all the Columbia's blueback came from Idaho, but a good many did. They spawned in places like the Payette Lakes, Alturous Lake, Stanley Lake, Yellow Belly Lake, Pettit Lake, and Redfish Lake. So plentiful were the fish in these high Idaho waters that entrepreneurs sold thousands of pounds to nearby mining camps, shipped out more salted and barreled, and at one time even considered a cannery on Redfish Lake. On the Payette Lakes, commercial operators salted down as many as seventy-five thousand sockeye annually in the 1870s.[2]

As early as the 1890s residents of Idaho's mountain country noticed dramatic deterioration in sockeye runs. Commercial fishing operations in Idaho had all but ceased by then, and one resident reported on the declines in the Payette Lakes: "There used to be millions of them here. So thick were they that often, in riding a horse across at the ford, I have been compelled to get off and drive them away before my horse would go across. . . . [There have been] very few during recent years."[3]

In the twentieth century, people—including fish and game biologists—all but exterminated what remained of Idaho's sockeye salmon. On the Payette, a series of small irrigation dams virtually wiped out the runs, and the Bureau of Reclamation's Black Canyon Dam, 183-feet high with no fish-passage facilities, finished the job in 1924. At Alturas and other lakes feeding the Salmon River system, small irrigation projects likewise blocked access to most spawning grounds. Continued commercial harvest on the Columbia and irrigation blockages in Idaho, later combined with fish-passage problems at the huge Corps-built dams along the Columbia and Snake rivers, probably would have been enough to doom most of the sockeye. But the Idaho Department of Fish and Game decided to make sure of the extinction in all but Redfish Lake.

Although hundreds of people annually traveled to Idaho's sock-eye-rearing lakes to gaff, trap, or net the redfish, sockeye rarely took a hook, and sports fishers pressured the Idaho department to provide more opportunity to catch "game" fish. In other words, they wanted trout in their lakes, not worn-out salmon about to spawn and die. So the department—charged not so much in those days with protecting species as with appeasing a powerful sports fishing lobby—abetted the fishers by destroying sockeye. At Pettit, Yellow Belly, and Stanley lakes in the 1950s and 1960s it dumped so much poisonous taxophene that nothing could survive for a year or two. Having wiped out the sockeye and all other native fish, department officials then restocked the lakes with introduced species of catchable trout. Then, to insure that the few sockeye that escaped the holocaust by being at sea could never return, department workers blocked all entrances to the lakes and prevented the sockeye from spawning.

Redfish Lake, for some reason, escaped the Idaho Fish and Game onslaught. Redfish, however, had its own problems. In 1910 the Golden Sunbeam Mining Company constructed a dam on the Yankee Fork to produce power for its Sunbeam Mill. The dam never worked effectively except to block fish. Idaho Fish and Game recommended the company provide fishways, but they didn't work well either. Indeed, it is questionable whether or not any spawning sockeye between 1910 and 1934 made it past the dam. A small tunnel in the dam might have allowed some sockeye to make their way to Redfish Lake, although biologists debate the point: some say the dam completely blocked access to the lake and that no historic run of distinct Idaho sockeye remains. In any event, the Idaho Department of Fish and Game for once did something right by the sockeye when it blew up a portion of Sunbeam Dam in 1934 and restored a free-flowing river.

In the meantime, the department had planted foreign fish in Redfish Lake beginning in the 1920s. Over the next six decades it introduced thousands of sockeye and their land-locked cousins, the kokanee, bringing them in from throughout the Northwest. Some people claim that a few kokanee, perhaps breeding with the introduced sockeye, began migrating to the ocean and created an entirely new species of fish. The original gene pool of the Snake River sockeye—if it still exists—is highly diluted by now, and some biologists, particularly those working for hydropower interests, argue that the Snake River sockeye does not deserve endangered species listing because it is a species indistinct from the plentiful Redfish Lake kokanee and not a true historic stock. Others, less concerned with hydropower profits, believe that any fish that survives an eighteen hundred mile roundtrip to the ocean deserves protection, whether a pure historic species or not.

In any event, when things became so bad that only one Snake River sockeye returned over Ice Harbor Dam in 1990, Idaho's Shoshone-Bannock Indians had had enough. They petitioned the government and the Snake River sockeye, whether a unique species or not, would join the list of America's endangered species.

The spotted owl crisis in the Pacific Northwest has pitted loggers against environmentalists and might have cost George Bush the electoral votes of Oregon and Washington in the 1992 presidential election. By claiming Democratic vice presidential candidate Al Gore would have "us up to our necks in owls," Bush failed to realize that most Northwesterners supported the spotted owl endangered species listing and its recovery. As heated as the spotted owl issue became, however, Idaho Fish and Game biologist Steve Pettit believes, "The issue of endangered species for salmon could make the spotted owl controversy look like a pillow fight." [4]

There are dramatic differences between the owl and salmon issues. For one, the owl touches the livelihood of a few thousand woods workers. The salmon potentially affects the lifestyles of anyone in the West who uses Snake or Columbia river hydroelectricity. Beyond that, the spotted owl issue proved relatively simple to isolate. Determining the owl's endangered status was a straightforward task: scientists came up with estimates of how many breeding pairs existed and at what point the population would drop so low the species could not perpetuate itself. But in the salmon issue, even defining a "species" creates contention.

Each tributary of the Columbia and Snake is believed to produce a genetically distinct run of salmon specifically adapted for the peculiar needs of migrating to and from its particular stream. These are fish that, for the most part, breed only with their neighbors from the same stream. Under Endangered Species Act language, a distinct fish population in a specific geographic spot is eligible for protection. There are, therefore, literally hundreds of "species" of salmon in the West, and in 1991 the American

Fisheries Society reported that 214 of these faced potential extinction.[5]

In an earlier time, when biological science played no role in fishery management, Idaho's Shoshone-Bannock Indians came to rely upon the dependable annual return of sockeye to the Salmon River region. Of course, the Sho-Bans were not alone in that. Native American lifeways in the Northwest evolved with the salmon; religion,, world view, traditions, and history revolved around the annual salmon runs. Downstream tribes closer to the Columbia and Snake rivers naturally depended more upon the fish than did southern Idaho's distant Shoshone-Bannock. The annual hunt of salmon in prehistoric and historic times, however, took the Sho-Bans from desert homes to wooded, mountainous country in search of the plentiful fish. They speared and trapped chinook, coho, and sockeye with relative ease in the days before irrigation and dams and state-supported fish poisonings.

All Northwest tribes suffered as salmon runs declined. The most famous regional Indian fishing grounds at Celilo Falls on the Columbia—where the Corps of Engineers labored so long in the nineteenth century to create a canal opening the river to navigation—now lies inundated beneath the backwaters of The Dalles Dam. But at least downstream tribes can still fish along the river, although catches have dramatically waned in the twentieth century. With the exception of a few chinook that still manage to struggle to the mountains of Idaho, the Sho-Bans are reduced to spearing hatchery salmon trapped by Idaho Department of Fish and Game personnel, trucked over the mountains, and carefully planted at selected spots specifically for the tribal fishery; virtually no wild fish enter Idaho's once-abundant salmon streams.

As one example of Ed Chaney's "box within a box," the salmon crisis in the Northwest has pitted tribe against tribe. When the Shoshone-Bannock petitioned to place Snake River sockeye on the endangered species list in 1990, other tribes became concerned. Such a listing might further reduce downstream fishing or in other ways alter lifestyles. The endangered species listing could, for instance, affect northeastern Washington's Colville Indians. They, too, once depended upon salmon, catching them at the second most famous fishing spot in the Northwest, Kettle Falls. Grand Coulee Dam, however, put a stop to that by blocking all anadromous fish migrations. In the decades since the 1940s the Colvilles adapted by building marinas and renting houseboats on Lake Roosevelt, the reservoir behind Coulee Dam. Proposals to flush juvenile fish to sea by reducing Lake Roosevelt's water level worry the tribe. They fear that such a drawdown could leave a primary source of Colville tribal wealth high and dry by creating unusable marinas during much of the tourist season.

For their part, Sho-Bans claim that in petitioning for endangered species listing they only sought what was fair. The salmon once came to their lands and they want them to return. The downstream tribes should be willing to share what limited bounty remains. Indeed, some Shoshone-Bannock, who do not fish commercially, are as upset at downstream Indian commercial fishers as they are at their white counter-parts, the Bonneville Power Administration, and the Corps of Engineers: all, in their view, have contributed to the virtual elimination of Idaho salmon. "We don't sell our [fish]," says Sho-Ban salmon hunter Danny Edmo. "They [downstream tribes] have got the big numbers where they can rely on it for profit. We get the very limited number for ceremonial use."[6]

Congress passed the Endangered Species Act in 1973 and, six years later, the first petitions arrived to list selected Columbia River salmon. Officials concerned about the federal government imposing actions in what they considered a regional problem put off a decision on those petitions and instead encouraged Congress to establish the Northwest Power Planning Council to enhance the Columbia Basin's fish and wildlife. The council wrote ambitious goals to more than double then-existing runs of Colum-bia/Snake river salmon, and for a while it appeared its emphasis on hatcheries, bypass systems, and fish barging might work. In the period from 1985-87, annual salmonid fish counts over Columbia and Snake river dams more than doubled from their levels in the 1970s. But by 1988 it became apparent that these figures represented a glitch, not a trend. The increase in returns actually resulted *not* from council-backed sophisticated fish technology but from a few years of abundant water in a region facing an era of drought. By the 1990s most runs had declined to their 1970s levels or below, although a few fish, particularly hatchery steelhead, showed some improvement under the council-inspired recovery efforts.[7]

In 1988, during a time when the Corps and BPA attempted to convince people that the region had turned the corner in its fish crisis by citing the increased returns, other federal officials quietly declared the Snake River coho salmon extinct. Runs had declined from as many as six thousand an-nually in the 1960s to nothing by 1986. With little fanfare, the Snake River coho thus joined the upper Columbia River summer chinook, Lewis River spring chinook, Klickitat River sea-run cutthroat, Sandy River sum-mer steelhead, and more than sixty other Columbia River native species now extinct.

In 1962 nearly a hundred thousand chinook salmon entered the Snake River; by the late 1970s that number had plummeted to less than fourteen thousand before showing a rebound created by hatchery-produced fish. By 1991, however, chinook runs had dropped again to fewer than fourteen thousand and in 1990 fish counters recorded only seventy-eight fall chinook—this on a river that once averaged more than two-and-a-half million wild chinook returnees annually. The Snake River sockeye had no luxury of artificial hatchery stimulous and its numbers dropped even more precipitously: from more than a thousand annually in the early 1960s to one in 1990. On the verge of becoming extinct, Idaho's Shoshone-Bannock in the spring of 1990 petitioned the National Marine Fisheries Service (NMFS) for an endangered species listing for the sockeye. Two months later several organizations—Oregon Trout, Oregon Natural Resources Council, Northwest Environmental Defense Center, American Rivers, and the American Fisheries Society—petitioned to list Snake River spring, summer, and fall chinook.[8]

Ignoring opinions that the Snake River sockeye is an "impure" species, NMFS in 1991 declared it endangered, basing its decision on two factors. First, Redfish Lake kokanee and sockeye spawn at different places and different times. That fact alone significantly decreases the chances that the sockeye are really just a form of kokanee that started swimming to the ocean once Idaho Fish and Game officials blew away part of Sunbeam Dam in 1934. Second, after conducting DNA research on the two fish, NMFS became convinced that Redfish sockeye were genetically distinct from their neighboring kokanee. In 1991 four sockeye returned to Redfish Lake, three males and one female. Biologists carefully extracted all of the female's eggs and began rearing her offspring in two hatcheries in an effort to reintroduce the Snake River runs. In 1991 NMFS also declared Snake River chinook threatened. (In 1994, NMFS changed the chinook's status to endangered.) The endangered and threatened listings required the federal government, in consultation with Northwest states, to develop a plan to help the fish recover.[9]

The endangered species rulings had an immediate impact. For the first time since the Corps began contemplating dams along the Columbia River system, fish gained equal priority with hydropower, navigation, and other river interests. Over the years biologists had warned about ebbing fish runs once the rivers became plugged, and many federal agencies paid lip-service to fish protection. But never had anything stirred so much action as the threat of the Endangered Species Act. "One of the main reasons that we in

the Northwest enjoy extraordinarily cheap power and cheap water is because we're putting the real cost on the salmon and the bill has come due,"
said Jim Pissot, director of the National Audubon Society in Washington
state. Oregon congressman Ron Wyden put the issue more bluntly: "The
evidence shows over the years that when Bonneville [Power Administra-
tion] wanted to go with a nuclear project or capital project, it moved like
grease through a duck. But when [biologists] were talking about promoting
natural fisheries stock, they [the BPA] just did not give it the type of com-
mitment that was needed."[10]

The endangered species listing brought immediate gloomy forecasts
from the BPA, which predicted drastic electricity price increases even
before NMFS had a chance to consider recovery alternatives. The BPA,
port officials, aluminum companies, and some politicians—who hoped that
spreading alarm about the dire impacts of salmon listing might provide an
opportunity to gut the Endangered Species Act—pointed to similarities
between the spotted owl and salmon crises. The comparisons, however,
are disingenuous. True, the salmon controversy does indeed have the
potential to make the spotted owl controversy look like a "pillow fight." But
the very size of the salmon issue, affecting virtually everyone who lives and
works in the Pacific Northwest, also has the potential to diffuse its direct
effects. Unlike the owl controversy, where woods workers must shoulder
the bulk of recovery costs, salmon recovery can spread across a much
broader spectrum. While the BPA and some industry officials quickly
predicted regional economic doom, the listings could have quite a different
result. As Dan Silver, an aide to former Washington governor Booth
Gardner noted, "The economic impacts will be not nearly as severe as the
spotted owl was. . . . We're not facing an economic calamity, we're not
facing economic disaster. The net effects will be higher power costs and
some market adjustments as far as moving products to market."[11]

There is no doubt that salmon recovery will have dramatic effects in the
Northwest and beyond. Southern Idaho irrigators might have to use less
water. Hydropower generation will probably decrease and electricity rates
rise. Drawing down reservoirs to increase river velocity to help flush juvenile
fish to sea could disrupt barge traffic and increase shipping expenses. Commercial fishing harvest by both white and Indian fishers will be severely
limited. Sports fishers might have to do without catching salmon at all. The
ramifications of that would reverberate throughout the region at a time
when tourism is the area's primary growth industry. In short, the salmon
issue has far-reaching implications, and its impacts could affect everything

from the cost of air-conditioning in California to the availability of wood pulp shipped down the Columbia/Snake waterway for Japan's cloth industry. Indeed, for many individuals, the fate of the salmon is the most overriding concern of their lives. It influences everything from how they make a living to where they live. For people like Kent and Irene Martin, who reside four hundred miles from Idaho, the Snake River salmon crisis has all the drama anyone could want and most people would just as soon avoid.

Kent Martin attended college in Washington state and Newfoundland before ending up in a doctoral program in marine anthropology at Rutgers, where his research focused on people who had made their livings by fishing. A fourth-generation resident of Skamokawa, Washington, located on a sharp bend of the Columbia River just about twenty-five miles upstream from the Pacific Ocean, it never occurred to Martin until later that he was actually studying himself. You tend to think of anthropologists as being "interested in exotic cultures," Kent says, and it took him a while to include himself in that category.[12]

Kent and Irene Martin and their two daughters live across the road from land Kent's great-grandfather farmed. Four generations of family lie buried in the local cemetery. He stores fishing equipment in a logging warehouse his father built. Kent had cousins and uncles who fished commercially and he knew plenty of farmers and loggers. "Most of the people I grew up with could talk about setting steam chokers for logging and milking a cow," Kent remembers. They could also talk about gillnetting for salmon in the Columbia. "Fishing attracted me more than logging or farming," he admits, but he also recognized the value of education. So he set off in pursuit of an academic career. After a while at Rutgers he realized he could never abide the politics of a college campus and returned to Skamokawa to fish.

To walk into Irene and Kent's home one would never guess, judging by the collection of original art depicting fish and fishing that adorns every wall, that salmon are endangered. Fish literally surround you. But it doesn't take long to discover that declining fish runs are a threat not only to the fishery resource, but also to this family, to a way of life, and to communities like Skamokawa. During the course of an afternoon with the Martins, fellow fisherman Dean Badger comes to discuss his and Kent's upcoming season in Alaska, where Kent has journeyed for a few months of work every year since 1970. Those were the days when he and folks like Badger discovered they could no longer piece together a living from the declining seasons imposed on Columbia River gillnetters. In Alaska, Columbia River fishers now join seventeen hundred others in the largest commercial salmon fishery in the world, part of a Pacific Rim industry that annually harvests about $5 billion in salmon.[13]

Badger wears an extra-large T-shirt covering huge shoulders, arms, and an ample girth. It pictures a fishing boat circled in red with a diagonal slash through the middle. It reads "Endangered Species," and you soon get the feeling that any endangered species listing for Snake/Columbia river salmon also ought to include people like Badger and the Martins.

Kent Martin understands better than most that Columbia River fish are on the decline. You don't invest tens of thousands of dollars in fishing equipment in Alaska and uproot from your family every summer just for fun. You make those kinds of adjustments and investments because you've got a problem making a living off fish at home. Kent recognizes the problem, but he differs with a lot of people on the cause.

"Fishermen haven't done much about public relations," he admits. "They are aloof. This aloofness has in many ways crippled us." Martin points out that commercial fishers have become scapegoats for the Pacific Northwest salmon crisis. Most everyone seems out to get them. "Recreational fishermen are hostile toward us. 'We cheat; we use nets,' they say. The power companies have taken up a lot of this rhetoric to get the issue focused on us and not on dams. State fishery agency directors serve at the pleasure of the governor, and the governor listens to people. Most of the power used in the Pacific Northwest goes to the population bases in Oregon's Willamette Valley and Washington's Puget Sound. So the governors dance to the tunes of these population bases. In order to appease the voters, the state agencies blame commercial fishermen for declining fish runs, and each time they take a whack out of our season this seems to confirm people's suspicions that fishermen are the problem."

"On top of that," Martin continues, "we have to battle the image of high-seas drift nets. A Columbia River gillnet is pretty selective. You can vary the mesh size so that smaller fish can go through uncaught; you can select what days you are on the river and allow threatened stocks to go upstream untouched. There is no totally clean fishery, but gillnets are pretty clean. High-seas drift nets catch everything, and most people tend to equate all nets. So that makes us out to be evil—the same as someone catching those cute dolphins in the ocean. Actually, no biologist I know will tell you that high-seas drift nets have any appreciable impact on endangered Snake River salmon. They catch some steelhead, but Snake River salmon stay too close to shore to be caught by those nets. But now people are trying to blame high-seas drift nets for part of the salmon problem. That is misdirected attention. All it does is focus on harvest and create a smoke screen to cloud the *real* problems—dams and upriver development."

Martin points to statistics that agencies like the Bonneville Power Administration and Corps of Engineers have only recently, and then only reluctantly, come to admit, that dams claim 95 percent of fish mortalities on the river system. "If I get caught over-fishing, I can go to prison," Martin says scornfully. "But the Corps can destroy thousands of fish with impunity." The Corps, BPA, and aluminum companies that thrive on the region's cheap hydropower continue beating the tired old horse of overfishing. In the spring of 1993 ten aluminum manufacturers and 114 public utilities filed a federal suit to halt all commercial fishing in the lower Columbia and to close all federal lands in the Columbia Basin to logging, grazing, and recreation. The suit, conveniently, said nothing about dams and the 95 percent mortality they cause. On the contrary, the suit concentrated on a fraction of the 5 percent mortality caused by habitat degradation and fishing. The aluminum companies specifically avoided challenging Indian and sports fishers, who are responsible for a good portion of that 5 percent mortality not brought by dams. Instead, the companies focused on a tiny portion of the problem. No one except aluminum and utility company officials believed that a court victory would make any substantive progress toward saving salmon. The aluminum firms obviously want cake and frosting. They cavalierly suggest that fishers like Kent Martin retire their nets while the BPA continues to subsidize their aluminum operations with below-cost hydropower.

Martin sees many misplaced resources wasted in the efforts to further wrench down commercial catches. In the early 1990s the Bonneville Power Administration funded a $10 million program to apprehend Columbia and Snake river salmon poachers, aiming a disporportionate amount of its resources at commercial fishers. The BPA even provided the fish police with night-vision equipment left over from Operation Desert Storm in Kuwait. The initial effort in October 1991 caught no poachers and did nothing to preserve fish runs. "I don't have any time for poaching," Martin says, "but again, this is just an attempt to blame harvest." Seconded another lower Columbia gillnetter, Frances Clark, "We view it as a publicity stunt by Bonneville."[14]

"Recreational fishers see us as competitors, but we're not," Martin claims. "Once at a public meeting a woman said, 'I can only catch three fish a day, but gillnetters can catch all they want.' Aside from the fact I've never caught all I wanted, we have different motivations. I am fishing for a market and a livelihood. Besides, only some types of salmon will take lures as they move up the river—only 10 percent or so will bite. Gillnetters can catch those that don't bite; recreational fishers can't."

Martin watched agonizingly as neighboring Oregon voted in November 1992 on a proposition to ban all commercial gillnetting by Oregon fishers, a proposal bankrolled by recreational fishing groups and supported by electric utility companies. It was similar to a 1942 ballot measure brought by recreational fishers in Oregon and it was, in Martin's view, an unnecessary fight. There were once and would once again be plenty of fish for both recreational and commercial fishers if the fish could survive the gauntlet of a river choked with dams. Oregon voters defeated the 1992 measure just as they had in 1942, but proponents vowed to try again, next time coordinating efforts with anti-gillnetting groups in Washington in an attempt to pass measures eliminating all non-Indian commercial fishing in the river.[15]

Martin views recreational fishing groups as part of a larger threat that would change places like Skamokawa into tourist towns catering to bed-and-breakfast escapees from urban America. Skamokawa, a town of a few dozen people, is the kind of place a California magazine writer would inevitably call quaint. Steep-roofed frame houses hug Skamokawa Creek, which flows into quiet Skamokawa Harbor. A couple of generations grew up in this town living completely on the water, rowing from house to house and business to business and home to school in what locals called "The Venice of the Columbia," a town for many years without streets. There are roads now, but the creek, the harbor, and the river remain the focus of the community. Wooden docks extend from most houses, and a still-considerable fishing fleet ties up in the harbor.

It is the kind of quiet, nostalgic setting that could attract tourists, and Irene Martin has invested much of her life attempting to do just that. She has helped transform the town's most prominent structure into an interpretive center that will explain to those visitors just how the loggers, farmers, and fishers of Skamokawa made their livings and raised their families in this place. But that doesn't mean Kent and Irene want their town to become a rustic Columbia River resort. "These asses come down here from the state capitol and say, 'Your salvation is tourism,'" Kent

Martin mocks. "I'm supposed to wait tables? The I-5 corridor [from Portland to Seattle] wants to turn these communities into cutsey places so they can have fun coming to recreate while we starve. They want to tie up all this area for themselves. And that's part of the mentality we're dealing with on the fish."

Kent Martin sees the demise of commercial fishing destroying both his way of life and his community. More than that, however, he speaks passionately of the total collapse of the Snake/Columbia river fishery resource: "I think the intent is to destroy commercial fishing. If you have a commercial fishery, you've got to explain to the fishermen why there are no fish coming into the river. With no commercial fishery, you can put in a few riffles by a dam and have tourists come and see a handful of fish. Commercial fishermen are the watchdogs for fish and environmental protection. The commercial fishery has a vested interest in fish. I've got $100,000 in Columbia River equipment. It is not in my interest to over-fish or deplete the runs."

"If we lose the commercial fishery, we're going to lose the ballgame," Martin maintains. And he is not optimistic. "I'm very cynical that we have the will to save the fish. The hydropower people want to kill us, so then it will be easier to kill the fish. The technology exists to turn the Columbia/Snake fishery around, but we're not seeing the will to do it."

To Kent and Irene Martin the fish issue is far bigger than Skamokawa, the Columbia and Snake rivers, or even the Pacific Northwest. The fish are threatened because of an insatiable national appetite. "We as a society think everyone can have several cars, a boat, a hot tub—and that there is no cost other than money," says Kent. Seconds Irene, an ordained Episcopal minister, author, and historian: "We have to get past the mindset that we can give money to environmental groups and we can volunteer to pull weeds and we can recycle, and so therefore we can have a swimming pool in our yard. There is a necessary connection between dwindling resources and our ways of life that people just don't seem to understand. We think its OK to buy toys to reward ourselves for hard work, but we don't look at the real costs of those toys." Her words reminded me of a statement Northwest conservationist Bill Bakke made a couple of years ago: "Turn on a light switch and kill a fish."

We have not quite reached that point where every flick of a switch kills a salmon, but there is no doubt Northwesterners cannot have both fish and ever-rising electrical consumption. Some residents of the region are beginning to make that connection; energy conservation seems to have some chance for success in the future. Whether that conservation comes soon enough to save the salmon or people like the Martins remains to be seen, but Kent and Irene Martin are skeptical.

"Until recently," Kent mused, "the Columbia River represented 40 percent of my income. But there is nothing to come home to now. You hear about the big years, the big jag, but you don't hear about the in-between years." And recently, it seems every year on the Columbia has been in-between for commercial fishers like Martin. The day after my visit he would investigate the prospects of moving his family to Prince Rupert, British Columbia, closer to his Alaska fishing waters. The thought depressed him. And why not? In Skamokawa he leads a cherished way of life, surrounded by so much family history. This is a safe place for him to raise his daughters and visit daily with friends of a lifetime. "I don't want to leave this country, but every time I roll the dice I turn up a loser."

To people like Kent Martin, salmon are more than a commodity and salmon fishing is more than a business. "It's a religion, it's my whole life, it's my identity," he says. The statement recalls some of those Irene included in a video she produced about Columbia River gillnetting. "Fishing is in my blood," said one interviewee. "Nothing I like better than the sight of a salmon coming over your roller." Or another: "There are times when I fish for long periods of time that the boat, and I, and the water, and the sky, and the net—the whole works—become one. I'm part of that. It's a marvelous oneness that occurs."[16]

Back in the 1930s Columbia River gillnetters forced the Army Corps of Engineers to include more sophisticated fish-passage equipment at Bonneville Dam than the Corps had originally intended. Commercial fishers fought against fish-killing river pollution and forced irrigators to screen diversion canals to prevent smolts from dying in farmers' fields. Commercial fishers encouraged upstream habitat improvements. And they did, for a good many years, overfish the river.

But Kent Martin is right. Overfishing by commercial fishers is not now the problem for Columbia/Snake river salmon, and it hasn't been for decades. Commercial fishers have become scapegoats for power companies and Army Engineers and port officials and recreationists and a host of others who want to pass along the sacrificial buck and who have plenty of money to spend in an effort to kill gillnetting along the Columbia. And they probably will destroy commercial fishing, and people like the Martins will have to move on. The destruction of the commercial fishery will not bring the salmon back, however, and it might well doom the fish, for when Kent Martin leaves there will be one less watchdog keeping an eye on dwindling salmon. We will probably always have a few salmon to gawk at, like caged animals in a zoo, but that is not a resource. The Martins, like the salmon, truly are endangered, but one is not the most serious threat to the other. Both the Martins and the fish could survive. Fishermen and the fish once did coexist on this river system, but that was before dams and cheap power. Now a whole region has grown used to ignoring the real consequences of flipping a light switch.

Cory Eagen and Eldon Crisp are not threatened in the same way as the Martins, but some fish-saving proposals—particularly an annual drawdown of Snake River reservoirs to help flush smolts to sea—could disrupt their lives for months every year, perhaps seriously eroding their earning potential.[17]

Cory Eagen began working on tugs and barges along the river in 1948. "It was the year of the Vanport flood that killed all those people near Portland," he recalled one spring evening as he piloted the tug *Idaho* down the moonlit canyons of the lower Snake River. "I got initiated in a hurry."

"I worked for twenty-eight years on the river and never got farther upstream than Washougal—never saw Bonneville or any of the other dams," he remembers. But he sees them regularly now, hauling wheat, petroleum, wood chips, logs, and container barges for the Brix navigation company, pushing five or six barges at a time, loads 84 feet wide and more than 650 feet long. The lower Snake and Columbia river locks are 86 feet wide. Maneuvering barges 84 feet wide into them is like trying to park a Cadillac in a space better suited to a Honda. "When you've got 650 feet of barges in front of you," he says, "sometimes the fog is so thick you can't even see the front end." It can take all day getting through Bonneville Dam, the only one on the system with locks narrower than 86 feet. Pilots like Eagen must tie up outside the locks and haul barges through one at a time. Soon, new locks will eliminate this bottleneck in the heavily navigated Columbia/Snake waterway. The "sea locks" that groups like the Inland Empire Waterways Association successfully advocated in the 1930s have long since become outmoded.

Eagen has been making the trip up the lower Snake from Portland for more than a dozen years, working shifts six hours long, taking six hours to rest and catch some sleep before going back to the wheelhouse, working seven days straight, taking seven days off. His grandfather operated the first tug on Coos Bay, Oregon. "There's been a member of my family in the maritime business for the last 150 years," he says proudly. "But when I retire, it's the end of a line. None of my kids are interested. All they know about it is how much time I had to spend away from home when they were growing up."

Chances are Cory Eagen will retire before the Snake experiences a permanent annual closing of navigation, if that day ever comes. Many conservationists in the Northwest advocate a Snake River drawdown that would halt navigation for two months each spring while smolts make their way downstream. The drawdown would increase river flows. Conservationists see this as the only way to obtain the velocity required to flush fish safely and quickly to the ocean.

Herbert West must be rolling over contemplating an annual cessation of navigation. West's vision, and that of others like him, brought the Pacific Northwest a navigational system, one that moves more than seventeen million tons of commodities annually and exports more cargo than any other port on the West Coast. It handles $10 billion in import and export goods each year. It is a system that transports approximately one-third of the nation's total wheat crop at about a sixth the price it would cost if the crop went by truck. Tamper with this system and you tinker not only with the earnings potential of individuals like Cory Eagen, but also with the economic health of an entire region. The State of Washington is the most trade-dependent state in the nation. As much as cheap hydroelectricity, its late-twentieth century economy depends upon an open Columbia/Snake riverway. A drawdown would temporarily put many tugs out of business, sending crew members home to live off savings or unemployment.[18]

The drawdown also greatly concerns Eldon Crisp and his boss at the Port of Whitman County, Jim Weddell. The port at Wilma, operated by Whitman County just across the river from Clarkston, Washington, is the lower Snake's largest. Here you can see Herbert West's dream come true. Eldon Crisp lives there in a house overlooking the river where he watches the water traffic and dreams of how much more the Snake could handle. He is Wilma's port superintendant and he wore a Port of Whitman T-shirt, jeans, and Nikes on the spring day we met. He drove me around the 250-acre Wilma site in his pick-up.

We went past the Bennett Lumber Products' planing mill and Stegner Grain's elevators: "Lots of times we'll have thirty-five to forty trucks lined up here during wheat harvest, stacked bumper-to-bumper clear to the road, waiting to unload at the elevators." We drove to the Mountain Fir

Lumber Company, by the factory assembling log home kits for shipment to Japan, past the concrete block manufacturer.

Build the dams and development will come, Herbert West said. And here, where Lewis and Clark camped on May 4, 1806, development has come. But Eldon Crisp envisions more. He wants to extend the port downstream to lure even more industry, a restaurant, maybe a hotel: "I don't see Lewiston and Clarkston becoming a major metropolitan area, but with increased river transportation they could become more of a hub." If you shut down this and the seven other ports between here and Ice Harbor Dam for several months each year, however, you might forget about expansion. Indeed, you could forget about some of the current businesses remaining, because most of them claim they need a reliable and steady mode of transportation to ship goods in and out. They depend upon the year-round open river. Close the ports part of each year and you not only disrupt business but you probably eliminate jobs. Yet to an environmental activist like Ed Chaney, a lower Snake River drawdown appears the only reasonable alternative if the salmon are to survive.

As you enter Ed Chaney's home office on the outskirts of Eagle, a tiny bedroom community near Boise, Idaho, two things become readily apparent. First, Chaney has little time for housework. Dishes totter uncertainly in the sink; the expansive yard might most charitably be called wild. Second, one need not have money or a huge staff to play a principal role in the Pacific Northwest fish wars. The loner Ed Chaney has more than occasionally brought the fear of God to bureaucracies like the Army Corps of Engineers and the Bonneville Power Administration. He has sat on virtually every significant panel and board contemplating the Northwest salmon crisis. He speaks with an unwavering voice as a fish advocate, and when he speaks, reporters, bureaucrats, politicians, and environmentalists listen. And he accomplishes all this virtually single-handedly from his ramshackle house using little more than a telephone and home computer.[19]

Chaney came to the Pacific Northwest on a whim in 1966. Raised in the Midwest, he picked up a map one day, saw a place nearly all green, and decided to move west. He landed a job managing commercial fisheries with the Oregon Fish Commission. In 1968 he ran headlong into the Army Corps of Engineers, which had brought John Day Dam on the

Columbia into operation without adequately testing its fish-passage facilities. The resulting fish kills brought the fury of environmentalists and the investigation of reporters, and Ed Chaney helped lead the charge. "I caught the Corps red-handed burying fish, trying to hide them while publicly denying any wrongdoing," Chaney recalls. "The Corps went after me, a young lowly bureaucrat, with a vengeance. This made me a student of why we do these things. What drives people to lie and manipulate and intimidate in order to deceive the public? That's what got me started on the Columbia River fishery issues."

The Corps won that battle; a chastened Ed Chaney left the Oregon Fish Commission and moved to Washington, D. C., as information director of the National Wildlife Federation. But he returned to the Northwest, and the Engineers have probably regretted their vendetta ever since. Ed Chaney never forgot or forgave. John McKern, biologist with the Corps' Walla Walla District since 1971, will admit—in proper Corps understatement—only that Ed Chaney is "outspoken." But body language at the mention of his name clearly indicates that there is today, a quarter of a century after the John Day incident, little mutual respect between the environmental gunslinger and the agency that operates the dams.[20]

Ed Chaney refuses to cut the Corps of Engineers much slack: "In the 1940s fishery agencies told the Corps that if they built the lower Snake dams fish would probably not survive. Before the first lower Snake dam, we recognized the problems slackwater caused smolts, and we knew about the negative cumulative impacts of dams. But the Corps is *still* in a state of denial. They admit that dams kill some fish, but in the same breath they always say that 'commercial fishing kills fish, too.' They will say that 'barging fish helps smolts' when all evidence indicates that chinook salmon smolts do poorly when barged. They blatantly manipulate the data and reasonable people are caught off guard. Reasonable people are intimidated because the Corps appears to have the expertise."

Even so, Chaney believes the Corps might actually end up saving the salmon. "The irony is that the only thing that might save the fish is the Corps' instinct for survival," he admits. "I hate to think the fish are now in the hands of the world's biggest fish killers. But the Corps might start proselytizing to save the salmon in order to save itself. The marketplace has changed and not even the Corps is imperious to the marketplace. The Corps' days of scattering reservoirs like seeds are over. The Corps is going to change because nothing is more frightening to them than running out of work. So in time the Corps will become a constructive force. They are trying to head in that direction now through their innate sense of survival."

In 1990 Oregon Senator Mark Hatfield called together a "salmon summit" of representatives of resource agencies throughout the Northwest to hammer out ways the region could address fish needs in anticipation of the upcomng endangered species listings. Hatfield wanted nothing of another spotted owl "debacle" where the federal government imposed preservation regulations because the region had not prepared a formula of its own to protect the birds. Ed Chaney attended those salmon summit meetings as a primary advocate of what became known as the "Idaho plan," a proposal to draw down the lower Snake reservoirs every year when the smolts make their way to sea.

"Governor Andrus asked me to get some interested parties together and decide on some concrete alternatives we could take to the salmon summit meetings," recalled Andy Brunelle, who was Cecil Andrus's special assistant for natural resources. "The biologists like Ed attending that meeting said that if you could increase the river's flow, you could get the smolts through the reservoirs, past the predators, and to the ocean on time." The lower the velocity of the river, the fewer smolts survived. Once the fish reached the Columbia, river manipulators like the Corps and Bureau had a variety of options to speed them on their way past the next four dams, including releasing water from Canada and Grand Coulee's reservoir. Once in the Columbia, in other words, there would be enough stored water to increase velocity to assist fish without totally disrupting irrigation or navigation. So the problem Andy Brunelle's group faced was getting the salmon smolts down the lower Snake.[21]

Most people believed that the only way to increase the Snake's flow was to drain irrigation reservoirs in Idaho and rush that water downstream. Irrigators—and politicians like Andrus who depended upon their votes—were not about to listen to that alternative. "Besides," continued Brunelle, "the water simply did not exist to create the velocity we needed." Especially not in the midst of one of the West's most severe and long-term droughts.

"We had to come up with an alternative," Brunelle remembered, "and Keith Higginson said, 'If you need that much velocity, the only way to get it is to draw down the river.'" Environmentalists and biologists latched onto the drawdown concept, something that might have surprised R. Keith Higginson, for he is not always on the side of environmentalists.

Higginson moved to Idaho from Utah in 1964 when Republican Governor Robert Smylie appointed him to the state Department of Water Resources. Republican Governor Don Samuelson reappointed him, as did Democrat Cecil Andrus in 1971. Andrus and Higginson worked together well, and when Andrus moved to Washington, D. C., as Secretary of the Interior under Jimmy Carter in 1977, Higginson went along to head the Bureau of Reclamation. When Andrus returned, winning election as governor once again in the 1980s, he reappointed his old friend to head the state Department of Water Resources. Higginson has always identified with irrigators and understands their point of view, a necessity for retaining his job in an irrigation-dependent state like Idaho.

"There is nothing Idaho is now doing that is endangering the salmon," Higginson maintains. "Idaho is holding water for irrigation, but it is not a lack of water that is harming smolts, it is a lack of velocity. Downriver interests in Washington and Oregon want people to think that Idaho irrigators are to blame for the fish crisis. We say the fish are fine until they get to the dams. The lower Snake dams are killing the fish. The bulk of the resolution of the problem should not fall on Idaho farmers."[22]

So, the Idahoans meeting with Higginson and Chaney and Brunelle came up with the Idaho drawdown plan: drop down the reservoirs behind the four lower Snake dams, thereby reducing the width of the river and increasing velocity in the narrower stream. The lower Snake would once again look something like a river instead of a lake, and the smolts could again ride to the ocean in a timely fashion rather than wander around in still water and become snack food for predators.

It did not take long for the Corps to criticize the proposal. Said Corps biologist McKern: "The concept to pull the plug on the reservoirs and let the river run naturally is simplistic. It won't work. Navigation will halt; turbines won't be able to operate properly and will kill more fish; fish bypass systems will be left high and dry, stranding both adults and juveniles." Indeed, the Engineers came up with a host of reasons to condemn the drawdown even before they gave it an experimental chance. The Corps even threatened that it might need to get reauthorization from Congress—a time-consuming proposition—to implement drawdowns, because the dams were constructed primarily to aid navigation. Drawdown proponents, however, noted that Congress also intended that fish runs be preserved and that congressional authorization stated nothing about the riverway being navigable every month of the year. "The Army Corps of

Engineers failed to properly design the four lower Snake River dams as Congress intended," bluntly stated a publication of Idaho governor Cecil Andrus's office. "The dams must be modified so reservoirs periodically can be drawn down to speed water and young salmon . . . to the ocean."[23]

The Engineers projected problems ranging from the loss of nearly a million visitor days of recreation annually at the lower Snake reservoirs—a conclusion that surprised some local residents who wondered where so many recreationists originated from in this lightly populated region—to threatened kills of adult migrating fish because fish ladders could no longer operate, to the loss of millions of dollars worth of hydropower. The Corps, the Bonneville Power Administration, and port officials quickly seized the idea of a drawdown lasting three, four, even six months, with dire economic consequences. They ignored the fact that the Idaho plan called for a two-month drawdown in the spring when 80 percent of juveniles go downstream—and long before the peak recreational period on the river.[24]

The Corps and BPA response did not surprise proponents of the Idaho plan. "I can envision the Corps coming up with a whole laundry list of problems, then throwing up their hands and saying, 'See, the drawdown won't work. Let's get water out of Idaho,'" said Higginson. Ed Chaney had little patience with Corps' efforts to censure the drawdown before even trying it: "The Corps is looking at it the wrong way. They want to find problems. 'Oh, look, you draw down, and adult fish ladders and juvenile bypasses don't work.' But they should look at solutions—what *can* we do. We need a 'can do' attitude and the Corps doesn't have it. They're trying to poison the well. They are handing out disinformation. For example, no intelligent people would propose a drawdown without also proposing to fix fish ladders." Added Governor Cecil Andrus: "We have to tell the Bonneville Power Administration and the Army Corps of Engineers that they've had a microchip in their head on how to run the river. That should be removed and replaced with a new chip in which you say, 'You will maintain this river for the fish, as well as power generation.'"[25]

It's easy to understand the BPA's concern with drawdowns. Lower the river too much and the Corps would shut down turbines for fear of damaging them at a replacement expense of millions of dollars. During the Reagan/Bush years the BPA came under increasing pressure to sell all the electricity Northwest dams could produce in an effort to generate as much revenue as possible. Reduce hydropower production, the BPA warned, and the only alternatives would be more coal-fired power plants, increasing air pollution, or more nuclear plants, with their own potential environmental problems.

It is also easy to understand the Corps' reservations about drawdowns. For more than a century the Corps closely allied itself with navigation interests along the Columbia/Snake waterway. When open river adherents sought a solution to the rivers' many navigational obstacles, they looked to the Corps. And when the Corps needed help passing the idea of the massive dam and lock system through Congress, it asked the open river advocates to provide the necessary lobbying power. When ports began to predict economic catastrophe shortly after Idahoans proposed a drawdown, the Corps listened, as it always has, to these navigation interests.

For a time, the ports attempted to pose as fish advocates when denouncing drawdowns, claiming the lower Snake reservoirs provided spawning beds for Chinook salmon and that drawing down the river would eliminate these. Some Chinook do spawn in the main stem, but in numbers insignificant compared to upstream tributary spawners. The real issue was getting fish through the reservoirs to and from more active spawning beds. Taking another tack, the Port of Whitman County's manager questioned, "why we should hurt one kind of fish [bass particularly] to save another?" It was a classic case of comparing apples and oranges. The Port wanted people to believe a fish is a fish, but few people other than port officials seemed willing to stake the lives of endangered Pacific salmon against common warm-water bass. But the Port manager pressed the argument: "We believe that more weight should be given to recreation interests than has been shown to date. Giving more weight to resident [warm water] fish and wildlife resources would help." The Lewiston and Clarkston chambers of commerce took a similar approach in full-page newspaper ads showing dead fish on a dry reservoir bottom. Such a sight, they maintained, would become common during drawdowns. Andrus pointed out that the carcasses in the newspaper ads were trash fish that preyed on salmon smolts. "Not a bad deal," he retorted.[26]

All of the talk about fish, however, was only a subterfuge, and the ports soon retreated to their hard case—the economic impacts of shutting down the river. Immediately, they focussed on a six-month drawdown—something no one had seriously contemplated. Noted the Port of Whitman County, "A drawdown . . . for six months . . . would force a dozen elevator and other firms to abandon their facilities . . . on or near Port [of Whitman] owned river properties. . . . A drawdown of this magnitude would not only result in an $18 million loss for these 12 firms but would have a devastating impact on farmers because of the discontinuance of low-cost water transportation for getting grain to highly competitive markets overseas."[27]

A six-month drawdown would bring economic turmoil. But the ports had created a strawman. Champions of the Idaho plan proposed drawdowns lasting two months. Since the river system already shuts down two weeks annually for lock inspections and maintenance, the Idaho plan added only six weeks to this schedule—a proposal that probably did not endanger any ports or permanent jobs, especially since lower Snake barges do not ship perishables. The ports would suffer some financial losses and should be compensated for them, said the drawdown adherents. In the words of the outspoken Ed Chaney, "Port districts are a public welfare system already. They would not exist were it not for federal construction of dams and locks and continued federal assistance that allows barges to move goods toll-free. So let's write them some more checks. The net social benefits with fish will exceed the net social benefits of not having fish." But this concept, of course, cuts across our ideological grain: tell a port official that she or he lives off welfare and you'll hear more than mild remonstration.[28]

In one of the most objective analyses of the drawdown idea, economists from the University of Idaho, Washington State University, and Oregon State University concluded there would be economic ramifications with a two-month drawdown: farmers living closest to the river with fewer shipping alternatives would suffer, and port districts might not enjoy continued expansion. Nevertheless, the economists concluded that only 5.4 percent of the wheat shipped from Portland to international markets arrives from the lower Snake during the two months proposed for a drawdown and that Portland could meet export goals during that time with shipments from other sources. Further, some people would gain financially by the drawdown, particularly railroads and truckers. The drawdowns might, in essence, be an economic wash. "We conclude," they wrote, "that shippers who presently depend on the Lower Snake ports are likely to be very creative in modifying the time and mode of their shipments in response to any drawdown of the river. They have a strong economic incentive to do so. These market-driven adjustments are likely to mitigate some of the impact of a river drawdown. Those estimates which predict devastating impacts on the region's shippers should be seen as exaggerations or negotiation postures."[29]

In the short run, the ports lost their battle. Faced with public and political pressure to save fish, and with the recommendation of the salmon summit and the Northwest Power Planning Council that it try the Idaho plan, the Corps in 1992 agreed to an experimental drawdown to determine its effects on dam equipment, river banks, roads, marinas, ports, and other facilities along the lower Snake.

In March 1992 the Corps began lowering the river behind Lower Granite Dam, dropping the reservoir two feet a day. By the end of the month the Snake had sunk thirty-seven feet. Freshwater mussels, carp, bass, cars, fishing equipment, soda machines, an airplane, human remains, cash registers, guns, house foundations, old railroad beds—all lay exposed in vast mud flats. All of that proved interesting to visitors, but what concerned port and governmental officials more was the cracking of road pavements, marina docks left stranded on beaches of muck, and eroding river banks—all in all, a loss of $1.3 million in damages. "If this keeps up year after year, you can kiss shipping goodbye, you can kiss agriculture goodbye," fumed Port of Clarkston commissioner John Givens. Not necessarily, countered former Idaho Fish and Game commissioner Keith Stonebraker. Ports in the Midwest annually shut down several months for winter weather and dredging, yet shippers and ports there manage to thrive. "I don't think these people are any less capable."[30]

Faced with no politically palitable alternative, Cecil Andrus continued to encourage drawdowns as the only feasible solution to the lower Snake fish crisis. Andrus would willingly incur the wrath of a few Idaho port officials and navigators. He would not irritate Idaho irrigators.

If the Pacific Northwest economy depends upon inexpensive hydroelectricity and an open Columbia/Snake riverway, it also relies on agriculture, and in a dry country—for only that fraction of the Northwest lying between the Cascade mountains and the Pacific Ocean matches the regional stereotype of a land of abundant rainfall—agriculture means irrigated crops. Millions of Northwest acres receive their water from irrigation and annually produce crops valued at more than $2 billion. These crops account for five of the top ten products exported from the Columbia River. Agriculture also provides the Pacific Northwest with its positive balance of foreign trade. In Idaho, irrigation enables the state to rank third in the nation in production of sugar beets, hops, and mint; second in barley; and first in potatoes. Idaho ranks fourth among states in water used for all purposes, behind only the huge states of California, Florida, and Texas. Idaho easily leads the nation in per capita use of water—about nineteen thousand gallons per day as opposed to a national average of two thousand. Writer Tim Palmer has noted that Idaho "has the highest rate of [water] use on the planet, by far." All but a small portion of it goes to irrigate crops. Indeed, Idaho is the nightmare John Wesley Powell feared. Powell, one-armed director of the U. S. Geological Survey, authored one of the classic (although too-often ignored) documents of nineteenth-century Western history, *Report on the Lands of the Arid Region of the United States*. Powell well understood that only a fraction of the West's land is really suitable for irrigation, but boosters ignored his pleas for sanity, and the Reclamation Bureau, in states like Idaho, went on an irrigation binge. It dammed far too many rivers and drained far too many aquifers, all in an effort to produce subsidized crops that often found a market only as surplus commodities. Irrigation, despite Powell's warnings, today accounts for 80 to 90 percent of all water used in the West, and much of that, in Idaho and elsewhere, is sadly wasted. The irrigated West of the 1990s often lacks logic, but the irrigation society has many powerful adherents, and for a governor like Cecil Andrus to mess with Idaho irrigators—folks like Sherl Chapman and the Idaho Water Users Association—is to invite political suicide.[31]

The Idaho Water Users Association consists of more than 125 agribusinesses and municipalities and 130 irrigation and canal companies. Chapman is the group's executive director, and his association came on board the drawdown plan early because it moved the focus of creating more velocity from upstream Idaho irrigators to downstream ports. "Downstream interests in Washington and Oregon are saying we need to add much more water to the Snake system from Idaho. This also seems to be the mindset of the National Marine Fisheries Service as they attempt to deal with endangered and threatened species," Chapman said a few days before the 1992 drawdown experiment began. "So we hope the drawdown works. It might save Idaho agriculture."[32]

"If you drained every reservoir in southern Idaho you'd only get about half of what the biologists say they need to flush smolts to the Columbia River," he went on. "And you would eliminate three million acres of irrigation in Idaho." And then Sherl Chapman begins to sound something like Kent Martin, the Skamokawa fisherman: "If you don't want Idaho to go back to sagebrush, then we can't eliminate irrigation. We've got a lot of people saying we can eliminate irrigation. We have national crop surpluses, so we can bring in light industry and tourists instead of having agriculture. But light industry is very polluting and tourists are not going to come to a desert. Idaho has the quality of life it has primarily because of irrigation."[33]

Just as much as Idaho irrigators wanted the drawdown to work, navigators and port officials sought to defeat the idea before giving it a chance. They threatened lawsuits; they complained to Congress; they poured out thousands of dollars worth of negative publicity. And they proposed alternatives—none of them novel. Crank down on commercial fishing, they said; improve hatchery production; barge more fingerlings. To a fish advocate like Ed Chaney, those all seemed like tired and unworkable suggestions. In December 1994 the Northwest Power Planning Council, reacting to the 9th Circuit Court of Appeals ruling earlier that year that the council had done too little to fulfill its salmon preservation responsibilities, tried to reach a compromise. The council agreed with the idea of an immediate drawdown of Lower Granite's pool, with other reservoir drawdowns to be phased in over several years. Yet even this 6-2 compromise decision seemed unlikely to end the controversy. Seven of the Northwest's eight United States senators immediately criticized the plan. They argued instead that biologists conduct more studies, a scenario that could literally study the salmon to death, conveniently and finally ending the controversy. And a Republican, Phil Batt, won the governorship of Idaho in the 1994 elections. He pledged to appoint planning council representatives more friendly to navigation interests. The 6-2 majority seemed soon to become a 4-4 deadlock just as one of the region's most powerful salmon advocates, Cecil Andrus, lost his political influence.[34]

As of this writing the region has yet to reach a final decision on drawdowns. At a time of increasing concern over federal expenditures, however, it is easy to see the attraction of barging. The Corps estimated it would cost between $1.3 and $4.9 billion to retrofit its four lower Snake dams to safely pass fish in drawdown conditions—figures that dwarfed the dams' original construction costs and flabergasted many observers. They so flabergasted Cecil Andrus that he hired his own analyst who concluded that the Corps' estimates were at least twice as high as actual retrofitting would cost. Even so, all agreed changing the dams would be expensive. On the other hand, the Corps spends a comparatively piddling $2.2 million annually on its juvenile fish transportation system. The ports eagerly publicized this economic imbalance to advocate barging over drawdowns, especially since biologists had been unable to empirically demonstrate that drawdowns would help fish. But most biologists agreed on one thing: increased emphasis on barging wouldn't help the fish, either. Indeed, a team

of experts assembled by the Columbia Basin Fish and Wildlife Authority
went so far as to say barging imperilled them. As Ed Chaney noted, the
Corps has been hauling more and more fish in this unnatural way each
year, but the numbers of salmon surviving to adulthood continues to
dwindle.[35]

The drawdown was not the only fish-saving proposal outlined at the salmon summit or in public hearings before federal agencies. It was merely
one of dozens. In its complexity, however, in the number of interest
groups on all sides of the issue, the drawdown proposal exemplifies the
difficulty of resolving the fish crisis in the Northwest, the problem, as Ed
Chaney put it, of dealing with infinite "boxes within boxes."

For those people bent on deflecting public opinion away from drawdowns, increased hatchery production became the key suggestion. Hardly
a new idea. Nonetheless, as the Northwest faced the endangered species
threat in the 1990s, alliances made up of port officials continued to advocate hatchery production. But by then virtually all biologists had come to
believe that, while hatcheries played a role in preserving runs, over-reliance
on them had to end.[36]

In the mid-1970s, forty-four hatcheries in the Columbia Basin annually
produced 151 million salmon and steelhead smolts. The hatcheries contributed about 50 percent of the adult salmon and steelhead then in the
region's rivers. With the addition of the nine Lower Snake River Compensation Plan hatcheries, along with several others, by 1992 hatcheries annually
produced nearly 200 million fish, and hatchery stock had come to com-
prise 95 percent of coho runs, 70 percent of steelhead, 80 percent of summer chinook, 70 percent of spring chinook, and 50 percent of fall
chinook.[37]

In a typical hatchery, fish grow in concrete tanks, usually segregated by
size, in dense concentrations, under unnatural light and temperature—not
all that different from feedlot cattle or hothouse plants. They eat a
specially prepared meal and get used to the humans who toss it to them.
Under these conditions fish rushing fastest to the food survive and prosper.
When released into wild streams the fish that possess these characteristics
seldom survive. Rush to food without looking and a fish can suddenly
become predator fodder; dart around willy-nilly after food and fish soon
run out of energy. Biologists discovered other problems with hatcheries.
Fish raised *en masse* proved prone to diseases that could wipe out millions

at a time. And survivors could spread the malady to other fish once they began mingling in wild waters. Hatchery fish, raised in convivial conditions, also proved less able to survive the rigors of nature. In other words, while hatcheries produce millions of fish a year, relatively few survive. About 8 percent of wild fish live to spawn; only about 2 percent of hatchery fish last that long. Even more important, since hatchery fish compete with wild strains for food and space, biologists fear a drastic reduction of the salmonid gene pool.[38]

By the 1990s biologists had seen enough. Robert Francis, director of the Fisheries Research Institute at the University of Washington, wrote that hatcheries "have become a narcotic served to pacify society." Even a Corps biologist like Sarah Wik came to recognize the downside of overzealous hatchery production: "We learned the hatcheries can't solve the problem. It's a big puzzle. You have to look at all the pieces. If you look at one piece and not the other, you can't solve it."[39]

But, in the best boxes in boxes tradition, no one wanted to eliminate hatcheries either. James Lannan, a salmon geneticist at Oregon State University, derided the idea that Northwest wild stocks are "somehow wonderfully adapted" to the region's rivers after thousands of years. "Their previous evolution is irrelevant," he claimed. "The conditions they evolved in no longer exist." And even Bill Bakke, whose Oregon Trout was one of the organizations that petitioned for endangered species protection for Snake River chinook, agreed hatcheries would play a role in preserving Northwest fish runs. "Hatcheries are not undesireable," he said. "They just need to be operated better within the ecosystem as a whole." Among the practices biologists wanted to eliminate was the hatchery tendency to select only the largest fish for brood stock and to select those fish that arrived first, a practice undertaken in good faith to ensure adequate egg takes and to allow the fry to hatch earlier, begin to feed earlier, and thus enjoy a better chance to grow to larger size before release. Now fish researchers want hatcheries to take eggs and sperm from a much larger number of brood stock, stock as diverse in size and time of arrival as possible in order to insure the greatest diversity.[40]

The Northwest Power Planning Council adhered to the biologists' concerns in its 1992 comprehensive plan for salmon survival. It asked agencies to study the juvenile fish-carrying capacity of the Columbia River system to ensure that hatchery releases did not exceed those limits; to work with geneticists to sustain the diversity of salmon runs; and to improve hatchery practices to assist fish to better survive in natural waterways.[41]

The planning council listened to many other ideas about how to save the salmon. The Bonneville Power Administration at first tried to bluster its way through the endangered species threat. Shortly after the Shoshone-Bannock tribe and Oregon Trout sent in their petitions, the BPA claimed, despite all scientific evidence to the contrary, that declines in chinook salmon runs "have been reversed and are now trending upward." Aware that such reassurance probably wouldn't wash, the BPA also tried threats: declare these runs endangered, it warned, and electricity rates would skyrocket. By the fall of 1990, however, even the BPA could see that people would no longer tolerate either scare tactics or implausable reassurance. So the agency, in what it termed "a major shift in BPA policy and responsibility toward fish" came out with a $3 billion plan to save dwindling stocks of wild salmon. The BPA advocated improved upstream habitat, better-run hatcheries, and—not surprisingly—reducing commercial harvests. Although a relatively small part of the proposal, the idea that drew the most attention was BPA's plan to pay bounties for catching squawfish, voracious salmon smolt predators.[42]

The problems predators like squawfish would cause once the rivers became reservoirs really did not surprise biologists, although development agencies like the Corps and BPA ignored early warnings. Noted the U. S. Fish and Wildlife Service as early as 1963 in commenting upon the effects of slackwater created by Little Goose Dam: "Populations of nongame fish are expected to increase in the reservoir within a few years after initial filling. Competition between game and nongame fish populations for food and space will increase. Increased predation on the young of game fish by nongame fish will occur. This situation will detract from the sport fishery, and also create fishery management problems."[43]

Squawfish are native to the system, and in the days before dams they played a roll in keeping populations of other fish—even salmon—in balance. But the reservoirs created an ideal situation for the predators, who like to sit near a dam and capture young smolts emerging confused and disoriented from the turbines, spillways, or bypass systems. The BPA proposed to spend $5 million or more annually on squawfish control. It would pay professionals to fish eight-hour days at Corps dams, Indians to catch the fish using long lines of hooks, and sports anglers for each squawfish they brought in. "The squawfish bounty is part of the equation," says Kent Martin. "But it is still a smoke screen. We're putting money into this bounty program that could be spent on the *real* problems." Still, the power planning council agreed with the BPA and proposed to reduce squawfish numbers by 20 percent.[44]

Idaho Trout suggested building a small canal alongside the Snake and Columbia rivers that would allow young fish to swim past the dams. Scientists at the Idaho National Engineering Laboratory proposed floating a long plastic tube in the water the length of the river system to shoot smolts downstream. Both of these alternatives came with their share of critics. Some wondered if adult salmon would return up a river having gone downstream in a pipe or ditch. Others questioned whether a separate canal or pipe might give the equivalent of *carte blanche* permission to further pollute the mainstem river once fish became isolated. Everyone questioned how to gather the smolts into the canal or tube in the first place, and some, like Ed Chaney, dismissed the whole concept as absurd. "These animals don't just use the river as part of a conduit from point A to point B," he said. "They use it to feed, to reach a certain physiological change from river water to saltwater. . . . This isn't a transportation problem, it's an ecological problem. . . . You can't put elk in a bus and move them to a winter range and hope it works out."[45]

Some people have touted energy and water conservation as potential ways of helping the salmon. The Northwest attempted energy conservation programs in the 1970s and 1980s without abundant success. One reason for their failure is a lack of incentive on the part of power marketers to enthusiastically support the measures. After all, each kilowatt of energy saved represents lost revenue to a power supplier. Too many power companies still urge ever more consumption despite the salmon crisis. However, energy conservation does hold considerable promise.

On the surface, conserving irrigation water along the Snake River likewise seems a plausible way to provide more water for fish. Southern Idaho farmers could convert part of their land to crops requiring less water. Surprisingly, almost three times as much irrigated land on the Snake River Plain is devoted to alfalfa and pasture than potatoes, yet alfalfa and grass take many times more water. Grow spuds in Idaho and hay somewhere else, say the critics. Some go even farther. Noting the dramatic shift of agriculture to the West with irrigation—the South alone saw its cropland reduced by one-third in the twenty years after World War II—historian Donald Worster has called for a national rethinking of agricultural priorities. The East and South have the capability of growing crops such as potatoes, sugar beets, and fruit without wasting precious water. The nation would be better off to cut irrigation subsidies and thus provide an economic incentive for farmers to raise such crops where they do well with natural rainfall. Worster goes so far as to suggest a new "Homestead Act" that encourages farmers to "Go East, young man or woman." More farmers in the irrigated West could convert to sprinkler irrigation rather than the traditional and highly inefficient ditch and furrow system still used by more than half of Idaho's irrigators. Those who retain ditches could line them to prevent water loss through seepage. Farmers could convert to drip irrigation, effectively shown to work elsewhere, and could irrigate their crops using interactive computers that precisely determine the amount and time water is needed. Irrigators could save tremendous amounts of water by simply cutting a few days off the irrigation season without any damage to crops, according to agricultural researchers. These changes in a system that wastes millions of gallons of water daily appear not only doable, but also cheap compared to some other solutions suggested for assisting fish. That is, until a person starts talking to those with a vested interest in protecting Idaho irrigators.[46]

It soon becomes apparent that irrigators do not want to talk seriously about conservation. "You can conserve all you want, but you are not adding water to the system," says the Idaho Water Users Association's Sherl Chapman. "The only thing conservation can do is affect timing." Seconds Keith Higgenson of the Idaho Department of Water Resources, "Conservation is not a panacea. Making the Idaho farmer more efficient is not the solution." And then both quickly come around to an argument that is, at best, curious to the uninitiated. It goes something like this, and if its logic at first escapes the outside observer, it is the Holy Grail of arguments to Idaho irrigators: it is important that we pump more water onto irrigated lands than the crops require because this water seeps into the aquifer. To stop "wasteful" irrigation might dry up the aquifer.[47]

The Snake River aquifer is huge, among the world's most productive. It runs as much as nine hundred feet beneath the surface and roughly parallel to the river. Groundwater from the aquifer irrigates about one-third of Idaho's farms, and irrigation accounts for 95 percent of Idaho's groundwater use. As early as 1960, the Bureau of Reclamation—often thought of only as an agency that manipulates surface water through dams and canals—had sunk 170 wells to tap the aquifer, and private individuals had drilled hundreds more. Groundwater pumping continued to increase. Today, approximately 8 million acre-feet of water is pumped out of the aquifer annually, with about 7.8 million acre-feet flowing in. The argument from Idaho irrigators is that they help the aquifer by taking excess water from the Snake River, overwatering their crops, and allowing what's left to revive the underground supply. "The Snake River aquifer is largely recharged by irrigation leakage," claims Chapman. "So if you seal up everything, then you don't replenish the aquifer." It is a curious argument, and leads one to question how the aquifer got along so well for so many years before irrigators moved to Idaho. But it is repeated relentlessly by irrigation interests in the state. Says Higgenson, "Downstream irrigators use water that seeps into the aquifer from upstream irrigators. So the excess water put on crops is not wasted. If we conserve water upstream, we affect downstream users because there will be less water in the aquifer. Excess irrigation water is not 'lost.' We say we will support conservation if it can be done without hurting others." Indeed, Idahoans pump so much river water that the mighty Snake virtually disapears at Milner Dam. It reappers again only at the Thousand Springs area, courtesy of discharges from the aquifer. In other words, irrigators essentially pump the river dry. Then they justify their excessive water use by claiming their waste recharges the aquifer. Further, they state, if the aquifer were not so robust from all that irrigation overflow, it could not replenish the irrigation-drained Snake. Only Idaho irrigators and politicians fail to see the absurdity.[48]

The "others" Higginson worries about hurting, of course, are Idaho irrigators, not downstream interests along the lower Snake and Columbia rivers, and certainly not salmon. The premise of Higginson's argument against irrigation conservation is that using less water will damage the aquifer. But the argument taxes logic. In the first place, if the aquifer requires replenishing, there are more effective means of replenishing it than pumping too much water onto crop lands—where some water evaporates and therefore is "lost" to the system. Second, if Idaho irrigators wasted less groundwater, the aquifer would not need replenishing. Third, water that escapes southern Idaho is not "wasted." "From Idaho's standpoint, water is wasted when it flows under the Lewiston-Clarkston bridge" into Washington, says Higginson. This ethnocentric argument fails to recognize that the Snake and Columbia need vital downstream flows to remain biologically viable. Higginson's rationale is the same as the thirsty southern Californian who longingly looks at water rushing out the mouth of the Columbia and claims it is merely "wasted," hoping to turn the Columbia into another Colorado, a river pumped and dammed so excessively that it now dies in a sandy desert before reaching the ocean. Fourth, although they speak softly about it, even people like Chapman and Higginson admit that conservation can affect the timing of water releases from upstream reservoirs. This timing can make all the difference to juvenile fish. If a little conservation saves water that can be forced downstream in the spring, it could very well significantly benefit the entire system. Finally, the argument ignores the fact that Idaho irrigators raise excess crops that the nation does not need. At the very least, farmers elsewhere could raise these crops without irrigation. Should we extinguish a species of fish so farmers can continue to raise surplus commodities?[49]

As an alternative to irrigation conservation, people like Higginson would like to build more dams "just for the fish." Idaho irrigators could keep all their reservoirs. Meanwhile, dam builders would create some additional reservoirs in the state's few undammed areas strictly to store a water supply to help flush fish to the ocean. The Corps and Bureau of Reclamation love this idea, although they do not talk about building more dams in their public meetings and publications. Instead, in bureaucratic double-speak they state that "additional upstream storage" could benefit the fish. But in an irrigated kingdom like southern Idaho that so far has found no way to ease its thirst for ever more water, one can only suspect that water set aside for "wasting" on fish would soon be appropriated by irrigators. Beyond that, even the thought of more dams, for whatever purpose, flies in the face of the contemporary political climate. "Upstream storage" advocates must have been dozing for the past twenty years if they believe they will once again get to build dams on Idaho streams.

Many other proposals have been and will be suggested to assist fish. The Corps, the Bureau, and the BPA, for example, studied ninety alternatives under their 1992 systems operation review. And, of course, various organizations and agencies have already tried many fish-saving ideas. On the Umatilla River, a tributary of the Columbia that enters below the Snake, volunteers painstakingly attempted to create better fish habitat by super-gluing logs to rocks. While that experiment was more exotic than most, by 1990 the Corps and BPA spent about $100 million annually on preserving fish runs. Regardless, the salmon runs have continued to decline. Some people began to worry that the costs of preservation might threaten the region's economy, in which case environmentalists might lose their chief ally in the fight to save salmon: public opinion. "People want to save the salmon in the abstract," claimed Washington's Republican Senator Slade Gorton. Gorton wants to modify the Endangered Species Act to include economic as well as biological considerations prior to listing. "We need a serious discussion of the costs of saving that species," he says. Stated Tom Trulove of the Northwest Power Planning Council, "The worst thing you could do for salmon is something so radical that you ruin the economy and lose the support of the public."[50]

To a biologist like Steve Pettit of the Idaho Department of Fish and Game, salmon are worth the economic investment. "These fish are the canaries of the river," he says, alluding to the miner's safety tocsin. "If the river isn't fit for fish, it won't be fit for humans. I hope people are willing to pay to have salmon in Idaho. Most people come to the Pacific Northwest for the quality of life, and that includes having wild species, like salmon, in our rivers." People also come to the Northwest because of affordable living—traditionally dependent upon cheap hydroelectricity. And even a few biologists have begun to question whether saving wild salmon is worth sacrificing Northwesterners' standard of living. "I'm not sure the cost of preserving these fish is going to be worth it," says Eastern Washington University fish biologist Allan Scholtz. Some local politicians are following that lead. "Why not just abandon the fish?" asks Idaho legislator James Lucas. "Give it up as not worth the costs? Why is the fish vital to the South Idaho farmer?"[51]

That kind of talk leaves a lot of fish advocates, who have lost battle after battle along the lower Snake since the 1930s, feeling pessimistic. "In 1980, Congress gave the Northwest Power Planning Council a mandate and a blank check: 'Save the Salmon,'" laments Ed Chaney. "But more than a decade later, we have nothing. They spend money and the fish keep dying. It need not be that way. It is difficult not to be cynical. Having been through five or six 'Save the Salmon' campaigns, I don't think we have the will to save them. The aluminum industry, barge operators, the BPA—all create a culture too powerful to overcome."[52]

Chaney places his survival hopes on the Endangered Species Act and its authority to force the Northwest's most powerful economic institutions into a new way of doing business. But many congressional representatives from the Northwest and elsewhere are plotting ways to weaken it. The act might have had smoother sailing had the Northwest not faced both a spotted owl and Snake River salmon crisis simultaneously. In other words, the act regional environmentalists used to help preserve species has aroused so much publicity and controversy that the federal government now might weaken it. History along the lower Snake River has never played itself out in a vacuum. From the time of government explorations to the time of government dams, what happens in Washington, D. C., has always impacted the region. And now the Northwest sees that history is a two-way path: reactions to the Snake River salmon crisis influence national politics.

After spending billions of dollars to save salmon will politicians say "enough," and abandon the fish along with the Endangered Species Act? That possibility greatly concerns Ed Chaney. What bothers him more, however, is the thought that we will continue to whittle elegant species to death because we have neither the desire to sacrifice to the extent necessary to allow them to thrive nor the courage to say, "Kill them." "If we won't do what is right, then let's close the fish ladders at Ice Harbor Dam and give the fish an honorable death," he says. It is an important issue with him. "If we are going to kill them, let's not do it with phony data and press releases. Let's quit lying to the public. Let's quit pissing away public money. The honorable thing is to have a last salmon feast and kill them. The fish have done so much for the Northwest that they deserve this. But the bureaucracies responsible for the fish crisis are gutless. So they will grind the fish to death slowly."[53]

Ed Chaney is a pessimist, but he is also a realist. If we are honest, we must admit that we are slowly grinding the fish away. We've spent millions of dollars but the fish continue to die. Nothing has worked so far, and one gets the feeling that the Endangered Species Act is the salmon's Armageddon. If we fail this time, it well might be too late to save them. It is an issue with the potential to touch every person in the Northwest, not just the Kent Martins, Cory Eagens, Ed Chaneys, and Eldon Crisps. The question Northwesterners face for the first time in the region's history—both individually and collectively—is whether or not they are willing to save the salmon. We've paid lip service to sacrifice until now and the salmon has managed to survive, only because it is an incredibly strong and adaptable fish. But it has nearly reached its limits. The question now is whether the preservation of a species that we could survive without is worth real cross-societal sacrifice.

Epilogue

After waving goodbye to Ed Ferrell on the fish barge and climbing up the navigation lock on that spring evening when I rode downstream from Lower Granite Dam, I got in my car and started the drive back to Pullman from Ice Harbor Dam. It was by now past midnight. The trip down the lower Snake on the tug *Idaho* had taken twelve hours. The same full moon that had lit our path through the Snake's canyons now shown over irrigated fields of asparagus and onions and potatoes on the outskirts of Pasco. I had plenty of time to reflect on the river and its salmon on that quiet drive home along isolated country roads.

I found it virtually impossible to consider anything new about the Snake River and its salmon, anything beyond the thousands of pages of newspaper articles, magazine essays, public hearing transcripts, and governmental studies devoted to these topics since the 1930s. Of all the pages I had read and of all the opinions I had heard in the years researching this topic, one phrase came to mind. It surprised me, for a politician with whom I seldom agree uttered it. Yet I thought about how it was perhaps the only topic concerning the Snake that has not seen enough ink; has not been contemplated sufficiently. "People want to save the salmon in the abstract," Washington Senator Slade Gorton once said. But they do so without considering the disruption to lifestyles that salvation might bring.[1]

I liked to believe I had done some serious speculation about the potential human consequences of saving salmon. I had spoken to commercial fishers who might lose their livelihood and be forced off homes occupied for generations. I had discussed the issue with port employees and tugboat crews who faced seasonal layoffs if politicians opted for annual river drawdowns. I had interviewed irrigators who might lose water rights. I had spoken to wheat farmers concerned about increasing freight charges in an era when the price they receive for a bushel of crop sometimes does not equal the expense of harvesting it. I had chatted with senior citizens on fixed incomes fearful of hydroelectric price increases. I had considered all of this and still come down in favor of the salmon.

But then I admitted, on that nighttime drive through eastern Washington, that Gorton was right. Even after talking to these people and thinking about their stories, I was still only ruminating in the abstract. As I probed deeper, I began to wonder if I really was willing to save the salmon. Some people say we have sacrificed too much for the fish already, that we have invested hundreds of millions of dollars that could have been better spent. They are wrong, however, on at least one count. We have not really sacrificed at all. We paid for all those fish-salvage efforts while continuing to enjoy the cheapest electricity in the nation, while continuing to support, at little personal expense, a huge toll-free navigable waterway. We have not even begun to make the regional lifestyle changes that might actually be required to save these fish. And if we are too afraid to even discuss such sacrifices, it is safe to assume we will not undertake them. I realized that I was guilty as charged by Senator Gorton.

As much as anyone in the Pacific Northwest, I am a child of cheap electricity. My father rode the rails of freight trains from North Dakota to western Washington during the Great Depression. He sought an opportunity to make a living, something impossible on the dust-swept family farm he left behind. He arrived in time to join the work crews that helped Franklin Roosevelt fulfill his dream of constructing the great Bonneville Dam, a dam that would revitalize a depressed economy. For our family, that dam became much more than an abstract beacon of hope and pride. For when workers finished it, the Alcoa Aluminum Company chose Vancouver, Washington, as the site of the Northwest's initial aluminum plant, and my father was among the first employees through the door. He worked there for nearly forty years. That huge power-guzzling plant along the Columbia River and the dam that fed it electricity were significant icons in my formative years. We lived in an all-electric house and we owned a farm where a boy could roam to his heart's content and we ate good food and we wore new clothes and we took vacations. All of that we owed to cheap hydropower and the dams that had made so many dreams come true in the Northwest.

In those days, if someone had asked me if we should sacrifice my father's job so that more salmon could make their way to Idaho streams I would have laughed at the absurdity of it. My parents were proud of dams and electric power lines and massive industrial plants like Alcoa. They had helped, in their way, to bring such development to the Northwest, and they admired the way the place had taken shape. They knew well the limited prospects for raising a family the country had offered before the dams. But my father grew up on the near-empty plains of Dakota and my mother in the isolated wheat country of eastern Washington, and they also instilled in me an appreciation for unsettled land and unteathered animals and the abundant fish we still then enjoyed. In those days of growing up in the 1950s and 1960s, it never occurred to me—or probably to them—that we would not always enjoy both nature and development. My parents had told me stories of pitch-forking salmon along a small stream near our home, salmon so bounteous that you might, indeed, have walked on their backs. That abundance influenced my childhood, for I had seen salmon rolling thick in spawning streams; they were a part of the Northwestern mythology I grew up with. It would have seemed absurd to question whether we wanted jobs or salmon not only because we were confident in those days of the primacy of people over fish, but also because we really believed we would never have to choose. It seemed to us that we could have both—indeed, the Army Corps of Engineers told us we could have both—and that was part of the beauty of living in the Northwest in those years, part of the attractiveness that has lured so many people to the region since.

Alcoa not only bought our clothes and paid for our food and gave us a house, but when it came time for me to go to college, Alcoa also provided me with a scholarship. So, at eighteen I set off for school, and while I doubt that I seriously thought about it, had anyone asked, I could have then given a long litany of reasons why we needed dams and cheap electricity and plants like Alcoa. I literally owed my life to them. But I landed in college at the dawn of what we now think of as the modern environmental era; my first year in school I attended the teach-ins during Earth Day commemorations. And my thinking, partially formed by an Alcoa-paid education, began to gradually shift, so that I have now reached a point where my family refers to me—sometimes charitably and sometimes not—as an environmentalist. I have never been a man-the-barricades type of environmentalist, but I think the label is appropriate to me, as it is to many members of my generation. We have learned to view the world through different lenses than our parents.

So, my immediate reaction to Slade Gorton's challenge was, "You are wrong. I have contemplated the issues; I have studied them. There is nothing abstract in my views. The salmon must continue to run." As I wrestled with the subject, however, I discovered what a safe response that was. My father had long since retired from Alcoa; he no longer required its wages. I knew port employees and commercial fishers and irrigators who might be forced into serious financial sacrifices. I thought of myself as sacrificing, too. I was willing to pay higher electricity rates to save the salmon. But I had to confess that I was still dealing in the abstract. My sacrifice would be minimal; my decision, therefore, easy.

But what if that sacrifice became greater? What if we, as a society, opted for a total save-the-salmon effort that turned out to be as disruptive and expensive in the short-term as port officials and power companies would scare us into believing? What if freight rates climbed so high that, combined with slashes in agricultural price support programs, Palouse farmers went bankrupt and, with their money removed from my community, drove many businesses into bankruptcy, forcing people to leave, lowering the tax base, gutting the public schools we rely on for our childrens' educations? What if electricity rates skyrocketed so that our town's university, the one where I had learned environmental consciousness and that now employs me, had to make layoffs to meet spiraling expenses during an era of state budget cutting? What if I lost my job and could no longer support my family and had to move from this rural area in which we have chosen to live precisely because it is still possible here to savor natural abundance while enjoying the economic prosperity that the dams have brought?

Now I was no longer thinking in the abstract, and suddenly I had no quick retort to the question of how much sacrifice we should endure in order to save fish.

As in other endangered species confrontations, part of the problem is that we have placed an economic value on flaura and fauna in order to weigh the costs and benefits of saving it. When the snail darter temporarily blocked Tellico Dam or when forest products firms fought measures to save the spotted owl, economics came down clearly on one side of the debate. The darter and the owl have no economic value. We chose to build the dam at the expense of the darter; we are still leveling ancient forests at the expense of the owl. There are many writers and philosophers who tell us that this is all wrong; that until we forego our tendency to save only those species with potential value to humans—be it economic, medicinal, scientific, or other—we view the world with impaired vision. Other species have a right to exist whether or not they have utility for us.[2]

Historian Richard White laments the fact that we have reduced the rivers and their fish to benefit/cost ratios, that we have given fish a price tag, that we have come to view both salmon and kilowatts as commodities. Indeed, one of the earliest, most passionate, and most influential pleas in defense of the salmon came from Oregon naturalist William Finley in the 1930s. By couching his arguments in cost/benefit terms, Finley laid the foundation for what has since been a largely economic discussion. Regardless of White's lament, Snake and Columbia river salmon exist today precisely because they have economic value. If salmon provided no economic benefit, commercial and sports fishers would not have insisted upon functional fish ladders at Bonneville Dam, and the Columbia/Snake fish runs, except for those below Bonneville, would now be extinct. End of controversy. Today, commercial and sports fishing in the Northwest comprises a billion dollar annual industry (at least in years when fishing is allowed), and it provides about sixty thousand jobs. A good part of that business depends upon getting fish over the eight lower Columbia and lower Snake dams. Economics always has been and always will be part of the equation when dealing with salmon.[3]

Yet an economist viewing this issue would find something askew. Economic logic would indicate that decisions on the Columbia/Snake system should have been more two-dimensional, that two large economic forces like salmon and hydropower, even considering both strictly as commodities, should have reached a better balance. We have spent some money on saving the fish, to be sure, but we have spent much more in a pell-mell effort to destroy them in order to create more kilowatts. Economist Phillip Meyer has speculated that throughout the long history of Columbia/Snake development this occurred because dam builders and power planners consistently—and knowingly—understated the value of salmon and "significantly underestimated present [power] capability and overestimated future demand. [Thus] fishery valuation has been conservative, while estimation of power benefits is usually inflated. It follows that an unbiased decision-maker, considering the value results of such calculations . . . would conclude that fish must give way to power on each occasion." Which is what has happened.[4]

That is not the whole story, of course. The history of how we came to build the dams is longer and more politically complicated than that. But Meyer's analysis does go a long way toward explaining why we are where we are today. What it does not help us do is chart a direction for the future. For if salmon and hydropower economics were once relatively balanced, that balance is now totally askew. The salmon still is no snail darter; a billion-dollar-a-year industry has some economic punch. If we are to decide the fate of the salmon on economics alone, however, the fish is doomed, for the salmon industry today is a tiny drop in a huge bucket of Northwest economy fueled largely by inexpensive hydropower.

So the real decision will come down to sacrifice and our views about our responsibility to nature and to our children. These are topics we are still uncomfortable discussing; it is difficult to stand up in a Corps of Engineers public meeting and spout phrases like "we have a moral obligation to save all plants and creatures, great and small." That is not a quantifiable argument, and the Snake/Columbia river is now a series of reservoirs largely because of quantifiable decisions made by people who crunched numbers and found economic benefits at the end of their equations. If we are serious about saving the salmon we must find a way to leap this intellectual chasm; we must wean ourselves from the comforts of quantification. We must, as historian Donald Worster has said, stop viewing a river as a commodity "bulked here as capital to invest some day, spent freely when the market is high." We must adopt a water ethic like the land ethic Aldo Leopold proposed, one that views a river as the lifeblood of the land. Roderick L. Haig-Brown provided a model for this viewpoint as early as 1946. His book about Columbia River salmon, *Return to the River: A Story of the Chinook Run*, saw the fish as a symbol essential to the spirit of Northwesterners, despite any economic value salmon might have.[5]

To many Native Americans who have and continue to live near the rivers, the salmon have always had both economic and spiritual value. From California to Alaska and inland as far as the salmon swam, native residents developed beliefs about the fish that were remarkably similar for peoples so widely scattered. The salmon appeared every year, different species at different times, following a constant rhythm. Native peoples explained this by evolving the belief that the fish were really Salmon People who, most of the year, lived in houses beneath the ocean or in a land across the sea. At the appropriate time they temporarily stepped out of their human form and became fish, deliberately sacrificing themselves in order to feed those who caught them. Once caught, their spirits returned to their homes to await the next year's run. To honor the Salmon People and ensure their annual return, natives of the West developed elaborate rituals. Culture dictated the precise words to be spoken when a fisher caught a fish. Some bands prescribed the method by which to transport salmon to a village. Many groups developed detailed rituals for preparing, cooking, and eating the fish. Most natives returned salmon bones to the river so the Salmon People would not arrive home missing an arm or leg. Native people ate the first fish caught—assumed to be the Salmon Chief who led the Salmon People up the river—at an elaborate first-salmon ceremony and believed that the success or failure of the salmon harvest rested on the respect given this first salmon. Many Native Americans continue to hold the salmon as sacred. Notes Allen Slickpoo, historian for the Nez Perce, declining salmon runs are destroying native culture. "The sense of the loss is like going to church and all of a sudden somebody has removed all the Bibles," he says.[6]

Although I respect Native American beliefs, I cannot fully appreciate them. Yet I commiserate with Slickpoo when he says "The salmon is being destroyed for the convenience of special interest groups. Just because they have special interests I don't feel I should be denied my birthright." Still, I look at Native American beliefs primarily in the abstract: their faith is not mine; we grew up in different cultures. Abstractly I want the salmon runs to continue, partially because of their spiritual value to Native Americans. But to me Indians are something like commercial fishers and Idaho irrigators: their sacrifice would not be mine. I am sympathetic, but if I am to convince myself of the moral necessity of saving the salmon I must find reasons to do so in my own beliefs.[7]

Much of our American value system stems from Christian philosophy and theology. That theology, as it regards people and nature, has seemed clear cut to some who have studied the Bible. For *Genesis* states very early on:

> So God created man in his own image. . . .
> And God said unto Them, Be fruitful and multiply, and replenish

the earth, and subdue it: and have dominion over the fish of the sea,
and over the fowl of the air, and over every living thing that moveth
upon the earth (*Genesis* 1: 27-28).

But there has been over-emphasis on the "dominion" and "subduing" pas-
sages in *Genesis* to the near exclusion of other biblical teachings about
nature. Perhaps the Latter-day Saints, who settled both in Utah and
abundantly along the Snake River in southern Idaho, carried this view to
its zenith among Westerners. Noted Mormon hierarch John Widtsoe
during the height of irrigation campaigns in the West: "The destiny of man
is to possess the whole earth; the destiny of the earth is to be subject to
man. There can be no full conquest of the earth, and no real satisfaction to
humanity, if large portions of the earth remain beyond the highest
control."[8]

Such a view obliterates the "Christian" characteristics other
species exhibit and leads us to question if there is room in Christian ideolgy
to accept and appreciate the religious significance of a salmon's lifecycle.
When adult salmon swim upstream they make the ultimate sacrifice. They
spawn and die so that their children might live, and their bodies float
downstream to nourish the river and provide food to other animals—from
eagles to grizzlies—who come to the streamside to feast on their bodies.
The salmon, therefore, seems to be a sacrificial fish in the most Christian
of terms.

Perhaps it is too much to expect dominion theorists to see Christian
values in a fish. But at least they should read the entire Bible when
developing their views of nature and human relationships to it. Some
people have tended to ignore significant parts of the Bible. They tend to
forget that it is also *Genesis* that describes the greatest effort to preserve
wildlife species ever undertaken:

> Of clean beasts, and of beasts that are not clean, and of fowls, and of
> every thing that creepeth upon the earth,
>   There went in two and two unto Noah into the ark, the male and
> the female, as God had commanded Noah (*Genesis* 7: 8-9).

And what of "For that which befalleth the sons of men befalleth beasts;
. . . yea, they have all one breath; so that a man hath no preeminence
above a beast: for all is vanity" (*Ecclesiastes* 3: 19).
Or:

> But ask now the beasts, and they shall teach thee; and the fowls of
> the air, and they shall tell thee:
>   Or speak to the earth, and it shall teach thee: and the fishes of the
> sea shall declare unto thee (*Job* 12: 7-8).

And what of that phrase so often used by those who claim humans stand
at the pinnacle of a pyramidal view of earth? What exactly does it mean to
have "dominion" over other species? Dominion is "the power or right of
governing and controlling; sovereign authority; lordship, sovereignty; rule,
sway; control, influence. The lands or domains of a feudal lord." There is
no doubt we can interpret dominion as domination, as people's intrinsic
superiority to all other life forms, just as feudal lords held a superior
position to those under their dominion.

But feudal lords—at least those desiring to retain power—interpreted
dominion in such a way as to preserve the livelihoods of those over whom
they ruled. Survival dictated that they hold dominion over *live* species,
otherwise their domain would soon be conquered. Will we have a domain
if we continue eradicating the species over which we have been entrusted
with dominion? *Genesis* told us to subdue, and any logical person can see
that we have accomplished that. There is no place left to subdue. Now
that we have tranquilized nature, how are we to perform our role as the
earthly species holding dominion?

Are we to interpret dominion as manipulation and exploitation?
Historian H. W. Nibley has said, "Man's dominion is a call to service, not
a license to exterminate." If "God were to despise all things beneath him,
as we do," Nibley asks, "where would that leave us?" We must, as Richard
White proposes, move beyond comparing salmon to kilowatts if we are to
save the fish; we must learn to value such lives for their own sake, not for
what they can provide us. Difficult as it is to envision government
bureaucrats making decisions based upon moral reasoning, quite simply
that is the salmon's—and thousands of other species'—only hope. For we
will never be able to demonstrate that the salmon has more economic
value than the water in which it swims.[9]

We have made this leap beyond economics in regards to the eagle,
probably for whales, and possibly for grizzly bears. But what of fish? Roger
Caras in his book about salmon stated up front, "A fish is not the easiest
animal to relate to." As he notes, we enjoy communion with other
vertebrates. Many mammals enjoy our touch; birds appreciate it when we
feed them. But a fish lives in a mysterious and independent world; it is

happiest having no contact with us. We can admire the tremendous strength, endurance, and survival instinct of the Pacific salmon, as Northwesterners have always done. To save this species, however, we must feel more than admiration. Somehow we have to find a way to move beyond the medieval chain of being that places humans first, all other mammals next, birds below, and so on down to "everything that creepeth upon the earth." That is a social value system destined to extinguish many more thousands of species, including Snake River salmon.[10]

Much hangs on our decision about the fish, most obviously the destiny of the salmon, so long nurturer of and symbol for a Northwest way of life. Then there is the fate of the Endangered Species Act itself. Politicians short on biology and long on demagoguery will continue their efforts to gut that law, using scare tactics fueled by economic and societal cost estimates provided by agencies like the Bonneville Power Administration and the Corps of Engineers, bureaucracies with storied histories of disseminating inaccurate projections. Even beyond the future of the Endangered Species Act in this country, decisions we make along the Snake River have potential worldwide consequences. Americans have long taken a sanctimonious attitude toward preserving nature. It has been easier for us to set aside islands of wilderness than it has for many nations; we have enjoyed an abundance of land, a sparsity of population, and a wealth of money that most world citizens cannot fathom. We have also been duplicitous. While exporting dollars to preserve the Amazon rain forest we blithely go about leveling our own ancient woods. The rest of the world has now caught onto our secret and they are watching. The American example, on the Snake and elsewhere, could be pivotal in worldwide decisions concerning endangered species. We still have reasonable, oftentimes even "cost effective" options here. If we are to convince other nations to defend nature we must first demonstrate a willingness to sacrifice—be it hot tubs or jobs—for our endangered species. As Thomas Lovejoy of the World Wildlife Fund once said, "Our American collection of endangered flora and fauna really represents but part of the forward contingent of a great rush to extinction."[11]

It is hard to figure how to convince society of the need to save salmon; how to instill a sacred feeling that is real and not abstract. But there is some room for optimism. Wallace Stegner noted that Americans have proven themselves "the most efficient and ruthless environment-busters in history." Yet while we were "slashing and burning and cutting our way through a wilderness continent, the wilderness was working on us."

Humans are still a wild species. No dominant beings have domesticated us, and while, as Stegner said, we have come close to domesticating ourselves, there is still a part of each of us, ingrained through millions of years of evolution, that senses an almost mystical attachment to nature. And at no time is this unlearned association stronger than when we stand near water. "Who hears the rippling of rivers will not utterly despair of anything," wrote Henry Thoreau. We emerged from water. Indeed, we are, for the most part, water packaged inside a carton of skin. "As for men," wrote naturalist Loren Eiseley, "those myriad little detached ponds with their own swarming corpuscular life, what were they but a way that water has of going about beyond the reach of rivers?" If we do have a chance of preserving nature, we should be most sanguine about saving our waterways, for our connection to them runs the deepest. And if we preserve our waters, we will also protect their fish.[12]

The key to conserving nature is to make ourselves think of the long term. "It pays to know there is just as much future as there is past," Eiseley once wrote. But there are places, and the lower Snake River is one, where we must douse some short-term fires before we can properly plan for a long-term future. First, we must get beyond the belief that once people have altered a landscape it is no longer worthy of our environmental attention. We need to retain our few remaining wild spots. But we also must learn to live and work with altered spaces. "The conservation movement has . . . concentrated too much on scenic places," Wendell Berry has written. "To preserve only the scenic places is to invite their destruction, either in the process of the destruction of their surroundings, or by the overcrowding of people who have no other places to go." Seconded Stegner: "I am not moved by the argument that those wilderness areas which have already been exposed to grazing or mining are already deflowered, and so might as well be 'harvested.' . . . They are only wounds; they aren't absolutely mortal. Better a wounded wilderness than none at all."[13]

I would say better a wounded Snake River than no river at all. The lower Snake dams have killed fish, destroyed wildlife, and ravaged nature. We domesticated this river in order to ship wheat more cheaply and provide inexpensive hydropower the region did not then need and might not ever need if we practice real energy conservation. We should legitimately question whether we made the right decision when we dammed the Snake. But wistful wishing about a free-flowing river will not bring it back. In the short-run—that is, in our lifetimes—the lower Snake will undoubtedly remain a chain of reservoirs. We need to live with that fact and make the most of it—for the fish, for the wildlife, and ultimately, for ourselves.

Although we might rather be gazing onto a stream roaring over rapids, we do ourselves no injustice if we can manage to look upon the dammed Snake River and still see some beauty. For if we can find that grace, we will be more inclined to preserve the nature that still exists there.

The lower Snake remains the essential strand in a complex natural web that includes all its tributaries. Under its placid waters swim fish as wild as any. Exterminate this stem, prevent these fish from migrating up and down, and you kill all of the streams in one of the nation's largest river basins, symbolically if not literally. For—well beyond the dammed lower Snake River—there remain the unconfined mountain streams that feed it, places where water foams white in pools and flows through evergreens, below jagged peaks, as it has for thousands of years. There remain spots where moss clings to granite rocks and trails downstream, waving in the current, and where waterbugs skip undisturbed across glassy surfaces. There are places in the mountains where, if you cup your ears, the rattling river takes on a sound distinctly similar to ocean waves and beach wind, a beckoning to the distant sea that, perhaps in some small human way, approximates the unequalled urge that lures three-inch fish to leave this comforting home and journey through hundreds of miles of water to an alien ocean.

And there are still watery pools in these streams where fish take rest in calm water before continuing their struggle upstream; shallows where you can see their silvery sides reflecting sunlight as they slash along. There are places where tiny pebbles, crumbled from boulderous mountainsides, have come to rest in a soft, gravelly sediment that entices a salmon to tail-scoop a nest for her eggs. Part of the mystique of these unspoiled places, hundreds of miles from the sea, is that this special fish, the Pacific salmon, still returns to lay eggs in gravel beds and begin one of nature's most magical stories, a tale of unequalled endurance, strength, and stamina, an inspiring mystery of refinding their exact gravel home after years of journeying thousands of miles in river and ocean, a feat unrivaled by any other animal, including humans.

If we lapse into saying "We have already desecrated this place, let's protect something more sacred," then we have condemned those fish to die. And if the salmon die—the canaries of the Snake—so too will the countless creeks and small ecosystems upstream, because if we kill off the king of the Snake there will no longer be an indicator species of significant economic or symbolic value to prevent us from completely destroying this complex river system.

We must preserve what is left of the lower Snake and its fish because of the long-term consequences of our actions. Most assuredly, this river will not look in the distant future as it does today. How long, after all, will these dams last? The river is already at work washing them away, as rivers do with all obstacles placed in their paths. The Corps, when figuring project economics, plans their dams for fifty or one hundred years, although they believe they should survive longer. But the truth is, no one really knows how long the massive Western dams constructed between the 1930s and 1970s will last. How long will they withstand harsh climates and unrelenting pressures from the reservoirs they back? Metal must some day rust. Concrete must turn soft and crumble. Yet none of the Western dam-building agencies estimated the costs of decommissioning, dismantling, or replacing these structures when presenting their glowingly positive cost/benefit ratios to Congress. Congress did not then and does not now require that information. But it is an issue with which future generations will surely have to grapple.

The Corps of Engineers dislikes such talk. "Man, in fact, does control, or at least constrain, parts of natural processes. The questions . . . are for how long, at what cost, and at what risk," wrote Paul Walker, chief of the Corps' Office of History when he read my comments above. "Nobody is able to predict long-off 'what-ifs,'" seconded Harry Drake, former chief of the Walla Walla District's engineering division. "The life of most structures depends on maintenance, lack of earthquakes and destructive wards. Note the existing Roman aqueducts, various cathedrals and mosques. . . . We do not consider the cost of decommissioning. Neither do we consider such costs for our national capital, our highways, our churches, or even our homes."[14]

But huge floods along the Missouri and Mississippi rivers in the summer of 1993—rivers even more clogged with Corps-built dams than the Snake—should once again remind us that, continued Corps assurances to the contrary, man cannot always control, or even constrain, nature. And while money to maintain dams obviously prolongs their lives, and while the lower Snake dams have been well-kept so far, the issue of a never-ending flow of federal funds to maintain structures in the sparsely populated Inland Northwest is one we should consider. Technology may well provide us with a more reliable, less expensive means of generating electricity than dams. When that happens, who will support the costly maintenance of aging edifices along the Snake River? Already, the Corps has had to renege on some promises it made about permanently maintaining boat ramps and recreational sites along the lower Snake. "Perpetual" federal recreational funds anticipated at the time of construction have withered. Obviously, there is a qualitative difference between cutting money for recreation and eliminating funds for dam maintenance. But we need to think long term, and as structures age and maintenance costs increase, will the government continue to pour money into the dams?

What will happen, for example, if silt clogs the reservoirs, rendering dams useless?

When Congress prohibited dam construction at Asotin, it created an unanticipated problem for the Army Engineers. The Snake washes tons of sand and mud downstream each year. The Corps thought Asotin would trap much of this. With no dam at Asotin, the sediments now collect behind Lower Granite. Approximately two million cubic yards of material end up in the Lower Granite reservoir each year, lessening the Lewiston levees' flood control capability and creating navigation hazards. Dredging is the most feasible means of ridding the river of detritous, but dredging is very controversial. Let the channels clog by slacking off on dredging, and the Corps angers tug operators and threatens homes and businesses in Lewiston. Clear the channels, and it potentially endangers fish and wildlife.[15]

If the Corps dumps the dredged spoils on land, it can destroy wildlife habitat. So in the early days the agency created artificial Snake River islands with its dredged materials. That assisted geese, but researchers came to believe it damaged fish. The Corps had only one other alternative: deep-water deposition.

Placing dredged materials in deep river water provided some initial benefits for salmon and steelhead. Upstream migrating adults used the shallower spots to rest and feed, and downstream migrating smolts also lingered there. But deep-water dumping poses potential problems. Will these smolt-friendly shallows also attract predators such as bass and squawfish? Will altering the river bottom disrupt invertebrate life? Will increased turbidity brought by dredging harm anadromous fish? Early studies indicated that some deep-water zones attracted greater concentrations of sturgeon than originally believed, and researchers worried about the effects to sturgeon of dumping dredge waste in these deep-water holes. In addition, wildlife agencies and Indian tribes insisted that the Corps dredge only in winter when the river is little used by anadromous fish. But winter dredging is frequently delayed because of ice and inclement weather. Further, dredging in January and February, while best for fish, is the worst time for navigation. Nearly as soon as the channel is opened, it can fill again with wastes brought downstream during spring run-off.[16]

Even if the tests determine that environmental benefits of deep-water disposal outweigh disadvantages, someday all such sites will be filled. Then there will be no alternatives but very costly removal of dredged spoils to land or allowing the reservoirs to silt up.

We must in the future weigh real long-term costs against real long-term benefits before deciding to "develop" a river. It is foolhardy to even contemplate a project with a fifty or one hundred year lifespan without also figuring into those equations what happens when that time is up. Project benefit/cost ratios are now skewed toward construction. Any huge, multipurpose dam should show a profit in a fifty-year time span. It does not take an economic genious to figure how to make those estimates come out in the black, for—after fifty years—the dam is still, relatively speaking, spanking new and working well. But what if we project benefits and costs over a longer period, when dams begin aging and maintenance—or removal—costs rise? Would we come up with the same rosy benefit/cost scenarios that in the past enabled developers to dam virtually every river in America for the "economic good" of the country? Agencies like the Corps are hiding the true costs to society when they do not account for what to do with their dams once they age.

Thinking long term should give us a whole new sense of our obligations to nature. The fact of the matter is that while people have *altered* nature along the lower Snake, it is impossible, despite sophisticated technology and engineering capability, to *control* it. Even the Corps—though they are the last to admit it—cannot forever engineer nature into something it doesn't want to be. Of what consequence are four man-made concrete dams to a river that has known the Missoula floods? The Snake has always adjusted to impediments thrown in its way. It will again. While we cannot control nature, we can dictate a great deal of its future. When the Snake River adjusts to the Corps' impediments, will the wild fish of the river still remain? That is a choice we will largely determine in the near future, although our decision will affect all those generations that come after us.

That means that, while always thinking long term, we must make wiser short-term decisions than we often have in the past.

In the short run, we need realistic incentives to encourage energy conservation in the Pacific Northwest. With the nation's lowest electricity prices, it is no wonder that Northwesterners use—and waste—more electricity than any other Americans. We have sacrificed fish and wildlife to inexpensive convenience, and it is time that energy conservation—implemented through a realistic rate structure and serious public education—become something more than a lip-service ideal.

We need irrigation conservation. We must recognize arguments about depleting a river's flow to stabilize an aquifer for the phony excuse to avoid conservation that they are. The Snake River aquifer continues to shrink despite some of the most intensive river irrigation in America. Surely, if we were going to replenish the aquifer with river pumping we would have done so by now. Irrigators must receive educational—and financial—assistance in converting to irrigation methods that conserve water. Some irrigated land must be eliminated in favor of moving agriculture once again to a moister part of the country. And we must place societal values ahead of the values of individual agriculturalists. Nostalgic romance about yeoman farmers have led to immeasurable societal harm in the arid West. Thomas Jefferson's ideal does not work so well in a dry country. There is no logical reason why deserts need always bloom. A good case can be made that cactus and sagebrush sometimes have a greater societal value than do surplus crops that cost taxpayers millions of dollars in subsidy programs while they waste water and destroy fish and wildlife.

We need to halt short-sighted subsidies that cause irreparable harm to the environment. For example, the Bonneville Power Administration should eliminate its practice of offering low-rate electricity to utilities that sell this cheap power to irrigators. In addition to being the West's largest water user, irrigators are the second largest user of electric power in the Northwest, behind only aluminum companies. This practice of providing cheap power to irrigators only encourages wasteful pumping and provides no incentive to conserve. And the BPA should gradually raise electricity rates to fair-market values for aluminum companies, still by far the biggest power users in the region. One economist has projected that it costs the average household in the Northwest $3.75 a month to subsidize aluminum company electricity rates. Raising rates will no doubt force some aluminum companies to relocate elsewhere, and that could temporarily hurt the region economically. But just as we need to focus on the long term, we need also think more in terms of societal good rather than regionalism. It is time to stop sacrificing fish to subsidize an industry that does not pay its own way. We are no longer in the 1940s when BPA clammored for any industry willing to move in and consume excess energy. It is unfair to continue playing favorites by subsidizing aluminum company profits. America can exist with a few less aluminum companies in the Northwest, with a few less irrigated farms. It can exist if Pacific Northwesterners begin paying a fair price for electricity. Indeed, not only can American society exist in such an atmosphere, it will improve—at least if we truly believe that saving some natural things has value.[17]

We need to stop sacrificing fish in the name of redundant science. No biologist is satisfied with our current knowledge of the complex lives of salmon and steelhead. But organizations such as the Pioneer Ports River Alliance, a lobbying group made up of various Snake River ports and other development organizations, use science as a club. "There is no scientific proof that drawdowns will help fish," they say, insisting that we undertake years more study before attempting any action. That would truly result in studying the fish to death—perhaps literally. Notes biologist Steve Pettit, "The number of fish required for ongoing and proposed mainstem research and monitoring will exceed the total number of fish produced. They'll have to take every damn smolt out of the river and mark them just to study them." We do need to continue studies, for each year we learn more about anadromous fish. But in the meantime we need to be bold, to initiate some activity, if we are to preserve the fish in order to retain some to study. The ports do a societal disservice when they spend thousands of dollars promoting the concept that we do not yet know enough about salmon to take any action. We know that we must increase river velocity when smolts travel downstream. And we know the most cost-effective, least disruptive way of doing that is to drawdown the lower Snake reservoirs. Yet permanent drawdowns hold little hope of saving the salmon unless we speed up the drawdown testing process. According to current plans it will be at least 1996 before the Corps even begins drawdown experimentation on an annual basis, and years of testing will follow that. "The Corps is proposing about 10 years of testing. By that time all the endangered salmon will be dead," criticizes James Baker of the Sierra Club. The Corps will admit to only three years of necessary testing (taking us to approximately 1999), but concedes that completing dam modifications to allow permanent annual drawdowns once the tests are concluded will be "many years in the future." Such delays are not propelled by science, but rather by politics. Port officials, pumping thousands of dollars into negative publicity, have made it politically difficult for federal bureaucrats to move more quickly. But those who oppose the drawdowns are in the minority and if the drawdown means that we have to pay a subsidy to some ports unable to do business a couple of months a year, then that is what we should do, for society will benefit in the long run.[18]

We need to stop looking for scapegoats. Commercial fishers, for example, have shouldered too much criticism for the salmon crisis. We need to recognize that we all—power users, recreational boaters, ports, irrigators, sports and commercial fishers—share in the death and destruction we have caused.

We need to tell the Corps of Engineers that they exist to serve the public good, not merely to perpetuate their own existence. We—and Congress—need to insist that innovative suggestions be discussed seriously by the Corps, not summarily dismissed as unworkable. Throughout the early 1990s, as people proposed a drawdown, the Corps traveled into the region armed with pessimistic slide shows depicting dire consequences should drawdowns come. The glass was always half empty, never half full. Obviously, drawdowns will only work with modifications to dams. But the Corps for years painted disastrous scenarios of the consequences of drawdowns on existing projects, as if anyone had proposed lowering the river without making necessary alterations. When they did finally agree to examine retrofitting, they pegged an astronomical price to it. We need more optimism and far less pessimism from this agency built upon a foundation of "can do" engineering. Northwest Corps pioneers used to grab onto dreams and turn them into reality. The Corps did not drag its feet when asked to tame one of the world's mightiest river systems. Surely, providing the short-term engineering required to improve fish passage at dams so that a river might be drawn down is an easier task than was damming the Columbia and Snake in the first place. This generation of Corps leadership seems hobbled by bureaucratic lethargy, and it is killing fish and wildlife.[19]

We need to eliminate doublespeak from the Corps and other agencies. We should not refer to slackwater reservoirs as "lakes." We should not call plugging a stream with dams and lining its edges with riprap "river improvement." We should not say we are "enhancing the fishery" when we erect a hatchery to pump out millions of feedlot fish to serve as dam fodder while they compete with wild fish for food. We must stop talking about the benefits of "upstream storage" and begin telling people that this fancy term is really just a metaphor for building more dams. We should stop calling a stream dammed to the limit an "open river." Language counts. When we rely on euphemisms to smooth the very rough edges of destroying a river, we tend to accept such destruction too easily.

We need to demand leadership, not sound bites, from our elected officials. When someone like Idaho congresswoman Helen Chenoweth panders to certain constituents by questioning why she should take the endangered salmon issue seriously because "you can buy a can [of salmon] in Albertson's," we should question how we can take someone like her seriously. It is true that, in 1994, there was a short-term glut of Alaskan salmon on the market. But Chenoweth's disingenuous statement begs two important questions. First, although there are still salmon in Alaska, should we destroy Northwest runs merely because we can find canned Alaskan salmon in grocery stores? Second, does Chenoweth understand anything about the history of natural resource extraction in America? Her comments sound precisely like early twentieth century timber barons and politicians who knowingly smokescreened people into believing the Northwest had limitless old-growth forests. Now, of course, those forests are nearly depleted. So will we deplete Alaskan salmon runs if all the nation's salmon harvest focuses in that one region, the last tiny remnant of a vast West Coast salmon fishery that once seemed as inexhaustible as Northwest timber.[20]

We need to eliminate some of the "boxes within boxes" in the Northwest fishery. There is such a maze of bureaucracy that no one is in charge. The Corps of Engineers, Bureau of Reclamation, Bonneville Power Administration, National Marine Fisheries Service, Northwest Power Planning Council, Pacific Fishery Management Council, numerous Indian tribes, and state departments of fish and game are just some of the players, with overlapping and often conflicting authorities. In essence the maze has created a leadership void. Not only is nearly everyone afraid to act, no one can legally act without redundant consultation. This failed effort at attempting to control the rivers by "consensus" is perhaps the greatest threat to fish. Governors from Oregon, Washington, California, and Idaho have called for the appointment of a salmon czar, and this might be the only hope the fish have.

We might even need to consider dismantling a Lower Snake dam—an unthinkable possibility until recently. But on the Elwha River in Washington's Olympic Penninsula, the Department of Interior in 1993 recommended removing two dams in order to restore fish runs. Environmentalists in southern Oregon are hopeful of someday tearing down the half-built, unnecessary, and uneconomical Corps of Engineers Elk Creek Dam on a tributary of the Rogue River, a boondoggle leftover from the grand pork-barrel days that even the Corps has since admitted has no justification. The Oregon Natural Resources Council has called for the removal of fifteen dams in the Northwest. Even Secretary of the Interior Bruce Babbit has uttered what, only a few years ago, would have been unthinkable for a person in his position: "I would love to be the first secretary of the interior in history to tear down a really large dam." It is time to seriously consider the societal value of removing Lower Granite Dam. If the fish had one less dam to cross, would survival rates substantially improve? Would dam removal assist in developing the flows necessary to help smolts over the remaining three dams? Is there any real reason, other than convenience and community pride, that ports could not relocate farther downstream? Lewiston would no longer be a "seaport," but would society as a larger whole benefit?[21]

None of this should suggest that solutions—even short-term ones—will be easy. We must take care of the fish, but we must do so without gutting the economic prosperity that dams have brought. People are willing to sacrifice to protect the Northwest's foremost wildlife symbol. We all should pay higher power rates and there must be some economic shifting—probably a few less aluminum plants in the region, acres taken out of irrigated production, and ports closed part of the year. These are difficult but doable choices. But if we tinker so much that we bring vast disruption to a region built upon these dams' benefits, we will destroy the most important ally the fish have—public good will. Still, if we are to save the salmon, we must be creative. We must take some action and not watch fish continue to die while we lapse into a stupor of bureaucratic handwringing. We have the scientific knowledge to begin taking some action now. As a society, we know what must be done in the short term to save the fish. The only question is whether or not we have the courage to take the necessary steps.

As much as anything, the Snake has become a river of compromise. This river of compromise, reshaped by the Army Corps of Engineers, brought benefits: irrigation, increased recreation, flood control, navigation, and, most of all, hydroelectricity. It brought change: archaeological sites, towns, and farms buried; rapids submerged. And the benefits and change came at a cost: hundreds of millions of dollars spent; wildlife habitat inundated; wild fish extinguished and threatened.

Each action of the Corps along the lower Snake seemingly required a reaction to maintain the delicate balance of compromise. Archaeologists, farmers, developers, conservationists, river pilots, railroads, power companies—each, in their turn, accused the Corps of moving either too fast or too slow. The diversity of that criticism in itself indicates the complexity of the issues raised and the concessions made.

Each step the Corps took along the river came with debate, criticism, conciliation; also plaudits, praise, awards. The river looked considerably different in the 1990s than the Corps originally envisioned in the 1940s. The Engineers built one less dam than they had planned, developed wildlife habitat units, and provided expensive fish-passage facilities. The final product probably did not completely satisfy anyone. But that is the nature of compromise.

Yet, after years of meticulously planned development, after the Corps had built all the dams it was going to build along the lower Snake, the potential remained that the compromises of the past would pale before those necessary in the future.

In 1990 California had 26 percent more people than in 1980. Its population dwarfed all the Pacific Northwest states combined, as did its energy requirements. Its requests for Columbia/Snake power will continue to rise, and with each demand that dams generate more electricity will come the need to merge power requirements with those of fish and wildlife.

California's increasing population, combined with a long drought, also activated old schemes to divert Columbia River water to the south. For perhaps the first time in the modern environmental era, after people had learned the ecological necessity of fresh water dumping into salt at places like the Columbia's mouth, California politicians, facing meetings filled with irate constituents, spoke again of all that water pouring out to sea as "wasted." Few people living in the state where the Colorado River dies before reaching the ocean, a river exhausted on irrigation and hydropower, would have dared call fresh water entering the ocean "wasted" just a few years ago. But the complexities of drought, combined with a mushrooming population, made some people desperate. Columbia/Snake water diversion, a concept most Northwesterners thought dead in the 1980s, had reappeared. The prospect of channeling water to help meet California's thirsty desires still seemed distant in the early 1990s, but people took it seriously enough that the governors of Washington, Oregon, and Idaho spoke out boldly against the idea, attempting to squelch the concept before it gelled.

Even if the Northwest proves able to hold off Californians and their increasing energy and water appetites, it faces a myriad of compromises of its own. In places like the lower Snake River it is time to begin planning for the distant future. For this is a river that has already been a lifeline to humans for eleven thousand years. Provided people still live here eleven thousand years from now, it will of necessity continue as a lifeline. And the decisions we make, the compromises we choose—about salmon and wildlife and energy and transportation and the balance between them—will affect not only our children, but theirs, and theirs, distant generations we seldom contemplate, but people who, nonetheless, will thank us if we choose wisely. We need to personalize those future generations, to think of them as *our* children, just as we need to think of the Marmes Rockshelter inhabitants as *our* parents. It is difficult to perceive our responsibility to nature only in abstract terms. But if we look to human life as a continuum, as a chain of hands that links the generations of the distant past with those of the distant future, then we can personalize our responsibility for nature, for ourselves, and for our children. Only then will we be able to say no to short-term greed in favor of long-term society good. Only then can we make the short-term decisions that will enable nature and humans to co-exist along the lower Snake far into the future.[22]

The Timbavati Nature Reserve in South Africa has adopted the following motto: "The wildlife of today is not ours to dispose of as we please. We have it in trust. We must account for it to those who come after." So it is with the salmon of the Snake and the river they swim in: we manage it in trust for future generations. We might not today appreciate all that Herbert West and an earlier generation of politicians, developers, and Engineers wrought, but we should recognize their skill, tenaciousness, and audacity. And while they did alter the river beyond what many of us might today prefer, they did not destroy it as a living organism. They left us enough of nature to appreciate and enough of engineering technology to dazzle. It is now our responsibility to muster their strength, their innovative spirit, their can-do attitude, to ensure that we pass on a worthy legacy. For our decisions will, in the final analysis, determine whether this stream of compromise will ultimately be branded a river of life or a channel of death. And those decisions can no longer be made in the abstract. Each of us will need to struggle with the issues of fish and power and checkbooks and jobs. The easy choices on the lower Snake have all been made.[23]

Endnotes

Endnote Abbreviations

Andrus Papers: Papers of Idaho Governor Cecil Andrus, Idaho State Historical Society, Boise

Brock Evans Papers: Papers of the Sierra Club's Brock Evans, University of Washington Library, Seattle

BSU: Boise State University Library

CBIAC: Papers of the Columbia Basin Interagency Committee, University of Washington Library, Seattle

Church Papers: Papers of Idaho Senator Frank Church, Boise State University Library

EDF: Engineering Division Files

EWSHS: Eastern Washington State Historical Society, Spokane

EWU: Eastern Washington University Library, Manuscripts and Archives Section, Cheney

IDFG: Idaho Department of Fish and Game Library, Boise

IEWA: Papers of the Inland Empire Waterways Association, Whitman College Library, Walla Walla

ISHS: Idaho State Historical Society, Boise

Jackson Papers: Papers of Washington Senator Henry M. Jackson, University of Washington Library, Seattle

Jordan Papers: Papers of Idaho Senator Len Jordan, Boise State University Library

LCHS: Latah County Historical Society, Moscow, Idaho

Magnuson Papers: Papers of Washington Senator Warren G. Magnuson, University of Washington Library, Seattle.

May Papers: Papers of Washington Congresswoman Catherine May, Washington State University Library, Pullman

Morse Papers: Papers of Oregon Senator Wayne Morse, University of Oregon Library, Eugene

Nat. Arch.: National Archives, Washington, D.C.

NPD: North Pacific Division, U.S. Army Corps of Engineers

NPPA: Papers of the Northwest Public Power Association, University of Washington Library, Seattle

PAO: Public Affairs Office

RG: Record Group

RHA: Records Holding Area

Seattle FRC: Federal Records Center, Seattle

Seattle NA: National Archives—Pacific Northwest Region, Seattle

Smylie Papers: Papers of Idaho Governor Robert Smylie, Idaho State Historical Society, Boise

UISC: University of Idaho Special Collections, Moscow

UO: University of Oregon Library, Eugene

UW: University of Washington Library, Seattle

Wash. Arch.: Washington State Archives and Records Center, Olympia

White Papers: Papers of Idaho Congressman Compton White, Jr., University of Idaho Library, Moscow

WSU MASC: Manuscripts, Archives, and Special Collections section of the Washington State University Library, Pullman

WWD: Walla Walla District, U.S. Army Corps of Engineers

Notes for Prologue

1 Donald Worster, *Rivers of Empire: Water, Aridity, and the Growth of the American West* (New York: Pantheon Books, 1985), p. 19.

2 Steve Pettit, interview with the author, Lewiston, Idaho, 26 Sept. 1990.

3 See especially Worster, *Rivers of Empire*; Marc Reisner, *Cadillac Desert: The American West and Its Disappearing Water* (New York: Penguin Books, 1986); and Richard Lowitt, *The New Deal and the West* (Bloomington: Indiana University Press, 1984).

4 The statistics come from Worster, *Rivers of Empire*, pp. 266, 269.

5 Quotations are from oral history interviews in a videotape written by Irene Martin, "Work is Our Joy: The Story of the Columbia River Gillnetter" (Corvallis: Oregon State University, 1989).

6 Among her writings see, for perhaps the best examples of this view, Limerick's *The Legacy of Conquest: The Unbroken Past of the American West* (New

York: W. W. Norton & Co., 1987); and "The Significance of Hanford in American History," in David H. Stratton, ed., *Washington Comes of Age: The State in the National Experience* (Pullman: Washington State University Press, 1992).

7 Worster, *Rivers of Empire*, p. 11. For more on Worster's view of the hydraulic society, and his debt to German historian Karl Wittfogel, see Worster's book of essays, *The Wealth of Nature: Environmental History and the Ecological Imagination* (New York: Oxford University Press, 1993), particularly pp. 30-44.

8 Limerick, *Legacy of Conquest*, p. 39.

Notes for Chapter One: Fire and Water

1 For the most accessible sources on the Missoula Floods see J Harlen Bretz, *Washington's Channeled Scabland*, Bulletin no. 45 (Olympia: Washington Division of Mines and Geology, 1959); Bretz, "The Lake Missoula Floods and the Channeled Scablands," *Journal of Geology*, 77:5 (Sept. 1969), pp. 505-43; *The Channeled Scablands of Eastern Washington: The Geologic Story of the Spokane Flood* (Washington, D. C.: Government Printing Office, 1976); and John E. Allen, Marjorie Burns, and Sam C. Sargent, *Cataclysms on the Columbia: A Layman's Guide to the Features Produced by the Catastrophic Bretz Floods in the Pacific Northwest* (Portland, Or.: Timber Press, 1986). Other useful sources, more technical in tone, include Bretz, "The Channeled Scablands of the Columbia Plateau," *Journal of Geology*, 31:8 (Nov./Dec. 1923), pp. 617-49; "Glacial Lake Missoula . . . ", *Guidebook for Field Conference E* (International Association for Quaternary Research, 7th Congress), pp. 68-89; Bruce D. Cochran and John H. Bush, "A Channeled Scabland Field Trip, Eastern Washington," in Patricia Beaver, ed., *Tobacco Root Geological Society llth Annual Field Conference* (Spokane: Tobacco Root Geological Society, 1986), pp. 52-65; and Donal R. Mullineaux, et. al., "Age of the Last Major Scabland Flood of the Columbia Plateau in Eastern Washington," *Quaternary Research*, 10:2 (1978), pp. 171-80. I am also indebted to geologist Pat Seward for his kind assistance.

2 Unless otherwise cited, the following discussion of the Bretz controversy comes from Allen, *Cataclysms on the Columbia*; Stephen Jay Gould, "The Great Scablands Debate," in Gould, *The Panda's Thumb: More Reflections in Natural History* (New York: Norton & Co., 1980), pp. 194-203; and J Harlen Bretz, "Alternative Hypotheses for Channeled Scabland," *Journal of Geology*, 36:3 (Apr./May 1928), pp. 193-223; 36:4 (May/June 1928), pp. 312-41. For a brief biographical sketch of Bretz see *American Men of Science: A Biographical*

Directory; The Physical and Biological Sciences, 11th ed. (New York: R. R. Bowker Co., 1965).

3   For background on the Bonneville Flood see G. K. Gilbert, "The Ancient Outlet of Great Salt Lake," *The American Journal of Science and Arts*, 15:3 (Apr. 1878), pp. 356-9; Harold E. Malde, *The Catastrophic Late Pleistocene Bonneville Flood in the Snake River Plain, Idaho*, Professional paper no. 596 (Washington, D. C.: Geological Survey, 1968); and Eric Craig Swanson, "Bonneville Flood Deposits Along the Snake River Near Lewiston, Idaho" (unpublished master's thesis, Washington State University, 1984).

4   For the importance of aerial photography in redeeming Bretz see Bretz, "Lake Missoula Floods and Channeled Scablands," p. 508.

5   While information on the Missoula floods is accessible to lay audiences, an easily understood description of most Snake River geology remains to be written. The best overview for non-specialists is Eugene H. Walker, "The Geologic History of the Snake River Country of Idaho," *Idaho Yesterdays*, 7:2 (Summer 1968), pp. 18-32. For Columbia River basalts see Newell P. Campbell, *Geology of the Yakima Area* (Yakima, Wa.: self published, 1981; rev. ed. 1984). Also useful for understanding the geology of the region are: John C. Reed, "The Fiery Floods That Formed the Inland Empire," *Natural History*, 47 (April 1941), pp. 200-10; T. L. Vallier and P. R. Hooper, *Geological Guide to Hells Canyon, Snake River* (Pullman: Washington State University Department of Geology, 1976); Hallett H. Hammatt, "Late Quaternary Stratigraphy and Archaeological Chronology in the Lower Granite Reservoir Area, Lower Snake River, Washington" (unpublished Ph.D. dissertation, Washington State University, 1977); Mark Thomas Wheeler, "Late Cenozoic Gravel Deposits of the Lower Snake River, Washington" (unpublished master's thesis, Washington State University, 1980); Louis Don Ringe, "Geomorphology of the Palouse Hills, Southeastern Washington" (unpublished Ph.D. dissertation, Washington State University, 1968); and Edwin H. McKee, et. al., "Duration and Volume of Columbia River Basalt Volcanism, Washington, Oregon, and Idaho," *Geological Society of America Abstracts with Programs*, 9:4 (February 1977), pp. 463-4. Also very useful are the several field conference guidebooks published for annual conferences of Spokane's Tobacco Root Geological Society, available in most major regional libraries. For recent evidence of the Columbia River basalt flows being the largest in geologic history see *Spokane Spokesman-Review*, 12 Dec. 1990.

Notes for Chapter Two: The Ancients

1   Richard Daugherty, interview with the author, Pullman, Washington, 27 Sept.

1990. Unless otherwise noted, information on Marmes, Daugherty, Fryxell, and WSU archaeology along the lower Snake River comes from this interview.

2 For Lind Coulee see Richard Daugherty, "Archaeology of the Lind Coulee Site, Washington," *Proceedings of the American Philosophical Society,* June 1956, pp. 223-278.

3 Fryxell, *The Interdisciplinary Dilemma: A Case for Flexibility in Academic Thought* (Rock Island, Ill.: Augustana College Library, 1977).

4 Wormington is quoted in *The National Observer,* 12 Mar. 1969; and Martin P. Works, "Throwing Cold Water on Marmes Man," *Esquire,* 73:1 (Jan. 1970), pp. 59-64.

5 Despite the significance of the Marmes Rockshelter discoveries, little scientific work has been done since materials uncovered there were transported to Washington State Univesity. Indeed, most of the artifacts still remain packaged as they arrived from the field. For an outstanding popular account of the excavation—written primarily for children but useful and entertaining for all readers—see Ruth Kirk, *The Oldest Man in America: An Adventure in Archaeology* (New York: Harcourt Brace Jovanovich, Inc., 1970). Also helpful is Kirk and Richard Daugherty, *Discovering Washington Archaeology* (Seattle: University of Washington Press, 1978), esp. pp. 34-7; and Gerald H. Grosso, "Cave Life on the Palouse," *Natural History,* 72:2 (Feb. 1967), pp. 38-43. Most regional newspapers regularly covered news of the excavation, particularly in the period from August 1968 through March 1969. For more technical background see David G. Rice, *Preliminary Report: Marmes Rockshelter Archaeological Site, Southern Columbia Plateau* (Pullman: Washington State University Laboratory of Anthropology, 1969); David G. Rice, "The Windust Phase in Lower Snake River Region Prehistory" (unpublished Ph.D. dissertation, Washington State University, 1972); and Alan Gould Marshall, "An Alluvial Chronology of the Lower Palouse River Canyon and Its Relation to Local Archaeological Sites" (unpublished master's thesis, Washington State University, 1971). For biographical information on Fryxell, in addition to Richard Anderson's foreword to Fryxell's *The Inter-disciplinary Dilemma,* see Fryxell's obituary in *The Pullman Herald,* 23 May 1974, and Washington State University *Daily Evergreen,* 21 May 1974.

6 For various theories on the settling of the Americas see Brian M. Fagan, *The Great Journey: The Peopling of Ancient America* (London: Thames and Hudson, 1987), esp. pp. 25-40. Jose de Acosta's quotation is on p. 28. Also very helpful in detailing the history of "early man" theories and research is Jose Luis Lorenzo, "Early Man Research in the American Hemisphere: Appraisal

and Perspectives," in Alan Lyle Bryan, ed., *Early Man in America From a Circum-Pacific Perspective*, Occasional Papers No. 1 of the Department of Anthropology, University of Alberta (Edmonton: Archaeological Researches International, 1978), pp. 1-9.

7   This is only a cursory summary of Beringia and various theories about when people made the crossing from Siberia. For some of the better sources on ancient man studies, particularly for non-specialists, see Fagan, *The Great Journey*; Bryan, *Early Man in America*; David M. Hopkins, ed., *The Bering Land Bridge* (Stanford: Stanford University Press, 1967); Frederick Hadleigh West, *The Archaeology of Beringia* (New York: Columbia University Press, 1981); Jesse D. Jennings, ed., *Ancient Native Americans* (San Francisco: W. H. Freeman and Co., 1978); Richard Shutler, Jr., ed., *Early Man in the New World* (Beverly Hills: Sage Publications, 1983); L. S. Cressman, *Prehistory of the Far West: Homes of Vanished Peoples* (Salt Lake City: University of Utah Press, 1977); and an issue of *Artic Anthropology*, 8:2 (1971) devoted to early man in North America. For recent evidence indicating the first American settlers might have arrived as early as 20,000 B.P. see Virginia Morell, "Confusion in Earliest America," *Science*, 248:4954 (27 Apr. 1990), pp. 439-41.

8   While the above description of the route covered in the peopling of the Americas is today the most accepted theory, there are some with other opinions. For example, some archaeologists believe the first migrations came down the west coast rather than through the ice-free corridor, and some archaeolgists believe the peopling of North and South America took many thousands of years. For some of these "contrarian" views see Knut R. Fladmark, "The Feasibility of the Northwest Coast as a Migration Route for Early Man," pp. 119-28, and Lorenzo, "Early Man Research in the American Hemisphere," pp. 1-9, both in Bryan, *Early Man in America*.

9   This scenario is not the generally accepted view. Most archaeologists think the lower Snake river area was settled from the south, ancient wanderers first going down the east side of the Rockies and then filtering back up to the Snake from the Great Basin, or perhaps from California and southern Oregon. Obviously, because the Missoula floods destroyed most, if not all, evidence of any earlier occupation it is speculative to determine the exact migration route to the lower Snake, whether very early from the north or later from the south.

10   For details on the frantic work activity see Kirk, *Oldest Man in America*, esp. pp. 38, 45-6, 65; Grosso, "Cave Life on the Palouse," p. 40; *Spokane Daily Chronicle*, 23 Feb. 1969; and Fryxell and Daugherty to Col. Robert Giesen, Walla Walla District Engineer, 16 Aug. 1968. For the first quotation see Giesen

to North Pacific Division Engineer, 25 Sept. 1968. For the second quotation see Drake to District Engineer, 27 Je. 1968. The three latter references are in RG 77, Acc.–T77-85-0022, WWD files, box 21, Seattle FRC.

11 For the Corps' initial rejection of a dike see "Daily Log, Technical Engineering Branch," 21 Aug. 1968. For the Corps' attempts to dissuade Magnuson from pursuing the levee see H. L. Drake, telephone record of conversation with Chief of Engineers Gen. William Cassidy, 19 Oct. 1968. For efforts to dissuade Johnson see Maj. Harold Matthias, record of telephone conversation, 17 Oct. 1968. All are in RG 77, Acc. –T77-85-0022, WWD files, box 21, Seattle FRC. For additional background see *Seattle Times*, 27 Oct. 1968.

12 Donald E. Weitkamp and Max Katx, "Dissolved Atmospheric Gas Supersaturation of Water and the Gas Bubble Disease," 1977, available at U. S. Army Corps of Engineers Library, Ft. Belvoir, Virginia, Civil Works File IV, box 31.

13 The quotations are from P. W. Schneider, Director, Oregon State Game Commission, telegram to Hatfield, 30 Oct. 1968; and John Woodworth, Director, Idaho Fish and Game Department to Church, 24 Sept. 1968, RG 77, Acc. –T77-85- 0022, WWD files, box 21, Seattle FRC. Also see the *National Observer*, 12 Mar. 1969.

14 Drake, interview with the author, Walla Walla, Washington, 27 Apr. 1992.

15 The quotation is in Sydney Steinborn, Chief, Engineering Division, memo 1 Oct. 1968, RG 77, Acc. T77 85 0022, WWD files, box 21, Seattle FRC. For groundbreaking ceremonies see *Tri-City Herald*, 3 Nov. 1968.

16 Daugherty interview.

17 For background on constructing the levee and reaction when water seeped behind it see Kirk, *Oldest Man in America*, pp. 80-91; Works, "Throwing Cold Water on Marmes Man;" and the following newspaper accounts: *Seattle Post-Intelligencer*, 11 Mar. 1969, 16 Mar. 1969; *Seattle Times*, 11 Mar. 1969; *Spokane Daily Chronicle*, 23 Feb. 1969; *Spokane Spokesman-Review*, 12 Mar. 1969; *National Observer*, 12 Mar. 1969. Also see Col. R. E. McConnell, Seattle District Engineer, interdepartmental memo, 5 Mar. 1969, RG 77, Acc.– T77-85-0018, WWD files, box 7, Seattle FRC.

18 The following description of early lifestyles is taken from numerous published and unpublished materials by archaeologists who have worked in or know of the lower Snake region. See, among sources previously cited, Cressman, *Prehistory of the Far West*; Kirk, *Oldest Man in America*; Kirk and Daugherty, *Exploring Washington Archaeology*; C. Melvin Aikens, "The Far West," in Jennings, *Ancient Native Americans*; Rice, *Preliminary Report: Marmes Rockshelter Archaeological Site*; and Rice, "The Windust Phase in Lower Snake River Region Prehistory." Also see David G. Rice, "A Resource Protection Plan-

ning Process Identification and Evaluation for Prehistoric Archaeological Resources of the PaleoIndian Study Unit" (unpublished resource document prepared for the Washington State Office of Archeology and Historic Preservation, 1985); Charles R. Nance, "45WT2: An Archaeological Site on the Lower Snake River" (unpublished master's thesis, Washington State University, 1966); Martha E. Yent, "The Cultural Sequence at Wawawai, Lower Snake River Region" (unpublished master's thesis, Washington State University, 1976); Glen S. Greene, "Prehistoric Utilization in the Channeled Scablands of Eastern Washington" (unpublished Ph.D. dissertation, Washington State University, 1975); Hallett H. Hammatt, "Late Quaternary Stratigraphy and Archaeological Chronology in the Lower Granite Reservoir Area, Lower Snake River" (unpublished Ph.D. dissertation, Washington State University, 1977); Madge L. Schwede, "An Ecological Study of Nez Perce Settlement Patterns" (unpublished master's thesis, Washington State University, 1966); Jerry R. Galm, et. al., "An Archaeological Overview of the Mid-Columbia Study Unit, Benton, Franklin, Klickitat, and Walla Walla Counties" (unpublished resource document prepared for the Washington State Office of Archaeology and Historic Preservation, 1985); John D. Combes, "Burial Practices as an Indicator of Cultural Change in the Lower Snake River Region" (unpublished master's thesis, Washington State University, 1968); and Paul E. Nezbitt, "Petroglyphs of the Snake River, Washington" (unpublished master's thesis, Washington State University, 1968).

19   This discussion of horses among lower Snake Indians comes primarily from Francis Haines, *The Nez Perces: Tribesmen of the Columbia Plateau* (Norman: University of Oklahoma Press, reprnt., 1975), pp. 17-25; and Alvin M. Josephy, Jr., *The Nez Perce Indians and the Opening of the Northwest* (New Haven: Yale University Press, 1965), pp. 27-30, 648-649.

20   Contrary to popular myth, there is no evidence the Nez Perce or Palouse bred their horses for spots. Nez Perce and Palouse tribes did have spotted horses—which became known as Appaloosas, supposedly a condensation of the phrase "a Palouse horse." But spotted horses were known in other cultures dating well before the Nez Perce and Palouse people, and these Snake River residents had horses with a wide diversity of coloring. The Appaloosa Horse Club, with national headquarters in nearby Moscow, Idaho, is primarily responsible for fostering this bit of mythology about the Appaloosa being the "war pony of the Nez Perce." The Nez Perce and Palouse were shrewd and skilled horse breeders. They depended on horses with speed, stamina, and strength. If a strong horse happened to have spots, fine. But to claim these people bred for pretty spots perpetuates a stereotype about their simplicity

similar to the one that ridicules native people for trading away land for pretty beads. Both are myths developed for the convenience of whites and have their origins in half-truths at best. For a discussion of how the myth began and various views on the Apppaloosa controversy see an amazingly frank discussion in the Appaloosa Horse Club's journal, Nella Peterson, "What is an Appaloosa," *Appaloosa Journal* (Oct. 1990), pp. 46-53.

21 See Combes, "Burial Practices in the Lower Snake River Region," and Kirk and Daugherty, *Exploring Washington Archaeology*, p. 70.

22 For details on lifestyles of lower Snake residents during the Numipu phase see David Ray Brauner, "Alpowai: The Culture History of the Alpowa Locality" (unpublished Ph.D. dissertation, Washington State University, 1976); "The Granite-Goose Cultural Resource Management Unit" (unpublished report prepared for the U. S. Army Corps of Engineers, Walla Walla District, by Western Heritage, Inc., n.d.); Combes, "Burial Practices as an Indicator of Cultural Change," esp. pp. 5-7; and Josephy, *The Nez Perce*, pp. 15-39. Also see "The Ice Harbor Cultural Resource Management Unit" (unpublished report prepared for U. S. Army Corps of Engineers, Walla Walla District, by Western Heritage, Inc., n.d.); Galm, et. al., "An Archaeological Overview of the Mid-Columbia Study Unit," pp. 38-40; and Nance, "45 WT 2," pp. 2-9.

23 Daugherty interview.

24 For the difficulties of the Marmes families and the two quotations see *Walla Walla Union Bulletin*, 9 Dec. 1973. For Fryxell's death see Washington State University *Daily Evergreen*, 21 May 1974; *Pullman Herald*, 23 May 1974.

Notes for Chapter Three: The Seekers

1 Grace Jordan, *Home Below Hell's Canyon* (Lincoln: University of Nebraska Press, rprnt., 1962), p. 10.

2 For original journal entries of the expedition along the lower Snake and adjacent country see Reuben Gold Thwaites, ed., *Original Journals of the Lewis and Clark Expedition, 1804-1806* (New York: Antiquarian Press, rprnt., 1959), vol. 3, pp. 101-122; vol. 4, pp.348-62; vol. 5, pp. 11-13. For Sergeant John Ordway's account of the lower Snake passage see Milo M. Quaife, ed., *The Journals of Captain Meriwether Lewis and Sergeant John Ordway* (Madison: State Historical Society of Wisconsin, rprnt., 1965), pp. 268-72; 323-25. Unless otherwise noted, details of the Lewis and Clark expedition along the lower Snake are taken from these two sources, although readers should be aware that the literature on Lewis and Clark is voluminous.

3 Lewis and Clark partially misidentified some of the Indians who lived along

the lower Snake, believing they were all Nez Perce. It was a mistake others would often repeat in coming years. Actually, this was also the home of the Palouse Indians. They shared the river with other groups, including the Nez Perce in the upper area nearest its confluence with the Clearwater. But the Palouse predominated. See Clifford E. Trafzer and Richard D. Sheuerman, *Renegade Tribe: The Palouse Indians and the Invasion of the Inland Pacific Northwest* (Pullman: Washington State University Press, 1986).

4   The quotation is in A. W. Thompson, "New Light on Donald McKenzie's Post on the Clearwater, 1812-13," *Idaho Yesterdays*, 18:3 (Fall 1974), p. 25. For general overviews of early explorations along the lower Snake see also Erwin N. Thompson, "Men and Events on Lower Snake River," *Idaho Yesterdays*, 5:3 (Fall 1961), pp. 10-15, 18-19; Albert W. Thompson, "The Early History of the Palouse River and Its Names," *Pacific Northwest Quarterly*, 62:2 (April 1971), pp. 69-76; Jean C. Neilson, "Donald McKenzie in the Snake River Country Fur Trade, 1816-1821," *Pacific Northwest Quarterly*, 31:2 (1940), pp. 161-79; and an excellent guide to all historic sites along the river, David H. Stratton and Glen W. Lindeman, *A Cultural Resources Survey for the United States Army Corps of Engineers, Walla Walla District*, Project Report no. 28 (Pullman: Washington Archaeological Research Center, 1976).

5   Douglas's quotation is in Thompson, "Men and Events on Lower Snake," p. 12.

6   William Stanton, *The Great United States Exploring Expedition of 1838-1842* (Berkeley: University of California Press, 1975), p. 258.

7   The quotations are in Thompson, "Men and Events on Lower Snake," p. 12; and D. W. Meinig, *Great Columbia Plain: A Historical Geography, 1805-1910* (Seattle: University of Washington Press, 1968), pp. 119-120.

8   Alvin M. Josephy, Jr., *The Nez Perce Indians and the Opening of the Northwest* (New Haven: Yale University Press, 1965), pp. 274-76; Trafzer and Scheuerman, *Renegade Tribe*, pp. 27-30.

9   For Stevens see Kent D. Richards, *Isaac I. Stevens: Young Man in a Hurry* (Pullman: Washington State University Press, rprnt., 1993); and U. S. Congress, *Reports of Explorations and Surveys to Ascertain the Most Practicable and Economical Route for a Railroad from the Mississippi River to the Pacific Ocean*, 35th Cong., 2d Sess., 1859, Sen. Ex. Doc. No. 46.

10   Numerous accounts trace the history of the war of 1855-58. For some of the more accessible writings see Benjamin Franklin Manring, *Conquest of the Coeur d'Alenes, Spokanes & Palouses* (Fairfield, Wash.: Ye Galleon Press, 1975); Jerome Peltier, *Warbonnets and Epaulets* (Montreal: Payette Radio Limited, 1971); *We Were Not Summer Soldiers: The Indian War Diary of Plympton*

J. Kelly, 1855-1856 (Tacoma: Washington State Historical Society, 1976); Trafzer and Scheuerman, *Renegade Tribe*, pp. 60-92; Josephy, *The Nez Perce*, pp.
333-85; and Meinig, *Great Columbia Plain*, pp. 152-68.

11 Quoted in Thompson, "Men and Events on Lower Snake," p. 19. Also see
Mullan, *Report on the Construction of a Military Road from Fort Walla Walla
to Fort Benton* (Washington: Government Printing Office, 1863); Louis C.
Coleman and Leo Rieman, *Captain John Mullan; His Life Building the Mullan
Road* (Montreal: Payette Radio Limited, 1968); and "The Granite Goose Cul-
tural Resource Management Unit" (unpublished report prepared for the U.S.
Army Corps of Engineers, Walla Walla District, by Western Heritage, Inc.,
n.d.), p. 36.

12 Randall V. Mills, *Stern-wheelers Up Columbia: A Century of Steamboating in the
Oregon Country* (Palo Alto: Pacific Books, 1947), pp. 80-81.

13 The story of Pierce and Idaho's first gold discovery has been well documented. This account is taken from the following sources: J. Gary Williams and
Ronald W. Stark, eds., *The Pierce Chronicle: Personal Reminiscences of E. D.
Pierce as Transcribed by Lou A. Larrick* (Moscow: Idaho Research Foundation,
1975); Ralph Burcham, "Reminiscences of E. D. Pierce, Discoverer of Gold
in Idaho" (unpublished Ph.D. dissertation, Washington State College, 1958);
Josephy, *The Nez Perce*, pp. 386-442; Merle Wells, *Rush to Idaho*, Bulletin No.
19 (Moscow: Idaho Bureau of Mines and Geology, 1963); and William J.
Trimble, *Mining Advance Into the Inland Empire*, Bulletin No. 638 (Madison:
University of Wisconsin, 1914).

14 The quotation is from *Pierce Chronicle*, p. 79.

15 *Ibid.*, p. 80.

16 The quotation is from Josephy, *The Nez Perce*, p. 429.

17 The quotations are from the Introduction, *Pierce Chronicle*.

18 For statistics on numbers of miners entering the region see Dorothy O. Jo-
hansen and Charles M. Gates, *Empire of the Columbia: A History of the Pacific
Northwest*, 2nd ed. (New York: Harper & Row, 1967), p. 267. Unless otherwise noted, the following description of early navigation on the lower Snake
is taken from the following: Mills, *Stern-Wheelers up Columbia*, esp. pp. 40-3,
80-3; Fritz Timmen, *Blow for the Landing: A Hundred Years of Steam Navigation on the Waters of the West* (Caldwell, Ida.: Caxton Printers, 1973), esp.
pp. 2-21, 141-2; Fred W. Wilson and Earle K. Stewart, *Steamboat Days on
the Rivers* (Portland: Oregon Historical Society, 1969), esp. pp. 2-10, 59-60,
84-7; Carole Simon-Smolinski, *Clearwater Steam, Steel, & Spirit* (Clarkston,
Wash.: Northwest Historical Consultants, 1984); Bill Gulick, *Snake River
Country* (Caldwell, Ida.: Caxton Printers, 1972), pp. 136-43; Henry Miller,

"Letters From the Upper Columbia," *Idaho Yesterdays*, 4:4 (Winter 1960-61), pp. 14-25; Lulu Donnell Crandall, "The Colonel Wright," *Washington Historical Quarterly*, 7:2 (Apr. 1916), pp. 126-32; and John E. Akins, "History of Steamboat Navigation on Snake River," typescript, 1927, Cage 1599, WSU MASC. *The Colfax Gazette*, 21 Mar. 1957, carried excellent articles on early Snake River navigation. For a fine descriptive account of steamer travel up the river to Lewiston see Carole Simon-Smolinski, *Journal 1862: Timothy Nolan's 1862 Account of His Riverboat and Overland Journey to the Salmon River Mines, Washington Territory* (Clarkston, Wash.: Northwest Historical Consultants, 1983). Simon-Smolinski's account is fictionalized, but is based on original research in first-person accounts and includes an excellent list of sources for those interested in additional information on this subject.

19   The quotation is from Miller, "Letters from Upper Columbia," p. 16. Also see Simon-Smolinski, *Journal 1862* for good details on the luxurious early steamers.

20   Miller, "Letters From Upper Columbia," p. 17.

21   The quotation is in Merle Wells, "Steamboat Down the Snake: The Early Story of the 'Shoshone,'" *Idaho Yesterdays*, 5:4 (Winter 1961-62), p. 23.

22   *Ibid.*, pp. 24-5; Mills, *Stern-Wheelers up Columbia*, pp. 81, 84. For a first-hand account of the *Colonel Wright's* trip up the canyon see Fred Lockley, ed., "Reminiscences of Captain William Polk Gray," *Oregon Historical Quarterly*, 14:4 (December 1913), pp. 321-54.

23   For cattle raising in the region see J. Orin Oliphant, *On the Cattle Ranges of the Oregon Country* (Seattle: University of Washington Press, 1968); Oliphant, "Winter Losses of Cattle in the Oregon Country, 1847-1890," *Washington Historical Quarterly*, 23:1 (January 1932), pp. 3-17; Meinig, *Great Columbia Plain*, pp. 220-23; Marjorie Hales, "The History of Pasco, Washington, to 1915" (unpublished master's thesis, Washington State University, 1964), pp. 19-20; and Alexander Campbell McGregor, *Counting Sheep: From Open Range to Agribusiness on the Columbia Plateau* (Seattle: University of Washington Press, 1982).

24   For some of the better sources on the agricultural development of the region see Meinig, *Great Columbia Plain*; Keith R. Williams, "The Agricultural History of Latah County and the Palouse: An Overview and Three Case Studies" (unpublished master's thesis, Washington State University, 1984); Kirby Brumfield, *This Was Wheat Farming: A Pictorial History of the Farms and Farmers of the Northwest Who Grew the Nation's Bread* (Seattle: Superior Publishing Co., 1968); Thomas B. Keith, *The Horse Interlude: A Pictorial History of Horse and Man in the Inland Northwest* (Moscow: University Press of Idaho, 1980);

Selma Yocom, "History of Crops in the Palouse, 1880-1930," unpublished research report in Rural Life in the Palouse, Binder 2, LCHS; Philip R. P. Coelho and Katherine H. Daigle, "The Effects of Developments in Transportation on the Settlement of the Inland Empire," *Agricultural History*, 56:1 (January 1982), pp. 22-36; Frank Gilbert, *Historic Sketches of Walla Walla, Whitman, Columbia, and Garfield Counties, Washington Territory* . . . (Portland: A. G. Walling, 1882); and *An Illustrated History of North Idaho* (Chicago: Western Publishers, Inc., 1903). In addition, many of the local historical societies of the region publish journals that regularly carry invaluable information about the area's agricultural history. For the better of these see *Latah Legacy* (Latah County Historical Society); *Bunchgrass Historian* (Whitman County Historical Society); *The Golden Age* (Nez Perce County Historical Society); and *Franklin Flyer* (Franklin County Historical Society).

25   Information for this discussion of transporting wheat down the Snake canyon by various means comes from June Crithfield, *Of Yesterday and the River* (Self-published, 1964); Arthur Earl Victor, "The May View Tramway," *The Pacific Northwesterner*, 9:3 (Summer 1965), pp. 33-47; Norma Gimlin, "May View Tramway Tragedy," *The Record*, 34 (1973), pp. 61-5; Keith C. Petersen and Mary E. Reed, "Tramways," *Latah Legacy, the Quarterly Journal of the Latah County Historical Society*, 14:2 (Summer 1985), pp. 21-4; Glen Lindeman and Matthew Root, "The Interior Grain Tramway," *Bunchgrass Historian*, 16:3 (Fall 1988), pp. 3-11; Glen Lindeman, "Canyon Grain Bin and Chutes," *Bunchgrass Historian*, 16:4 (Winter 1988), pp. 3-8; and George M. Gage, "The Bucket Tramway," *Pacific Monthly*, 12:3 (Sept. 1904), pp. 149-50. For more technical detail on the workings of tramways see the David Stearns papers, Cage 4148, WSU MASC.

26   For excellent descriptions of the international grain trade of the nineteenth century and its impact on Inland Empire farmers see Donald W. Meinig, "Wheat Sacks Out to Sea," *Pacific Northwest Quarterly*, 45:1 (January 1954), pp. 13-18; and Mills, *Stern-Wheelers up Columbia*, pp. 99-113.

27   For a description of a lower Snake River warehouse see William Hampton Adams, "Silcott, Washington: Ethnoarchaeology of a Rural American Community" (unpublished Ph.D. dissertation, Washington State University, 1976), p. 102.

28   For the first shipment and development of the lower Snake wheat fleet see *An Illustrated History of Whitman County, State of Washington* (W. H. Lever, 1901), p. 105; and typescript of speech delivered by June Crithfield, 9 Jy. 1967, Cage 1820, WSU MASC.

29   Ben E. Kelley, "Over the Hills and Far Away," unpublished reminiscences,

Ben E. Kelley papers, Cage 140, WSU MASC. For other reminiscences of life along the river, in addition to sources already noted in this chapter, see June Crithfield papers, Cage 2018, WSU MASC; Mary Staley Carpenter, "Strawberry Island: The Way it Was," *Franklin Flyer*, 12:1 (April 1979), pp. 4-5; and Irene Standley Harrison, "Memories of the Gale Bar School," *Bunchgrass Historian*, 4:2 (Summer 1976), p. 10. For Lewiston see Gene Mueller, *Lewiston: A Pictorial History* (Lewiston: Chamber of Commerce, 1986); and Margaret Day Allen, *Lewiston Country: An Armchair History* (Lewiston: Nez Perce County Historical Society, 1990). For Clarkston see Elgin V. Kuykendall, *Historic Glimpses of Asotin County Washington* (Self published, 1954), pp. 50-51; and Ted Van Arsdol, "Brief History of Jawbone Flat and Early Clarkston," typescript, n.d., Ted Van Arsdol papers, Cage 117, WSU MASC. The papers of the Lewiston-Clarkston Improvement Company, which provide excellent detail on the founding and development of Clarkston, are also available at WSU MASC.

Notes for Chapter Four: An Open River

1 For the best background on the long struggle to complete Cascade Locks see two works by William F. Willingham, *Army Engineers and the Development of Oregon: A History of the Portland District, U. S. Army Corps of Engineers* (Portland: U. S. Army Corps of Engineers, Portland District, 1983), pp. 28-36, and "Engineering the Cascade Canal and Locks," *Oregon Historical Quarterly*, 88:3 (Fall 1987), pp. 229-257. Also see Randall V. Mills, *Stern-Wheelers Up Columbia: A Century of Steamboating in the Oregon Country* (Palo Alto, Ca.: Pacific Books, 1947), pp. 75, 143-4; and Stewart H. Holbrook, *The Columbia* (New York: Rinehart and Co., 1956), pp. 286-87. For some typical editorials urging Congress to authorize construction of the canal see Boise *Idaho Statesman*, 19 Oct. 1876; and *Lewiston Teller*, 25 Nov. 1876.

2 For the Celilo Canal see Mills, *Stern-Wheelers Up Columbia*, pp. 148-52; Holbrook, *The Columbia*, pp. 289-92; and Gordon Lee Merritt, "Prelude to Slack Water" (unpublished master's thesis, University of Idaho, 1973), pp. 26-8.

3 The quotations are in *Oregon Historical Quarterly*, 16:2 (June 1915), pp. 124 and 131, respectively. The entire issue is devoted to the open river celebrations of May, 1915. For more on the commemorations see Walter A. Oberst, *Railroads, Reclamation and the River: A History of Pasco* (Pasco, Wash.: Franklin County Historical Society, 1978), pp. 81-5; Oberst, "Open River Celebrations Held in 1915," *Franklin Flyer*, 8:1 (April 1975), pp. 2-3; and

Carole Simon-Smolinski, "Lewiston's Greatest Day," *The Golden Age*, 12:1 (Spring/Summer 1992), pp. 8-15.

4   For the decline in shipping see U. S. Congress, *Columbia and Snake Rivers*, 73rd Cong., 2d Sess., 1933, House Doc. No. 16, p. 3; and U. S. Congress, *Snake River and Tributaries*, 73rd Cong., 2d Sess., 1934, House Doc. No. 190, pp. 3, 47.

5   For background on the history of American canals see William J. Hull and Robert W. Hull, *The Origin and Development of the Waterways Policy of the United States* (Washington, D. C.: National Waterways Conference, Inc., 1967); Dwight M. Blood, *Inland Waterway Transport Policy in the U. S.* (Prepared for the National Water Commission, 1972); and William H. Shank, *Towpaths to Tugboats: A History of American Canal Engineering* (York, Penn.: The American Canal and Transportation Center, 1982).

6   U. S. Congress, *Preliminary Report of the Inland Waterways Commission*, 60th Cong., 1st Sess., 1908, S. Doc. No. 325, pp. iii-iv.

7   Summaries of these early Corps programs can be found in Forest G. Hill, *Roads, Rails, and Waterways: The Army Engineers and Early Transportation* (Norman: University of Oklahoma Press, 1957); Frank N. Schubert, ed., *The Nation Builders: A Sesquicentennial History of the Corps of Topographical Engineers, 1838-1863* (Ft. Belvoir, Va.: U. S. Army Corps of Engineers, Office of History, 1988), and Frank N. Schubert, *Vanguard of Expansion. Army Engineers in the Trans-Mississippi West, 1819-1879* (Washington, D. C.: Historical Division, Office of the Chief of Engineers, 1980). For the Corps' early history generally see Paul K. Walker, *Engineers of Independence: A Documentary History of the Army Engineers in the American Revolution, 1775-1783* (Washington, D. C.: Historical Division, Office of the Chief of Engineers, 1981). And for a succinct summary of the development of the Corps see Todd Shallat, "Engineering Policy: The U. S. Army Corps of Engineers and the Historical Foundation of Power," *The Public Historian*, 11:3 (Summer 1989), pp. 7-27.

8   See Martin Reuss, "Andrew A. Humphreys and the Development of Hydraulic Engineering: Politics and Technology in the Army Corps of Engineers, 1850-1950," *Technology and Culture*, 26:1 (Jan. 1985), pp. 1-33; Martin Reuss, "The Army Corps of Engineers and Flood-Control Politics on the Lower Mississippi," *Louisiana History*, 23:2 (Spring 1982), pp. 131-48; and, for a popular account of the story, John McPhee, *The Control of Nature* (New York: Farrar Straus Giroux, 1989), pp. 3-92.

9   For Bonneville Dam see William F. Willingham, *Water Power in the "Wilderness": The History of Bonneville Lock and Dam* (Portland: U. S. Army Corps

of Engineers, Portland District, 1988). For the importance of the Flood Control Act of 1936 on the Corps see Howard Rosen and Martin Reuss, eds., *The Flood Control Challenge: Past, Present, and Future* (Public Works Historical Society, 1988).

10 For the role of the Corps of Engineers in the region generally see Charles McKinley, *Uncle Sam in the Pacific Northwest: Federal Management of Natural Resources in the Columbia River Valley* (Berkeley: University of California Press, 1952); Estella Dee Brown, "The Corps of Engineers in the Pacific Northwest, 1866-1890" (unpublished bachelor's thesis, Reed College, 1952); Gordon B. Dodds, *Hiram Martin Chittenden: His Public Career* (Lexington: University Press of Kentucky, 1973); *The History of the North Pacific Division, U. S. Army Corps of Engineers, 1888 to 1965* (Portland: U. S. Army Corps of Engineers, North Pacific Division, 1969); Mary E. Reed, *A History of the North Pacific Division* (Portland: U. S. Army Corps of Engineers, North Pacific Division, 1992); *History of the Seattle District, 1896-1968* (Seattle: U. S. Army Corps of Engineers, Seattle District, 1969); *The History of the Portland District, Corps of Engineers, 1871-1969* (Portland: U. S. Army Corps of Engineers, Portland District, 1970); Willingham, *Army Engineers in the Development of Oregon*; Howard Preston, *A History of the Walla Walla District, 1948-1970* and *Walla Walla District History, 1970-1975* (Walla Walla: U. S. Army Corps of Engineers, Walla Walla District, 1971 and 1976); and John R. Jameson, Keith C. Petersen, and Mary E. Reed, *Walla Walla District History, 1975-1980* (Walla Walla: U. S. Army Corps of Engineers, Walla Walla District, 1982).

11 For the state appropriation see various pieces of correspondence from the War Department, the United States Engineer Office in Portland, and Walla Walla commercial interests to Washington Governor Albert Mead in the period January through April 1907, Governor Albert Mead papers, box 2E-2-27, Wash. Arch. For background on Corps activity along the lower Snake in the late nineteenth and early twentieth centuries see U. S. Congress, *Columbia and Snake Rivers*, 73rd Cong., 2d Sess., 1933, H. Doc. No. 16, pp. 11-12, 23-4; June Crithfield, typescript of speech delivered 9 Jy. 1967, p. 7, June Crithfield papers, cage 1820, WSU MASC; and Caroline D. Carley and Robert Lee Sappington, *Archaeological Test Excavations of the Historic Component of 45-WT-1, Texas City/Riparia, Whitman County, Washington, 1983*, Anthropological Research Manuscript Series No. 77 (Moscow: University of Idaho Laboratory of Anthropology, 1984), p. 6.

12 1932 review of report on Columbia and Snake rivers as given in U. S. Congress,

72nd Cong., 2d Sess., 1931, H. Doc. No. 440, RG 77, Civil Works Projects Construction Files 1925-48, box 2, Seattle NA.

13 The comparative freight rates are quoted in "To the Corps of Army Engineers: Farm Markets and Transportation," typescript, c. 1936, cabinet V, drawer 1, "Agriculture" file, IEWA. For other similar statistics and pleas for Snake River development see the statements of J. W. Shepard and Arthur Ward, U. S. Congress, *Snake River, Oreg., Wash., and Idaho*, 78th Cong., 2d Sess., 1944, Hearings before the House Committee on Rivers and Harbors, pp. 5, 18.

14 Quoted in Marshall Dana, "The Celilo Canal—Its Origins—Its Building and Meaning," *Oregon Historical Quarterly*, 16:2 (June 1915), p. 122.

15 The quotation is in an insightful story written by Ward about the history of Columbia and Snake river improvement organizations, *Lewiston Morning Tribune*, 7 Jan. 1934. For additional information on the plethora of improvement associations see Merritt, "Prelude to Slack Water;" U. S. Congress, *Snake River and Tributaries* (1934), pp. 51-2; and Wallace R. Struble to John Haines, Governor of Idaho, 10 Jan. 1914, in Governor Ernest Lister papers, box 2H-2-86, Wash. Arch.

16 The first quotation is in a brief of the Western Inland Waterways Corporation to the board of Engineers for Rivers and Harbors, 1933, RG 77, NPD files, box 6, vol. 8, Seattle NA. The second is from an editorial in the *Lewiston Morning Tribune*, 14 Feb. 1934.

17 Details on the Lewiston meeting and the subsequent formation of the IEWA can be found in numerous news stories in the *Lewiston Morning Tribune* for the dates February 7-25, 1934. For a good summary of the meeting and IEWA formation see Merritt, "Prelude to Slack Water," pp. 61-69.

18 West to Union Warehouse and Supply Co., Grangeville, 11 Oct. 1934, cabinet V, drawer 4, "Grain Growers, 1934-50" file, IEWA.

19 Merritt, "Prelude to Slack Water," pp. 69-70.

20 The quotation is in *Spokane Spokesman-Review*, 15 Oct. 1967. For other biographical sketches of West see *Walla Walla Union-Bulletin*. 14 Jy. 1959; IEWA 25th anniversary party booklet, cabinet XI, drawer 2, "Herb West" file; Correspondence Files, "Lower Monumental—H.G. West Lake" folder, PAO WWD; and Ted Van Arsdol, "History of Ice Harbor Dam," typescript, 1962, cage 117, folder 2, Ted Van Arsdol papers, WSU MASC.

21 Merritt, "Prelude to Slack Water," pp. 68-69; Willingham, *Water Power in the Wilderness*, pp. 13-14. While West and the IEWA deserved considerable credit for the larger locks at Bonneville, one could exaggerate their influence

in obtaining them. The IEWA at this time was still a young organization; its most dramatic years of influence lay ahead. The advocacy of Oregon Senator Charles McNary was more influential. But the IEWA did play a role, and it was not above the boosteristic Herbert West in later years to take abundant credit for convincing the government to install larger locks.

22   Tonnage statistics from M. J. Vennewitz, "Navigation on the Columbia River, 1897-1939," typescript, 1940, cabinet VI, drawer 4, "Navigation" file, IEWA.

23   Statement at Corps of Engineers public meeting, Lewiston, 15 May 1935, RG 77, Civil Works Projects Construction Files 1925-48, box 4, Seattle NA.

24   Various letters attesting to the close personal and professional relationship between West and Walla Walla District Engineers can be found in cabinet VI, drawer 1, "Walla Walla District" file, IEWA.

25   See West to Oregon Representative Walter Pierce, 18 Dec. 1936, and Pierce to West, 27 Dec. 1936, Walter Pierce papers, "Columbia River, General Correspondence," box 1, UO; and Giesen, interdepartmental memo, c. Feb. 1970, RG 77, Acc.—T77-85-0018, WWD files, box 9, Seattle FRC.

26   Programs outlining lobbying activities and accounts of lobbying trips by delegates can be found in numerous places in the IEWA papers, usually under the file heading "Mission (or Delegation) to Washington," followed by the appropriate year. The quotation is in Portland *Journal*, 2 Dec. 1956.

Notes for Chapter Five: "Construct Such Dams"

1   Mendell to Chief of Engineers, 8 Oct. 1895, RG 77, entry 103, box 1112(3), Nat. Arch.

2   Board of Engineers, "Public Notice Relative to the Proposed Improvement of the Snake and Columbia Rivers, March 1923," file 24443(1667); Wallace R. Stubble, Lewiston Commercial Club, to Senator William Borah, 23 Jy. 1912, file 24443(1644); Congressman Burton French to Chief of Engineers, 2 Aug. 1912, file 24443(1644); Senator Weldon Heyburn to Secretary of War Henry Stimson, 7 Aug. 1912, file 24443(1642). All in entry 103, box 522, Nat. Arch.

3   Barden to Chief of Engineers, 3 Nov. 1923, file 2334(9); 4 Dec. 1924, file 2334(22); 2 Jan. 1924, file 2334(11). All in entry 103, box 575, Nat. Arch.

4   U. S. Congress, *Columbia and Snake Rivers*, 73rd Cong., 2d Sess., 1933, H. Doc. No. 16.

5   For the quotations see Arthur E. Ward, "General Presentation in Support of Senate Bill No. 2670," typescript, 1932, cabinet VI, drawer 3, "Snake River Improvement Hearing" file, IEWA; and Roy Huffman, Traffic Manager,

Potlatch Forests, Incorporated, to Major O. O. Kuentz, Portland District Engineer, 22 Mar. 1932, RG 77, Civil Works Projects Construction Files 1925-1948, box 2, Seattle NA. For an earlier version of the "build and development will follow" argument see *Lewiston to Portland by Water in 1905: Resolutions Demanding the . . . Opening of the Upper Columbia and Snake Rivers to Navigation, Adopted . . . 1901* (Portland: Chamber of Commerce, 1901).

6   *Lewiston Morning Tribune*, 7 Sept. 1932; U. S. Congress, *Hearings on a Bill to Provide for the Improvement of the Columbia and Snake Rivers . . . S. 2670 and S. 4408*, 72d Cong., 2d Sess., 1932.

7   U. S. Congress, *Snake River and Tributaries*, 73d Cong., 2d Sess., 1933, H. Doc. No. 190. The complex efforts by developers in the 1930s to lobby for slackwater, the role of IEWA, the numerous public hearings, and the role of the Corps of Engineers and Congress, is conveniently summarized in Gordon Lee Merritt, "Prelude to Slack Water" (unpublished master's thesis, University of Idaho, 1973), esp. pp. 38-87.

8   Merritt, "Prelude to Slack Water," pp. 72-73.

9   U. S. Congress, *Columbia and Snake Rivers, Oreg., Wash., and Idaho*, 75th Cong., 3d Sess., 1938, H. Doc. No. 704. Also see *Lewiston Morning Tribune*, 12 Je. 1938, and, for hearings in Lewiston prior to Robins's report, *Lewiston Morning Tribune*, 17 Feb. 1937.

10   *Columbia and Snake Rivers*, 1938, H. Doc. No. 704.

11   For examples of protests by Puget Sound interests see Ferd Schaaf, Director, Department of Public Service, memorandum to Gov. Clarence Martin, 3 Feb. 1937, box 2K-2-25, Clarence Martin papers, Wash. Arch.; and John Ulrich to "Director of Information," 12 Mar. 1959 memo on hearings in Lewiston, box 100, NPPA.

12   The letter appeared in the Boise *Idaho Statesman*, quoted in Lt. Col. C. R. Moore, Portland District Engineer to A. L. Alford, Lewiston, 1 Dec. 1941, cabinet VIII, drawer 2, "Snake River Improvements" file, IEWA. Also see Representative Compton White to E. W. Rising, Southwestern Idaho Water Conservation Project, 11 Mar. 1944, RG 77, WWD files, box 7, Seattle NA.

13   Moore to Herbert West, 9 Jan. 1942, RG 77, WWD files, box 5, Seattle NA.

14   Southern Idaho opposition to the lower Snake project continued even after Congress authorized the dams. In 1957 the IEWA, Lewiston Chamber of Commerce, and Washington congressional representatives carried on a rather protracted battle with Idaho congressman Hamer Budge of Ada County, a representative with strong ties to southeast Idaho's irrigation interests, regarding congressional appropriations for lower Snake dam construction. At the time, Budge sat on the House Appropriations Committee and, again citing

fears that lower Snake navigation might harm irrigationists, proved unenthusiastic about the lower Snake project. Proponents always feared such oppositon from Pacific Northwest congressional representatives; they worked diligently—and usually successfully—for a positive united front. See Representative Don Magnuson, Washington, to Herbert West, IEWA, 3 Apr. 1957; and Budge to Herbert Powell, Lewiston Chamber of Commerce, 14 May 1957. Both in cabinet VIII, drawer 1, "Lower Granite Dam, 1956-1959" file, IEWA. Also see *Lewiston Morning Tribune*, 30 Apr. 1957.

15   Ickes, foreword to Maass, *Muddy Waters: The Army Engineers and the Nation's Rivers* (Cambridge: Harvard University Press, 1951).

16   E. K. Burlew, Acting Secretary of the Interior to Representative Joseph Mansfield, Chairman, House Committee on Rivers and Harbors, 8 Oct. 1941, RG 77, WWD files, box 5, Seattle NA.

17   Herbert West to Portland District Engineer Col. Ralph Tudor, 20 Mar. 1944, RG 77, WWD files, box 7, Seattle NA.

18   Portland District Corps of Engineers, "Supplement to Special Report on Selection of Sites, Lower Snake River," 14 Mar. 1947, RG 77, Civil Works Projects Construction files 1925-1948, box 9, Seattle NA.

19   The railroad history of the Pacific Northwest in general and the Snake River in particular is complicated, but has been well documented. See especially: D. W. Meinig, *The Great Columbia Plain: A Historical Geography, 1805-1910* (Seattle: University of Washington Press, 1968), pp. 241-83, 382-83; Peter J. Lewty, *To the Columbia Gateway: The Oregon Railway and the Northern Pacific, 1879-1884* (Pullman: Washington State University Press, 1987); Enoch A. Bryan, *Orient Meets Occident: the Advent of the Railways to the Pacific Northwest* (Pullman, Wash.: Students Book Corporation, 1936); John T. Gaertner, *North Bank Road: The Spokane, Portland & Seattle Railway* (Pullman: Washington State University Press, 1990); Walter R. Grande, *The Northwest's Own Railway—Spokane, Portland & Seattle and Its Subsidiaries* (Portland: Grande Press, 1992); Charles R. Wood and Dorothy Wood, *Spokane, Portland and Seattle Ry, the Northwest's Own Railway* (Seattle: Superior Publishing Co., 1974); James L. Ehernberger and Francis G. Gschwind, *Smoke Along the Columbia: Union Pacific, Oregon Division* (Callaway, Neb.: E. G. Publications, 1968); and James B. Hedges, *Henry Villard and the Railways of the Northwest* (New York: Russell & Russell, 1967).

20   See, for example, the testimony of John T. Corbett, National Legislative Representative of the Brotherhood of Locomotive Engineers, U. S. Congress, *Columbia and Snake Rivers, Oreg., Wash., and Idaho: Hearing Before the Committee on Rivers and Harbors*, 78th Cong., 1st Sess., 1943, pp. 36-40.

21 See West to J. B. Fink, Director, Washington Department of Conservation and Development, 26 Nov. 1937, box 2K-2-25, Clarence Martin papers, Wash. Arch.

22 See, for example, Portland District Engineer Major Oscar Kuentz, address before the annual meeting of the Columbia Valley Association, Lewiston, 15 Feb. 1932, RG 77, Civil Works Projects Construction files 1925-1948, box 2, Seattle NA.

23 For the Corps' quotation see U. S. Congress, *Snake River and Tributaries*, 1934, H. Doc. No. 190, pp. 4-5.

24 For a synopsis of the growth of the aluminum industry in the region see *Columbia River Power & The Aluminum Industry: A Research Report* (Portland: Bonneville Power Administration, 1953). Also see Richard L. Neuberger, "Feud in the Northwest: The Vendetta Against Aluminum," *Frontier*, (Feb. 1954), pp. 15-16; *Aluminum in the Northwest and What It Means to You* (Walla Walla: Inland Empire Waterways Association, c. 1953); *Spokane Spokesman-Review*, 16 Dec. 1991; and Vancouver (Wa.) *Columbian*, 4 Je. 1991. For the Bonneville Power Administration see Gus Norwood, *Columbia River Power for the People: A History of Policies of the Bonneville Power Administration* (Portland: Bonneville Power Administration, 1981); and Vera Springer, *Power and the Pacific Northwest: A History of the Bonneville Power Administration* (Portland: Bonneville Power Administration, 1976).

25 The quotation is in *Columbia River Power & The Aluminum Industry*, p. 8.

26 For background on the issue over the number of dams see "Legislative History of Fight for Ice Harbor Dam," Inland Empire Waterways Association press release, 10 Aug. 1955, cabinet VIII, drawer 1, "Ice Harbor" file, IEWA; U.S. Congress, *Snake River, Oreg., Wash. and Idaho*, 77th Cong., 1st Sess., 1941, Hearings Before the House Committee on Rivers and Harbors, p. 7; and "Special Report on Selection of Sites, Lower Snake River," Apr. 1947, RG 77, WWD files, box 9, Seattle NA.

27 Comments from various fishery agencies as to the number of dams, written in November and December 1946, can be found in RG 77, Acc.-T77-82-0060, WWD files, box 4, Seattle FRC. The quotation is in James O. Beck, Director, Idaho Department of Fish and Game to Corps, 25 Nov. 1946. For the Chief's decision see Chief of Engineers to North Pacific Division, 23 Apr. 1947, RG 77, WWD files, box 9, Seattle NA.

Notes for Chapter Six: Battle for Ice Harbor

1 Details on the early history of the Walla Walla District come primarily from Howard Preston, *A History of the Walla Walla District, 1948-1970* (Walla Walla:

U. S. Army Corps of Engineers, Walla Walla District, 1971), esp. pp. 39-68.
Also see the fortieth anniversary issue of *Intercom*, 19:6 (Oct. 1988), the in-
terdeptartmental publication of the Walla Walla District; and William F. Willingham, *Army Engineers and the Development of Oregon: A History of the Portland
District U. S. Army Corps of Engineers* (Portland: U. S. Army Corps of Engineers, Portland District, 1983), esp. pp. 150-51.

2 Harry Drake, interview with the author, Walla Walla, Washington, 27 Apr.
1992.

3 Details on the Ice Harbor dedication can be found in RG 77, Acc.–
T77-85-0034, box 4, and Acc. –T77-85-0022, box 16, WWD files, Seattle
FRC. Additional dedication information and materials are in series 1.1, box
121, folder 13, Church Papers. Also see *Walla Walla Union Bulletin*, 10 May
1962.

4 The story is recounted in Walter A. Oberst, *Railroads, Reclamation and the
River: A History of Pasco* (Pasco: Franklin County Historical Society, 1978),
p. 20.

5 Details on the Palouse Irrigation Project can be found in Alexander Campbell McGregor, *Counting Sheep: From Open Range to Agribusiness on the Columbia Plateau* (Seattle: University of Washington Press, 1982), p. 220; Marjorie
Hales, "The History of Pasco, Washington to 1915" (unpublished master's
thesis, Washington State University, 1964), pp. 55-64; and Oberst, *Railroads,
Reclamation and the River*, p. 64.

6 For details on the Burbank Project see *Burbank*, a promotional brochure published by the project's backers, c. 1913. A copy is available for researchers
at EWSHS. Also see Hales, "History of Pasco," p. 64; and, especially, two
excellent historical pieces by journalist Ted Van Arsdol: "History of Ice Harbor Dam," 1962 typescript, Ted Van Arsdol Papers, Cage 117, WSU MASC;
and his outstanding seventeen-part history of Ice Harbor that ran in the *Tri-
City Herald*, Oct.-Nov. 1961.

7 For the long history of the Five Mile project see the two Van Arsdol pieces
cited above. Hopson's 1916 report is in VF 2740, WSU MASC. There are
two outstanding sources of primary materials relating to the Five Mile Rapids
project. See cabinet VII, drawer 14, "Five Mile Dam" file, IEWA; and detailed
correspondence concerning the project between the State of Washington, the
Reclamation Service, and local promoters, in Washington State Department
of Conservation Irrigation Files, "Five Mile Rapids Project, 1919-26," box
2, Wash. Arch.

8 Technical research studies on salmon are voluminous and growing rapidly;
our knowledge of their ways is consequently increasing, though many mys-

teries remain. For some popular accounts of salmon lifestyles see Atsushi Sakurai and John N. Cole, *Salmon* (New York: Alfred A. Knopf, 1984); Jere Van Dyk, "Long Journey of the Pacific Salmon," *National Geographic*, 178:1 (Jy. 1990), pp. 3-37; and two intriguing books written from the perspective of a salmon, Henry Williamson, *Salar the Salmon* (New York: The New American Library, 1936); and Roger A. Caras, *Sockeye: The Life of a Pacific Salmon* (Lincoln: University of Nebraska Press, 1975). Also very helpful in understanding the various species of Pacific salmon is C. Groot and L. Margolis, eds., *Pacific Salmon Life Histories* (Vancouver: University of British Columbia, 1991).

9   The myth probably started with Anthony Netboy, a prolific writer and one of the strongest advocates of fisheries protection in the Pacific Northwest. His books and articles are insightful and have helped increase awareness of the many difficulties Columbia River anadromous fish face. But in his advocacy Netboy sometimes overstates his case. For example, in his important 1958 book, *Salmon of the Pacific Northwest: Fish vs. Dams* (Portland: Binfords & Mort), he states, pp. 43-4: "Such strenuous objections were raised by fishery people to the blockading of the river by Bonneville dam that the Corps of Engineers was forced to include fish-passage facilities in the plans for this structure. At first they were to consist of only four conventional ladders of moderate size . . . estimated to cost $800,000. When fishery biologists demonstrated that they would be palpably inadequate to handle the large fish traffic using this stretch of the river, an elaborate system of traps, locks, elevators, canals and ladders was devised which added $7 million to the cost of the dam." As detailed below, the remark—later repeated by Netboy and numerous other writers. Contrary to Netboy's intimations, fishery people were open in their praise for the cooperative attitude of the Corps at Bonneville. See, for example, William F. Willingham, *Water Power in the Wilderness: The History of Bonneville Lock and Dam* (Portland: U. S. Army Corps of Engineers, Portland District, 1988), pp. 47-8.

10 Lukesh to Chief of Engineers, 8 Mar. 1929, RG 77, Records of the Chief of Engineers, Columbia River, File -7249, Nat. Arch.; Kuentz, "The Lower Columbia River Project," *Military Engineer*, 25:139 (Jan.-Feb. 1933), p. 44.

11 For background on fishways at Bonneville see U. S. Congress, *Columbia River and Minor Tributaries*, 73rd Cong., 1st Sess., 1933, H. Doc. No. 103; U.S. Army, Chief of Engineers, *Review of Report on the Columbia River, Washington and Oregon*, 73rd Cong., 2d Sess., Sen. Comm. Print; Harlan B. Holmes, *The Passage of Fish at Bonneville Dam*, Oregon Fish Commission Contribution no. 2 (Salem: Oregon Fish Commission, 1940); "Fishways at Bonneville

Dam to Cost $3,500,000," *Engineering News Record*, 116 (Feb. 1936), p. 235; and Willingham, *Water Power in the Wilderness*, pp. 47-53. Unfortunately, Frank N. Schubert's "From the Potomac to the Columbia: The Corps of Engineers and Anadromous Fisheries," has never been published. However, a 1978 type-script is available for researchers at the Office of History, U. S. Army Corps of Engineers, Ft. Belvoir, Va. Schubert, pp. 40-58, offers the most detailed history of the fishery problem at Bonneville yet written. For the cooperation between the Corps and fishery people see Charles E. Jackson, Bureau of Fish-eries to Senator Charles McNary, 9 Nov. 1933, box 33, McNary papers, UO.

12 U. S. Congress, Commissioner of Fisheries *Report on Bonneville Dam and Pro-tection of the Columbia River Fisheries*, 75th Cong., 1st Sess., 1937, Sen. Doc. No. 87; Schubert, "From the Potomac to the Columbia," pp. 56-7.

13 *Ibid.*

14 For background on the hearing and the IEWA conversion see the considera-ble correspondence of Feb.-Mar. 1937 on this issue in Acc. –68-A-92, Depart-ment of Fisheries papers, "Stream Improvement" files, box 746, Wash. Arch.; and cabinet VI, drawer 3, "Lewiston Hearing, 1937" file, IEWA.

15 W. S. Nelson, The Dalles Chamber of Commerce to Herbert West, 19 Dec. 1945, cabinet VI, drawer 2, "Fish, Through 1951" file, IEWA.

16 U. S. Congress, *Snake River Oreg., Wash., and Idaho*, 77th Cong., 1st Sess., 1941, Hearings before House Committee on Rivers and Harbors, pp. 14-15.

17 The Department's proposed moratorium came in a memorandum from Warner W. Gardner, Assistant Secretary of the Interior to the Federal Inter-Agency River Basin Committee, 24 Mar. 1947, cabinet VI, drawer 3, "Miscellane-ous Hearings" file, IEWA. For additional background on the proposed morato-rium see Roy Scheufele, "History of the Columbia Basin Inter-Agency Committee," typescript, n.d., pp. 22-8, copy in the library, Portland District, Corps of Engineers; Roy Scheufele, *The History of the North Pacific Division, U.S. Army Corps of Engineers, 1888 to 1965* (Portland: U. S. Army Corps of Engineers, North Pacific Division, 1969), pp. 23-4; and Charles McKinley, *Uncle Sam in the Pacific Northwest: Federal Management of Natural Resources in the Columbia River Valley* (Berkeley: University of California Press, 1952), pp. 386-7, 429-31, 473-5. Also see Acc.–1659-2, box 14, CBIAC. The CBIAC's decision against a moratorium is outlined in a 24 Nov. 1947 news release in this box.

18 Col. O. E. Walsh, Portland District Engineer to Leo Laythe, Fish and Wild-life Service, 26 Mar. 1947, RG 77, WWD files, box 9, Seattle NA.

19 *Columbia River Basin Fish and Wildlife Program* (Northwest Power Planning Council, 1982), p. 4 -1.

20 Ed Chaney, interview with the author, Eagle, Idaho, 26 Feb. 1992.

21 U. S. Fish and Wildlife Service, *Review Report on Columbia River and Tributaries; Appendix P: Fish and Wildlife* (Portland: U. S. Army Corps of Engineers, North Pacific Division, 1948), pp. 100-01; "Presentation by Col. F. S. Tandy Before the Sportsmen's Jamboree, Idaho Falls, 12 Feb. 1954," Gov. Len Jordan papers, AR 2/23, box 15, ISHS; Ray Oligher, telephone interview with the author, 12 May 1992. For Grand Coulee and juveniles see Paul C. Pitzer, *Grand Coulee: Harnessing a Dream* (Pullman: Washington State University Press, 1994), p. 224. For Harlan Holmes's two early studies and the Corps cover up, see Lisa Mighetto and Wesley J. Ebel, "Draft Report, Saving the Salmon: A History of the U. S. Army Corps of Engineers' Role in the Protection of Anadromous Fish on the Columbia and Snake Rivers," typescript done on contract (DACW68-91-0025) with the Army Corps of Engineers, Oct. 1993, pp. 84-85.

22 The quotation is in Alvin Anderson, Director, Washington Department of Fisheries to Congressman Cecil King, 25 Jy 1950. For the Oregon arguments against the dams see John Veatch, Chairman, Oregon Fish Commission to House Sub-committee on Civil Functions, 16 Apr. 1951. Both are in Acc. -73-7-675, Department of Fisheries papers, Central files 1948-64, box 1010-42, Wash. Arch.

23 The Corps' estimates from its "Letter Report, Lower Snake River Project," 20 Oct. 1948, are quoted in "Report Showing How the Army Engineers Have Juggled the Figures in Attempting to Justify the Four Lower Snake River Dams," n.d., *ibid.*

24 The first quotation is in Robert Schoettler, Director, Department of Fisheries to Senator Kenneth McKellar, 16 Jy. 1951; the second in John Hurley, Department of Fisheries to J. H. Cellars, Columbia River Packers Association, 12 Je. 1950; both *ibid.*

25 These arguments are made in several background papers and pieces of correspondence to be found in Acc.-73-7-675, Department of Fisheries papers, Central files 1948-64, box 1010-42, Wash. Arch. For particularly good examples see C. L. Anderson, Director to Congressman Henry Jackson, 24 Feb. 1949; and Alvin Anderson, Director to Herbert West, 3 Apr. 1950. Also see Robert Hicks, Executive Secretary, Columbia River Fishermen's Protective Union to Charles Baker, President, IEWA, 2 Nov. 1953, cabinet VI, drawer 2, "Fish, 1951-55" file, IEWA; and Lars Langloe, "Memorandum,

Lower Snake River Dams," 6 Jy. 1950, Control –36-A-1-b, Department of Conservation papers, Director's General Correspondence, box 3, Wash. Arch.

26 The quotations are in, respectively, Biggs to Charles Baker, President, IEWA, 3 Apr. 1952; and Hurley memorandum to Director Robert Schoettler, 13 Je. 1951. Both in Acc. –73-7-675, Department of Fisheries papers, Central Files 1948-64, box 1010-42, Wash. Arch.

27 The first quotation is in Hurley memorandum. For the direct approach to friendly congressmen see Arnie Suomela, Master Fish Warden, Fish Commission of Oregon to Alvin Anderson, Director, Washington Department of Fisheries, 5 Apr. 1950; and Representative Thor Tollefson to Anderson, 21 Sept. 1950. For other lobbying and pressure tactics see Alvin Anderson, Director, telegram to President Harry Truman, 29 May 1950; and Anderson to "Dear Fishermen," 1 Mar. 1950. All in *ibid.*

28 The first quotation is in West to Idaho Governor Robert Smylie, 4 May 1955, box 5, Smylie papers, ISHS. The second quotation is in Robert Schoettler, Director, Department of Fisheries to Members of the Public Works Subcommittee of House Appropriations Committee, 27 May 1955, Acc. –73-7-675, Department of Fisheries papers, Central Files 1948-64, box 1010-42, Wash. Arch. For various news stories about West's 1955 testimony and the resulting controversy see *Walla Walla Union Bulletin*, 21 May 1955; Pasco *Tri-City Herald*, 22 May 1955 and 23 May 1955. For an example of the argument that dams can help fish see *The Log*, newsletter of the IEWA, 7:6 (July 1955), p. 5.

29 Walla Walla District news release, 2 Sept. 1955, RG 77, Acc. –T77-85-0018, WWD files, box 25 Seattle FRC. For a summary of fish run declines in the 1800s see U. S. Congress, *The Salmon Fisheries of the Columbia River Basin*, 53d Cong., 2d Sess., 1894, S. Misc. Doc. No. 200. Salmon catches always show considerable fluctuation. However, they were as stable in the 1920s and 1930s as they ever had been. See U. S. Congress, *Bonneville Dam and Protection of the Columbia River Fisheries*, 75th Cong., 1st Sess., 1937, S. Doc. No. 87.

30 The quotations are in M. T. Hoy, Oregon State Fisheries Director to Walla Walla District, 31 Oct. 1955; James Cellars, Executive Secretary, Columbia River Salmon & Tuna Packers Assn. to Maj. Gen. Charles Holle, Chairman, Board of Engineers for Rivers and Harbors, 27 Sept. 1955; and Neuberger to Brig. Gen. Louis Foote, North Pacific Division Engineer, 20 Sept. 1955. All in RG 77, Acc. –T77-85-0018, WWD files, box 25, Seattle FRC. The *Astorian Budget* quotation is in an editorial in that newspaper, 27 Sept. 1955.

31   See Foote to Walla Walla District Engineer Col. Myron Page, 26 Sept. 1955, RG 77, Acc.–T77-85-0018, WWD files, box 25, Seattle FRC.

32   West to Robert Hicks, Columbia River Fishermen's Protective Union, 24 May 1952, cabinet VI, drawer 2, "Fish, 1951-55" file, IEWA; West to Anderson, 7 March 1950; West to John Biggs, Director, Washington Department of Game, 14 May 1952. Both the latter in Acc. –73-7-675, Department of Fisheries papers, Central Files 1948-64, box 1010-42, Wash. Arch.

33   See, for example, "Statement of Gus Norwood Relating to Appropriations for Corps of Engineers Civil Functions," 18 Apr. 1952, box 128, NPPA.

34   *Power for Defense* (Walla Walla: Inland Empire Waterways Assn., c. 1952).

35   M. W. Boyer, AEC to Magnuson, 27 May 1952, copy in cabinet VIII, drawer 1, "Ice Harbor Dam Power" file, IEWA. For the 1950 AEC effort see the seventh installment of Ted Van Arsdol's newspaper history of Ice Harbor that appeared in the Pasco *Tri City Herald*, Oct.-Nov. 1961.

36   Schoettler to Senator Kenneth McKellar, 15 Jy. 1951, Acc. –73-7-675, Department of Fisheries papers, Central Files 1948-64, box 1010-42, Wash. Arch.

37   Wayne Morse to Robert Ballard, President, Sportsmen's Association, Yamhill, Oregon, 5 Jy. 1951, series A, box 125, Morse papers, UO.

38   The quotations are in, respectively, Warner W. Gardner, Assistant Sec. of the Interior, memorandum on Columbia River dams and salmon, 24 Mar. 1946, cabinet VI, drawer 3, "Misc. Hearings" file, IEWA; C. L. Anderson, Director, Washington Department of Fisheries telegram to Senator Kenneth McKellar, 15 Apr. 1949; and Anderson to Congressman Henry Jackson, 24 Feb. 1949. Both the latter in Acc. –73-7-675, Department of Fisheries papers, Central Files 1948-64, box 1010-42, Wash. Arch.

39   See Lloyd Royal, Chief Biologist, Washington Department of Fisheries to James Simpson, Fish Culturist, Idaho Department of Fish and Game, 10 Sept. 1948, Washington Department of Fisheries papers, Acc. –73-7-675, Department of Fisheries papers, Central Files 1948-64, box 1010-42, Wash. Arch.; Milo Moore, Director, Washington Department of Fisheries to Col. O. E. Walsh, Portland District Engineer, 28 Jy. 1948; and M.R. Litt, Head, Corps' Fish Facilities Section to Chief, Walla Walla District Engineering Division, 30 Nov. 1948. Both in RG 77, WWD Civil Works Project Construction Files, 1925-48, box 3, Seattle NA. The quotation is from Oligher's telephone interview, which also provided the information on the turbine design.

40   Summaries of the long struggle to obtain construction funds for Ice Harbor can be found in several places. The following account is taken from these sources: "Legislative History of Fight for Ice Harbor Dam Traced by IEWA,"

IEWA news release, 10 Aug. 1955, cabinet VIII, drawer 1, "Ice Harbor 1952-present" file, IEWA; and the Pasco *Tri-City Herald*, 14 Apr. 1957. In addition, copies of the IEWA's newsletter *The Log* carried summaries of annual legislative victories and defeats in this period.

41 Magnuson to Frederick Lawton, 29 Je. 1951, cabinet VIII, drawer 1, "Ice Harbor to 1952" file, IEWA.

42 The first quotation is in Netboy, *Salmon of the Pacific Northwest*, p. 79. The second is in the IEWA's "President's Address," 22 Nov. 1955, box 59, NPPA.

43 The first quotation is in the seventh installment of Ted Van Arsdol's newspaper history of Ice Harbor, Pasco *Tri-City Herald*, Oct.-Nov. 1961; the second in the *Walla Walla Union-Bulletin*, 6 Dec. 1961; and the third in *Columbia Basin News*, editorial, 18 Jy. 1957.

44 The Baker quotation is in Baker to Gus Norwood, Northwest Public Power Assn., 8 Dec. 1950, box 69, NPPA. For background on the construction history of Ice Harbor see *Spokane Spokesman-Review Magazine*, 20 Dec. 1957; Ted Van Arsdol, "History of Ice Harbor Dam," typescript, 1962, Ted Van Arsdol papers, Cage 117, WSU MASC; Van Arsdol's seventeen-part series on Ice Harbor history, Pasco *Tri-City Herald*, Oct.-Nov. 1961, esp. parts eight and nine; and Preston, *History of Walla Walla District, 1948-70*, pp. 215-29. Also see George C. Richardson, "Ice Harbor Navigation Lock," typescript, c. 1965, available at Army Corps of Engineers Walla Walla District Library.

Notes for Chapter Seven: A Seaport for Idaho

1 IEWA *Log*, 12:1 (Jan. 1960).

2 Magnuson to West, 27 Aug. 1960, cabinet VIII, drawer 1, "Lower Granite Dam, 1960-Present" file, IEWA.

3 For the naming of Lake Herbert G. West see *Walla Walla Union-Bulletin*, 16 May 1978. For an earlier movement to name the reservoir after Alice Clarissa Whitman see box 95, May papers, WSU MASC.

4 For the large contract see news release from the Office of the Chief of Engineers, 15 Je. 1965. A copy is in box 161, May papers, WSU MASC.

5 For the Columbia River Treaty and the intertie see John V. Krutilla, *The Columbia River Treaty: The Economics of an International River Basin Development* (Baltimore: The Johns Hopkins Press, 1967); *The Treaty With Canada: Handbook* (Portland: Bonneville Power Administration, 1965); Gus Norwood, *Columbia River Power for the People: A History of the Bonneville Power Administration* (Portland: Bonneville Power Administration, 1981), pp. 227-46; and Bill Gulick, *Snake River Country* (Caldwell, Ida.: The Caxton Printers, 1972), pp. 153-66.

6   *Lewiston Morning Tribune*, 25 Apr. 1964.

7   *Ibid.*; quotation in West to A. B. Martin, 17 Mar. 1964, cabinet VIII, drawer 1, "Lower Granite, 1960-present" file, IEWA. Also see *Lewiston Morning Tribune*, edit., 15 Aug. 1964; and Portland *Oregonian*, 17 Dec. 1964.

8   For BPA's 1965 estimates see *The Treaty with Canada: Handbook*, p. 22.

9   Howard Preston, *A History of the Walla Walla District, 1948-1970* (Walla Walla: U. S. Army Corps of Engineers, Walla Walla District, 1971), pp. 241-49.

10   The quotation is in *Lewiston Morning Tribune*, edit., 18 Dec. 1969. For early construction history see Preston, *History of Walla Walla District, 1948-1970*, p. 253; and *Pullman Herald*, 23 Jy. 1970. For background on the continuing construction delays caused by the Executive Branch's withholding of funds see Lt. Col. Lewis Pick, Jr., Corps of Engineers, to Magnuson, 1 Mar. 1967, Acc. -3181-4, box 196, Magnuson papers, UW; Catherine May to Paul Potter, Walla Walla, 22 Oct. 1969, box 342, May papers, WSU MASC; and *Lewiston Morning Tribune*, edit., 20 Mar. 1969.

11   *Washington Post*, 25 Mar. 1969.

12   See *Lewiston Morning Tribune*, 26 Je. 1969; and, for the amount spent to 1969, Col. Robert Giesen, Walla Walla District Engineer to Magnuson, Acc. -3181-5, box 146, Magnuson papers, UW.

13   A copy of Hatfield's letter to Nixon, 14 May 1969, is in Acc. -3181-5, box 146, Magnuson papers, UW. Idaho Senator Frank Church remained considerably more enthused about Lower Granite than he did additional power facilities at Grand Coulee, because Granite promised many more benefits for his state. But Church was also a Democrat with little influence over Nixon, and besides, he knew better than to do battle with the dean of Northwest senators when "Maggie's people are putting all their public works eggs . . . in the third powerplant basket at Grand Coulee." The quotation and good background on the Magnuson and Church positions is in a staff memo to Church, 15 Apr. 1969, series 3.3.3, box 49, Church papers, BSU.

14   *Lewiston Morning Tribune*, edit., 18 Dec. 1969; *Pullman Herald*, 23 Jy. 1970; Preston, *History of Walla Walla District, 1948-70*, p. 253.

15   The quotation is in Jordan to Don Modie, Lewiston, 25 Mar. 1969. Also see Modie to Jordan, 4 Mar. 1969 and 31 Mar. 1969; and typescripts of two Thomas broadcast editorials aired in the spring of 1969. All in box 218, Jordan papers, BSU.

16   The best background on the significance of the Flood Control Act comes in Howard Rosen and Martin Reuss, eds., *The Flood Control Challenge: Past, Present, and Future* (Public Works Historical Society, 1988). Higginson's quo-

tation came in his interview with the author, Boise, Idaho, 28 Feb. 1992.

17   See Reuss's introduction to Rosen and Reuss, *Flood Control Challenge*, pp. *ix-xiv*; and Luna B. Leopold and Thomas Maddock, Jr., *The Flood Control Controversy: Big Dams, Little Dams, and Land Management* (New York: The Ronald Press, 1954).

18   Carson, *Silent Spring* (Boston: Houghton Mifflin Co., 1962). For an excellent analysis of the impact of the book see Frank Graham, Jr., *Since Silent Spring* (Boston: Houghton Mifflin Co., 1970). Also see "Averting a Death Foretold," *Newsweek*, (Nov. 28, 1994), pp. 72-73.

19   Arthur E. Morgan, *Dams and Other Disasters: A Century of the Army Corps of Engineers in Civil Works* (Boston: P. Sargent, 1971); Martin Heuvelmans, *The River Killers* (Harrisburg, Pa.: Stackpole Books, 1974); Gene Marine, *America the Raped: The Engineering Mentality and the Devastation of a Continent* (New York: Simon and Schuster, 1969).

20   For some of the more thoughtful critiques of the Corps' benefit/cost analysis procedures see Carlos David Stern, "Hydropower vs. Wilderness Waterway: The Economics of Project Justification Through the Sixties," *Journal of Leisure Research*, 6 (1974), pp. 46-57; Constance Elizabeth Hunt with Verne Huster, *Down by the River: The Impact of Federal Water Projects and Policies on Biological Diversity* (Covelo, Ca.: Island Press, 1988); and Michael Frome, "Dam the Rivers, Full Speed Ahead," *Field and Stream*, a multi-part series running from October through December 1970.

21   For some of the glowing writings about the Corps see Daniel Mazmanian and Jeanne Nienaber, *Can Organizations Change? Environmental Protection, Citizen Participation and the Corps of Engineers* (Washington, D. C.: The Brookings Institution, 1979); and Jeanne Nienaber Clarke and Daniel McCool, *Staking Out the Terrain: Power Differentials Among Natural Resource Management Agencies* (Albany: State University of New York, 1985). For the impact of NEPA on the Corps see Jeffrey Kim Stine, "Environmental Politics and Water Resources Development: The Case of the Army Corps of Engineers During the 1970s" (unpublished Ph.D. dissertation, University of California at Santa Barbara, 1984); and Steven Weller, "Public Policy as Law in Action: The Implementation of the National Environmental Policy Act of 1969 by the U. S. Army Corps of Engineers" (unpublished Ph.D. dissertation, Cornell University, 1979).

22   The quotation is in Don Moser, "Dig They Must: The Army Engineers, Securing Allies and Acquiring Enemies," *Smithsonian*, (Dec. 1976), pp. 40-51, quote p. 45. For more on the Corps' insistence on pursuing old projects see Mazmanian and Nienaber, *Can Organizations Change*, pp. 11, 187-188; and Bea

trice Hort Holmes, *History of Federal Water Resources Programs and Policies, 1961-70* (Washington, D. C.: U. S. Department of Agriculture, 1979), pp. 113-117.

23 Weller, "Public Policy as Law," pp. 201-02.

24 Stine, "Environmental Politics," p. 198; Weller, "Public Policy as Law," p. 18.

25 Harry Drake, interview with the author, Walla Walla, Washington, 27 Apr. 1992.

26 For the suggestion that the Lower Granite reach be included in a middle Snake moratorium see Richard Lee, Vice President, Association of Northwest Steelheaders to William Hall, *Lewiston Morning Tribune*, 22 Mar. 1969, RG 77, Acc.–T77-85-0018, WWD files, box 9, Seattle FRC.

27 Information for this discussion of nitrogen supersaturation and gas bubble disease comes from the following sources: Carl Elling and Wesley Ebel, "Nitrogen Supersaturation in the Columbia and Snake Rivers—A Disaster or Blessing in Disguise?," typescript, 1973; and L. Richard Perry, "Supersaturated Nitrogen—Columbia River," typescript of testimony presented at U. S. House of Representatives Public Works Committee public hearing in Richland, Washington, 6 May 1972. Both of the above in Information Reference Papers Files, "Nitrogen Supersaturation Problem" folder, WWD PAO. Also see "Nitrogen Fish Kill Problem on Lower Snake and Columbia Rivers," informational release by Walla Walla District, Corps of Engineers, 31 Jy. 1970, cabinet VI, drawer 2, "Steelheaders vs. Corps" file, IEWA; Robert W. Schoning, "Nitrogen and Fish," typescript, 1971, Series 3.3.3, box 49, Church papers, BSU; and Norm Nelson, Jr. and Richard Furniss, "River on Its Deathbed," *Outdoor Life*, 149:4 (April 1972), pp. 61-3, 117-24.

28 Nelson and Furniss, "River on Its Deathbed," p. 118

29 Tussing, "The Fight to Save the Snake," *Field and Stream*, 76:6 (Oct. 1971), pp. 22-4, 126-7.

30 For historical background on studies about nitrogen supersaturation see a report submitted to the Idaho Power Company entitled *Resource & Literature Review Dissolved Gas Supersaturation and Gas Bubble Disease* (Seattle: Parametrix, Inc., 1973); Donald Weitkamp and Max Katx, *Dissolved Atmospheric Gas Supersaturation of Water and the Gas Bubble Disease of Fish* (Mercer Island, Wash.: Environmental Information Services, Inc., 1977); and a typescript of a North Pacific Division, Army Corps of Engineers public meeting held on 23 Mar. 1971, entitled "Nitrogen Supersaturation Problem." A copy is available at the University of Idaho library.

31 For fishery agencies' positive responses to Corps' actions see Donald Johnson, Regional Director, National Marine Fisheries Service to North Pacific Divi-

sion, 13 Mar. 1973, copy in Information Reference Paper Files, "Nitrogen Supersaturation Problem" folder, WWD PAO. Also see Elling and Ebel, "Nitrogen Supersaturation in the Columbia."

32   Connell to Division Engineer, 4 Jan. 1971, RG 77, Acc. –T77-85-0022, WWD files, box 18, Seattle FRC.

33   Various methods of alleviating the problem in the late 1960s and early 1970s are discussed in Elling and Ebel, "Nitrogen Supersaturation in the Columbia," pp. 9-12.

34   The first quotation is in a Corps' "Presentation to Snake River Editors Conference, 30 May 1974," in Information Reference Papers Files, "Nitrogen Supersaturation Problem" folder, WWD PAO; and the second is in Frank N. Schubert, "From the Potomac to the Columbia: The Corps of Engineers and Anadromous Fisheries," typescript, 1978, p. 77, available at Office of History, U. S. Army Corps of Engineers, Ft. Belvoir, Va. For congressional efforts to obtain funding see a joint news release from Idaho Senators Frank Church and Len Jordan and Congressmen James McClure and Orval Hansen, 29 Oct. 1970, in Series 3.3.3, box 49, Church papers, BSU. For IEWA support see Portland *Oregon Journal*, 31 Aug. 1971.

35   Packwood, cable to Lt. Gen. Frederick Clark, Chief of Engineers, 31 May 1972, Civil Works Projects files, "Nitrogen Supersaturation Program," box 44, NPD RHA.

36   For flip lips see "Presentation to Snake River Editors Conference," 30 May 1974; Schubert, "From Potomac to Columbia," p. 78; and Howard Preston, *Walla Walla District History, 1970-1975* (Walla Walla: U.S. Army Corps of Engineers, Walla Walla District, 1976), p. 64.

37   Quoted in Nelson and Furniss, "River on Its Deathbed," p. 63.

38   For statistics of the kills see *ibid.*; *Resource & Literature Review Dissolved Gas Supersaturation*, p. 14; Schubert, "From Potomac to Columbia," p. 71; and Tussing, "Fight to Save the Snake," p. 22.

39   The Sivley quotation is in Sivley to WWD PAO, Dec. 1991, commenting on an earlier draft of this manuscript. The Andrus quote is in Tussing, "Fight to Save the Snake," p. 22.

40   Quotation in Nelson and Furniss, "River on Its Deathbed," p. 63.

41   For background on the suits and the Corps' dismissal motions see Litigation Case File 410-01, "Steelheaders vs. U. S. Army Corps of Engineers and U.S. Fish and Wildlife Service," WWD RHA. Good background on the suit and copies of the court complaints can also be found in box 216, Jordan papers, BSU.

42   Background on the State of Washington suit can be found in cabinet VI, drawer

2, "Steelheaders vs. Corps" file, IEWA; Accession–79-7-480, Department of Fisheries papers, "Lower Snake River Compensation Plan" files, box 0061-76, Wash. Arch.; and RG 77, Accession–T77-85-0018, WWD Files, boxes 9 and 13, Seattle FRC.

43 Quoted in Seattle *Argus*, 23 Oct. 1970.

44 For the port districts' contemplated action see *Walla Walla Union-Bulletin*, 14 Jan. 1970 and Salt Lake City *Tribune*, 16 Jan. 1970. For action by the Clarkston Chamber of Commerce see *Lewiston Morning Tribune*, 10 Jy. 1970. For the IEWA brief see IEWA news release, 10 Je. 1970, cabinet VI, drawer 2, "Steelheaders vs. Corps" file, IEWA.

45 See "Meeting on Conservationists Attack," 9 Sept. 1969; and Max Tysor, Chief, Real Estate Divison to Public Affairs Office, 27 Apr. 1970. Both in RG 77, Acc.–T77-85-0018, WWD files, box 9, Seattle FRC.

46 Donald Johnson, Regional Director, Bureau of Commercial Fisheries and John Findlay, Regional Director, Bureau of Sport Fisheries and Wildlife to Walla Walla District Engineer, 31 Aug. 1970, RG 77, Accession–T77-85-0018, WWD files, box 9, Seattle FRC; Division Engineer Brig. Gen. Roy Kelly to Johnson, 29 Sept. 1970, Accession–79-7-480, Department of Fisheries papers, "Lower Snake River Compensation Plan" files, box 0061-76, Wash. Arch. Willard Sivley, interview with the author, Walla Walla, Washington, 28 Apr. 1992. The District's brochure, entitled *Facts About Lower Granite*, can be found in series 3.3.3, box 49, Church papers, BSU.

47 Robert F. Jordan, III, Special Asst. to the Sec. of the Army to Sen. Allen J. Ellender, 11 May 1970, Litigation Case file 410-01, "Steelheaders vs. Corps" WWD RHA.

48 As the Steelheaders' attorney admitted when first filing the suit, "There is no case law interpreting" NEPA. The Corps, the plaintiffs, and the courts were in untested legal territory. Lawrence Smith, Attorney, Spokane, to Brock Evans, Sierra Club, Seattle, 7 May 1970, box 25, Brock Evans papers, UW. *Spokane Spokesman-Review*, 17 Dec. 1971.

49 *Spokane Spokesman-Review*, 19 Jan. 1977; Robert Sweeney, Asst. U.S. Attorney, to Robert Heins, Walla Walla District Counsel, 1 May 1980, "Fish and Wildlife" file, book 8, WWD EDF; "Lower Snake River Fish and Wildlife Enhancement Study," Information Paper, 14 Dec. 1989, WWD PAO.

50 For details on the dedication ceremonies and the quotations see: *Lewiston Morning Tribune*, 16 Je. 1975, 10 Aug. 1980; *Spokane Daily Chronicle*, 19 Je. 1975; *Spokane Spokesman-Review*, 22 Je. 1975; "Remarks by Senator Magnuson, Snake River Dedication," Accession–3181-5, box 254, Magnuson papers,

UW; and "Schedule of Lower Snake Dedication Events," RG 77, Accession
-T77-85- 0018, WWD files, box 16, Seattle FRC.

51   For the economic impacts of navigation on the valley see *Lewiston Morning
Tribune*, 10 Aug. 1980, 11 Aug. 1980, 14 Aug. 1980, 25 Jy. 1982; *Tri-City
Herald*, 12 May 1988; "Navigation," Information Paper, 5 Oct. 1990, WWD
PAO; and John R. Jameson, Keith C. Petersen, and Mary E. Reed, *Walla
Walla District History, 1975-1980* (Walla Walla: U. S. Army Corps of En-
gineers, Walla Walla District, 1981), pp. 200-204.

Notes for Chapter Eight: Asotin

1   U. S. Congress, *Snake River and Tributaries*, 73d Cong., 2d Sess., 1934, H.
Doc. No. 190, esp. pp. 20-1.

2   For the 1950s plans see *Public Hearing, Review Report on Columbia River and
Tributaries, Boise, Idaho, 12 Jy. 1956* (Walla Walla: U. S. Army Corps of Engineers, Walla Walla District), pp. 12-13.

3   Itschner's arguments against the Asotin Dam are summarized in *The Log*, 12:1
(Jan. 1960), and 12:4 (Apr. 1960). The quotation is in the latter.

4   *The Log*, 12:1 (Jan. 1960).

5   For Smylie see Smylie to Itschner, 30 Aug. 1960, box 23, Smylie papers,
ISHS. For good background on IEWA lobbying and the engineering firm's
report see *Lewiston Morning Tribune*, 24 Apr. 1960.

6   The quotation is repeated in Walla Walla District Engineer Col. Frank McElwee to E. V. Lorenz, President, Lower Snake River Port Association, 29 Jan.
1965, *ibid*.

7   *Ibid*.; District Engineer Col. Frank McElwee, "Notice of Public Hearing in
Lewiston on 24 Mar. 1965," box 124, NPPA.

8   Port of Clarkston, "Economic Factors Bearing Upon the Question of: Asotin Dam Construction with Locks," n. d. (1965?), box 130, May papers, WSU
MASC; White to McElwee, 19 Mar. 1965, box 2, White papers, UISC; Magnuson and Church telegram read at Lewiston public meeting on Asotin locks,
quoted in *Tri-City Herald*, 25 Mar. 1965.

9   For the District study see Walla Walla District Engineer Col. Robert Giesen,
"Asotin Lock Study," memorandum to Division Engineer, 15 Sept. 1967,
RG 77, Acc.-T77-85-0022, WWD Files, box 24, Seattle FRC; and "Asotin
Lock Study: Summary of Report," n. d., cabinet VII, drawer 4, "Asotin Lock
and Dam—Misc." file, IEWA. For unanimous support at the Lewiston pub-
lic meeting see *Tri-City Herald*, 25 Mar. 1965. For additional background see
Lewiston Morning Tribune, 24 Apr. 1960.

10   The quotation is in U. S. Congress, *Hearings Before the Subcommittee on Parks*

and Recreation of the United States Senate Committee on Energy and Natural Resources: Outdoor Recreation Briefing, 95th Cong., 1st Sess., 1977, p. 124.

11 Clare Conley, "The Dam Shame," *Field and Stream*, (March 1959), pp. 57, 145-47.

12 Two books give a basic summary of the gradual evolution of the Corps in recreational activities. See Clayne R. Jensen, *Outdoor Recreation in America: Trends, Problems, and Opportunities* (Minneapolis: Burgess Publishing Co., 1973), pp. 70-75; and Phillip O. Foss, *Conservation in the United States, A Documentary History: Recreation* (New York: Chelsea House Publishers, 1971), pp. 418-60. Also see *Outdoor Recreation for America: A Report to the President and to the Congress by the Outdoor Recreation Resources Review Commission* (Washington, D. C.: 1962), pp. 4, 173; W. Clifford Harvey, "Waterfront at the Doorstep," in Pauline Madow, ed., *Recreation in America* (New York: The H. W. Wilson Co., 1965), pp. 124-26; Marion Clawson, *Land and Water for Recreation: Opportunity, Problems, and Policies* (Chicago: Rand McNally & Co., 1963), p. 70; Raynold Edgar Carlson, et. al., *Recreation and Leisure: The Changing Scene* (Belmont, Cal.: Woodsworth Publishing Co., 1979), p. 132; *The Third Nationwide Outdoor Recreation Plan* (Washington, D. C.: Heritage Conservation and Recreation Service, 1979), appendix III, pp. 112, 119; and William J. Hart, "Corps Lands: Is Anybody Minding the Store?," *National Parks and Recreation Magazine*, (Jan. 1980), pp. 16-19.

13 Davey Engineers, Inc., "Traffic Projections for Asotin Pool, Lower Snake River," Mar. 1965, p. 17, box 2, White papers, UISC.

14 Evans to Senator Warren Magnuson, 6 Dec. 1967, Acc.–2048 1776-1-6, box 25, Brock Evans papers, UW.

15 For Matthias see *Lewiston Morning Tribune*, 11 Dec. 1969. For the other quotation see Giesen to Magnuson, 17 Oct. 1967, RG 77, Acc.–T77-85-0022, WWD files, box 24, Seattle FRC.

16 For the 1973 study see *Spokane Daily Chronicle*, 31 Jan. 1973. The Evans quotation is in "Memo from Brock Evans to Snake River-Asotin Dam file," 25 Jan. 1973, Acc.–2048 1776-1-6, box 25, Brock Evans papers, UW.

17 *Lewiston Morning Tribune*, edit., 13 Oct. 1969.

18 The quotation is in *Lewiston Morning Tribune*, edit., 13 Mar. 1969. Also see the paper's editorials of 25 Feb. 1969, 13 Apr. 1969, and 16 Apr. 1969. The Portland *Oregonian* editorial appeared on 23 Mar. 1969.

19 Resolutions and clippings about various groups opposing appropriations for Asotin in 1969 can be found in box 339, May papers, WSU MASC. Also see *Spokane Daily Chronicle*, 19 Dec. 1969; and Thor Tollefson, Director,

Washington Department of Fisheries to Stanley Resor, Secretary of the Army, 1 Apr. 1969, Acc.–3560-4, box 84/3, Jackson papers, UW.

20   Deputy North Pacific Division Engineer Col. C. A. Carroll to Chief of Engineers, 29 Je. 1967, box 24. Also see Walla Walla District draft response to Sen. Warren Magnuson, Nov. 1969, box 16. Both in RG 77, Acc.–T77-85-0022, WWD files, Seattle FRC.

21   For samples of opposition mail see Acc.–3560-4, box 84, Jackson papers, UW; and box 339, May papers, WSU MASC. For Church's role in getting the Corps to drop its request see Church to George Nimmo, 24 Je. 1969, series 3.3.3, box 49, Church papers, BSU; and *Lewiston Morning Tribune*, edit., 16 Apr. 1969.

22   The quotation is in *Lewiston Morning Tribune*, 13 Jan. 1957. Also see Boise *Idaho Statesman*, 15 Feb. 1957. For some typical Church replies to environmentalists who unsuccessfully attempted to persuade him to oppose Lower Granite see Church to Christopher Kilmer, 10 Nov. 1971; Church to Mort Brigham, 3 Dec. 1971; and Church to Donald Thomas, 3 Je. 1971. All in series 3.3.3, box 49, Church papers, BSU. For an outstanding biography of Church, which details his changing ideas on environmental issues, see LeRoy Ashby and Rod Gramer, *Fighting the Odds: The Life of Senator Frank Church* (Pullman: Washington State University Press, 1994).

23   Despite its significance as one of the nation's longest battles between public and private power advocates, as well as between developers and conservationists, historians have given the long and complicated struggle over damming the middle Snake scant attention. For summaries of various parts of the story see Robert D. Tininenko, "Middle Snake River Development: The Controversy Over Hells Canyon, 1947-55" (unpublished master's thesis, Washington State University, 1967); Charles McKinley, *Uncle Sam in the Pacific Northwest: Federal Management of Natural Resources in the Columbia River Valley* (Berkeley: University of California Press, 1952); and Bill Gulick, *Snake River Country* (Caldwell, Ida.: The Caxton Printers, 1972), pp. 167-81.

24   See Jordan to Maj. Gen. I. D. Sturgis, Jr., Chief of Engineers, 1 Jy. 1954, box 5, Smylie papers, ISHS; Tussing, "Private Citizen Still Can Make His Voice Heard in the Capital," *Lewiston Morning Tribune*, 1 Mar. 1970; and "Statement of Senator Len Jordan, Introduction of a Bill Relating to a Moratorium for Dams on the Middle Snake River," 1 Feb. 1971, series 7.9, box 14, Church papers, BSU. Jordan's wife, Grace, wrote a moving account of their life on the river. See *Home Below Hell's Canyon* (New York: Thomas Y. Crowell Co., 1954).

25 See series 7.9, box 14, Church papers, BSU, for the long efforts of the Idaho senators to pass a middle Snake moratorium.

26 *Lewiston Morning Tribune*, 2 Jan. 1976, 3 Jan. 1976; 21 Je. 1976 (quotation). Seattle *Daily Journal of Commerce*, 3 Jan. 1976.

27 For the quotation see Church to Sen. Richard Russell, 3 Apr. 1969, series 3.3.3, box 49, Church papers, BSU. For Jordan's differing viewpoint about Asotin see John Knievel, Catherine May's administrative assistant, memo to May, 25 Feb. 1970, box 396, May papers, WSU MASC.

28 Packwood to Lt. Gen. Frederick J. Clark, 1 Dec. 1971, Acc. –2048 1776-1-6, box 25, Brock Evans papers, UW.

29 *Lewiston Morning Tribune*, edit., 2 Dec. 1971.

30 The first quotation is in Col. Thomas Nelson, Corps of Engineers, Washington, D. C. to Jordan, 24 Mar. 1972, box 216, Jordan papers, BSU; the second is in *Lewiston Morning Tribune*, 15 Mar. 1973; the third in Joint Testimony of Governors Straub, Evans, and Andrus Before House Interior Committee in Support of H. R. 30, 10 Apr. 1975, Cecil Andrus papers, Series III, box 24, ISHS. For the Walla Walla District's opposition to deauthorization see the *Lewiston Morning Tribune*, 25 Nov. 1974. For additional background see Seattle *Daily Journal of Commerce*, 3 Jan. 1976; and the *Lewiston Morning Tribune* for 2 Jan. 1976, 3 Jan. 1976, and 11 Jan. 1976.

31 The quotation is in *Lewiston Morning Tribune*, 6 Jan. 1979.

32 *Ibid.*, 15 Sept. 1977; 17 Apr. 1979.

33 Fredericks, memorandum to Engineering Division Files, 25 Mar. 1977. For the Corps' tepid agreement to get involved in the studies at all see Walla Walla District Engineer Col. Christopher Allaire to Maurice Lundy, Bureau of Outdoor Recreation, 20 Jan. 1977. Both in "Wild and Scenic River Studies" file, WWD EDF.

34 Allaire to Lundy, 2 May 1977; W. E. Sivley, Chief, Walla Walla District Engineering Division to Russell Dickenson, National Park Service, 3 Aug. 1977; Richard Pole, North Pacific Division Assistant Director of Civil Works to North Pacific Division Engineer, 26 Je. 1979. All in "Wild and Scenic River Studies" file, WWD EDF. Also see "Asotin Dam," Information Paper, 28 Aug. 1987, WWD PAO.

35 The quotation is in Moscow *Idahonian*, edit., 3 Mar. 1988. For other groups opposing the permit see *Lewiston Morning Tribune*, 25 Feb. 1988, 2 Apr. 1988, 3 May 1988, and 12 May 1988 (edit.); and Clarkston *Valley American*, 2 Mar. 1988, 25 May 1988.

36 The quotation is in *Lewiston Morning Tribune*, 3 Mar. 1988. For more on

the PUD see the *Tribune*, 18 Feb. 1988; and the Clarkston *Valley American*, 9 Mar. 1988.

37 "Asotin Dam," Information Paper, 28 Aug. 1987, WWD PAO.

38 *Lewiston Morning Tribune*, 1 Mar. 1988, 8 Nov. 1988.

Notes for Chapter Nine: Fish vs. Dams

1 The best background on the early years of the Columbia River fishery comes in U. S. Congress, *Bonneville Dam and Protection of the Columbia River Fisheries*, 75th Cong., 1st Sess., 1937, S. Doc. No. 87; and U. S. Congress, *The Salmon Fisheries of the Columbia River Basin*, 53d. Cong., 2d Sess., 1894, S. Misc. Doc. No. 200. Also very helpful is Francis Seufert, *Wheels of Fortune* (Portland: Oregon Historical Society, 1980), and Irene Martin, *Legacy and Testament: The Story of Columbia River Gillnetters* (Pullman: Washington State University Press, 1994), by far the outstanding work on the technology of gillnetting.

2 *Bulletin of the United States Fish Commission*, vol. 15, 1895, pp. 262-63.

3 The quotation is in *Salmon Fisheries of Columbia River Basin*, p. 5.

4 Still, many continued to believe hatcheries offered the best possible solution to the anadromous fish difficulties, and in 1938 Congress passed the Lower Columbia River Fishery Development Program to encourage more hatcheries. See *Review of the History, Development, and Management of Anadromous Fish Production Facilities in the Columbia River Basin* (Columbia Basin Fish and Wildlife Authority, 1990), pp. 15-18. Also see *Bonneville Dam and Protection of Columbia River Fisheries*, 1937. The quotation is on p. 59. Also helpful in tracing the story of early hatcheries and fishing regulations in the Northwest is Gordon B. Dodds, *The Salmon King of Oregon: R. D. Hume and the Pacific Fisheries* (Chapel Hill: University of North Carolina Press, 1959).

5 The quotation is from Kent Martin, interview with the author, Skamokawa, Washington, 4 May 1992. By the 1990s many others besides commercial fishers had come to recognize that continuing to emphasize reductions in commercial harvet would bring only limited results. "The status of the listed Snake River salmon is not a problem that can be solved simply by reducing harvest to meet annually increasing escapement goals," wrote Rollie Schmitten of the National Marine Fisheries Service in 1993, an opinion shared by many state and federal fishery officials. See John Harrison, "Paper Fish," *Northwest Energy News* (Nov./Dec. 1993), pp. 3-7. Helpful in providing commercial fishing statistics is Ted Bjornn, "The Salmon and Steelhead Stocks of Idaho," unpublished research report, 1976, at IDFG; *Review Report on Columbia River and Tributaries, Appendix P: Fish and Wildlife*, prepared by U.S. Fish and Wild-

life Service (Portland: U. S. Army Corps of Engineers, North Pacific Division, 1948); and *Columbia Basin Salmon and Steelhead Analysis, Summary Report* (Pacific Northwest Regional Commission, 1976).

6   For a detailed analysis of detrimental human impacts on fish habitat see Kenneth Thompson, "Columbia Basin Fisheries: Past, Present and Future," in *Investigative Reports of Columbia River Fisheries Project* (Pacific Northwest Regional Commission, 1976).

7   See Kirk T. Beiningen, "Compensation," *ibid.*; and Anthony Netboy, "Impact of Non-Fish Uses of the Columbia River," in Ernest Schwiebert, ed., *Columbia River Salmon and Steelhead*, Special Publication No. 10 (Washington, D. C.: American Fisheries Society, 1977), pp. 196-201.

8   Wesley J. Ebel, "Fish Passage Problems and Solutions: Major Passage Problems," in Schwiebert, *Columbia River Salmon and Steelhead*, p. 34; Beiningen, "Compensation," p. F-5.

9   Annual fish passage statistics at Columbia/Snake river dams are compiled each year by the Army Corps of Engineers and are available from the Walla Walla and Portland District offices. For a good analysis of prehistoric and post-dam fish runs see Kirk T. Beiningen, "Fish Runs," in *Investigative Reports of Columbia River Fisheries Project*. The quotation is in Ebel, "Fish Passage Problems," p. 34.

10 For background on federal compensation measures and controversies surrounding them see *The Mitigation Symposium: A National Workshop on Mitigating Losses of Fish and Wildlife Habitats* (Fort Collins, Col.: Rocky Mountain Forest and Range Experiment Station, 1979). The quotations are from Edward Mains, "Corps of Engineers Responsibilities and Action to Maintain Columbia Basin Anadromous Fish Runs," in Schwiebert, *Columbia River Salmon and Steelhead*, p. 40; and *Columbia Basin Salmon and Steelhead Analysis*, p. 4.

11 The quotations are in *Spokane Spokesman-Review*, 27 Oct. 1991, 13 Sept. 1994, and R. Keith Higginson, interview with the author, Boise, Idaho, 28 Feb. 1992. For additional background on the council see *Seattle Times*, 31 Mar. 1991. For brief background on the act see *Issue Backgrounder: Downstream Fish Migration* (Portland: Bonneville Power Administration, 1985); and Steve Crow, "Corps Dams Flow of Fish Funds," *Northwest Energy News*, (May/June 1988), pp. 22-4. In addition to hatcheries, the council experimented with spring reservoir releases to help flush juveniles downstream; improved certain spawning grounds; and funded the placement of screens at Corps dams to divert juveniles to bypass systems, among numerous efforts to increase runs. But the bulk of its effort went to hatchery production, and emphasis that an increasing number of biologists came to question in the 1980s and 1990s.

12   The first quotation is in Gen. G. B. Pillsbury, Chief of Engineers, to McNary, 11 Je. 1937, box 37, McNary papers, UO. The second is in Kelley to Walla Walla District Engineer, 20 Nov. 1970, RG 77, Acc.–T77-85-0022, WWD files, box 18, Seattle FRC.

13   Ray Oligher, telehone interview with the author, 12 May 1992.

14   For the Paulus and Hatch quotations see Portland *Oregonian*, 3 Jy. 1988. For Valentine see E. Paul Peloquin, Corps Wildlife Biologist, memorandum, "Office of Environmental Oversight Site Inspection," 3 Je. 1987, "Lower Snake River Compensation Plan—General" file, book 24, WWD EDF.

15   The cost figures for the compensation plan are from "Lower Snake River Fish and Wildlife Compensation Plan," Information Paper, 4 Oct. 1990, WWD PAO.

16   For background on the history of the plan see Walla Walla District Engineer Col. Richard Connell to Division Engineer, 13 Apr. 1973, RG 77, Acc.–T77-85-0022, WWD files, box 27, Seattle FRC; Walla Walla District Engineer Col. Nelson Conover to Ken Billington, Washington Public Utility Districts' Assn., 25 Aug. 1975, Acc. –3181-5, box 170, Magnuson papers, UW; and Conover to Donald Hodel, Bonneville Power Administration, 18 Jy. 1975, Acc. no. 88-1-16, box 3, "General Files," Washington State Game Department papers, Wash. Arch. Also see John R. Jameson, Keith C. Petersen, and Mary E. Reed, *Walla Walla District History, 1975-1980* (Walla Walla: U. S. Army Corps of Engineers, Walla Walla District, 1981), pp. 94-100, 292-93.

17   Willard Sivley, interview with the author, Walla Walla, Washington, 28 Apr. 1992.

18   For the gradual buildup of environmentalists nationally between 1938 and 1977 see Richard H. Macomber, "What is Happening Now in the Environmental Area in the Corps of Engineers," in John Cairns, Jr. and Kenneth Dickson, eds., *The Environment: Costs, Conflicts, Action* (New York: Marcel Dekker, 1974), esp. pp. 123-24; Daniel Mazmanian and Mordecai Lee, "Tradition be Damned! The Army Corps of Engineers is Changing," *Public Administrative Review*, 35:2 (Mar./Apr. 1975), pp. 166-72; and *Spokane Spokesman-Review*, 29 Jy. 1979. For the development of the recreation and environmental branch see Lt. Gen. William Casidy, "A New Look at Water-Resources Development," *Military Engineer*, 58:385 (Sept./Oct. 1966), pp. 323-25; and Albert Cowdrey, "Pioneering Environmental Law: The Army Corps of Engineers and the Refuse Act," *Pacific Historical Review*, 46:3 (Aug. 1975), esp. p. 346.

19   See, for example, Division Engineer Brig. Gen. Roy Kelley to Donald Johnson, Regional Director, Bureau of Commercial Fisheries, 29 Sept. 1970. Also

see J. Horvell Brown, Field Supervisor, Planning Committee of the Steelhead Study Group, River Basin Studies to Walla Walla District Engineer, 16 Je. 1969. Both in Acc.–179-7-480, Department of Fisheries papers, "Lower Snake River Compensation Plan" files, box 0061-76, Wash. Arch.

20 See J. L. Coniff, Washington State Asst. Atty. Gen. to Walla Walla District Engineer Col. Richard Connell, 17 Nov. 1971, RG 77, Acc.–T77-85-0022, WWD files, box 27, Seattle FRC.

21 Sawyer to Walla Walla District Engineer, 26 Jan. 1972, *ibid*.

22 For Corps' support of the final proposal and the agency's desire to see that Congress pass it see Connell to Division Engineer, 13 Apr. 1973, RG 77, Acc. –T77-85-0022, WWD files, box 27, Seattle FRC; and Conover to Billington, 25 Aug. 1975, Acc. –3181-5, box 170, Magnuson papers, UW. The quotation is from the Sivley interview.

23 Sivley interview.

24 The quotations are in Billington to Conover, 1 Aug. 1975, and Hodel to Conover, 3 Sept. 1975. Also see Chief of Engineers Lt. Gen. W. C. Gribble, Jr. to Sec. of the Army, 27 Apr. 1976; Billington to members of the State of Washington congressional delegation, 4 Sept. 1975; Hodel to Billington, 12 Aug. 1975; Conover to Billington, 25 Aug. 1975; and Billington to Conover, 29 Aug. 1975. All in Acc. no. 3181-5, box 170, Magnuson papers, UW.

25 Water problems impeded Corps progress in finding hatchery sites. A reliable water source within a specific temperature range is the most important consideration in fish-rearing operations. Walla Walla estimated it needed the equivalent of a water supply sufficient for a city of two million people to feed its nine hatcheries. In addition, different fish need different types of water. Steelhead can be ready for release in a year if raised in water at fifty to fifty-five degrees; consequently steelhead hatcheries should have a groundwater supply because water usually exits the ground at about the right temperature. Spring and summer chinook salmon, however, have an eighteen-month rearing cycle and need colder water. So the Corps preferred river water for its chinook hatcheries.

The District quickly found suitable water supplies for four hatcheries, but even with this success, by 1980 the District once again came under fire, with fishery agencies pressing it to complete the momentous task of replenishing fish runs. The Engineers had actually completed only one hatchery by then, and costs had already greatly exceeded expectations. To make matters worse, the selection of sites became more difficult after the Corps found the original four.

In southern Idaho the Corps paid $3.4 million for twenty-five acres and an exisiting trout farm known as Crystal Springs. The purchase ignited protests when local residents alleged that a private company later purchased a more modern facility nearby for considerably less money. Because of the controversy, Congress requested the General Accounting Office (GAO) to investigate.

The GAO's report concluded that the Corps' appraiser had over-valued the site. It also encouraged the Army Engineers to contract with commercial hatcheries to produce steelhead, estimating that fish from these hatcheries would cost one-sixth the amount of those raised by the state or federal government.

The Walla Walla District strongly disagreed. It not only stood by its real estate appraisal but also doubted whether commercial hatcheries could produce sufficient numbers of healthy steelhead over long periods of time, especially at cost figures suggested by the GAO. Despite the ruckus, the Corps did construct its proposed hatchery, which produces nearly 1.5 million steelhead juveniles annually.

Sometimes the Corps found adequate water and faced no local opposition, but still ran into difficulties. Infectious Hematopoietic Necrosis—IHN— stalled construction of the biggest hatchery complex.

When the Walla Walla District completed Dworshak Dam in northern Idaho in the 1970s, it set at its base the world's largest steelheead brooder, Dworshak National Fish Hatchery, with a water supply stemming from the Clearwater River. But by the early 1980s the hatchery had deadly IHN problems. Fish inflicted with the disease lose their abilty to swim and eventually die. The disease plagued other hatcheries in the Northwest, but the scale of Dworshak's losses dwarfed others. Sometimes only a few thousand fish died there, but some years IHN killed millions. Scientists speculated that water supply was a key to the disease: hatcheries served by wells rather than rivers generally saw fewer IHN deaths.

The Corps needed a chinook and steelhead hatchery along the Clearwater, a vital breeding tributary of the Snake. When Dworshak hatchery officials told the District they could rearrange schedules to rear some chinook, the Corps grasped the opportunity, despite the IHN problems.

Still, the Corps would eventually need a larger facility, and it planned to construct a huge steelhead and salmon hatchery just across the Clearwater and run river water into the complex. Originally scheduled for a mid-1980s construction start, the Corps delayed the project for years while researchers sought a solution for IHN. Finally, the Corps discovered it could obtain better temperature control with fewer IHN deaths by using water from the reservoir behind Dworshak Dam. Having finally solved the water supply issue, it began construction in 1989 and completed it in 1991 as the last hatchery built for the Lower Snake Compensation Plan authorized by Congress fifteen years earlier. And by the time officials dedicated the Clearwater Hatchery, construction costs for this facility alone totaled $43 million—nearly as much as the Corps had originally envisioned for the entire compensation plan.

See minutes of 5 Dec. 1979 meeting between Walla Walla District and North Pacific Division on funding for Lower Snake Compensation Plan, Program Development files, "Lower Snake River Fish and Wildlife Compensation Plan," NPD; Walla Walla District Engineer Col. Henry Thayer to Division Engineer, 18 Jan. 1980, *ibid*; Joseph McMichael, Lower Snake River Compensation Plan project manager, interview with the author, Walla Walla, Washington, 29 Apr. 1991. For background on the Crystal Springs controversy see *Corps of Engineers' Acquisition of Fish Hatchery Proves Costly*, CED-81-109 (Washington, D. C.: General Accounting Office, 1981); and *Twin Falls Times-News*, 28 Je. 1987. The Corps' response to the GAO report can be found within the report, and also in various inter-departmental memos and correspondence for the period from 1981-83 in "Lower Snake River Compensation Plan," file 3, Correspondence Files, WWD PAO. Also see Joseph McMichael, "Magic Valley Hatchery GAO Report," typescript, 1985, Lower Snake River Fish and Wildlife Plan office files, WWD. I also relied on the McMichael interview for background information. Finally, see "Magic Valley Hatchery," Information Paper, 5 Je. 1907, WWD PAO. For HIN and the Clearwater Hatchery see *Lewiston Morning Tribune*, 26 Nov. 1984, 27 Nov. 1984, 23 Je. 1988, 14 Jy. 1988, and 10 Aug. 1989; and Orofino (Id.) *Clearwater Tribune*, 24 Aug. 1989. Also see *Spokane Spokesman-Review*, 24 Aug. 1992.

26   Good summaries of the impact of the dams on Snake River riparian habitat can be found in the numerous project environmental impact statements published by the Walla Walla District in the 1970s and 1980s, available at the District library. For a detailed analysis of the impact of dams on riparian zones generally see Constance Elizabeth Hunt, *Down by the River: The Impact of Federal Water Projects and Policies on Biological Diversity* (Covello, Calif.: Island Press, 1988). The numbers of birds and animals to be affected are cited in Norm Nelson, Jr. and Richard Furniss, "Disaster on the Snake," *Outdoor Life*, 149:5 (May 1972), p. 100. Also see *Special Report for Congress: Lower Snake River Fish and Wildlife Compensation Plan* (Walla Walla: U. S. Army Corps of Engineers, Walla Walla District, 1983); David Mudd, "High Living, Canada Goose Style," *Washington Wildlife*, (Spring 1987), pp. 9-11; and "Lower Snake River Fish and Wildlife Compensation Plan," Information Paper, 4 Oct. 1990,

WWD PAO. Also helpful for more technical information is the Walla Walla District's *Design Memorandum for Wildlife Habitat Development* and its various supplements, all available at the District library. For the Corps' assessment of the infeasability of compensating for many non-game species see statement of District Engineer Col. Richard Connell, 22 May 1973, *Record of Public Meetings: Special Lower Snake River Report* (Walla Walla: U. S. Army Corps of Engineers, Walla Walla District, 1973), p. I-7. Federal agencies have frequently been criticized for concentrating mitigation efforts on game species at the expense of "minor" wildlife.

27   R. Neil Sampson, "Agriculture and Mitigation," in *The Mitigation Symposium*, p. 36.

28   *Ibid*.

29   See "Lower Snake River Fish and Wildlife Compensation: Wildlife Compensation," Information Paper, 4 May 1988, WWD PAO.

30   Sivley interview.

31   *Lewiston Morning Tribune*, 3 Aug. 1976.

32   Chief of Engineers Lt. Gen. W. C. Gribble, Jr. to Sec. of the Army, 27 Apr. 1976, Acc.–3181-5, box 170, Magnuson papers, UW; *Walla Walla Union-Bulletin*, 27 Aug. 1976; *Waitsburg* (Wa.) *Times*, 15 Jy. 1976.

33   Norman Hatley to Gov. Daniel Evans, 27 May 1976, box 25-2-1095, Daniel Evans papers, Wash. Arch.

34   Board of Columbia County Commissioners to Gov. Daniel Evans, 29 Jy. 1976, *ibid*.; Magnuson, Jackson, and McClure to Sen. Mike Gravel, Chairman of Senate Water Resources Subcommittee, 27 Aug. 1976; Governors of Washington, Oregon, and Idaho to Sec. of Defense Donald Rumsfeld, 28 Je. 1976. Both in Acc.–3181-5, box 170, Magnuson papers, UW. For additional background see *Dayton* (Wa.) *Chronicle*, 15 Jy. 1976, 9 Sept. 1976; *Lewiston Morning Tribune*, 26 May 1976; *Spokane Spokesman-Review*, 27 May 1976; *Walla Walla Union-Bulletin*, 21 Feb. 1978, 5 Apr. 1979; *Pullman Herald*, 5 May 1979. Also helpful in providing background was the Oligher telephone interview.

35   *Special Report for Congress: Lower Snake Compensation Plan*, p. 12.

36   *Ibid*., pp. 13-14.

37   North Pacific Division Engineer General George Robertson memo to Chief of Engineers, 30 Jan. 1987, "Lower Snake River Compensation Plan— General" files, book 23, WWD EDF. Also see "Lower Snake River Fish and Wildlife Compensation Plan: Wildlife Compensation," Information Paper, 7 Dec. 1989, WWD PAO.

38   Quoted in *White Salmon* (Wa.) *Enterprise*, 29 Jan. 1987. Also see Smith to Walla Walla District Engineer Col. James Royce, 29 Dec. 1986, "Lower Snake

River Compensation Plan—General" files, book 23, WWD EDF.

39   Carlton memorandum to Chief, Engineering Division, 12 Sept. 1990. This correspondence was found in papers that had not yet been filed at the time of research, WWD EDF.

40   *Ibid.*

41   Oligher telephone interview.

42   For a descripton of the Ice Harbor bypass system and alterations to the sluice-way over the years see "Columbia River Juvenile Fish Mitigation Program: Ice Harbor Lock & Dam," Information Paper, 5 Oct. 1990, WWD PAO; and "Environmental Assessment, Ice Harbor Lock and Dam, Permanent Juvenile Fish Facilities," in "Ice Harbor Fishways" file, book 4, WWD EDF.

43   "Columbia River Juvenile Fish Mitigation Program: Lower Monumental Lock and Dam," Information Paper, 19 Oct. 1990, WWD PAO; "Juvenile Fish Facilities," Information Paper, 3 Mar. 1987, WWD PAO.

44   For descriptions of how the screens work and how they were invented see "Juvenile Fish Transportation," Information Paper, Oct. 1990, WWD PAO; *Issue Backgrounder: Downstream Fish Migration*, pp. 7-8; *Dayton* (Wa.) *Chronicle*, 12 Je. 1988; and *Spokane Spokesman-Review*, 17 May 1992.

45   For background on changes in the Little Goose bypass system see "Little Goose Bypass Facilities," 7 Nov. 1984, and Brig. Gen. James van Loben Sels, North Pacific Division Engineer, draft reply to Sen. Robert Packwood, Feb. 1984, both in "Little Goose Project Fish Facilities" file, book 6, WWD EDF; and Howard Preston, *Walla Walla District History Part II 1970-1975* (Walla Walla: U. S. Army Corps of Engineers, Walla Walla District, 1976), p. 11. Also helpful was John McKern, Walla Walla District fisheries biologist, interview with the author, Walla Walla, Washington, 28 Nov. 1990.

46   "Columbia River Fisheries," Information Paper, 30 Jy. 1986; "Juvenile Fish Facilities," Information Paper, 3 Mar. 1987, both in WWD PAO.

47   For background on Operation Fish Run see Frank N. Schubert, "From the Potomac to the Columbia: The Corps of Engineers and Anadromous Fisheries," typescript, 1978, Office of History, U. S. Army Corps of Engineers, Ft. Belvoir, Va., pp. 79-88; Frank King, "Operation Fish Run," *Water Spectrum*, 9:4 (Fall 1977), pp. 7-11; "Juvenile Fish Transportation," Information Paper, Oct. 1990, WWD PAO; and Donn L. Park, *Transportation of Chinook Salmon and Steelhead Smolts 1968-80 and Its Impact on Adult Returns to the Snake River* (Seattle: National Marine Fisheries Service, 1980).

48   Ebel, "Fish Passage Problems and Solutions," p. 39.

49   Andy Brunelle, Governor Cecil Andrus's Office, interview with the author, Boise, Idaho, 25 Feb. 1992; Ed Chaney, interview with the author, Eagle,

Idaho, 26 Feb. 1992; *Snake River Salmon: National Treasure at Risk of Extinction* (Boise: Office of the Governor, 1993), p. 8; Lisa Mighetto and Wesley J. Ebel, "Draft Report, Saving the Salmon: A History of the U. S. Army Corps of Engineers' Role in the Protection of Anadromous Fish on the Columbia and Snake Rivers," typescript prepared for Army Corps of Engineers, contract no. DACW68-91-0025, 1993, p. 125.

50 *Spokane Spokesman-Review*, 1 Nov. 1992; *Lewiston Morning Tribune*, 21 Oct. 1993.

51 For background on flume testing and construction see numerous pieces of correspondence between the Walla Walla District and fishery agencies and tribes between 1983 and 1985 in "Little Goose Project—Fish Facilities" file, book 6, WWD EDF; and "Corps of Engineers Unveils . . . Fish Flume," News Release –90-19, 19 Apr. 1990, WWD PAO.

52 The long and complicated debate in the late 1980s over how best to expend federal appropriations to preserve Columbia and Snake River fish has not been succinctly summarized. I am indebted to Steve Pettit of the Idaho Department of Fish and Game and John McKern, biologist at the Walla Walla District Corps of Engineers for providing background information. The best printed summary can be found in the Portland *Oregonian*, 3 Jy. 1988. The debate was the subject of much media attention in the Pacific Northwest in the period from 1987-89 and I have relied heavily on various newspaper reports.

53 The quotations are in, respectively, *Christian Science Monitor*, 29 Dec. 1988; and Pocatello *Idaho State Journal*, 27 Jy. 1989.

54 Quotations are from Steve Pettit, interview with the author, Lewiston, Idaho, 26 Sept. 1990.

55 The quotations are in, respectively, Boise *Idaho Statesman*, 18 Mar. 1988, 15 Apr. 1988, and 11 Mar. 1988.

56 The quotation is in a transcript of a videotape by KOAP TV, Portland, "The Millions That Got Away," 10 May 1988. A copy is in "Juvenile Fish" file, Correspondence Files, WWD PAO.

57 The quotation is in "Columbia River Juvenile Fish Mitigation Program: Ice Harbor Lock and Dam," Information Paper, 5 Oct. 1990, WWD PAO.

Notes for Chapter Ten: Endangered Species

1 For background on Snake River sockeye specifically see D. W. Chapman, et. al., *Status of Snake River Sockeye Salmon* (Final Report of Pacific Northwest Utilities Conference Committee, 1990), and *Snake River Sockeye Salmon Sawtooth Valley Project: 1993 Juvenile and Adult Trapping Program, Draft En-*

vironmental Impact Statement (Portland: Bonneville Power Administration, 1992). For excellent background on the unique characteristics of the sockeye generally see Roger A. Caras, *Sockeye: The Life of a Pacific Salmon* (Lincoln: University of Nebraska Press, 1975). A more scientific overview of the species can be found in R. E. Foerster, *The Sockeye Salmon, Oncorhynchus nerka*, Bulletin 162 (Ottawa: Fisheries Research Board of Canada, 1968).

2   Barton W. Evermann, "A Preliminary Report Upon Salmon Investigations in Idaho in 1894," in *Bulletin of the United States Fish Commission for 1895* (Washington, D. C.: Government Printing Office, 1896), esp. pp. 277-82; Chapman, *Snake River Sockeye*, p. 13.

3   *Bulletin of Fish Commission, 1895*, pp. 279-80.

4   Steve Pettit, interview with the author, Lewiston, Idaho, 26 Sept. 1990.

5   Portland *Oregonian*, 13 Apr. 1991.

6   *Spokane Spokesman-Review*, 4 Aug. 1991. Downstream Indian fishers would claim they hardly have "big numbers" of salmon to harvest any more. For a moving novel about the contemporary plight of Columbia River commercial Indian fishers see Craig Lesley, *River Song* (Boston: Houghton Mifflin Co., 1989).

7   The Army Corps of Engineers maintains monthly, annual, and cumulative fish-count statistics for each of its Columbia/Snake river dams. It is somewhat risky to generalize about salmonid runs because a few did actually increase in some areas. Generally, however, with the exception of steelhead and three good years between 1985-87, the 1980s were not a good period for Columbia River anadromous fish and came nowhere close to meeting the Northwest Power Planning Council's recovery goals.

8   Counts of wild chinook stocks come from *Interim Columbia and Snake Rivers Flow Improvement Measures for Salmon*, Factsheet no. 1 (Walla Walla: U. S. Army Corps of Engineers, Walla Walla District, Oct. 1992), and from the Corps' annual fish passage reports.

9   For NMFS arguments in favor of listing sockeye as a distinct species see Moscow (Id.) *Daily News*, 6 Nov. 1992.

10 The quotations are in, respectively, the Vancouver (Wa.) *Columbian*, 3 April 1991 and 12 Aug. 1990.

11 The quotation is *ibid.*, 28 Apr. 1991.

12 Information on Kent and Irene Martin came in their interview with the author, Skamokawa, Washington, 4 May 1992. Also see Vancouver (Wa.) *Columbian*, 11 May 1992; and Portland *Oregonian*, 22 Mar. 1993, which details the impact of a federal lawsuit brought by aluminum companies and public utilities in the spring of 1993 recommending closure of the lower Columbia to

commercial fishing. And see Irene Martin's outstanding book on the history of gillnetting, with its eloquent appeal on behalf of gillnetters, *Legacy and Testament: The Story of Columbia River Gillnetters* (Pullman: Washington State University Press, 1994).

13   Jere Van Dyk, "Long Journey of the Pacific Salmon," *National Geographic*, 178:1 (Jy. 1990), pp. 3-37.

14   The Clark quotation and background on the anti-poaching measures comes in John Harrison, "Salmon Pirates," *Northwest Energy News*, 11:1 (Jan./Feb. 1992), pp. 34-39.

15   Portland *Oregonian*, 7 Nov. 1992. For the 1942 effort see Lisa Mighetto and Wesley J. Ebel, "Draft Report, Saving the Salmon: A History of the U. S. Army Corps of Engineers' Role in the Protection of Anadromous Fish on the Columbia and Snake Rivers," typescript for Army Corps of Engineers, contract no. DACW68-91-0025, 1993, p. 159.

16   "Work is Our Joy," video program written by Irene Martin (Corvallis: Oregon State University, 1989).

17   Information on Cory Eagen came in an interview with the author aboard the tug *Idaho*, Snake River, Washington, 9 May 1990; material on Eldon Crisp came in an interview with the author at the Port of Wilma, Clarkston, Washington, 10 May 1990.

18   For statistics on the Columbia/Snake waterway see Ron Mason, "Rivers Provide Economic Lifeline of Northwest," *The Great Waterway: The Columbia Snake River System* (Seattle: Marine Publishing, 1991), pp. 12-13; and Vancouver (Wa.) *Columbian*, 2 May 1991, 3 June 1991.

19   Information on Chaney came from his interview with the author, Eagle, Idaho, 26 Feb. 1992.

20   John McKern, interview with the author, Walla Walla, Washington, 28 Nov. 1990.

21   Andy Brunelle, interview with the author, Boise, Idaho, 25 Feb. 1992. For statistics on increased flow times when dams came see *Lewiston to Ice Harbor Water Particle Travel Time* (single sheet; no publisher; no date), and *The Relationship of River Velocity and Salmon Survival* (Boise: Idaho Department of Fish and Game, 1994), both provided to the author by Brunelle. In addition to increasing smolt survivability, a faster-flowing river would reduce water temperature. Some biologists have come to believe that a cooler entrance to the Snake will encourage more adult salmon to return up the stream rather than dying at the river's confluence with the Columbia because they refuse to enter the warm-water series of reservoirs. For the theorized benefits of a drawdown

for both smolts and adult fish see Executive Summary: Columbia River Salmon Flow Measures, Options Analysis/EIS (U. S. Army Corps of Engineers, Bureau of Reclamation, and Bonneville Power Administration, 1992), p. ES-3.

22 R. Keith Higginson, interview with the author, Boise, Idaho, 28 Feb. 1992.

23 McKern interview. The second quotation is in *Snake River Salmon: National Treasure at Risk of Extinction* (Boise: Office of the Governor, 1993), p. 7. For a legal analysis of whether or not the Corps would need to seek congressional reauthorization in order to provide for annual drawdowns, I am indebted to Andy Brunelle of Governor Andrus's office, who provided me with a copy of a memo addressing the legal aspects of this issue, completed by Jack Sterne, 22 Dec. 1992, entitled "Congressional Intent for Fish Passage in the Operation of Lower Snake Dams."

24 The Corps' initial analysis of various drawdown scenarios came in *Draft Columbia River Salmon Flow Measures Options Analysis/EIS* (Walla Walla: U. S. Army Corps of Engineers, Walla Walla District, 1991). The BPA and the Bureau of Reclamation also assisted in compiling the EIS. For local amazement at the Corps' recreational figures see *Spokane Spokesman-Review*, 19 Oct. 1991.

25 The Higginson and Chaney quotations came from their interviews with the author; the Andrus quotation is in the *Spokane Spokesman-Review*, 23 Jan. 1991. For a more detailed disection of the BPA and Corps concerns see Andy Brunelle to Governor Andrus, 16 Sept. 1991, copy in *Report to the Office of the Governor of Idaho: Update of Power Impacts to Protect Salmon* (Tallahassee, Fl.: Ben Johnson Associates, 1991).

26 For the Port of Lewiston's concern about Snake River salmon spawning grounds see *Spokane Spokesman-Review*, 28 Feb. 1992. For the Port manager's comments see Port of Whitman County *Port Progress*, Nov. 1991. For the newspaper ads and Andrus's response see Moscow-Pullman *Daily News*, 8 Mar. 1994.

27 *Port Progress*, Nov. 1991.

28 Chaney interview.

29 Joel R. Hamilton, Michael Martin, and Ken Casavant, *The Effect of Lower Snake Reservoir Drawdown on Barge Transportation: Some Observations* (University Task Force on Salmon and the Columbia River System, 1991).

30 The quotations are in *Spokane Spokesman-Review*, 22 Mar. 1992; the damage estimate comes in the 7 May 1992 edition. Virtually all regional newspapers carried daily stories about the drawdown in the spring of 1992.

31 Tim Palmer, *The Snake River: Window to the West* (Covelo, Calif.: Island Press, 1991), p. 103. For Powell see Wallace Stegner, *Beyond the Hundredth Meridian:*

John Wesley Powell and the Second Opening of the West (Boston: Houghton Mifflin Co., 1954).

32 Sherl Chapman, interview with the author, Boise, Idaho, 26 Feb. 1992.

33 *Ibid.*

34 *Spokane Spokesman-Review*, 14 Dec. 1994; 15 Dec. 1994.

35 For the Corps' economic statistics on retrofitting dams, the ports adherence to barging, and the findings of the Fish and Wildlife Authority team of experts, see the following editions of the *Spokane Spokesman-Review*: 17 May 1992; 9 Dec. 1992; 10 Dec. 1992; 5 Jan. 1993. For the economic study that differed drastically from Corps estimates see Edward L. McLean, *Lower Snake River Drawdown: Comparison Study of Estimated Construction Cost and Construction Schedule* (Boise: Idaho Department of Water Resources, 1993).

36 *Seattle Times*, 31 Mar. 1991.

37 *Columbia Basin Salmon and Steelhead Analysis, Summary Report* (Pacific Northwest Regional Commission, 1976), p. 9; *Salmon Passage Notes* (Portland: U. S. Army Corps of Engineers, North Pacific Division, Sept. 1992).

38 Portland *Oregonian*, 1 Nov. 1990; *Lewiston Morning Tribune*, 7 Mar. 1991; *Spokane Spokesman-Review*, 16 Aug. 1991; 16 Feb. 1992.

39 Portland *Oregonian*, 1 Nov. 1990; *Spokane Spokesman-Review*, 16 Feb. 1992.

40 Portland *Oregonian*, 1 Nov. 1990.

41 The plan is summarized in the Council's newsletter *Update*, 9:10 (Oct. 1992).

42 Vancouver (Wa.) *Columbian*, 12 Aug. 1990; *Spokane Spokesman-Review*, 10 Nov. 1990; 11 Nov. 1992.

43 U. S. Fish and Wildlife Service to Walla Walla District, Corps of Engineers, 7 May 1963 in "Lower Snake River Compensation Plan," Acc.–79-7-480, box 0061-76, Department of Fisheries papers, Wash. Arch.

44 Portland *Oregonian*, 31 Oct. 1990; *Spokane Spokesman-Review*, 12 May 1991; Martin interview. According to the results of a five-year study cited in the *Spokesman-Review* article above, 13 percent of all losses of juveniles along the system came from predators. Of these losses, bass accounted for 9 percent, walleye for 14, and squawfish for 77 percent.

45 *Spokane Spokesman-Review*, 14 Jy. 1991; Salem *Capital Press News*, 17 Sept. 1993.

46 For a good discussion on possible ways to conserve irrigation water on the Snake River Plain see Palmer, *Snake River*, pp. 83-140. Also see Donald Worster, *The Wealth of Nature: Environmental History and the Ecological Imagination* (New York: Oxford University Press, 1993), pp. 129-32.

47 The quotations are in the Chapman interview and the Higginson interview.

48   *Ibid*. Also see Carlos A. Schwantes, *In Mountain Shawdows: A History of Idaho* (Lincoln: University of Nebraska Press, 1991), p. 167.
49   Higgenson's quotation is in Palmer, *Snake River*, p. 119.
50   The systems operation review alternatives are summarized in *Screening Analysis: A Summary*, jointly published in 1992 by the Corps, Bureau, and BPA. Also see *Seattle Times*, 31 Mar. 1991, and *Spokane Spokesman-Review*, 18 Nov. 1990. For the Gorton and Trulove quotations see, respectively, the Spokesman-Review, 2 Apr. 1991 and 10 Feb. 1991.
51   Pettit interview;   Spokane Spokesman-Review, 22 Aug. 1990; Moscow *Idahonian*, 2 Dec. 1990.
52   Chaney interview.
53   *Ibid*.

Notes for Epilogue

1   *Spokane Spokesman-Review*, 2 Apr. 1991.
2   Many writers have taken this perspective. For one of the most passionate pleas in defense of species regardless of their human value, see Paul and Ann Ehrlich, *Extinction* (New York: Random House, 1981).
3   Richard White's comments came in an address at the "Great River of the West Conference," Vancouver, Washington, 2 May 1992. Also see Moscow/Pullman *Daily News*, 11 Aug. 1993. For William Finley see his two influential articles, "Salmon or Kilowatts· Columbia River Dam Threatens Great Natural Resource," *Nature Magazine*, 27 (Aug. 1935); and "Are Salmon Now Sold Down the River· What is the Attitude of the Commissioner of Fisheries?," *Nature Magazine*, 28 (Aug. 1936). For an analysis of Finley's significance see John J. Flancher, "Salmon, Dams and Concepts of Nature on the Columbia River, 1930-1980" (unpublished masters thesis, Western Washington University, 1993), pp. 72-75.
4   Phillip Meyer, *Fish, Energy and the Columbia River: An Economic Perspective on Fisheries Values Lost and at Risk* (Northwest Resource Information Center, 1982), p. 24.
5   Donald Worster, *The Wealth of Nature: Environmental History and the Ecological Imagination* (New York: Oxford University Press, 1993), pp. 124-26; Aldo Leopold, *A Sand County Almanac* (New York: Oxford University Press, 1949); Roderick L. Haig-Brown, *Return to the River: A Story of the Chinook Run* (1946; rprnt., New York: Crown Publishing, 1979); Flancher, "Salmon, Dams and Concepts of Nature," pp. 97-98.
6   Moscow/Pullman *Daily News*, 11 Aug. 1993.

  7 *Ibid.*

  8 Quoted in Wallace Stegner, *Where the Bluebird Sings to the Lemonade Springs: Living and Writing in the West* (New York: Random House, 1992), p. 86.

  9 H. W. Nibley, "On Subduing the Earth," in *Nibley on the Timely and the Timeless*, Brigham Young University Religious Studies Center, Religious Studies Monograph Series vol. 1 (Salt Lake City: Publishers Press, 1978), pp. 85-99.

 10 Roger A. Caras, *Sockeye: The Life of a Pacific Salmon* (Lincoln: University of Nebraska Press, 1975), p. viii.

 11 Thomas E. Lovejoy, "The Epoch of Biotic Impoverishment" in *The Endangered Species: A Symposium*, Great Basin Naturalist Memoirs No. 3 (Provo, Ut.: Brigham Young University, 1979), pp. 5-10.

 12 Wallace Stegner, *The Sound of Mountain Water* (Garden City, N. Y.: Doubleday and Co., 1969), pp. 147-46; Loren Eiseley, *The Immense Journey* (New York: Random House, 1957), p. 20.

 13 Eiseley, *Immense Journey*, p. 48; Wendell Berry, *The Unforeseen Wilderness: An Essay on Kentucky's Red River Gorge* (Lexington: University Press of Kentucky, 1971), p. 24; Stegner, *Mountain Water*, p. 151.

 14 Both comments were written in response to the above as it appeared in an earlier draft of this manuscript. Paul Walker to WWD PAO, 6 Je. 1991; Harry Drake to WWD PAO, n. d.

 15 For concise background on the dredging problem at Lower Granite see "Lower Granite Lock and Dam: Sedimentation Studies and Interim Dredging," Information Paper, 14 Dec. 1989, WWD PAO. Although there are several places along the lower Snake that require occasional dredging, the biggest problem is in the Lower Granite reservoir, home to the vast majority of sediment washed down the Snake and Clearwater. For additional background on the dredging at Lower Granite, the difficulties it causes, and various alternatives considered see *Lower Granite Environmental Impact Statement, Draft Supplement: Interim Navigation and Flood Protection Dredging* (Walla Walla: U. S. Army Corps of Engineers, Walla Walla District, 1988); "Record of Decision . . . Interim Navigation and Flood Protection Dredging," 20 Dec. 1988, "Lower Granite—Environmental Studies" file, book 5, WWD EDF; "Statement of Findings, Lower Granite Interim Navigation and Freeboard Maintenance Dredging," 31 Oct. 1989, "Lower Granite—Miscellaneous" file, WWD EDF; and David Bennett, "In-Water Dredge Disposal: Boon for Salmon & Steelhead?," in the University of Idaho College of Forestry, Wildlife and Range Sciences *Focus*, 13 (May 1988), pp. 22-3. There is also a considerable amount of correspondence and minutes from meetings pertaining to this issue in "Lower Granite—Sedimentation" file, WWD EDF.

16 Bennett, "In-Water Dredge Disposal," p. 23.

17 For the figure on the amount it costs an average household to subsidize aluminum companies see Paul Koberstein, "Northwest is Asked to Give Up 18 Dams," *High Country News* (Feb. 7, 1994), pp. 12-13.

18 Moscow/Pullman *Daily News*, 11 Aug. 1993; 23 Sept. 1993; 12 Aug. 1994.

19 Examples of pessimistic Corps presentations on drawdowns came during the series of "Public Scoping Meeting(s) for the Environmental Impact Statement on Improving Salmon Runs in the Columbia River Basin" held in various communities in the summer of 1990. In a meticulously prepared program the Corps showed slide after slide of incredible costs associated with most any alternative that might be chosen in an effort to adapt the lower Snake/Columbia system in order to save salmon. The unrelenting gloom they presented seemingly left little room for optimism—a tactic that backfired on the Corps as speaker after speaker chastised the agency for its negativity, often comparing this unfavorably to the "can do" attitude that had characterized the Army Engineers during the dam-building era.

20 For the Chenoweth quotation see *Newsweek* (12 Dec. 1994), pp. 79-80.

21 For the Babbit quotation see *Spokane Spokesman-Review*, 27 Sept. 1994. Also see *15 Damnable Dams* (Portland: Oregon Natural Resources Council, 1994).

22 I am indebted to Moscow, Idaho, writer Carol Ryrie Brink for the "chain of hands" image: "I like to think that the touch of life continues from the deep, dark origin of man forward into the deep, dark future. I touch another human being; but behind me was my mother's touch and all of those she touched; and behind her and behind her and behind her all the countless millions of seeking hands that touched, transmitting the mystery of a shared experience." Brink, *A Chain of Hands* (Pullman: Washington State University Press, 1993), p. 1.

23 Many authors have written compellingly about human efforts to control nature along rivers. The literature is thought-provoking and voluminous. The following are some places researchers might start if wishing to pursue this avenue of reading pleasure. Donald Worster's *Rivers of Empire: Water, Aridity, and the Growth of the American West* (New York: Pantheon Books, 1985), is the classic historical analysis of the impact of Western water developments upon people and nature. Worster's extensive documentation can lead readers to other less-comprehensive but valuable treatments of waterways history. Also see Marc Reisner, *Cadillac Desert: The American West and its Disappearing Water* (New York: Penguin Books, 1986), and the "sequel," Marc Reisner and Sarah Bates, *Overtapped Oasis: Reform or Revolution for Western Waters* (Covelo, Ca.: Island Press, 1990), which is much stronger than *Cadillac Desert* on legal issues.

Very insightful in detailing legal aspects of Western environmental issues for lay readers is Charles F. Wilkinson, *Crossing the Next Meridian: Land, Water, and the Future of the West* (Covelo, Ca.: Island Press, 1992). Many of the country's finest nature writers have set their skills to contemplating the impact of human actions on rivers and the impact of aridity on the development of the West, and they are often thought provoking—although rarely sympathetic to the Corps of Engineers and Bureau of Reclamation. Readers might begin their journey into this rich literature with the following: John Graves, *Goodbye to a River* (New York: Alfred A. Knopf, 1960); John Haines, *Living Off the Country: Essays on Poetry and Place* (Ann Arbor: University of Michigan Press, 1981); Edward Abbey, *Down the River* (New York: E. P. Dutton, 1982); Berry, *The Unforeseen Wilderness*; and almost any work by Wallace Stegner. Those interested in more technical literature on the environmental impacts of dams would do well to begin their research with William C. Ackermann, et. al., eds., *Man-Made Lakes: Their Problems and Environmental Effects*, Geophysical Monograph 17 (Washington, D. C.: American Geophysical Union, 1973); Edward Goldsmith and Nicholas Hildyard, *The Social and Environmental Effects of Large Dams, Vol. I: Overview* (Wales U. K.: The European Ecological Action Group, 1984); and James V. Ward and Jack A. Stanford, eds., *The Ecology of Regulated Streams* (New York: Plenum Press, 1979).

Acknowledgments

Thanks especially to Jim Hepworth at Confluence Press, whose enthusiasm kept this project alive during waning moments. Linda Vacura at Confluence also played a major role in keeping the book on schedule, and Tanya Gonzales put it all together in book form with her typesetting and design skills. Thanks too, to Mary Reed, as always, for the research and editorial help, and to my friends and colleagues Dave Hoyt for the beautiful cover design and Beth DeWeese for her marketing expertise.

I am indebted to several people who allowed me to interview them. From the U. S. Army Corps of Engineers: Rex Baxter, Bill Carter, Harry Drake (retired), Ed Ferrell, John McKern, Joseph McMichael, Fred Miklancic, Ray Oligher (retired), Willard Sivley (retired), Scott Sutliff, and Sarah Wik. From the Port of Whitman County: Eldon Crisp, Jack Thompson, and Jim Weddell. Also archaeologists Richard Daugherty and Robert Lee Sappington; geologist Patrick Seward; tug pilot Cory Egan; commercial fishers Kent and Irene Martin; biologist and fish advocate Ed Chaney; Sherl Chapman of the Idaho Water Users Association; Andy Brunelle, natural resources assistant in Governor Cecil Andrus's office; Steve Pettit of the Idaho Department of Fish and Game; Bill Knox of the Oregon Department of Fish and Game; and R. Keith Higginson of the Idaho Department of Water Resources. These people are all experts in their fields, and the book is better because of their knowledge and generous assistance.

I benefited from the suggestions of several who read the manuscript in its various stages, including William Willingham, historian at the Corps'

North Pacific Division; Martin Reuss at the Corps' Office of History; Andy Kerr, Executive Director of the Oregon Natural Resources Council; LeRoy Ashby, Claudius and Mary Johnson Distinguished Professor of History at Washington State University; Charles F. Wilkinson, Moses Lasky Professor of Law at the University of Colorado; Terry Tempest Williams, whose passionate writing on the Western environment has inspired so many; and Alvin Josephy, Jr., who has led the way for many of us who now study Western history.

Thanks also to historians Glen Lindeman and Craig Holstine for the assistance in uncovering helpful research materials, and to Mom for sending me every clipping she saw about fish and dams over the past half decade.

Many archivists and librarians helped during the project. Those I would especially like to thank are: Rose Marie Moore at the U. S. Army Corps of Engineers' Walla Walla District library; Martin Gordon at the Corps' Office of History library in Ft. Belvoir, Virginia; Lawrence Dodd, archivist at Whitman College's Penrose Memorial Library, Walla Walla; Patricia Hopkins and David Hastings at the Washigton State Archives and Records Center in Olympia; Terry Abraham at the University of Idaho Library Special Collections; Larry Stark at Washington State University Library's Manuscripts, Archives, and Special collections; Gary Bettis and Elizabeth Jacox at the Idaho State Historical Society in Boise; Joyce Justice and Scott Roley at the National Archives— Pacific Northwest Region, Seattle; Karyl Winn, Janet Ness, and Jo Lewis at the Archives and Manuscript Section of the University of Washington Library, Seattle; Richard Hobbs, Charles Mutschler, and Emma Meissner at Eastern Washington University Library in Cheney; and Alan Virta, archivist at Boise State University Library.

Some of the research for this project was undertaken while completing a contract for the Corps of Engineers. I would like to thank William Willingham, John Leier, Walla Walla District archaeologist, and James Hackett of the Walla Walla District's Public Affairs Office for their help on that project. These are just three of the many good, dedicated people who work for the Corps. But to be honest, I must admit that some people in the agency did not agree with what I believed to be objective history. As a result, that contract was, in some ways, frustrating. Having completed my contract obligations to the Corps, I undertook additional research, added new sections to this manuscript, and reworked others that the Corps found objectionable—but that I feel better reflect historical accuracy. One of the difficulties of that contract, I now understand, is that it was supervised by the agency's public affairs office. Sometimes historical accuracy and public relations can clash. Hopefully in the future the Corps will assign historians rather than public affairs officers to oversee all their historical contracts.

Index

About the Author

Keith Petersen is a native Washingtonian and award-winning historian who lives in Pullman with his wife, historian Mary Reed, and their daughters, Usha and Uma.

Cover design by Dave Hoyt
Interior desgin and production by Tanya Gonzales
Interior type is Janson with Janson Display
Printed at Cushing-Malloy
on acid-free paper